Abiayalan Pluriverses

Abiayalan Pluriverses

Bridging Indigenous Studies & Hispanic Studies

Edited by

Gloria Elizabeth Chacón

University of California San Diego

Juan G. Sánchez Martínez

Lakehead University

Lauren Beck

Mount Allison University

Amherst College Press

The complete manuscript of this work was subjected to a partly closed ("single-blind") review process. For more information, visit https://acpress.amherst.edu/peerreview/.

Published in the United States of America by
Amherst College Press
Manufactured in the United States of America

Library of Congress Control Number: 2023940786
DOI: https://doi.org/10.3998/mpub.14369000

ISBN 978-1-943208-74-6 (Print)
ISBN 978-1-943208-73-9 (OA)

CONTENTS

Introduction: Found and Fraught in Translation

In 1851, the Mexican army murdered the wife and three children of Geronimo, a Ndeé (better known as Apache) leader. He vowed to take revenge and led multiple raids against them. In response, Mexico issued a reward for his capture and any associates. Throughout the nineteenth century, Geronimo fought the US Calvary until his capture and subsequent imprisonment. As with many other tribes, his was divided between Mexico and the United States (Saldaña; Chaat Smith). Historical figures and life stories like those of Geronimo, who fought against Mexican and US forces, become symbolic of larger tensions between the empires of Spain and Britain, the nation-states of the United States and Mexico, and Indigenous nations. But these past and present entanglements also contest our desires for sanitized interpretations and divisions in our disciplines. What can we learn in Hispanic Studies from Geronimo, who not only spoke Nde and Spanish, but refused to speak English? How can we engage across our disciplines different resistances to colonizations—Spanish, Mexican, American—that overlap in the Indigenous territories of the Southwest through his 1906 multilayered and multilingual "autobiography," which he narrated in his native Apache language while captive in Oklahoma and that was later interpreted to English by Asa Deklugie and edited by Superintendent S. M. Barret? Similarly, should we really entertain the claim that he is "as Mexican as salsa verde" or even considered "one of the first Mexicans," as the Mexican novelist Álvaro Enrigue asserts?

Another complex figure, like the shipwrecked Spaniard Álvar Núñez Cabeza de Vaca, contribute to Indigenous Studies with his sixteenth-century account of tribes—the only account available—in what is today the southern United States? How does Cabeza de Vaca's reclaiming in Chicanx/Latinx historiography add another layer to his legacy?

Can the current perspectives of local tribes interpellated in the 1776 Domínguez-Escalante Spanish expedition throughout New Mexico, Colorado, Utah, and Arizona offer different points of departure for Indigenous agency beyond national identities and constructions of race across North America and Latin America in our disciplines? In considering Hispanic Studies in Canada, why don't wampum belts (the oldest books) and Maya glyphs merit study in Spanish-language courses? Or, why aren't local Indigenous languages or issues part of the Hispanic Studies curriculum? Decolonizing Hispanic Studies in Canadian contexts would problematize the fact that while printing presses didn't exist until 1751 in New France, Acadia, or Newfoundland, among Indigenous communities, wampums, birchbark scrolls, and other writing circulated as important components of diplomacy, "words functioned as presents" (Warkentin). These questions or concerns underpin the impetus for putting this anthology together.

While we recognize that we are working in the context of the Western academy, and acknowledge that the disciplines of Hispanic and Indigenous Studies came into existence along starkly different paths, we propose thinking of approaches and rationales for more dialogue between disciplines to further the goal of decolonizing knowledge in institutions of higher learning. In doing so, we not only point to how Hispanic Studies (also known as Spanish Studies or falling under the umbrella of Romance or Modern Languages and Literatures Studies) emerge largely in the German, British, and American academies of the nineteenth century but also emphasize its symbolic and material collusion with colonial hierarchies and taxonomies that need undoing. Historically, as others have also noted, the field entailed the study of literature, language, and culture primarily from Spain but eventually from Latin America (Beverley 7–16; Ramos and Daly 9). In the Global North, Spanish culture and language became objects of consumption and acquisition on the part of non-Hispanophone students and scholars.[1] These interests increasingly extended to Latin America, resulting in the Global North's colonizing of how and which knowledge about the Spanish-speaking world could be learned, including which texts are taught or excluded in degree programs (Altschul 11).

Furthermore, for more than a century, Hispanic Studies developed within the paradigm of Iberian and Latin American Studies as somehow coequal (Herlihy-Mera; Álvarez-Junco). Departments hired specialists in both disciplines as if they equally represented the complexity and variety of the literatures, languages, cultures, and peoples implicated by both geographical constructs, despite the evident population differences between Spain and the balance of Spanish-speaking countries worldwide. As a result, for many students and their professors who have trained in traditional Spanish and Portuguese departments in the Western academy, Iberian Studies takes up disproportionately more of their training. At the same time, the existing curriculum reinforces the colonizing gaze of the Global North that shaped Hispanic Studies in the nineteenth century. Bolstered by romanticized notions of past empires, and the settler-colonial imposition of European culture and language in the Americas, the field historically belies the fact that Indigenous cultures and languages continue to thrive (Codding 167). Adding to these genealogies is that the funding of many Spanish and Latin American Studies departments in the United States partly resulted from the rise of area studies tied to Cold War politics (Bartley). As Bartley points out, area studies emerge from the needs of foreign policy planners and geopolitical strategists. Of course, these foundations differ from the student movements that birthed Chicanx/Latinx Studies; thus, we are not necessarily engaging with that particular field formation, but we realize that more and more departments of Spanish and Portuguese feel compelled to include courses for heritage speakers and cater to a growing population of students who may be bilingual.[2]

Coloniality and language

Although "Latin America" takes up proportionately more geographical and cultural magnitude outside of Europe, until recently it remained undertreated in the discipline and usually confined to a settler-colonial construct, particularly in smaller programs where fewer faculty may influence the degree requirements. This means that precolonial cultural productions and works not written in Spanish remain parsimoniously studied in the classroom, and "Latin America" can be treated homogeneously as an undifferentiated cultural bloc, compared to the specificity with which Spain is treated (Castro-Gómez 47–58; Dussel 34). As a result, the richness and cultural diversity of this region tend to be confined to literatures and languages available to students who read Spanish: non-Spanish works are relegated to a past as precolonial artifacts rather than as thriving, contemporary bodies of literature, culture, and knowledge. Addressing this issue is the essay by Palacios, Worley, and Castillo Cocom, who, echoing Cree writer Womack, argue that there is no Hispanic Studies without Indigenous Studies. In their contribution, they point to colonial texts written in Indigenous languages that essentially give birth to Hispanic Studies. In concert with their assertion, we emphasize how epistemic biases have created a lacuna related to Indigenous knowledge in many Hispanic Studies curricula. That content void translates into a temporal dissonance by which Indigenous peoples and their cultural productions are simply positioned in the past or misunderstood by scholars who lack the training or familiarity with Indigenous contexts or knowledge systems relating to their discipline. Hence, Hispanic Studies, Latin American Studies, and Spanish departments more broadly frequently work in isolation from Indigenous Studies departments in Global North university contexts; rarely do the contributions of the latter influence the research and teaching of the former (Castro-Klaren). In fact, these disciplines have developed within Eurocentrically established American and Canadian universities in ways that continually obfuscate Indigenous perspectives (Beard). While Indigenous Studies as a field has gained traction in the twenty-first century, Hispanic Studies, Latin American Studies, and Spanish language programs slowly and grudgingly reflect on their own complicity with colonialism in higher education settings and beyond, trying to find ways of better including Indigenous scholarship.

Language is at the heart of the discipline's colonial oversight as Hispanic Studies emphasizes learning the Spanish language at the expense of Indigenous languages. Further complicating matters is that while English and Spanish are colonial languages, the primary language used by academic associations focused on Indigenous issues, such as the Native American and Indigenous Studies Association (NAISA) in the Global North, continues to be English. Despite attempts to include non-English speakers and scholars from south of the United States, English retains an unspoken official status in the association, with its professional meetings, conferences, and publications conducted mainly in English with very few exceptions. In contrast, Indigenous authors and other intellectuals from Abiayala/Latin America do not typically publish their work in English; rather, they do so in their native language and/or in Spanish. Thus, the Spanish language bridges Indigenous languages from Latin America, while English bridges Indigenous Languages from Canada, the United States,

New Zealand, and Australia. In effect, the linguistic disconnect between distinct but allied worlds and scholarly environments inevitably determines the texts we study in the university classroom, most of which have been produced by non-Indigenous writers and intellectuals for non-Indigenous audiences. How do we alter the academic conditions that perpetuate the invisibility of an entire corpus produced in Spanish and Indigenous languages by Indigenous peoples? Translation efforts between Indigenous languages from Latin America to Spanish and from Spanish to English respond to a profound transformation taking place between our disciplines.

Translation and translanguaging

Subjecting to scrutiny the inherent colonialism in the linguistic emphasis of Spanish departments at the university makes engaging with Indigenous thought produced and published in English or in Indigenous languages critical without forgoing the mission to teach and reinforce communicative abilities in the Spanish language. As noted by Castro-Klaren, literary and cultural analysis have limitations in the second language, and students may advance more in their intercultural competency while approaching Abiayala/Latin America's richness in translation (6). Today, professional and amateur translators work between Spanish, English, and Native languages with texts written by Indigenous authors from both hemispheres. Published in anthologies such as *Sing, Poetry from Indigenous America* (Hedge Coke) and *Poesía estadounidense contemporánea* (Hedeen and Rodríguez), or in curated online periodicals such as *Latin American Literature Today* and *Siwar Mayu: A River of Hummingbirds*, translators offer useful materials for educators and critics to disrupt geographic, linguistic, and disciplinary borders. However, as scholars, we must also grapple with the question of the untranslatability of Native languages and the limits of legibility in cross-cultural dialogues—all common themes in Indigenous Studies (see the chapters by Sánchez and Percia, Henne, and Zevallos-Aguilar). Despite the real, historical, and polemical issues of translation, it can play a critical role bilaterally, such that knowledge produced in the South or North can truly be horizontal and have consequences in political, philosophical, ontological, and aesthetic discussions.

While we recognize that the contents of this volume are offered in the colonial languages of English and Spanish, our initial idea included a call for Indigenous language scholarship, but we did not receive contributions in any Indigenous language. Of course, we agree that English and Spanish have also been appropriated by Indigenous intellectuals to further their political agendas and that it is for many an important vehicle for resistance, but we also see Indigenous languages as as one of the "unconquered cognitive spaces" as Mixe intellectual Yasnaya Aguilar points out. Nonetheless, we anticipate that our commitment to translations of the essays serves as a bridge between scholars in the North and the South. Linguistic knowledge and cultural forms of translation underline the contributions of Indigenous and non-Indigenous thinkers on a larger scale based on a different model of relating and knowing (see the essays by Henne, Tarica et al., Zevallos-Aguilar). Our political commitment to bilateral dialogues leads us to the potential role of translation. All essays in our collection will be available in translation and will be open access to aid scholars in this dialogue. Despite its polemics, translation as a political praxis becomes critical in both academic fields. We also aim to support more scholarship published in Indigenous languages or to see more works such as this one available in Indigenous languages, which is a consideration for the future of this anthology. Furthermore, any royalties generated by this volume will be dedicated to creating a scholarship for Indigenous scholars, writers, artists, or translators—in partnership with allied institutions—for them to produce multilingual material that guides and bridges Indigenous Studies and Hispanic Studies.

Transhemispheric Indigenous Studies

Decades of interdisciplinary programs—from Canadian Studies to Material Culture Studies—that strived to privilege Indigenous science, epistemologies, traditional ecological knowledge, histories, languages, cultures, and worldviews contribute to the vitality of Indigenous Studies in countries such as Canada and the United States (Battiste; Kovach). While still forged within (and at times in parallel to) the Western academy, the foundations of Indigenous Studies were built by Indigenous and, less often, non-Indigenous scholars (Tuhiwai Smith 211; Valaskakis 105; Wall Kimmerer). Indigenous Studies from the South figures less prominently in the Global North academy as even its standing in Latin American universities tilts toward more precarious conditions. We hope this anthology makes a strong case for Canadian and US scholars to engage with Indigenous thought, literature, and scholars from the South. As Heath Justice reminds us:

> Native lit scholars in Canada tend to be far more inclusive of and familiar with the literature and criticism coming out of the States than is evidenced by many of our counterparts in the United States, to the great detriment of the latter. Meaningful exchange is mutual, and just as scholarship in Canada is enriched by the insights of our southern colleagues, so too could more US-based scholars look farther beyond their borders to honor the knowledge and wisdom offered from the Land of Eh. (337)

His observation is relevant for those of us working with and through Indigenous literatures and knowledges in the US academy. We take special note of the influence of US Native/Indigenous critical thought informing the work of many contributors in this anthology (e.g., Huerta's, Catrileo and Carrión-Lira's, as well as Pineda's chapters). They represent a new generation of scholars thinking (trans)nationally and in multiple languages who hail from traditional Comparative Literature, Hispanic Studies, Latin American Studies, or Spanish and Portuguese departments. Offering students and scholars ways of thinking and learning through Indigenous knowledges about the Spanish-speaking and Indigenous worlds as well as their coexistence in Abiayala, Turtle Island, among its other names. These emergent scholars will transform Hispanic Studies/Spanish and Portuguese departments as they work across disciplines and languages. For instance, to Indigenous peoples whose ancestral land is today in between nation-states, the border between the US and Mexico is as arbitrary (Heath Justice) as the nation-state borderlines that divide the Wallmapu, the Mapuche territory across Chile and Argentina (see Carrión-Lira and Catrileo); the

Gunaiala, the Dule territory across Colombia and Panamá (see Haglund); or the Maya area whose original land is in present-day Mexico and various countries in Central America. It is not that there are not political and material consequences to consider, but these borders have divided Indigenous nations who maintain and preserve familial ties.

The volume juxtaposes the multilayered experience of Indigeneity across nation-states and disciplines. In tandem, as scholars in between hemispheres and disciplines, we seek to expand the conversation toward the South while involving scholars of Indigenous Studies in the North. For these reasons, we offer the volume's contents in Spanish and English so that broader audiences can benefit from our authors' thoughts and perspectives and animate new research methodologies and geographical foci. The editors of this volume have approached this project as a tapestry of varying, complementary, and sometimes discordant experiences as scholars of Hispanic and Indigenous Studies. Some of our contributors are Indigenous scholars who straddle both disciplines at the crux of identity and knowledge ways and who root themselves firmly into two fields that sometimes do not communicate with each other. Two of the Indigenous contributors are not academics but poets and language-based thinkers. Others are settler scholars who come to both disciplines as outsiders, choosing to learn languages and working to comprehend new-to-them worldviews. Most of these scholars are also of mixed background, and they have established relationships with Indigenous artists, writers, or elders, bridging disparate fields through Indigenous textualities. Scholars of Hispanic and Indigenous Studies themselves span an array of identities, races, worldviews, languages, and experiences. By working together, the editors and contributors to this volume attempt to bring into dialogue differences that might otherwise silo us as scholars of Hispanic or Indigenous Studies or as colleagues with different backgrounds and approaches to our research and teaching. In so doing, we—and by extension the chapters featured in this volume—nurture dialogues and exchanges that we hope will fortify bridges between us.

Contributing to North-South Indigenous dialogues

Abiayalan Pluriverses: Bridging Indigenous Studies and Hispanic Studies reveals the challenges to and benefits in understanding and engaging with Indigeneity comparatively and across Abiayala (the Americas) despite the constraints of defined scholarly disciplines and the linguistic, colonial differences they imply. What the collection cogently illustrates is how the literary, oral, and nonalphabetic Indigenous pluriverses of Abiayala traverse the ubiquitous linguistic perimeters that strictly segregate Indigenous Studies from the dominant Hispanic Studies (see the chapters by Sotelo, Roncalla, and Favaron in our volume). A handful of our contributors collectively propose a trans-Indigenous paradigm—building upon the work of Allen; Bianet Castellanos et al.; Cox and Heath Justice—that is facilitated by working through temporal geographies and texts (see the chapters by Carrión and Catrileo, Meneses, Pineda, and Sell). We hail trans-Indigenous as a methodology that juxtaposes Indigenous textualities and experiences to each other and also against the settler-colonial norm, implicating a quilted fabric of Indigenous nations and cultural practices that carpet Abiayala and opening the possibilities of expanding to global Indigenous Studies. The contributors to this volume offer three concrete methodologies that build bridges between Hispanic and Indigenous Studies (see the chapters by Huerta and Palacios et al.). First, as scholars involved in these fields, the authors generate dialogues between Indigenous and non-Indigenous paradigms, interweaving multimodal visual, material, and alphabetic textualities. Second, as educators, they question the periodizations, chronologies, and national narratives that promote the colonial perspectives on time and culture, which expropriate and inform the literary historiography of the Spanish-speaking world, while proposing alternatives that journey beyond the confines of a Spanish-speaking Hispanophone world. Finally, as scholars rooted to some place in Abiayala (the Americas), they theoretically reflect upon their own positionality while experimenting with various pedagogical tools they deem suitable for the study of Indigenous textualities within the framework of Hispanic Studies, particularly tools that resist any colonial trappings about language or literacy.

Some of the questions deliberated in our volume include the following: Which conceptual and practical adjustments can be made in the classroom or in the structure of a major or minor in Hispanic Studies to be able to better engage in dialogue with and understand the Indigenous voices and literatures so often silenced or isolated from the Hispanophone literary canon? What are the limitations and possibilities for non-Indigenous professors and critics to read, comment, and teach Indigenous texts and perspectives? How can we train students in Hispanic Studies or Latin American Studies to engage in dialogue with Indigenous texts and Indigenous research paradigms? How can we Indigenize the discipline of Hispanic Studies in the American and Canadian context? Or, if not "Indigenize," which pedagogical methodologies and tools help us to build intercultural and multilingual bridges? What is the role of translation and translanguaging in the classroom, whether in Hispanic or Indigenous Studies in the North? Concomitantly, how will the growing number of Indigenous peoples in the diaspora located in North America engage with these fields? How will the fields of Latinx/Chicanx Studies engage with Indigenous-informed scholarship seeping into non–area studies disciplines? And, how, if at all, do the bridges between Hispanic and Indigenous Studies facilitate efforts to decolonize in terms of epistemology, sovereignty, nation-states, and the relationships between the human and nonhuman worlds?

The essays model interdisciplinary pedagogical, methodological, epistemic, and ontological approaches and ways of reading texts and images that significantly indigenize the Hispanic Studies curriculum and the discipline to which it belongs. Through constant self-reflection within their classrooms and disciplines, this volume's contributors pose practical questions meant to provoke meaningful contemplation in the reader about their own positionality, objectives, and contributions to the goals this volume strides toward. The book also offers useful bibliographies to bridge cultural expressions, whether from Abiayala, Turtle Island, or the Spanish-speaking world. In questioning universal and national periodizations and timelines (see the chapter by Quiroz, Tarica, and Tello), this volume demonstrates how Indigenous textualities are adaptive and responsive while bringing new insights to the humanities that will address significant challenges of our time, from the Eurocentrism of the architecture of scholarly knowledge to our stated goal of Indigenization. The essays also underscore the linguistic conflicts haunting the origin of Hispanic Studies.

Furthermore, this anthology brings together Indigenous and non-Indigenous scholars, authors, and artists to stimulate, both within the book and in the future, dialogues between these fields and their demographics, who are often isolated from each other. Some essays are written as cross-cultural dialogues: the authors stand at the intersection of paradigms, constantly negotiating within Western academia while making space for Native sciences, languages, genders, sexualities, and spiritualities. Marco Antonio Huerta, for example, in his contribution to this volume, speaking on the disconnects between Indigenous Studies and queer theory, is in sync with Jodi Byrd: "Es por esta razón que es indispensable tomar en cuenta el territorio al momento de analizar la organización del género y la sexualidad al interior de naciones indígenas."

In gathering the chapters that form this volume, the editors found thematic convergences among authors and geographies that coalesce around the importance of the body, territory, and language. This triad informs many of the dialogues and analyses pursued in this volume's essays through foundational concepts such as affective rationalities, embodied territory, and grounded relationality. The nondialectic perspective from different Native languages brings richness, complexity, and simultaneity to Indigenous worldviews and experiences that Antonio Catrileo, Manuel Carrión-Lira, Víctor Quiroz Ciriaco, and others explore through Indigenous concepts and terminology, such as ch'ixi ("spotted gaze" in Aymara), epu rume ("double hearted" in Mapudungun), and kab'awil ("double gaze" in several Maya languages).

Our goal is to make this body of thought available for Native American and Indigenous Studies (NAIS) scholars who may otherwise not be able to read works of literature and theory in Spanish. In contrast, some contributors bring NAIS theory into dialogue with Spanish and Latin American literary and cultural contexts. Since most of this volume's contributors work between Indigenous and Hispanic Studies, their theoretical and critical frameworks—in Spanish, English, and Native languages—are from diverse disciplines. This volume expands conversations among non-Spanish speakers and scholars in North America, Australia, Aotearoa, the Pacific Islands, and Europe, as well as among non-Anglophone scholars in Latin America and Spain. We are conscious of the limits of translation. For instance, how can we discuss Abiayala's textualities and relational ways of being using the same Eurocentric categories that we fault for excluding Indigenous experiences and worldviews, as the university, textual culture, literacy, chronology, and ideations of what constitutes nature have been used to frame the legal rationale that continues to oppress Indigenous peoples? How can we maintain the "radical difference" while working in translation (see Zevallos-Aguilar's chapter on Quechua)?

Throughout the volume, the authors offer dynamic definitions and uses of poetic-cognitive strategies in Native languages to articulate Indigenous epistemologies and textualities within a Eurocentric academia (e.g., chumbe, utz kaslemal, waka, Tzamapänh'). At the same time, the essays bring critical thought and theory from Latin America into dialogue with analogous bodies of thought in the field of Indigenous Studies, particularly in North America. In the spirit of not positioning Indigenous languages as *other*, for instance, many of this volume's authors incorporate non-English and non-Spanish terminology without using italics into their essays and reject isolating non-Western terms. In this linguistic refusal, they assert Indigenous presence in settler-colonial institutional settings—in this case, publishing conventions—rather than contort non-Western language to fit within the confines of those conventions.

We hope that the trans-Indigenous literary paths charted throughout the volume are perceived as invitations to walk or engage in dialogue together, whether as Indigenous or Hispanic Studies scholars, regardless of our backgrounds and positionalities, to undo colonial legacies. Beyond making visible an Indigenous corpus, the authors envision trans-hemispheric cultural bridges between Indigenous sovereignty and cosmopolitanism while emphasizing the convergences in Indigenous ontologies. Despite the diverse sociopolitical context of the multiple Indigenous communities to which this volume refers, Abiayala—the land in full maturity—crisscrosses their languages, textualities, stories, and ceremonies, and it is in that space and time that our bodies battle, resist, think, feel, unlearn, remember, speak, write, and thrive. "We doubt, we know, we refuse," as Joseph M. Pierce writes in the afterword of our volume.

In the history of settler-colonial and settler-capitalist nation-states in the Americas (Speed; Bianet Castellanos), a modern, colonial economic system (Mignolo) has been imposed to control and exploit Abiayala and her inhabitants (humans and nonhumans). Throughout this volume, the heteropatriarchal, legal, and anthropocentric rationale at the core of this system is constantly revealed and challenged through stories of genocide, relocation, forced displacement, ethnic and racial constructions, tribal citizenship statuses, extractivism, and Indigenous resistance across reservations, resguardos, and cities. These layers of Indigenous and settler-colonial interactions have had a significant impact on the mode of expression some of the authors use in this book, as literate culture has paralleled and fortified the settler-colonial project while also proving itself a vehicle for Indigenous resistance, resurgence, and prosperity. Because alphabetic writing is at the heart of Western legal rationality, which influences constructions of race and gender, these contested layers of identity expressed through and with language over time have created complex and bifurcated concepts and names that this book's contributors negotiate. Hyphens and slashes populate the English/Spanish writing throughout this volume because colonial languages are stretched to accommodate nonbinary languages as well as Indigenous research paradigms. In this semiotic alteration, our volume challenges the hegemonic normativity regulating the relationships between land, nations, peoples, and language. John Beverley, in his reflection on the future of Hispanism and Latin Americanism, reminds us of Cornejo Polar's critique of Latin American nation-states' literatures as "contradictory totalities" in which Indigeneity both belongs to and disrupts "national unity" (Beverley 8). Our volume poses similar questions by crossing hemispheres and disciplines: What kind of discipline can scholars and educators imagine beyond Hispanic/American/Latinx/Canadian/Indigenous Studies? How can we decenter the colonialism implicated in the Euro-American Humanities and its chronologies, borders, genres, and epistemologies? As they engage with new and old land-based pedagogies, the authors in this volume offer clues and guidance cultivated from affective rationalities, reciprocity, relationality, and a multimodal and multilingual understanding of writing and poetics.

Thematic organization

We have divided the anthology into three thematic parts. The first, "Affective Rationalities: Thinking through the Body, Mind, Heart, and Spirit," contains five innovative chapters focusing on reciprocity and relationships between the human and nonhuman worlds through Indigenous epistemology. We acknowledge that renowned Indigenous writers of northern Abiayala, such as Leslie Marmon Silko (*Ceremony*, 1986; *Storyteller*, 2012), N. Scott Momaday (*The Man Made of Words*, 1997), Thomas King (*The Truth about Stories*, 2005), and Robin Wall Kimmerer (*Braiding Sweetgrass*, 2013), have devoted entire books to Indigenous storytelling, and its relationship with Native science, and the Indigenous epistemological principle of relationality. For decades and across academic fields, these books have been sharing the fact that the stories we tell—and the languages we use to tell them—are who and what we are. In *The Man Made of Words*, for example, Momaday observes: "We are what we imagine. Our very existence consists in our imagination of ourselves. … Man tells stories in order to understand his experience of him, whatever it may be. The possibilities of storytelling are precisely those of understanding the human experience" (87–88). Indeed, the instructions of a society to walk a "proper way" are embedded in its language, storytelling, and poetics. The chapters in this part are not just about aesthetics (literary criticism, art history) but also about ways-of-being and coming-to-know. They also engage with questions of visual sovereignty, knowledge and autonomy, and queer/cuir Indigeneity.

In the first part, we gather diverse voices who are disrupting obsolete dichotomies such as man/women, reason/emotion, body/spirit, Indigenous/non-Indigenous, and academic writing/storytelling. Instead of a binary oppositional thought based on European languages and concepts, these chapters reclaim Indigenous tongues and poetics from which they identify reciprocal poetic-cognitive strategies such as masanh tzame (zoque), kab'awil (maya languages), epu rume (mapudungun), and minga (quechua) to reorganize the body and our relationships with humans and nonhuman beings, and to reconnect with the territory. For instance, when Mikeas Sánchez, Violeta Percia, and Pedro Favaron speak about thinking through and with the heart, they are celebrating the Zoque and Shipibo-Konibo perspectives on words, which are not just for reasoning but also for imagining, healing, and bridging. In short, Indigenous textualities today represent a privileged space for cross-cultural dialogues beyond scholarly enterprise and its limited conceptualizations. This section reminds us of the need to literally cleanse our eyes and ears to see and listen to the languages of the land and to acknowledge the land and her keepers (e.g., Tzamapänh,' Chaikonibo). In the body, mind, heart, and spirit, knowledge is action-based, and words must be embodied.

In tune with these affective rationalities, in the chapter "Embodied Territory: Trans-Indigenous and Intercultural Practices," Miguel Rojas-Sotelo narrates the epistemological guidelines in organizing *Soberanía visual*, a 2018 exhibition of multigenerational and intertribal embodied practices and sovereign aesthetics. Confronting Colombian art history and criticism, Rojas-Sotelo deconstructs colonial ideas on literacy, aesthetics, and art itself through an intercultural and relational curatorial project that spans various Indigenous nations in Abiayala (the Americas). Similarly, in "El camino de una palabra que piensa con el corazón," Mikeas Sánchez and Violeta Percia contrast the colonial genealogy of the word "savage" (salvaje) with the Zoque expression Tzamapänh' ("the one who knows the mountain and protects her"). In activating the Zoque nonbinary perspective embedded in the language, the Western project of civilization reveals itself as weak and incoherent. The sacred Zoque word masanh tzame vindicates the force of speaking Native languages, remembering the ancestral names of the territory, and writing Indigenous oralitures. Untranslatability as central to Indigenous poetics becomes an invitation to enter Indigenous paradigms without the Western desire of knowing a priori.

Marco Antonio Huerta's "Hacia una relacionalidad cuir de la tierra: Géneros y sexualidades en Abiayala y Turtle Island" turns the reader's attention to a vibrant conversation about non-heteronormative sexuality. Huerta delves into the field of Queer Indigenous Studies from the North and places it into conversation with Cuir Indigenous Studies from the South, underlining the sociopolitical differences and acknowledging a lack of transhemispheric approaches. Huerta's research provides a fertile ground for future research where the south's relationship to non-heteronormative sexuality may inform new theoretical models in the North. Refracting American and Canadian identity politics that control Indigeneity among mixed-race individuals, in "Una conversación cosmoléctica a través de *Cherrufe, La Bola de Fuego*," Antonio Catrileo and Manuel Carrión-Lira demonstrate how the ideology of Chilean mestizaje and its literary implications imprison the possibilities implied by Mapuche textualities and identities. Reading Mariella Fuentealba Millaguir's novel through Gloria E. Chacón's "cosmolectics," Catrileo and Carrión illuminate a new path for an autonomous form of Mapuche literary criticism through juxtaposing Maya epistemes like "kab'awil" to the Mapuche "epu rume."

The final chapter in this section is inspired by Indigenous scholars from the North; Pedro Favaron reflects on an Indigenous research paradigm in "Desde el corazón de la cultura: Filosofía, investigación académica y racionalidad poética de las naciones amerindias de la Amazonía." Blurring the boundaries between a personal narrative (centered on thoughts and feelings) and academic inquiry, as well as between the disciplines of Anthropology, Indigenous Studies, and Hispanic Studies, Favaron invites scholars and educators to imagine Andean and Amazonian "affective rationalities" as well as science, art, and spirituality at the foundation of a land-based academy.

The second part of this anthology, "Reflections on Indigeneity, Translation, Pedagogies, and Epistemologies," contains five chapters that force readers to think with and through Indigenous epistemologies and ontologies. The connections between knowledge, philosophy, and Indigenous language become transparent in the classroom, and translation as a tool is imperative in understanding Indigeneity. Most answer the question that Heath Justice once posed: Why do Indigenous literatures matter? We evoke Lakota/Anishinabe educator Frances Washburn's insightful proposition that resonates in this part: "The best way for anyone to learn about other people's cultures is to learn their languages, but when that is not possible or practical, the next best way is to learn their stories" (427). In "*Man are' taj Utz k'aslemal la'*: Indigenous Ecologies and the Limits of Cross-disciplinary Translation," Nathan Henne reflects on teaching about Indigenous poetry and environmental humanities. He underscores the unintelligibility of Western concepts (e.g., animism, religion, nature) in teaching Maya and Quechua literatures and their originating ontologies and epistemologies—utz kaslemal and sumak kawsay. Henne's critique of "the Western ontological category of nature," as well as the inclusion or appropriation of untranslated Kichwa and Aymara concepts in the Ecuadorian and Bolivian constitutions, opens up an intercultural challenge for "decolonial translation" and the rejection of colonial languages equivalents for Indigenous cosmolectics.

In "Enseñanza de poesía y canto quechua: Castellanización y mantenimiento de la diferencia radical de la cultura y lengua quechua," Ulises Juan Zevallos-Aguilar, in conversation with Henne's treatment of language and cosmolectics and on the basis of his long experience teaching Quechua poetry in an American Spanish department, compares several translations from diverse Quechua dialects to Spanish in a kind of "archeology of translation." While pointing to academic discussions on Quechua phonetics and agglutination, Zevallos-Aguilar juxtaposes Andean genres such as traditional Huayno, Quechuañol urban poetry, and blues-influenced Huayno in Quechua. The themes explored in Zevallos-Aguilar's analysis reinforce the constant transformation of Native languages and the persistent renewal of Indigenous textualities as a recurring theme throughout our volume. The chapter also points to the injection of Indigenous languages in Hispanic Studies departments, contributing to their decolonization.

Similarly, in "Viven hasta ahora, canancamapas causan: El Manuscrito de Huarochirí como puente al futuro," Víctor Quiroz, Estelle Tarica, and Ana Lucía Tello revisit the "scriptural practices" (e.g., sacred geography, ceremony, the body) of the *Huarochirí Manuscript* through the Aymara ch'ixi—"motley" or "spotted" gaze (Rivera Cusicanqui). The authors invite Hispanists and Latin Americanists to destabilize their respective disciplines' graphocentrism while exploring Andean space poetics. In engaging with the sixteenth- and seventeenth-century Quechua manuscript—in an Andean gesture of nayrapacha ("pasado-como-por-venir," Muyolema 262)—its anonymous scribe or editor illuminates a multimodality and multitemporality that provides a guide for our present. In "Diálogos hispanos en América del Norte sobre video y cine indígena," Oswaldo Lara offers a necessary literature review of scholarly work in Spanish about Indigenous cinema from the North (a category that includes Mexico, Canada, and the United States). Lara connects an array of analyses on Indigenous video and film, ethnographic cinema, and visual anthropology while posing questions about their academic reception, communal forms of production, and mainstream expectations of Indigenous film. Following Lara's findings, open-ended questions remain for future analyses that make use of an Indigenous research paradigm: How does scholars' reception of Indigenous film change or coincide when speaking from Latin America rather than North America? What can creators and audiences from these two regions learn from one another's outlooks and interpretations of the world around them? What can we glean from the fact that no Indigenous films from the United States and Canada are studied in México, but the inverse is a growing field?

Because labeling, groupness, and assumptions about race, ethnicity, and gender occur in language, in this part's final chapter, "'We *Are* the Canon': On Reconceptualizing Hispanic Studies from Indigenous Studies," Rita Palacios, Juan Ariel Castillo Cocom, and Paul Worley remind us about the power relations between "lo hispano" and "lo indígena" among the settler-colonial intelligentsia. In resisting the current performance of "diversity and inclusion" (i.e., acknowledgment, reconciliation, and apology), Palacios, Castillo, and Worley call for imagining a land-based, transhemispheric, multilingual, and multiscriptural field beyond the narrow nationalistic and ethnic perspective of Hispanic/American/Canadian/Indigenous Studies. The chapter offers directives in thinking about curriculum changes at the institutional level from three different sites in the Americas.

The final part, "Indigenous Lands, Competing Found/(N)ational Narratives, and Governance," unpacks the profound connections between territory and the human and nonhuman worlds while exploring key concepts such as authority, identity, nation-states, and belongingness. Each chapter in this section questions, challenges, and engages with the paradoxes of bridging words and worlds through Indigeneity, race, land, nation, and geography. The first of these is "Huacas y lugares sagrados como poética indígena," in which Fredy Amílcar Roncalla revisits Peruvian literary historiography via "la huaca" to explore a form of Andean space-time poetics suitable for intercultural confluences. Beyond the avant-garde movement celebrated by European and Peruvian literatures, Roncalla invites us to delve into the non-graphocentric Andean forms of writing, such as quipu, ceques, taki, huayno, and ícaro. For Roncalla, a centuries-old continuance of anticolonial yanantin (meaning "complementarity") can be traced from Juan Choqne and the *Huarochirí Manuscript*, to Jorge Eduardo Eielson, Juan Ramírez Ruíz, Daniel Kirwayo, and contemporary Quechua literatures. In another reversal of national literatures, Roncalla concludes that huacas are foundational to Peruvian literature.

We continue this section with a chapter by the Guna scholar Sue Patricia Haglund. Currently, scholars and educators from Indigenous and Hispanic Studies conjure the "Abiayala" toponym borrowed from the Dulegaya language of the Gunadule people in Panamá and Colombia. Paradoxically, Haglund claims, scholarship commonly overlooks Gunadule multimodal textualities (e.g., Babigala/Dule narratives, healing songs, traditional molas) or misunderstands them via Eurocentric forms of anthropology, even by other Indigenous scholars outside the Gunadule community. Haglund's chapter, "*Iddisig, un poco más allá*: Dule Poetic Gatherings," addresses these challenges, bridges the *saglas* (Gunadule knowledge keepers), their traditional ways of governance, and contemporary Gunadule poets such as Aiban Wagua and Manipiniktikiya Abadio Green. In this conceptual reworking, she unsettles false dichotomies between oral and written expression ("writing as an extension of Gunadule oratory") and native and migrant producers (e.g., poets as urban saglas), while making visible the continuance of Gunadule "artful-political" cosmolectics.

Underlining the importance of positioning ourselves in contexts where multiple colonial narratives and languages overlap (e.g., Spanish-English, Mexican-American, Chicanx/Native), Carolina Bloem and James Courage Singer follow with "Utah, Aztlán, y otros reclamos colonialistas de colonos." This contribution is singular in addressing the (dis)connections between Chicanx/Latinx Studies and Indigenous Studies. Located in Utah, they engage with uneasy questions such as: How does a contemporary Navajo citizen perceive the Chicanx narrative of Aztlán? Or how does an Andean-mestizo settler in Utah reflect on her own identity in a settler-colonial society? The fourth chapter in this part underlines Sean Sell's trans-Indigenous literary juxtaposition of the Anishinaabe in the North to the Maya Tsotsil in the South. In "Restorative Indigenous Jurisprudence in

Anishinaabe and Tsotsil-Maya Fiction," Sell brings these two disparate geographies, languages, and nations together through the role of law in Indigenous communities. These novels feature more than just fiction; they boldly depict the injustices many Indigenous peoples face in their communities as a result of living within a colonial context, such as the recent murder of Tata Domingo Choc in Guatemala, whose body was set on fire because of his spiritual practice. Questions on sovereignty remain evident throughout Sell's essay: Is there a path for ancestral jurisprudence, autonomous Indigenous education, and nation-states' legal systems for working together toward a new and intercultural social or natural contract that promotes "growth and harmony" for all? And beyond revenge and incarceration, what can we learn, unlearn, and remember from Indigenous legal frameworks from both hemispheres?

Reaching to a different continent for comparison, in "Searching for Relatives: Assimilation and Global Indigenous Resistance to Boarding Schools in Xhon (Zapotec) and Jigalong (Martu) Fiction," Paulina Pineda contrasts two contemporary novels. She points to the fact that both the Zapotec and Jigalong novels examine oppression, forced assimilation, and intergenerational trauma in the context of settler-colonial boarding-school projects. In Pineda's analysis, oralitures and Indigenous experiences of womanhood link communities' reeducation processes in Australia and Mexico. Pineda's contribution expands the trans-Indigenous paradigm to a more global approach.

In the context of Indigenous literatures from Mexico, Native languages and communities such as the Maya Yucatec and the Biniza'a/Zapotec have a longer history of literary production and have received more critical attention than, for example, the P'urhepecha nation. In an attempt to rectify this omission, "Voces y tensiones entre mundos: Aproximación a algunos temas de la novela *Alonso Mariano* del escritor p'urhepecha Ismael García Marcelino," Sue Meneses Eternod analyzes the first novel ever written in P'urhepecha. She employs a translanguaging lens as well as the "visiones de cabeza" methodology applied by Miguel Rocha Vivas to Indigenous textualities from Colombia. Beyond the nation-state projects of Mexico and Colombia, Uwa/P'urhepecha literatures converge via trans-Indigenous literary criticism. Meneses leaves us with important critiques about monolithic perspectives on Indigeneity and "Indigenous literatures" based only on Indigenous languages, especially in contexts such as Mexico, where the nation-state's "educational" project of acculturation has marginalized Indigenous languages for centuries.

The final chapter in this part illuminates an understudied area of Hispanic Studies related to Brazil. "Literaturas indígenas en Brasil: Migrar a las letras," by Miguel Rocha Vivas, underlines the differences between Brazilian history and the rest of Latin America. Rocha Vivas considers the Portuguese Crown moving to Rio do Janeiro in 1822, the Amazonian ethnographers such as Ermanno Stradelli and Theodor Koch-Grünberg in the nineteenth and twentieth centuries, and an about-face in Brazilian art that occurred in 1922 during the Semana de Arte Moderna in São Paulo. Through a discussion of the latter event, which featured the work of five artists, including the women painters Tarsila do Amaral and Anita Malfatti, the poets Oswald de Andrade and Menotti del Picchia, as well as the spoken-word poet Mário de Andrade, Rocha Vivas argues it transformed how the country viewed itself. In particular, the discussion dismantles the stereotypes that locate Amazonian

Indigeneity exclusively in the forest and oral practices. In doing so, Rocha analyses the literary work of contemporary Indigenous writers from Brazil such as Eliane Potiguara, Daniel Munduruku, and Yaguarê Yamã, where cities function as a native villages and writings transcend the alphabet.

We hope this anthology inspires even more dialogues across, within, and beyond our hemispheres, ones in which linguistic barriers are confronted creatively so that we can collectively continue to disarm the colonial legacies that haunt our disciplines. Scholars of Afro–Latin American Studies (Rivera-Rideau et al.) argue that there is a need to juxtapose the Northern and Southern Hemispheres' constructions of race. As scholars traversing Hispanic Studies, Latin American Studies, Spanish, and Indigenous Studies, we are cognizant that more dialogues across our disciplines are needed in broader, multilingual, multiethnic modalities. Strikingly, it is clear that critical Indigenous thought from the North is having an impact on the work of scholars who are working in the South, and we hope Indigenous thought from the South can also have an indelible impact on the North as we lay down some building blocks for more dialogue. Last, although we do not engage directly with the formation of Chicanx/Latinx fields, we perceive its future involvement in Indigenous Studies from the South—and not just the North—will open other comparative horizons.

Notes

1. This turn did not seem to relate to the creation of "Hispanic" as a census category in the United States.

2. While Portuguese is usually taught in Hispanic Studies departments and arguably has gone through similar processes, our anthology mainly focuses on the founding and emphasis of Spanish because of its longer institutionalized history in Canada and the United States. Nonetheless, one of our contributors, Miguel Rocha Vivas, offers a panoramic view of Indigenous texts produced in Brazil that displays many similarities with the rest of Latin America. Another chapter, by Carolina Bloem and James Courage Singer, also touches upon the tensions between Chicanx and Indigenous Studies to give readers a sense of the divergences. However, most contributors of our anthology do not directly engage with the issues. We recommend the field of Critical Latinx Indigeneities for more discussion around these conceptual differences. A main issue in this anthology is the lack of Afro-Indigenous textualities or how Afro-descendants contribute to Hispanic Studies, but we hope that this is the start of a future conversation for our fields. New publications (Gómez Menjívar), offer new avenues to think about Afro-descendants' contributions to literature specifically.

Works Cited

Allen, Chadwick. *Trans-Indigenous: Methodologies for Global Native Literary Studies.* U of Minnesota P, 2012.

Altschul, Nadia R. *Geographies of Philological Knowledge: Postcoloniality & the Transatlantic National Epic.* U of Chicago P, 2012.

Álvarez-Junco, José. *Spanish Identity in the Age of Nations.* Manchester UP, 2011.

Bartley, Russell H. "The Cold War and Latin American Area Studies in the Former USSR." *Latin American Perspectives*, vol. 45, no. 4 (July 2018), pp. 115–140.

Battiste, Marie. *Decolonizing Education: Nourishing the Learning Spirit.* Purich Publishing, 2013.

Beard, Laura. "Decolonization and Indigenous Sovereignty: Coming to Terms with Theories in the Americas." *Decolonial Approaches to Latin American Literatures and Cultures*, edited by J. G. Ramos and T. Daly. Palgrave Macmillan, 2016, pp. 199–213.

Beverley, John. "The Pittsburgh Model and Other Thoughts on the Field (Hispanism/Latin Americanism." *Revista Hispánica Moderna*, vol. 74, no. 1 (2021), pp. 7–16.

Bianet Castellanos, M. "Introduction: Settler Colonialism in Latin America." *American Quarterly*, vol. 69, no. 4 (2017), pp. 777–781.

Bianet Castellanos, M., Lourdes Gutiérrez Nájera, and Arturo J. Aldama, editors. *Comparative Indigeneities of the Américas: Toward a Hemispheric Approach.* U of Arizona P, 2012.

Castro-Gómez, Santiago. *La poscolonialidad explicada a los niños.* Editorial Universidad del Cauca, 2005.

Castro-Klaren, Sara. "Notes from the Field: Decolonizing the Curriculum/The 'Spanish' Major." *Decolonial Approaches to Latin American Literatures and Cultures*, edited by J. G. Ramos and T. Daly. Palgrave Macmillan, 2016, pp. 3–18.

Chaat Smith, Paul. *Everything You Know about Indians Is Wrong.* U of Minnesota P, 2009.

Codding, Mitchell. "Archer Milton Huntington, Champion of Spain in the United States." *Spain in America: The Origins of Hispanism in the United States*, edited by Richard L. Kagan. U of Illinois P, 2002, pp. 142–170.

Cox, James H., and Daniel Heath Justice, editors. *The Oxford Handbook of Indigenous American Literature.* Oxford UP, 2014.

Dussel, Enrique. *The Invention of the Americas: Eclipse of "the Other" and the Myth of Modernity.* Continuum, 1995.

Enrigue, Álvaro. "El apache Gerónimo fue el primer mexicano." https://elpais.com/cultura/2018/11/28/actualidad/1543373959_232060.html

Gómez Menjívar, Jennifer Carolina. *América in Letters: Literary Interventions from Mexico to the Southern Cone.* Vanderbuilt UP, 2022.

Gómez-Moreno, Ángel. *Breve historia del medievalismo panhispánico (primera tentativa).* Iberoamericana, 2011.

Heath Justice, Daniel. "Currents of Trans/National Criticism in Indigenous Literary Studies." *American Indian Quarterly*, vol. 35, no. 3 (2011), pp. 334–350.

Hedeen, K. M., and Rodríguez Núñez, V. *Poesía Indígena estadounidense contemporánea.* La Cabra Ediciones, 2011.

Hedge Coke, Allison Adelle. *Sing: Poetry from Indigenous Americas.* U of Arizona P, 2011.

Herlihy-Mera, Jeffrey. *Decolonizing American Spanish: Eurocentrism and the Limits of Foreignness in the Imperial Ecosystem.* U of Pittsburgh P, 2022.

Kovach, Margaret. *Indigenous Methodologies: Characteristics, Conversations, and Contexts.* U of Toronto P, 2009.

King, Thomas. *The Truth about Stories: A Native Narrative.* U of Minnesota P, 2005.

Mignolo, Walter. *Local Histories/Global Designs: Coloniality, Subaltern Knowledge, and Border Thinking.* Princeton UP, 2000.

Momaday, N. Scott. *The Man Made of Words: Essays, Stories, Passages.* St. Martin's P, 1997.

Muyolema, Armando. "América Latina y los pueblos indígenas: Para una crítica de la razón latino-americana." *Teorizando las literaturas indígenas contemporáneas*, edited by E. del Valle Escalante. Contracorriente, 2015, pp. 233–274.

Ramos, J. G., and T. Daly. *Decolonial Approaches to Latin American Literatures and Cultures.* Palgrave Macmillan, 2016.

Rivera Cusicanqui, Silvia. *Un mundo ch'ixi es posible.* Tinta Limón, 2018.

Rivera-Rideau, Petra R., Jennifer A. Jones, and Tianna S. Paschel. *Afro-Latin@ Diasporas*. Springer Nature, 2016.

Rocha Vivas, Miguel. *Word Mingas: Oralitegraphies and Mirrored Visions on Oralitures and Indigenous Contemporary Literatures*, translated by Paul M. Worley and Melissa Birkhofer. U North Carolina P, 2021.

Saldaña Portillo, Maria Josefina. *Indian Given: Racial Geographies across Mexico and the United States*. Duke UP, 2016.

Silko, Leslie Marmon. *Ceremony*. Penguin Books, 1986.

———. *Storyteller*. Penguin Publishing Group, 2012.

Speed, Shannon. "Structures of Settler Capitalism in Abya Yala." *American Quarterly*, vol. 69, no. 4 (2017), pp.783–790.

Tuhiwai Smith, Linda. *Decolonizing Methodologies: Research and Indigenous Peoples*. St. Martin's P, 2012.

Valaskakis, Gail Guthrie. *Indian Country: Essays on Contemporary Native Culture*. Wilfred Laurier UP, 2005.

Wall Kimmerer, Robin. *Braiding Sweetgrass: Indigenous Wisdom, Scientific Knowledge, and the Teachings of Plants*. Milkweed, 2013.

Warkentin, Germaine. "In Search of 'The Word of the Other': Aboriginal Sign Systems and the History of the Book in Canada." *Book History*, vol. 2 (1999), pp. 1–27.

Washburn, Frances. "All That Is Native and Fine: Teaching Native American Literature." *The Oxford Handbook of Indigenous American Literature*. Edited by Jamex H. Cox and Daniel Heath Justice. Oxford UP, pp. 427–432.

PART 1

Affective Rationalities: Thinking through the Body, Mind, Heart, and Spirit

CHAPTER 1

Embodied Territory: Trans-Indigenous and Intercultural Practices

Miguel Rojas-Sotelo
Duke University

In 2018, as copresident of EILA V (Fifth Intercultural Encounter of Amerindian Literature and Art) in Bogotá, I co-organized and co-curated *Soberanía visual*, an exhibit on "trans-Indigenous and intercultural" art practices in Abiayala.[1] The intention of organizing such an exhibition was to bring into discussion embodied cultural practices in the field of Indigenous Studies. I understand as embodied practices not those that emanate from academic spaces and disciplinary constructs but the ones associated with situated and contextual knowledge and that are able to bring oral and local traditions into institutional spaces of the arts and culture. As a scholar currently living in the US and working frequently with Indigenous cultural producers (filmmakers, visual artists, oralitores, scholars, activists) and their work, I believe that transcultural and decolonial approaches are able to interrupt academic spaces such as universities, museums, galleries, conferences, and publications. The opportunity to contribute to this volume had me revisiting those ideas and pondering the ways our thinking and doing relate to the disciplinary divides across Latin American Cultural Studies, Indigenous Studies, and North American Indigenous Studies.

This chapter brings the embodied, situated aesthetic practice of a group of Indigenous and non-Indigenous cultural producers into dialogue with decolonial approaches and Indigenous and Native American Studies from the North American academy. The notion of embodiment derives from the way each subject literally carries its territory and develops a critical yet sensible individual and collective interruption in the way academic disciplines look at cultural products, categorizing and compartmentalizing them in taxonomical exercises of capture and control. I use trans-Indigenous and decolonial practices to identify critical departures from coloniality (the beyond, expressed in the prefix "trans-") and the points of origination in coloniality itself.[2] These producers work on intercultural dialogues and do not make what we consider art (in conventional terms) but mostly perform acts and events that interrupt spaces within and outside academic locations, supporting ways of exercising aesthetic sovereignty and forms of liberation. Their work, however, is read within the realm of visual studies.

I am a non-Indigenous scholar-activist writing in the field of decolonial aesthetics and Indigenous Studies, cognizant that the missing piece embedded in theoretical approaches to cultural production is the fact that rarely there is compensation to the communities we work with. This chapter, then, is a conscious effort to recognize the lack of compensation, and for instance, it should work as a form of *a'buru* (*pagamento, despacho*, or offering in Iku of the Indigenous-Koguis, Arhuacos, Wiwas, of Sierra Nevada de Santa Marta), a ritualized embodied, situated, and contextual cultural practice that otherwise would be a mere academic exercise.[3] To start with, I am aware that this chapter is a work in progress and that, by thinking and doing, I have learned, I continue to learn, and I keep engaging with those I work with.[4] What follows is an open reading of a group of multigenerational cultural producers. Their situated and relational practices are associated with visual, performative, and documentary work that make a territory legible. The Cree writer Craig Womack makes the distinction that Indigenous art is not purely aesthetic, "art for art's sake; rather, it invokes, evokes, and creates from, in, and on the communities where we live" (16).

Modern and colonial visuality erased our ability to read the material and cultural production of Indigenous peoples. On the one hand, by deterritorializing and marginalizing it. On the other, by emphasizing the realm of Kantian aesthetics (the beauty and sublime, a sphere outside life itself) and placing artistic products in places such as the museum, controlled by an institutionalized world of art. Most Indigenous peoples base their archival practices on incorporated/embodied forms (prácticas encarnadas) and continue to use orality and visuality based on material culture that is ideographic and functional in nature. Womack reminds us: "In mainstream culture, the Indian intellectual term is an oxymoron. Yet we have produced intellectual texts written for centuries, not to mention that indigenous-based intellectual knowledge is such an important part of oral tradition" (14).

The conceptual script of the exhibit *Soberanía visual* was based on an essay of the same title that won the 2016–2017 national prize on art criticism in Colombia. It was the first time that an academic contest recognized a text addressing Indigenous "artists." Here the prefix "trans-" functions as a form of translation or a way in which a constellation of cultural production moves across or through divides. In the essay, as well as in the exhibit, an ecocritical and epistemic reading of a group of cultural producers (I would rather not use the category "artist") and their practices are explored to expand the horizon of avant-garde aesthetic canons.[5] What brought them together? It was the fact that they seek to be in relation and tension with notions such as territory, the body, memory, and the expansion of extractivist agendas by using an array of visual, audiovisual, and textual tools derived from their lived experience as subjects living along the frontier of academic and nonacademic spaces. They function, both in their artistic practice and in their life experience, as Pedro Pablo Gómez asserts on an "aesthetic bordering," they inhabit rural and urban contexts, illiterate and literate ones, and as colonial subjects they have been imprinted by racial, civilizatory, gender, social, and moral modern/colonial traits.[6] Today, they are seekers of individual and collective sovereignty through their work. These bordering subjects are intervening in hegemonic spaces: art galleries, museums, cinema screens, books fairs (and books), festivals, schools and universities, the streets, and most importantly, their territories.

Earthing

The modern/colonial, north/south axis has defined power relations during modernity and established forms of relating to the land and its resources. Most Indigenous peoples in rural (but also in urban) settings preserve an earth/cosmos form of existence, establishing networks of relations within the earth, the human, nonhuman, the beyond human, and the cosmos. The sun rises in the east and continues to be the main protagonist in the Indigenous cosmovision. At the end of the first moon each June, peoples in Chile, Argentina, Bolivia, Peru, and Ecuador celebrate a new solar year. The We Xipantu or Nquillatún (Mapuche for "new year" or "sunrise of the new sun") and Inti-Raymi ("festival of the sun" in Quechua) are some of the most important celebrations of Indigenous peoples of the Southern Hemisphere.[7] The Incas worshipped Inti because they knew the value of its service: giving plants their life energy (photosynthesis). European conquerors followed traces of sun/gold temples and gold cities and all forms of its representation in violent and treacherous ways—the search for "El Dorado."

What follows are some examples (artworks) that build on such traditions from a contemporary visual practice. For his installation titled *CHINGAZA* (2018), the visual cultural producer of peasant origin Jeisson Castillo-Gutiérrez (Colombia, 1996) used 6,600 golden coins to write the name of a sacred mountain páramo (moorland) (Figure 1). The coins were installed directly on the central column of the gallery space facing east—the direction of the páramo and the rising sun, and reading "CHINGAZA," which in Chibcha means "mountain of the God of Night." Formally, the piece establishes an almost sacred relationship with the audience because of its manual construction (each coin was glued to the wall), its location (toward the east), its color (gold), its grand size, and the lighting, which generated an aura that seemed to emanate from the image/word itself, just like any sacramental altar of the American baroque. Conceptually, *CHINGAZA* makes a demand toward the threat of extractivism in ancestral territories and to the monetization of mother earth. This direct allusion occurs due to repetition, 6,600 golden coins and their value, which relates on the one hand to forms of production of material culture and art and on the other to the valuation and extraction of natural resources; in this case, gold mining in the páramos is positioned against their value as water sponges, filters, and reserves in addition to their ecological value as reservoirs of life. The golden COP$100 peso coin used in the installation has a frailejón (the representative plant of the páramo) printed on one of its sides, which reinforces the idea of an extractive economy on a natural space.

CHINGAZA is part of Castillo's *Páramo* project that includes scientific illustrations, ceramics, and installations.[8] Castillo's illustration has been used by the national park service in pedagogical pieces to conserve the fragile ecosystem. The series not only re-creates this geography, sacred for Indigenous peoples and valuable for its mineral and water

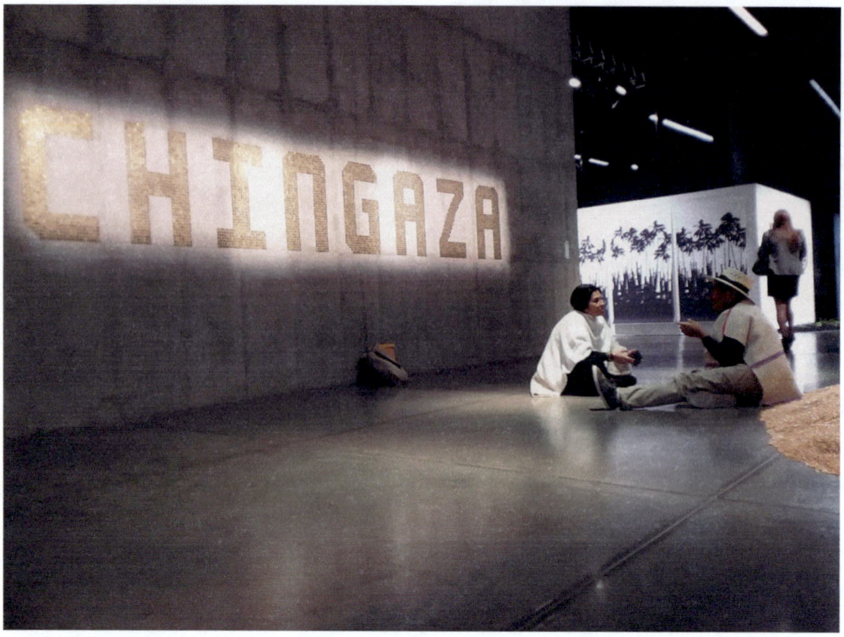

Figure 1. *CHINGAZA* by Jeisson Castillo, 2018, 6,600 coins on the wall. *Soberanía visual*, Exhibition Hall, Universidad Javeriana, 2018.

resources in the Andes, but also builds narratives in which scientific illustration and economics collide. In sum, the project reflects on the conflictive nature of this territory. The work captures the imposing geography using conventional artistic means, also via installations that portray the government's race for the exploitation and monetization of the ecosystem (Figures 2 and 3). The piece also makes reference to a canonical work by the famous conceptual visual artist Antonio Caro (1951–2021), titled *Diez-Pesos / San Andrés* (1997). Caro used COP$10 peso silver coins to draw the map of San Andrés and Providencia, the Caribbean archipelago located along the outer ring of Colombia. The piece was almost premonitory to what happens to this territory, immersed in a border conflict with Nicaragua since the times of New Granada and before the separation of Panama in 1903. The old 10-peso silver coins he used had the map of San Andrés and Providencia printed on one side; they were larger than other coins minted in Colombia, and consequently, they were made with a cheap metal alloy, giving them an ordinary appearance. The accelerated devaluation of the peso quickly put them out of circulation, testifying to the country's (de) appreciation for its island territories (historically inhabited by Afro Caribbeans that speak creole), and mistreated by the actions of the government recently after the destruction of Providencia by Hurricane Iota in 2020.

Castillo's *Páramo* series also documents plants, animals, peoples, and other nonhuman creatures in drawing, painting, photography, and ceramics. In his own words: "My art is experiential, so everything that happens in everyday life has an effect on the pieces in development. The project is also nourished by the continuous trips and explorations of this vast land in danger of extinction" (135). Castillo's approach to visuality takes him to

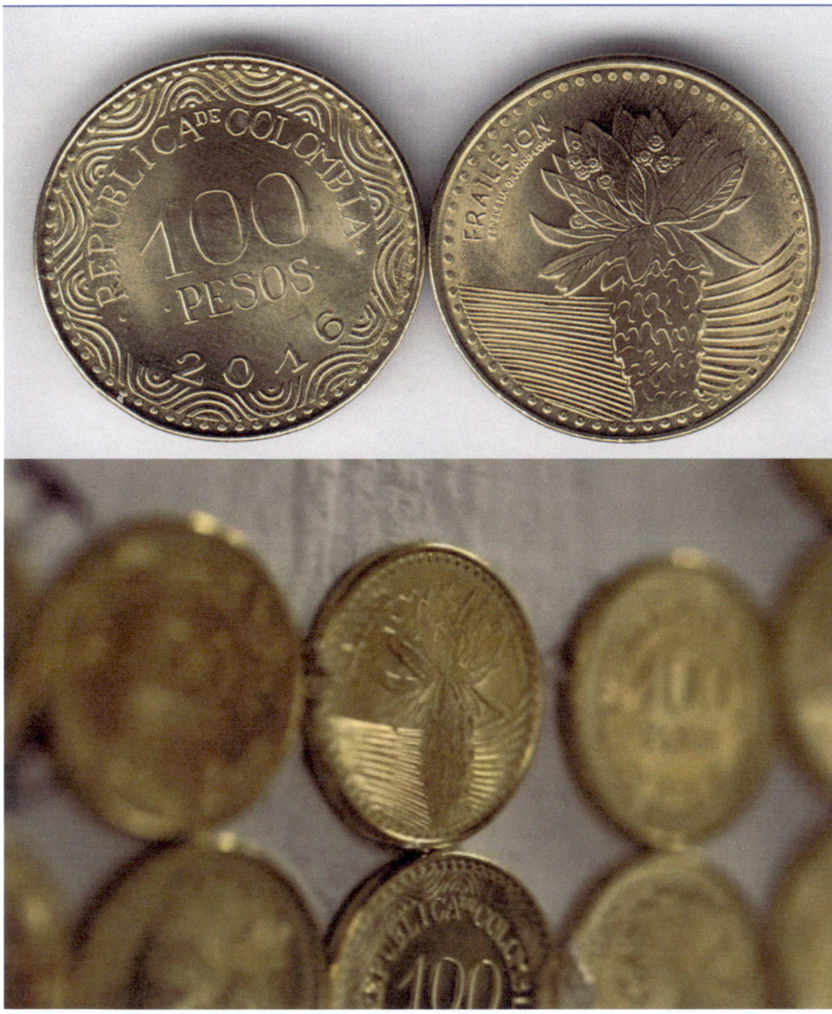

Figure 2. COP$100 peso coins. *CHINGAZA* by Jeisson Castillo, 2018, detail.

multiple territories and Indigenous nations. For this series, he traveled, interviewed peasant and Indigenous páramo dwellers, documented several páramos, and experienced a territory unique to this part of Abiayala, also reconnecting his rural upbringing in Boyacá, in the Andean highlands, with his training as a contemporary artist, researcher, and producer (Figure 4).

As a curatorial decision, in front of *CHINGAZA*, facing west, was *Maíz* (1994–2018), an installation piece by the historian, cultural administrator, and cultural producer Carlos Uribe (b. Colombia, 1964) (Figure 5). *Maíz*, in its simplicity, is a conceptual bombshell; five tons of yellow corn are deposited on the ground to form a mountain. Historically, after European conquerors took military control, pillaged, slaughtered, tortured, and raped peoples of territories in search of precious metals and gems, they turned to tribute. A direct form was to "kidnap" crops. Indigenous people had to pay with a measure of gold, a *millar*

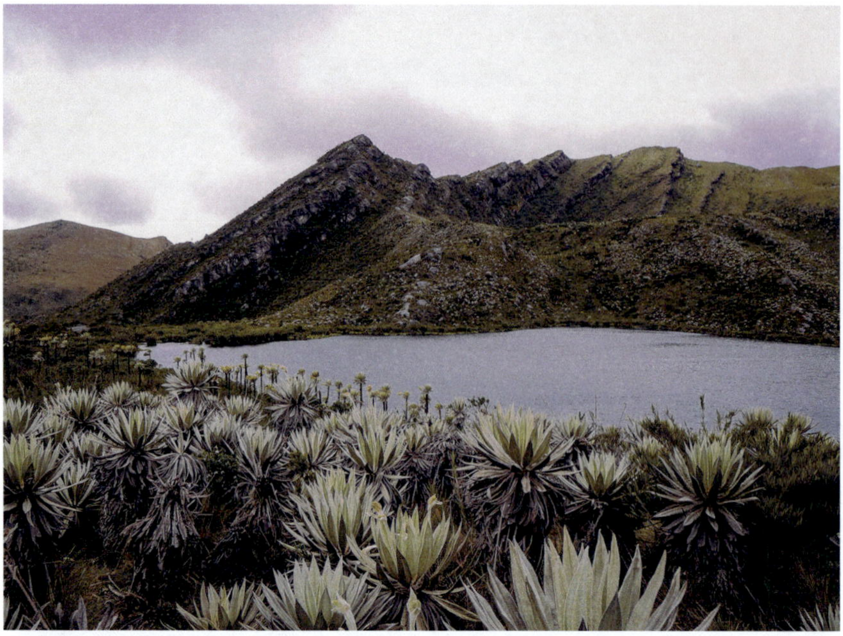

Figure 3. Chingaza páramo, see "frailejones," 2001, author's photo.

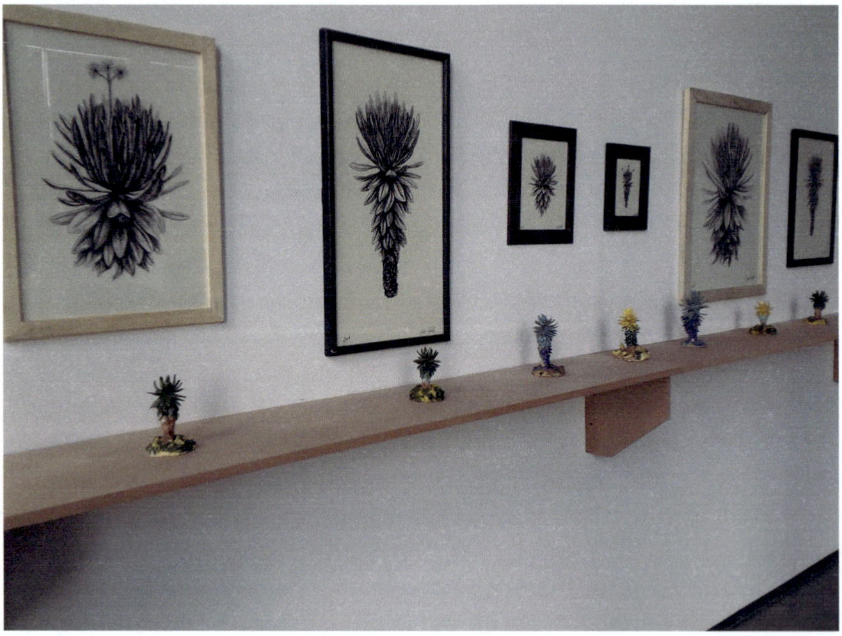

Figure 4. *Frailejón* by Jeisson Castillo, 2016–2017. Charcoal on paper, *Land of the Water That Is Cooked* (series of drawings and ceramic frailejones), variable dimensions, installation. *Soberanía visual*, Exhibition Hall, Universidad Javeriana, 2018.

(a colonial measurement according to Ramos and García), for their own grain that would guarantee the survival of their communities (84). This archaic form of tribute was added to the brutal forms of repression, cultural violence through evangelization, and the banning of local languages and culture. Formally, *Maíz* is a reenactment of a ransom payment, food for gold. Conceptually, it takes the spectator to a time and space outside the gallery, into coloniality and modernity itself, a place in which the colonial matrix of power exerts all control over the subject.[9] It reveals one of its darkest aspects: desire, the gaze of a golden mountain (the sundown).

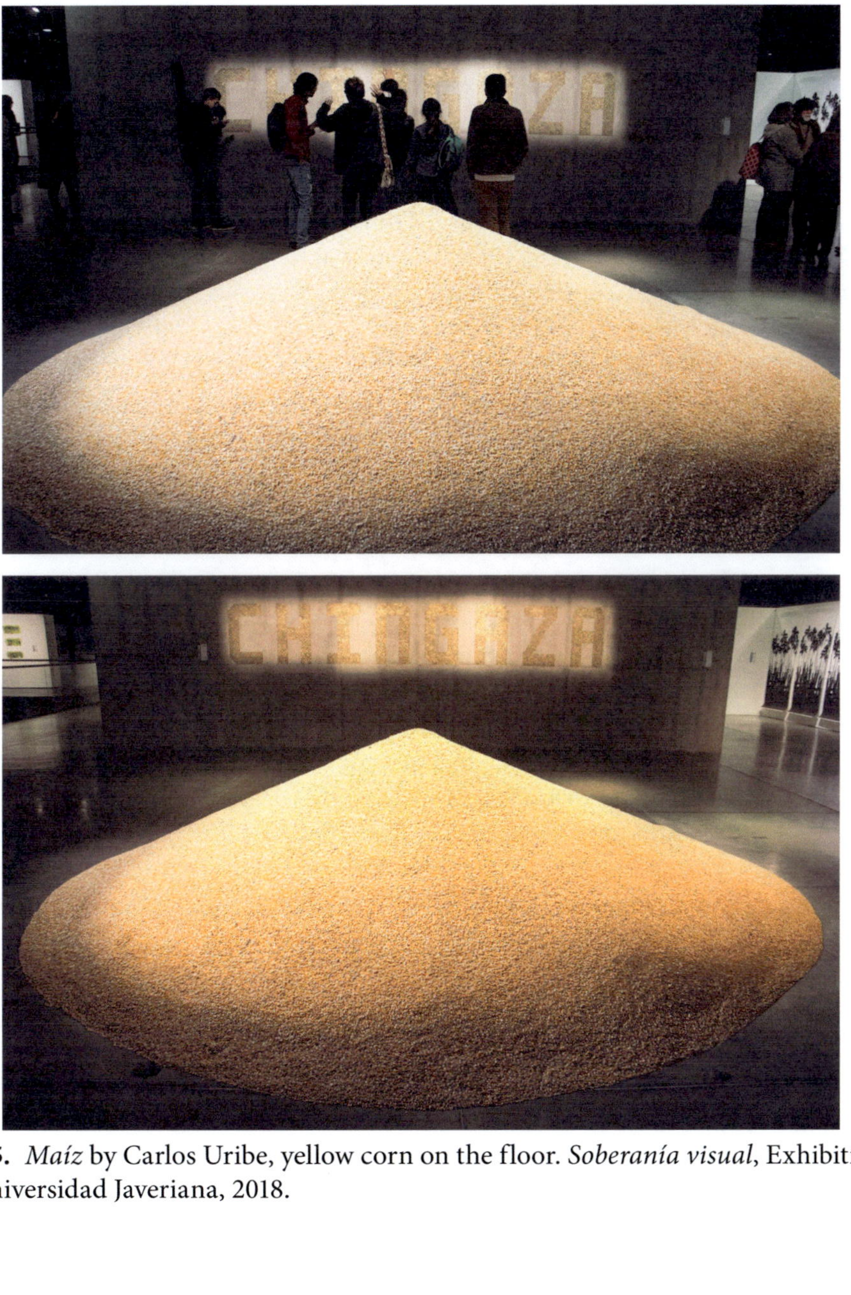

Figure 5. *Maíz* by Carlos Uribe, yellow corn on the floor. *Soberanía visual*, Exhibition Hall, Universidad Javeriana, 2018.

Here, an embodied territory emerges. Fernández mentions how geography is essentially a fact of power, as the landscape is identified, described, and conquered to be later exploited (246). Corn (maíz) and cane-sugar brick (panela) are some of the materials that Uribe has used in his career as a sculptor. He has also used materials such as oil, coal, earth, and water to make specific references to the economic and cultural geography of the Americas. Uribe's upbringing was in the mountains of Antioquia, where corn used to be a staple crop; today, most of it is imported from the United States, and *Maíz* a reminder of the colonial wound. As an art installation, it creates a bodily, almost sacramental experience (since corn is consumed), also linking the cosmogony and everyday life of the peoples of Abiayala.

Sowing

The landscape moves; it is transported in memories and the body of those displaced or exiled, but it is not uprooted. From the rural south of Colombia, trained in Medellín and later in Quito, Tirsa Chindoy-Chasoy (Inga, Putumayo, 1986), a member of the Inga nation from Putumayo, works in a continuous intercultural journey (Figure 6). This experience allows her to embrace other ways of thinking without neglecting the knowledge inherited from the traditions of her people. For a decade, Chindoy-Chasoy has been exploring what it is like to inhabit two spaces, rural and urban, what is carried and left behind, and what is always there. The processes of deterritorialization are multiple. For the new generation of Indigenous creators, it is loaded with memories, previous forced displacements, uprooting, echoes of past violence, and the certainty that in an intercultural education resides the key to inhabiting their own place, historically and physically.

In her performance and installation work, Chindoy-Chasoy explores displacement. She always carries and wears the *chumbe* that distinguishes her as an Inga woman.[10] Tirsa also brings along in her *mochila* seeds, photographs of her family, threads, and the textures and colors that recall weaving practices. She asks, what do we bring to the city? This was the idea force behind her video performance *Hilando historias*, produced as part of a workshop on intercultural creation in 2016.[11] For Quechua peoples (as the Inga), textiles are symbolic dictionaries; they declare who they are and where they are from by what they wear. With thread, Tirsa Chindoy-Chasoy weaves physically and symbolically. In *Entretejido* (2008–2018), she addresses the loss of life, "the death of a companion from Putumayo in the city of Medellín and the image of her remains reduced to a box of ashes impacted me in such a way that I could not give up the idea of rebuilding that feeling of abandonment and at the same time of rootedness that intermingled in my head" (51). By placing a photo of her feet clinging to the grass, connecting it both by means of a white thread to a circular fabric of different colors (purple, black, gray, and brown) and to a semicircular batch of earth on the floor, where seeds had been placed, Chindoy-Chasoy tries to rebuild a lost body and bring it, via memory, to its territory.

Thanks to the gallery guard (Doña Patricia), the seeds left by her containing plant life—which sustains her community in the form of food sovereignty in Putumayo—germinated

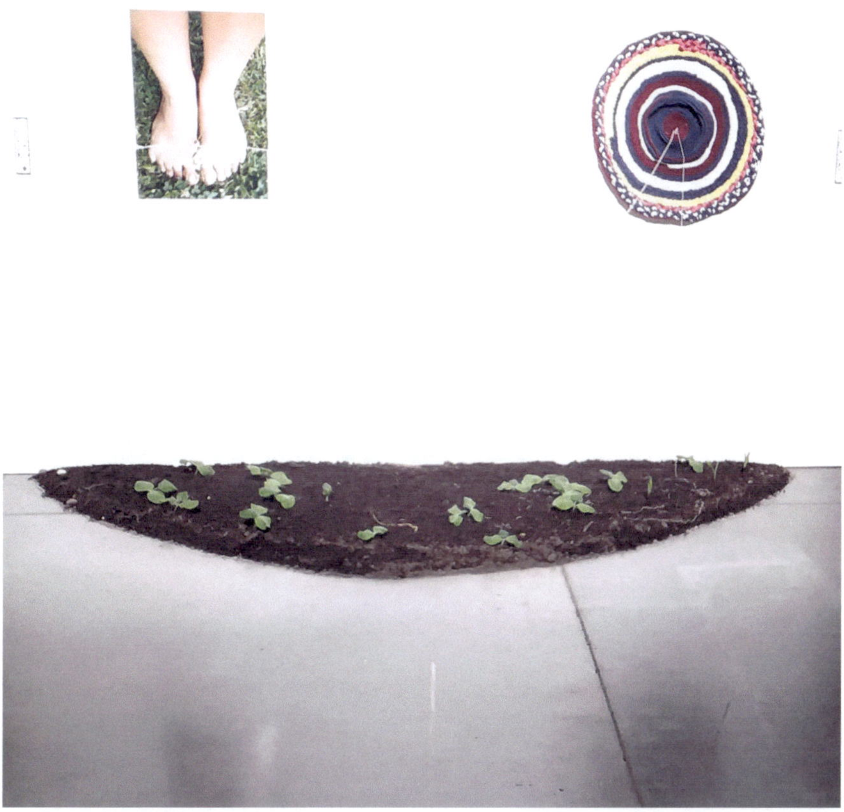

Figure 6. *Entretejido (Interwoven)* by Tirsa Chindoy-Chasoy, 2008–2018, photography, tissue, thread, soil, and seeds. *Soberanía visual*, Exhibition Hall, Universidad Javeriana, 2018.

(Figures 7 and 8). It is in this way that a feminine collaborative dimension occurs in the piece. Even in a cold and dead place—an art gallery—life finds its way, which reminds us of María Teresa Hincapié (1956–2008), a pioneer of situated performance art in Colombia and a mestiza from Ibagué who, with her piece *Divine Proportion*, won the 36th National Salon of Artists in 1996. This work consisted of an empty space in the exhibition, held in a pavilion of the International Fair of Bogotá, Corferias. Hincapié visited the space every day, tending it, inhabiting it, taking care of it, bringing seeds and water. Little by little in its cracks and corners, it began to germinate from within, to live.

Tirsa Chindoy-Chasoy uses her body as a communicative vehicle. In her movement between spaces, she gives recognition to her limbs since they are at the center of the cultural construction of the idea of the poor Indian (a *patirrajado*, or one who does not "wear shoes"), but at the same time, she connects the body to territory enacting an intercultural epistemology called *palabrandar* (walk the word).[12] "The feet as an element that unites

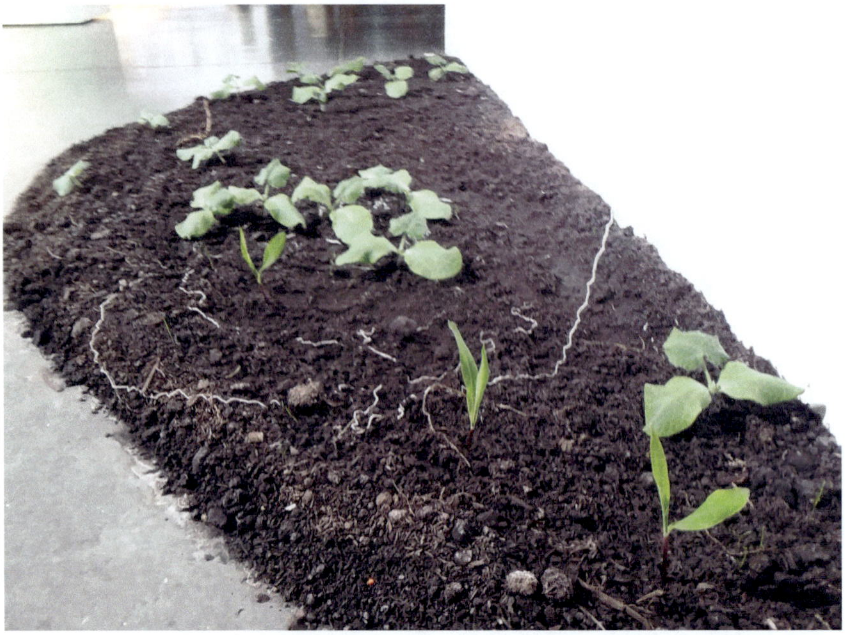

Figure 7. *Entretejido (Interwoven)* by Tirsa Chindoy-Chasoy, 2018, detail.

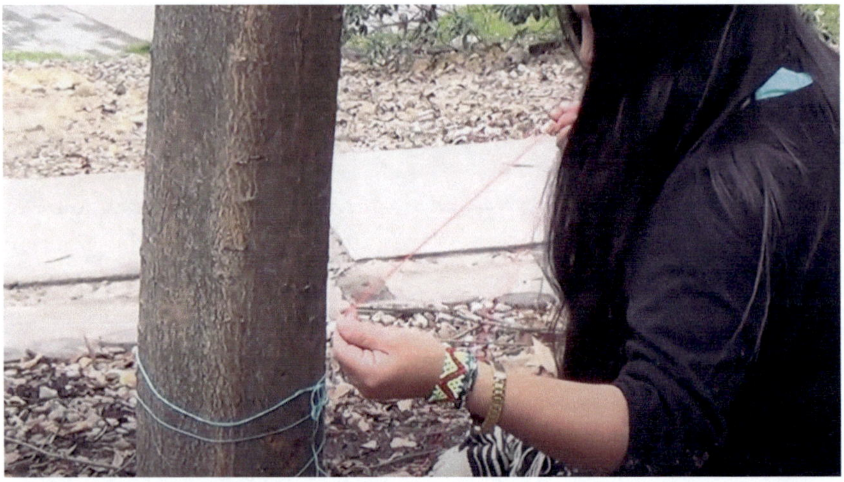

Figure 8. *Hilando memorias* by Tirsa Chindoy-Chasoy, still from the video performance. *Mingas de la imagen*, PUJ, Duke CLACS, Centro Ático, Bogotá Colombia, 2016.

me to that inhabited territory, a meeting point between two ways of perceiving the world. I immersed myself in the earth to get closer to her, to feel how with her delicacy she sheltered me like the warmest of hugs" (56).

A situated, ritual, incorporated, and inscribed drawing practice is present in the work of Rosa Tisoy-Tandioy (Inga, Putumayo 1986). Her series *Sara Indi* (2009–2014) inhabits an intermediate space between self-portrait and ethnography, and it emphasizes what is

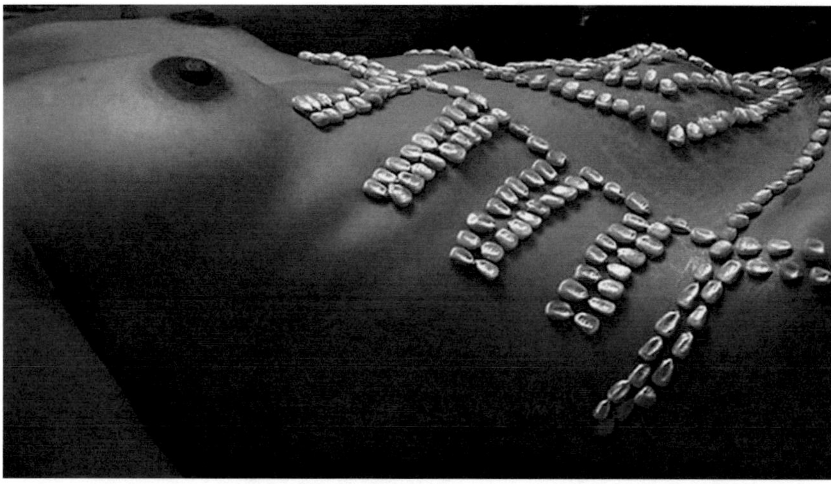

Figure 9. *Sara Indi* (Sacred Body Corn) by Rosa Tisoy-Tandioy, 2009–2014, body drawing and digital photography, courtesy of the artist.

hidden under the traditional *chumbe* and what is made public via drawing and photography (Figures 9 and 10). The *chumbe* is a protective belt that guards fertility and transmits traditional knowledge. In this work, self-documentation becomes a social landscape. The use of photography in the Indigenous world has been criticized for its exotic, ethnographic, marginal, and museographic character. Photography has been appropriated by Indigenous artists such as Rosa, where new paths are established. The Seminole artist Hulleah J. Tsinhnahjinnie calls this practice visual sovereignty—hence the title of the exhibit. Tsinhnahjinnie defines it as "a particular type of awareness rooted in trust that is exhibited as a force in cultural and visual presence" (xxiii). She also explains how "visual sovereignty does not ask for permission to exist, but ... it requires the responsibility to continue" (10–11). Tisoy-Tandioy decides to establish a *suyu* ("a place" in Inga), a geography where image and meaning find a new medium, using her own body also as *a'buru* or pagamento.[13] Photography is a practice that freezes time and is part of the colonial archive where political, economic, and cultural hegemony is exercised. At the same time, photography is part of the scientific arsenal (a physical and chemical innovation) that aims to replicate reality. These two dimensions, one semantic and the other scientific, keep photography contained as a space for the construction of power. Miranda Belarde-Lewis has written on the uses and abuses of photography in the Indigenous world and its documentation and exhibition in museum spaces. Through extensive research in archives, she reveals power differentials and argues that only elders can agree on what can be documented and exhibited (104). Rosa Tisoy-Tandioy's artworks function under this premise: they show respect for governance while she asks for permission from the community's elders as part of the construction of the works and their exhibition.

In her text *Cew Ete Haw I Tih: The Bird That Carries Language Back to Another*, the Native American art historian and curator Jolene Rickard asks audiences of historical and ethnic images to go beyond geographical, anthropological, and ethnographic visions to give

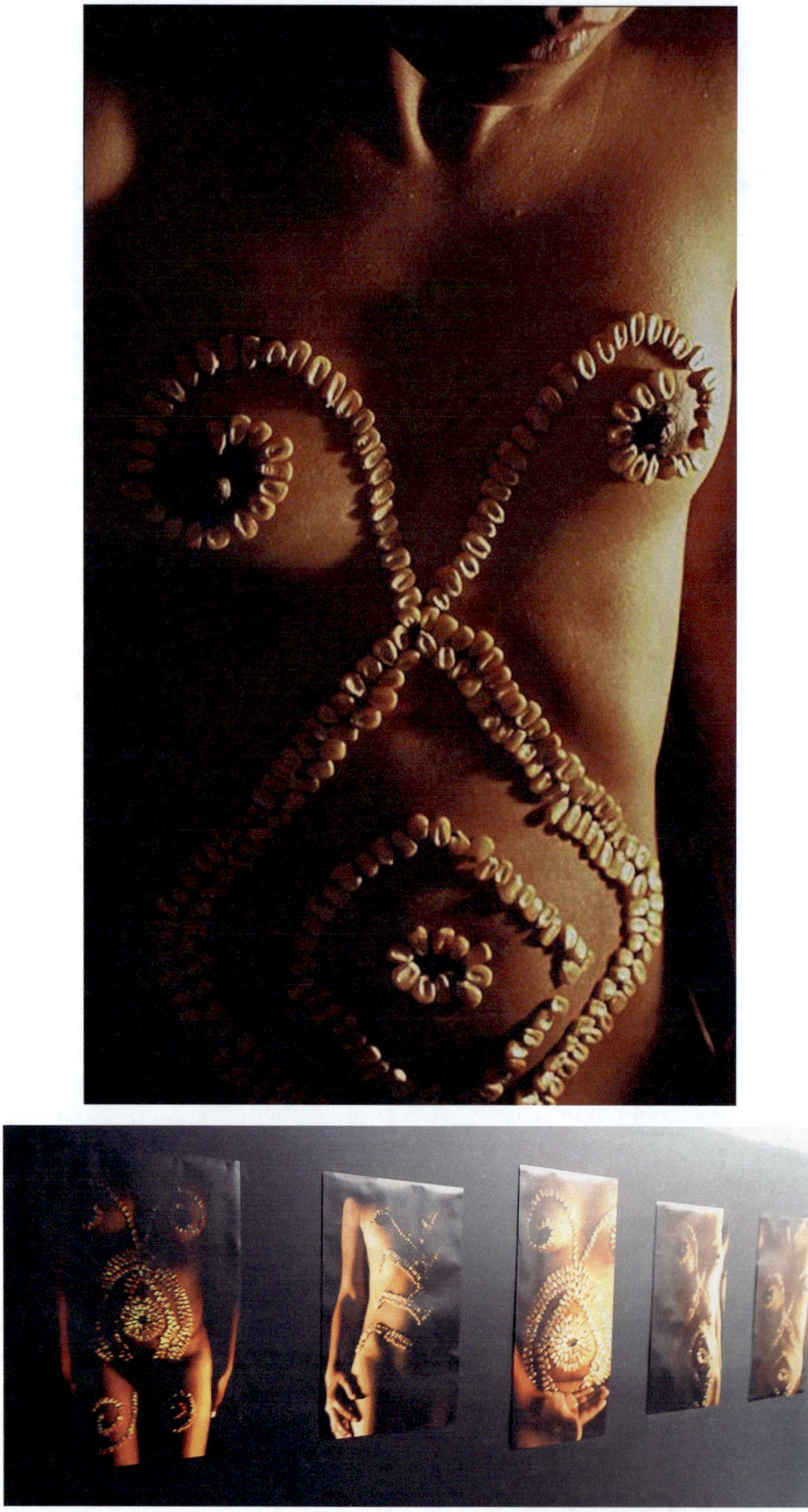

Figure 10. *Sara Indi* (Sacred Body Corn) by Rosa Tisoy-Tandioy, 2009–2014, body drawing and digital photography. *Soberanía visual*, Exhibition Hall Universidad Javeriana, 2018.

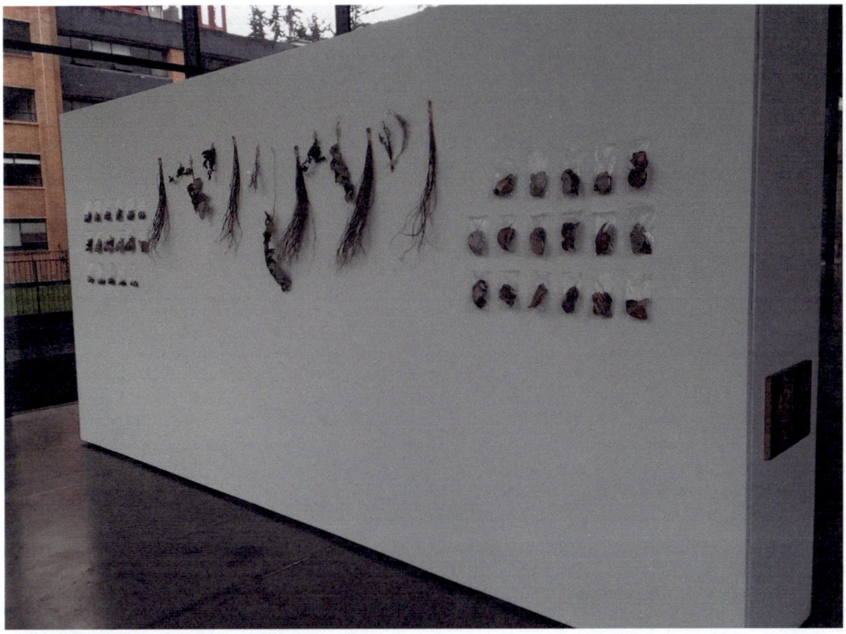

Figure 11. *Kalustrurinda-Tinii* by Rosa Tisoy-Tandioy, 2014–2018, medicinal plants from Rosa's chagra, installation. *Visual Sovereignty*, Exhibition Hall, Universidad Javeriana, 2018.

space to views that empower and build a sense of place and sensitive interpretation (109). This recognition of the relational is made explicit in communal practices of the Indigenous world today. For example, in *Kalustrurinda-Tinii* and *Tiagsamui* (2014 and 2016), Tisoy-Tandioy uses botanical products from her own *chagra* (small plots of cultivated land) that sustainably preserve a strength of these communities—food sovereignty and traditional medicine (Figures 11 and 12). Amid the loss of traditional forms of cultivation (for more technological ones), Tisoy-Tandioy's work recognizes and recovers the tradition of the *chagra* as a space of knowledge, resistance, autonomy, and in her case, as part of a situated artistic practice. In this way, her work becomes an imagined landscape that comes full circle as a process of reterritorialization that takes place as embodied territory through a practice that brings real sovereignty to her body and her land.

Sprouting

In the south of rivers and flows, in the Amazon basin, the legendary Nonuya elder Mogaje Guihu—Don Abel Rodríguez Muinane (Nonuya, Caqueta 1942)—creates fish traps and illustrations of forest cycles. As one of the last members of his people, he shares soft sculptural objects that float in space, like clouds, that remind us how elders recognize the three rivers that make up the Amazon at the falling of "the tree of life"—one that runs on the surface; one above, the climate system; and one that flows underground, the

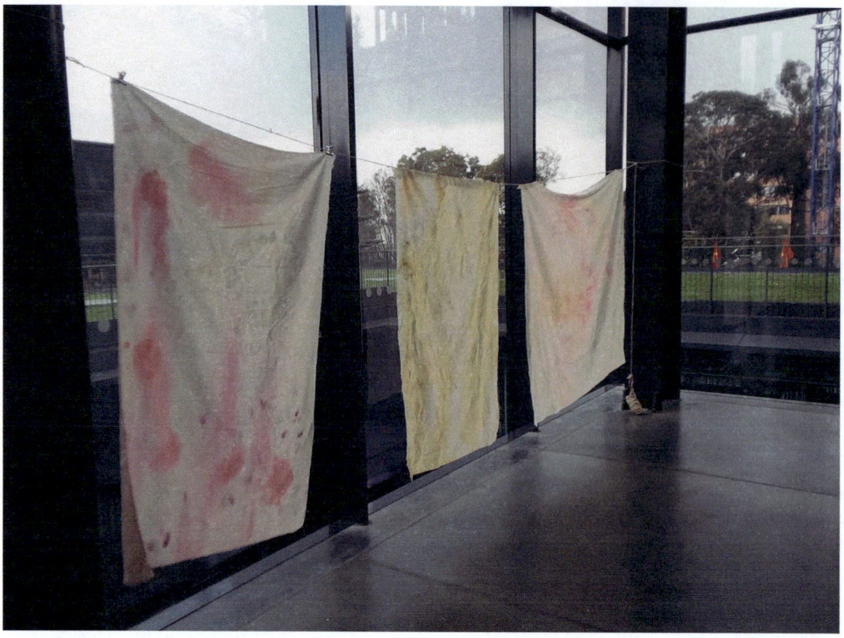

Figure 12. *Tiagsamu* by Rosa Tisoy-Tandioy, 2016–2018, painting with natural inks from Rosa'a chagra, installation. *Soberanía visual*, Exhibition Hall, Universidad Javeriana, 2018.

realm of spirits. Those three layers are where the original stories take place. According to Rodríguez-Muinane, van der Hammen, and Rodríguez, Indigenous peoples approach this world of water and plants from "an extensive and elaborate mythology, the definition of classification systems and local taxonomies" (1). This knowledge presents itself through material culture, which *Soberanía visual* intended to enact. For example, the showing of *manguarés* (ritual drums) in the exhibition may be linked to yagé rituals that involve their use to foster communication between worlds. The fabrics used by Mogaje are possible thanks to botanical knowledge. In the Nonuya tradition, drawings on *yanchamas* (a natural cloth) made with the bark of certain trees are used to carry children and are decorated with ideographics that represent different beings. In *balayes* (woven baskets) and woven sieves, or low wooden serpent benches (used for thinking), and even on the walls of the great *maloca*, different figures refer to the colors or markings of animals, their tracks, or their teeth. Mogaje Guihu, which in the Nonuya language means "hawk of bright feathers," is known as the notary of plants; he learned in a body-knowledge way—in the maloca and in the forest (Figures 13 and 14). He dominates hundreds of tree species from the tropical forest, and in addition to their names, he also recognizes their anatomical characteristics, their architecture, the distribution of their branches and leaves, the types of bark, flowers and fruit, and their ecological relationships with different animal species (4). As a situated subject, he is also a producer of material culture (no art). In contrast to his experience, in the last decade after his forced displacement to the city, Mogaje's illustrations were "discovered" by the art world, which has since taken him to the highest places of art and the art market.

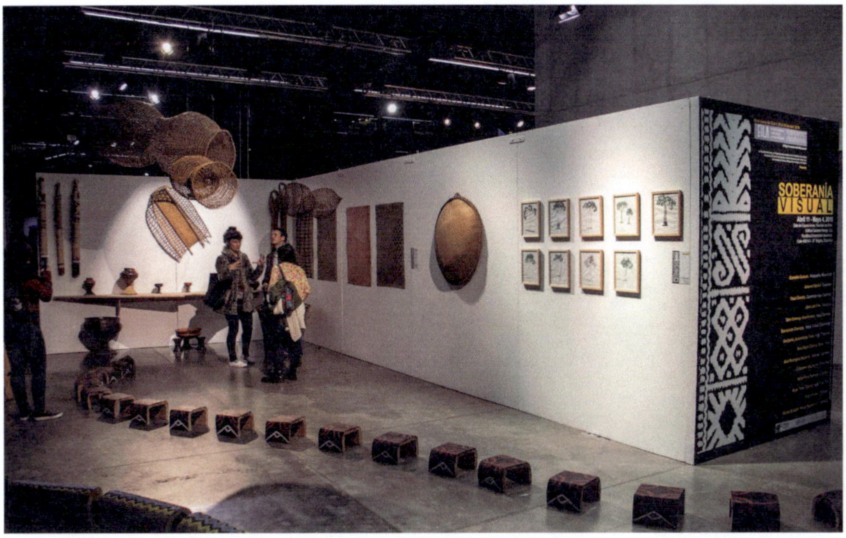

Figure 13. Tropenbos collection of Amazonian material culture, fish traps, ceramics, weavings, anaconda wooden benches, drums, and forest illustrations by Mogaje Guihu (Don Abel Rodríguez Muinane). *Soberanía visual*, Exhibition Hall, Javeriana University, 2018.

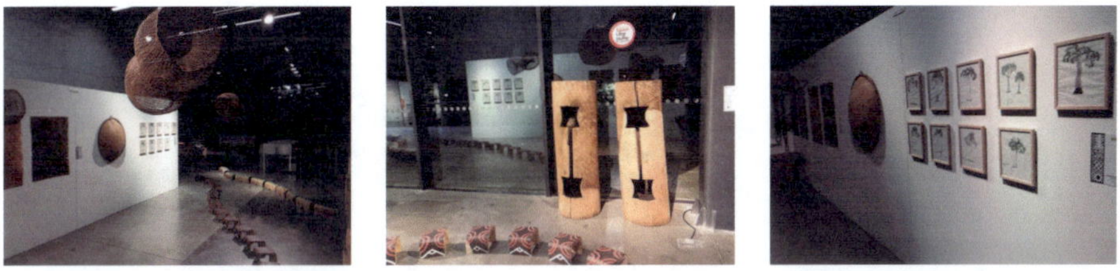

Figure 14. *Fish Traps* by Mogaje Guihu (left), *Manguarés* (wooden drums) (center), *Forest Illustrations* by Mogaje Guihu (right). *Soberanía visual*, Exhibition Hall, Javeriana University, 2018.

On the same register but living still in the territory (and traveling back and forth from it), Brus Rubio-Churay (Murui-Bora, Pucarquillo 1984) addresses the theme of shamanism embodied in the figure of the tiger grandfather, who, with the power of *ampiri* and tobacco, has the strength to preserve and maintain the balance of his environment (Figure 15). María Eugenia Yllia describes his work as a visual poetics that unifies symbolism and color (390). Rubio-Churay illustrates the path followed by the shaman to increase his power, maintain his strength, find allies, and—with the help of plants—defeat other shamans. The works made on canvas and also on yanchama (a natural textile from the Amazon) show the shaman at the moment when he begins to acquire the appearance of the tiger.

From his workshop on the banks of the Ampiyacu River in Peru, Rubio-Churay teaches material culture and art to the children of the town and keeps rescuing the traditional

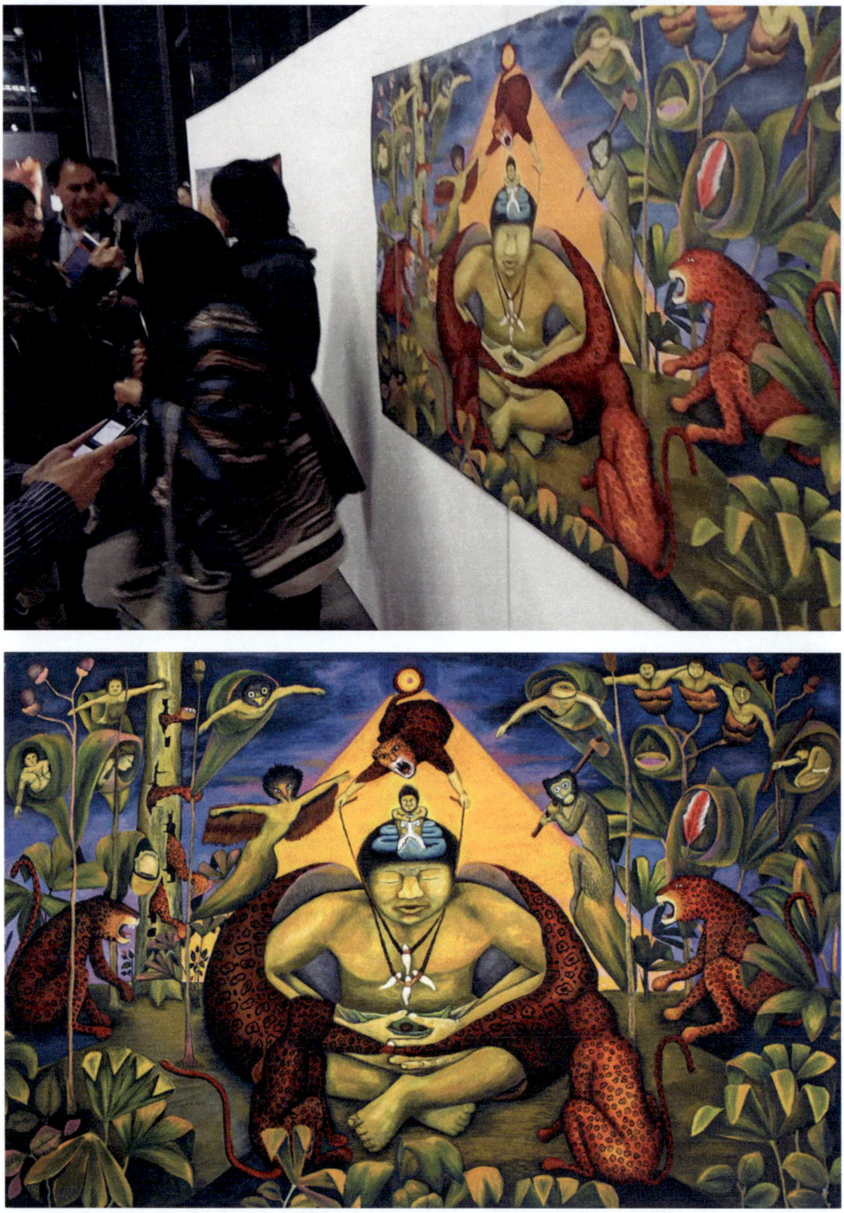

Figure 15. *Concentration* by Brus Rubio-Churay, 2017, acrylic on canvas. *Soberanía visual*, Exhibition Hall, Javeriana University, 2018.

knowledge of his community. His work reflects "a great cosmic joy because it is inspired by the gods and mythical characters, in the festivals and rituals, in the minga and agricultural work, in the magic and beauty of the fish and animals, in the song, the vision and the sacred word of my ancestors." His work also addresses social, historical, and political issues such as environmental pollution, the crimes of rubber tappers, corruption, and external threats imposed by development programs lacking knowledge of the local reality.

Spreading and Transindigeneity

In trips of abandonment and return, many of the participants in *Soberanía visual* reflect their border experiences that compress historical times and ancestral spaces between the urban and the rural. Benjamín Jacanamijoy-Tisoy (Inga, Putumayo 1965) is one of the most important exponents of the Indigenous rebirth in the arts in Colombia. He was born and raised in the Inga communities of the Sibundoy Valley, under the protection of his father, Taita Antonio Jacanamijoy, and his mother, Mercedes. As a designer and theorist of Inga art, he has produced multiple works of research that recover the feminine traditions of weaving (as in his books of 1993 and 2017). In his work as a visual producer, he uses multiple media: drawing, painting, digital constructions, objectual intervention (on boats, canes, benches), video, multimedia, and urban intervention. Starting with his work on the *chumbe*, a tradition that remains active in the narrative processes through weaving, Jacanamijoy-Tisoy has managed to make visible this living heritage of his people. Thanks to this practice, the women of the community have a place of learning that is decisive for their identity, because within the fabric, there is a relationship with the territory that is mediated by symbolic and material knowledge. The representations of the mountain, the tree, corn and coca leaves, the sun, the moon, and the stars—all are fundamental in the continuity of the Indigenous imaginary of Putumayo. These representations condense aesthetic and poetic form; they express a gendered practice that grants subjectivity and relevance to women in their rites of passage. With the *chumbe* he encompasses the cycles (*kutey*) of life. The Inga community has a unique history of encounters due in part to its having been a "contact zone" since before European colonization. Multiple layers of the cycles of life have been recorded. Piled on this history is the arrival of Catholic missions during the colonial period, the records left by Alexander von Humboldt in the early 1800s in his expeditionary journeys, and later the exploitation of rubber in the Putumayo at the turn of the twentieth century.[14] The Sibundoy Valley is not only considered the apothecary of the Amazonian foothills; it is also a place of contention, resistance, and reexistence, as Michael Taussig explores in his classic book, *Shamanism, Colonialism, and the Wild Man: A Study in Terror and Healing* (1987).

In Taussig's academic work, which is a kind of autoethnography mixed with iconographic research, Jacanamijoy-Tisoy indicates how the *chumbe* narrates events with images, taking as its basis the geometric figure of the rhombus (to him, a representation of the womb) from which territoriality emerges (Figure 16). Luis Alberto Suárez-Guava affirms how memory in the *chumbe* is a form of recording experience and that the symbols represent the river and death (87). As a river, it flows vertiginously between the hands of the weaver; its two banks contain life and wash the territory, reflecting it in its lakes and in the cosmos, and feeding the earth and its creatures. It is also death—it passes and ends. Jacanamijoy-Tisoy translates these concepts into his visual work and uses them as a cultural determinant, as seen in his urban intervention entitled *Kaugsay Auaska: Tejido de vida—Auaska Nukanchi Yuyay Kaugsaita: Tejido de la propia historia*, nominated for the 2015 Luis Caballero award in Colombia, where he created a digital *chumbe* for the lighting system of the Colpatria Tower in the Colombian capital (Rojas-Sotelo, "Adelante el pasado" 531) (Figure 17).

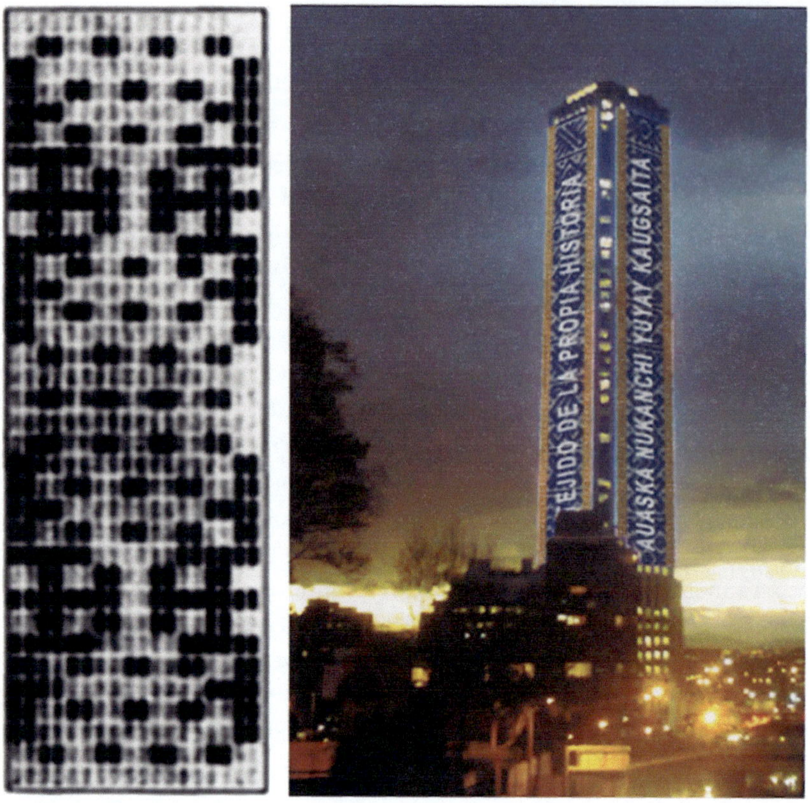

Figure 16. *Suyu kallarij. Uigsa Suyu. Lugar en donde todo se inicia, lugar del vientre. Chumbe. Kaugsay Auaska: Fabric of Life—Auaska Nukanchi Yuyay Kaugsaita: Fabric of Its Own History* by Benjamín Jacanamijoy-Tisoy, 2015, courtesy of the artist.

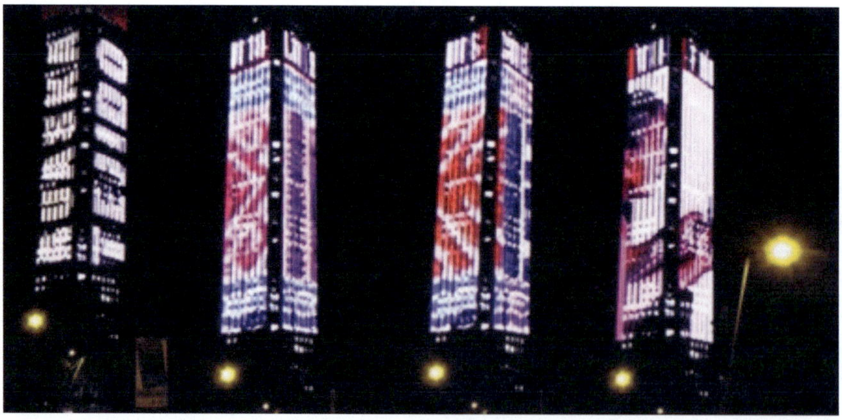

Figure 17. *Kaugsay Auaska: Fabric of Life—Auaska Nukanchi Yuyay Kaugsaita: Fabric of Its Own History* by Benjamín Jacanamijoy-Tisoy, 2015, Exterior lighting system, Torre Colpatria, Bogotá, Honorable Mention, VIII Luis Caballero Prize, courtesy of the artist.

The *chumbe* is written in a binary system (as computer coding); it is built in nine pairs, totaling eighteen *chullas*, where one point is filled and the other is empty, being a kind of coding. Each line is continued, and a network of columns constitute the image. When the image goes halfway, the viewer has to *kutey*, go back across to complete it (a conceptual, practical, and physical return to the origin).

Moving to the north of Abiayala, we encounter Cornelio Campos Vicente, a Mexican American artist of Purépecha origin, born in Cherán, Michoacán (1971). After the town of Cherán faced organized crime, environmental devastation, and the lack of action by governmental forces in the territory, it became one of a few autonomous Indigenous towns in Mexico. This was possible in part from the financial support of Purépechas living abroad, primarily farmworkers and migrants in the US. The most important thing about this autonomy is not that it is a response to those who opened the extractive frontier in the mountains of Michoacán to the arrival of green cartels (avocado growers and narcos); it is also an epistemic process of reconstitution.[15] This is a response to the Mexican cultural emasculation of Indigenous peoples. A long colonial story that reached its pinnacle after the Mexican Revolution and José de Vasconcelos's declaration of the cosmic race, which discursively flattened all possibility of Indigenous subjectivity while celebrating an imperial Indigenous past. Cornelio is not only Purépecha; he is also a migrant who lives in Durham, North Carolina (where he works as an electrician). Campos's journey influences his work as an artist, and he is a truly trans-Indigenous and intercultural (in a Northern academic sense) creator. Allen asserts how his work is "drawn from both indigenous and non-indigenous sources (135). Often, like other contemporary Indigenous art the products are the result of complicated and evolving networks of exchange. Vibrant, iconic colors and geometric patterns of pre-Columbian origin combine American symbols in a duality that at times becomes monumental—a reference to Mexican muralism (Figures 18 and 19). Through his paintings, he illustrates some of the harsh realities of immigration to the United States.

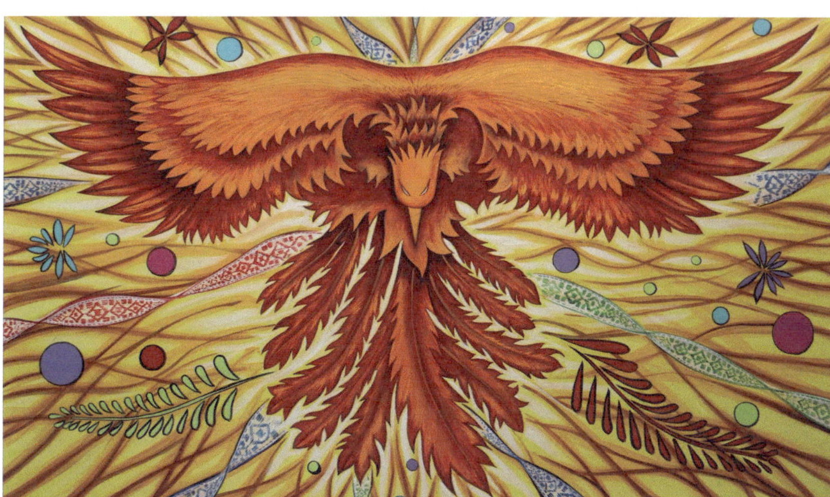

Figure 18. *Phoenix: Renacer Indígena* by Cornelio Campos Vicente, 2018, acrylic on canvas.

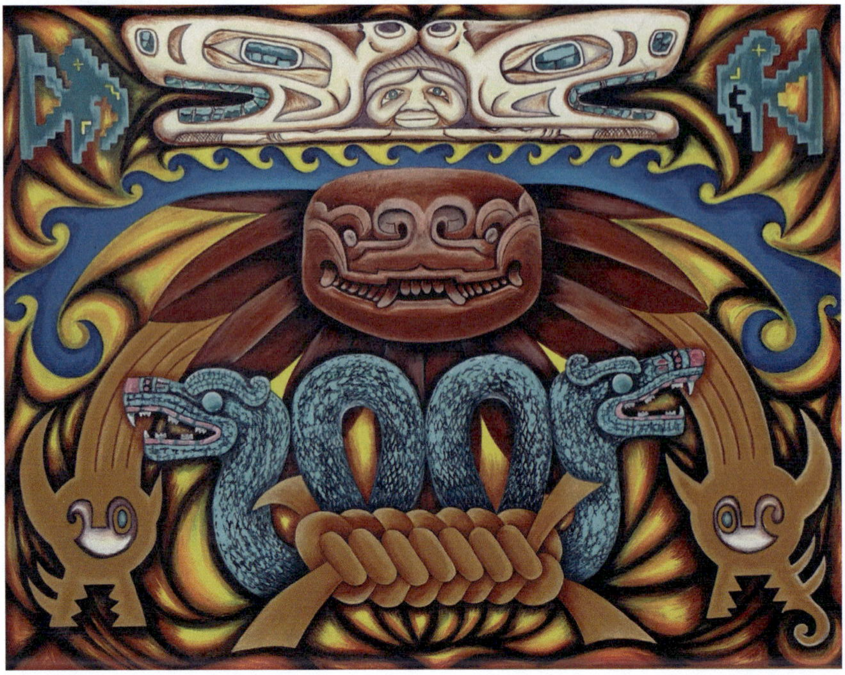

Figure 19. *Double Headed Snake* by Cornelio Campos, 2014, acrylic on canvas.

However, for *Soberanía visual*, Campos produced pieces loaded with Purépecha iconography in celebration and solidarity with his people.

Campos uses techniques that he has learned through observation and often challenges traditional color and design schemes. Through intercultural dialogue, Campos harmonizes two worlds, Indigenous and non-Indigenous (mixed/mestizo, Black, and white worlds). He always mixes iconographies that are relevant to the content of his pieces, exemplified by his *Phoenix: Renacer indígena* (2018), which celebrates the emergence of people from the ashes in a kind of reference to the Judeo-Christian myth of regeneration, but also in the Eastern millennial traditions (in China, the emperor is a dragon and the empress, a phoenix).

Pre-Columbian motifs, the national icons of Mexico (Coatlicue, Chac Mool, the double-headed serpent of pre-Columbian mythology, eagles, deer, butterflies, and corn, among others), are balanced in mirrored compositions that achieve a particular gravity. The coloring also refers to the design of Tarasco art (for which the Purépechas are also known). Campos's pieces are interwoven with time and space, as in his *Cherán soberano* (2018) (Figure 20). Direct references to *huanengos* (cloaks), *rebozos* (belts), and *huipiles* (dresses), along with techniques such as brocade and embroidery, produce symmetrical, repeated, and abstract images that share a direct relationship with the territory. This geometry of the image is clearly a Purépecha celebration in its search for autonomy. In that sense, a materiality based on tradition is visually translated, establishing a disjoined territoriality, a way of being in both words. On the one hand, dressing as Purépecha in the North challenges the homogenization of migrants that have to be assimilated, maintaining at the same time local markets of production for the material culture that resignifies cultural practices that

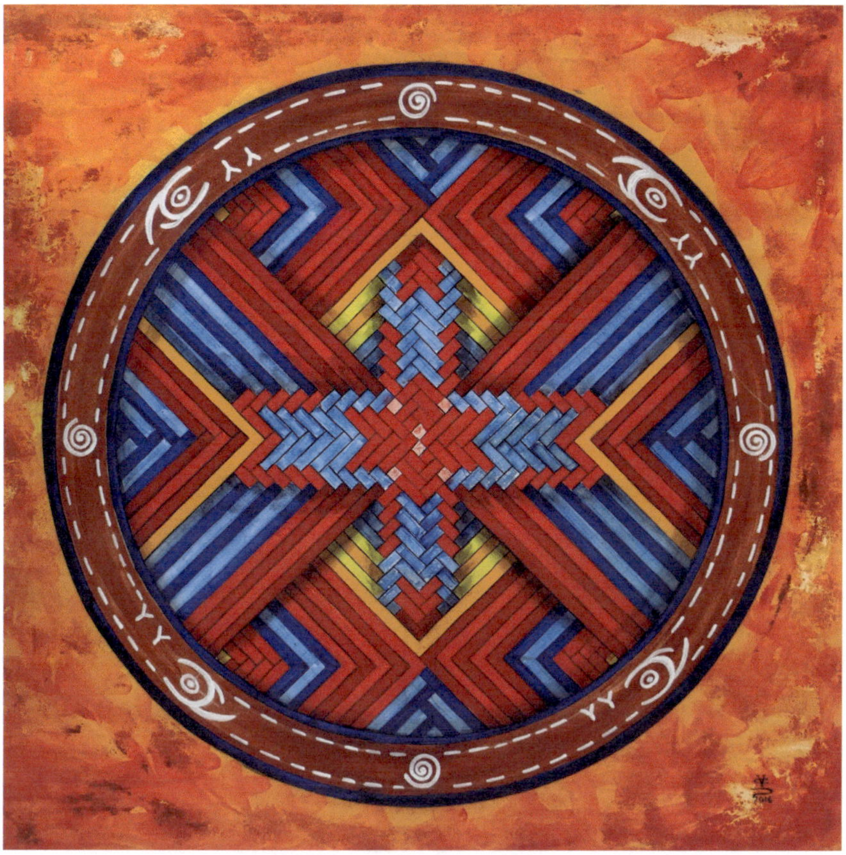

Figure 20. *Cherán soberano* by Cornelio Campos, 2018, acrylic on canvas.

contain ancestral knowledge (and a relation to the environment by the use of local source materials). On the other hand, the autonomy of Cherán is in part a product of its diaspora that keeps sending *divisas* and, with them, an economic dependency that reshapes the cultural makeup of the territory.[16]

Benvenuto Chavajay-Ixtetelá (Maya Tz'utujil, Guatemala, 1978) reflects on uses of language and the actions of the colonial matrix of power in his experience as a contemporary Indigenous artist (Figures 21 and 22). Thanks to his interaction inside and outside the art world, Chavajay makes his position clear regarding the colonial wound and his own containment strategies. In this way, he confirms his annoyance with basic concepts such as art or literacy, which were imposed on the original communities of the continent. Chavajay-Ixtetelá refers to the hegemony of alphabetic forms of language and the construction of universal history, and in particular to the idea of a rational or sublimated practice based on Kantian aesthetics.

And just as the word "art" has no translation in Tz'utujil (and in many of the original peoples' languages), this void is also an opportunity. This annoyance not only refers to the use of concepts, texts, and languages; it also refers to their places of enunciation, the supposed centers of production and circulation of culture. For Chavajay-Ixtetelá, as an individual and a visual producer, and as Latin American, Central American, Guatemalan, and

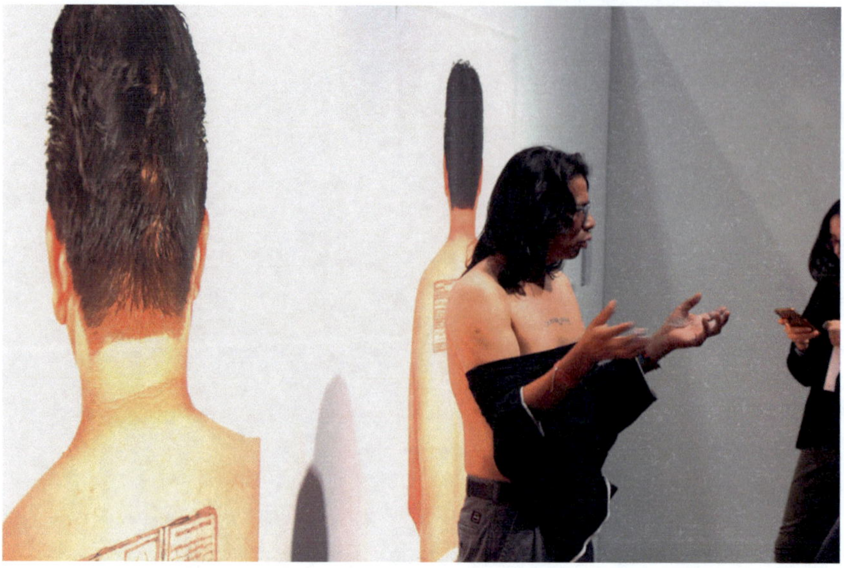

Figure 21. Benvenuto Chavajay-Ixtetelá in front of his pieces, *Doroteo Guamuche*, 2013. *Soberanía visual*, Exhibition Hall, Javeriana University, 2018.

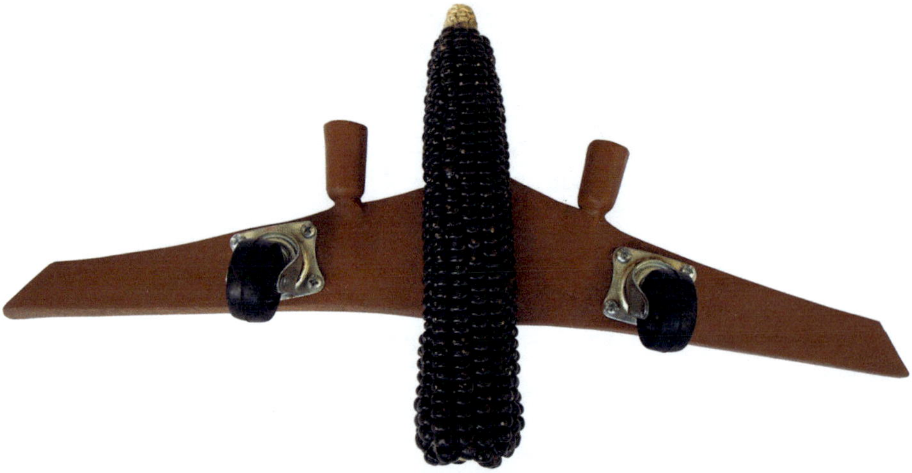

Figure 22. *Semillas (Seeds)* by Benvenuto Chavajay-Ixtetelá, 2012, assemblage. "The words 'chocolates' and 'seeds' were heard in codes in the mountains of Guatemala at the time of the War.... The military killed the chocolates and the seeds that were chocolate-skinned Mayan children. They had to destroy the seeds, now we have wings." Benvenuto Chavajay-Ixtetelá, courtesy of the artist.

Indigenous, these themes have become an obsession. He has chosen to work from a perspective of return, from a we (plural) and relational/situated position.

Chavajay-Ixtetelá works from a cultural translation platform, as a short circuit, in the middle of the colonial wound, entering and leaving—through the system. For Chavajay-Ixtetelá, illiteracy is not a problem of underdevelopment or the lack of public policies or education in their communities; rather, it is an indication of how the structures of coloniality are subject to a smaller group of romance languages of European descent. These languages, as Albán-Achinte argues, do not have the capacity to name "all the worlds," and because they are not appropriate in particular communities due to processes of cultural resistance, marginalization, or the weakness of the administrative apparatus, spaces of reexistence are established within the colonial matrix of power (89). Although nothing exists outside of it, within the matrix there are corners, cracks, and folds that allow the existence of vacuums that function as cultural islands within this hegemonic space. Chavajay-Ixtetelá's problematizes alphabetical knowledge: the word, the printed text and its archiving and legitimating mechanism that maintains privilege, economic, political, and cultural power (the law and the system of education), which he addresses with inscriptions—tattoos (letra encarnada). Benvenuto tattooed his Mayan name, which was not used in his government identification, along with the image of Doroteo Guamuch, on his back, as a letter of denunciation (he then took it to Congress and was able to rename the national stadium from Mateo Flores to Doroteo Guamuch, the original name of the Mayan athlete who won the 1952 Boston marathon). In addition, Chavajay-Ixtetelá has developed a series of erasure and fixation works that, through acts and events (performances in process), cancel (from the paper) and reinscribe texts (on the body) (Figures 23 and 24).

In a poetic/iconoclastic act, *To Annul, Suspend, Erase and Freeze, the Peace Accords*, the artist erases the text of the peace accords. The critical act clears not only the content of the text but also the use of the alphabetic language, Castilian, as the official language in a

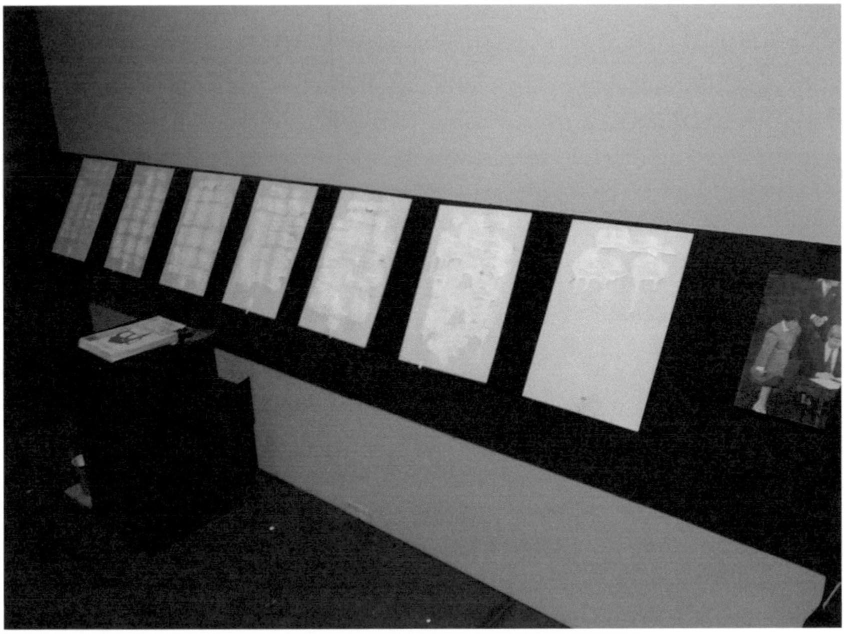

Figure 23. *To Annul, Suspend, Erase and Freeze, the Peace Accords, Signed on December 29, 1996, in Guatemala* by Benvenuto Chavajay-Ixtetelá, 2013–2018, seven sheets of watercolor paper, copy of the accords, photograph, lime and salt, installation and performance. *Soberanía visual*, Exhibition Hall, Javeriana University, 2018.

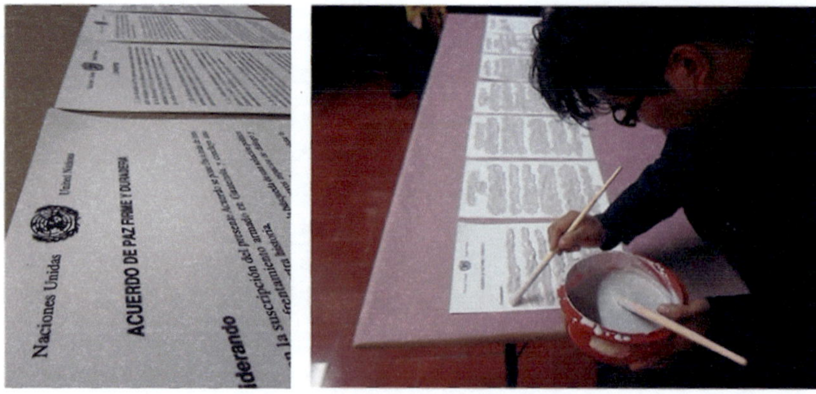

Figure 24. *To Annul, Suspend, Erase and Freeze, the Peace Accords, Signed on December 29, 1996, in Guatemala* by Benvenuto Chavajay-Ixtetelá, 2013, seven sheets of watercolor paper, copy of the accords, photograph, lime and salt, installation and performance, Mérida, Yucatán.

country where the majority is Indigenous (an illiterate—in Spanish). It also recalls the public consultation necessary to approve constitutional changes at the end of the Guatemalan civil conflict, when the peace accords were voted into effect through a referendum. When a consultation was finally held on May 16, 1999, to ratify the peace accords in Guatemala, the violent no campaign dominated the national scene. Of the 18 percent of Guatemalans who voted, little more than half of them voted against constitutional reforms. The piece was reenacted in *Soberanía visual* because of the particular and direct connection to what happened in Colombia. After more than half a century of internal conflict, the government and the Revolutionary Armed Forces of Columbia (FARC, by its Spanish initials) signed a peace agreement (September 25, 2016). However, on October 2, 2016, during the ratification of the peace accords, via referendum, the no campaign using strategies of fear and lies managed, by a small margin (0.4 percent), to defeat the endorsement, with the aggravation that 63 percent of voters did not exercise their right to vote.[17]

Sacbé / Kutey

A conclusion is an end of a road; however, there is no linearity in the Indigenous world. In Maya, *sacbé* means a "white path" (the root "beh/bey/bej" also means "destiny"). It takes people from location to location and connects (in a web of paths) relevant places. To the Inga, *caminar* (to walk) is also related to *kutey* (return to an origin), both of which have cosmological and physical implications that show a way to be trans-Indigenous and in need of intercultural dialogue. At the center of the new social contracts in many territories of Abiayala are Indigenous peoples, who are not one but many; by reexisting, they are also being recognized as subjects in history. In this chapter, thanks to their embodied and relational cultural practices, the Western notion of art encounters practices that bring attention to situated, bodily, and sovereign cultural production. As subjects, they are enacting notions of trans-Indigeneity, visual sovereignty, plurinationality, interculturality, and forms of reexistence. As the art world separated the realm of aesthetics from the one of everyday life (Kantian aesthetics, I mean), Nicole Blalock reminds us how objects created for everyday and ceremonial use incorporate visual markers to relay information about ways of being in and with the world (85). I want to suggest, as Womack does, that beyond the problem of material culture and orality in Indigenous literature in relation to the issue of cultural canons, "without Native American literature, *there is no American canon*" (7)—its extension would sound like "without indigenous cultural production, *there is no canon*." Indeed, my scholarly position builds upon decolonial aesthetics; these relational and intercultural (visual and embodied) cultural producers are beyond the visual arts and are trans-Indigenous thinkers and doers. In fact, their narratives are intertwined with the objects, actions, and territories they produce; their relational and situated (body knowledge) aesthetics allow us to walk not toward the future but to face the past in a sort of *kutey* (cycles) on white paths that look directly and intentionally to heal the colonial wound.

In relational terms, there is an obligation to help continue the flow. So in many cases, those other worlds that are not accessible to our senses must be dreamed via plants (with the guidance of spiritual or shamanic practices) and need forms of reciprocity, *a'buru* (pagamento, despacho). Arturo Escobar defines this with a clear example when he affirms: "The enaction of an ontology within which the mountain is a discrete and inert being, a lifeless object, leads to its eventual destruction, as in open-pit mining for gold or coal. If the mountain is seen as a sentient being, the treatment given to it is completely different" (57). This last idea affirms that Indigenous people also use and even extract resources from the earth, but with a measure of respect, which is what modernity/coloniality and its economic system, and capitalism, have lost.[18] Epistemic reconstitution starts, then, with *a'buru* as a form of relationality enacted in trans-Indigenous embodied cultural practice, even if not in conscious ways. An *a'buru* is not symbolic but also physical: it always implies work, even more so from our positionality of privilege in the equation of interculturality, a *kutey*.

On the path, looking back also gives a perspective, offering light and guidance (and forms of nonrepetition) along the way. Through the use of language, text, image, and acts and events (embodied practices), many creators from the Indigenous world find common lines of action. Today, trans-Indigenous peoples continue to affirm their stories through new languages. They are present in and out of the white "box" (the gallery, museum, or a book); they establish territories of sense and share old forms of embodied knowledge. These exercises of autonomy and sovereignty are situated and contextual, and are enacted by individual and social body territories from the indigenous world in Abiayala. They offer to those trapped in disciplinary divides and urban mazes some clues for a path that we must walk together toward a *sacbé*—a white path of healing. Here is my offering...

Notes

1. I cannot assert ownership over the congress or the exhibit. I consider myself a "collaborator" instead of a "curator," someone who connects rather than defines. I do not isolate but accompany processes of communication. Abiayala literally means "land in full maturity" or "land in bloom"; it is

the oldest name so far known referring to the American territory in the Guna Dule (Kuna) language of Panama and Colombia. In 1977, the World Council of Indigenous Peoples admitted "Abya Yala" as the name of the continent to identify the lands colonized since the fifteenth century by Europeans that they would later call America. Etymologically, "Yala" means "land" or "territory." "Abya" means "blood hole," "mature mother," "mature virgin," or "in full maturity."

2. Regarding "trans-Indigenous," I follow Allen's definition (2012): "*Trans*-Indigenous may be able to bear the complex, contingent asymmetry and the potential risks of unequal encounters borne by the preposition *across*. It may be able to indicate the specific agency and situated momentum carried by the preposition *through*" (xiv). Because it goes beyond Indigeneity, and across geographies and nations, into intercultural practices, where we, non-Indigenous people, can operate and at times translate/transmit knowledge, in academic spaces.

3. *A'buru* or *pagamento* in the Indigenous tradition of the Andes is a step toward restoring dignity to the land. The Arhuaco of Sierra Nevada in Colombia make offerings, which are expressions of a conscious relationship of reciprocity nature. My work (this chapter in particular), because of my deterritorialized condition, is an offering to restore Indigenous dignity, a recognition of their relationship with the land, as a form of retribution.

4. This work has led to a manuscript that tries to construct a collaborative genealogy on Indigenous art in Colombia from before contact to contemporary times. Edited and published by the Universidad Distrital doctoral program on artistic practice and Centro de Estudios Ecocríticos e Interculturales (CEI), Universidad Javeriana (both in Bogotá, Colombia), as *Territorio encarnado: Ejercicios de soberanía visual. Visualidades, textualidades y estéticas situadas en la producción artística indígena en Abya Yala*.

5. I used the proceedings of the prize to invite seventeen creators (Indigenous and non-Indigenous) from multiple Amerindian nations and regions of Abiayala. The exhibition took place between April and June 2018 as part of EILA V, organized with my friend and collaborator Miguel Rocha Vivas, and cofunded by the Universidad Javeriana in Bogotá. What follows is a journey through some of the situated work of those creators.

6. In decolonial theory, there is no escape from the colonial matrix of power. As Walter Mignolo has expressed about "the modern and secular nation-State: they did not escape to internal colonialism...internal colonialism is just one corner of this complex structure [the colonial matrix of power] of its management and historical mutations" (174).

7. According to their latitude, there are small differences in date and times of celebrations that connect diasporic communities across the continent. Mayas in Mesoamerica also use the solar calendar system; the Haab cycle is 365 days and celebrates each new year approximately each July in Yucatán (the Sac Ha', Cha'a Chac, and Wajkol) and Guatemala (during the Wayeb short month).

8. Páramos (moorlands) are strategic for the sustainability of Andean nations. Plants on these landscapes, which are located more than three thousand meters (9,800 feet) above sea level, collect water from clouds, filter it, and distribute it via waterways all over the region. They are revered by Indigenous peoples in South America.

9. In Quijano's 2007 text "Coloniality Modernity/Rationality," the coloniality of power constitutes a matrix that operates through control or hegemony over authority (the nation-state), labor (the means of production), sexuality (gender identity), race (dehumanization), and subjectivity (ontology). It was developed in the conquering of the Americas as the cornerstone of modernity with an economic system based on accumulation, desire, and capitalism (171).

10. The *chumbe* is a woven belt that protects the womb of women in the Inga communities of southern Colombia.

11. *Hilando historias* was part of the first workshop on audio visual creation produced by the intercultural collective Mingas de la Imagen in Bogotá (https://www.mingasdelaimagen.org).

12. Palabrandar is a category of the Nasa epistemology that means the ability to "walk the word." According to Simone Ferrari, this notion or practice was developed by the Nasa-Misak writer, communicator, and activist Vilma Almendra-Quiguanás. It is the result of a long history of

searching for autonomous discursive models for the struggles of the Indigenous peoples of southern Colombia (195). Almendra-Quiguanás proposes palabrandar as a resistant and alternative way of thinking, communicating, and acting from Indigeneity.

13. For a more in-depth reading of Rosa Tandioy-Tisoy and Benvenuto Chavajay-Ixtetelá's work, see my essay "Soberanía visual en Abya Ayala," in *Premio nacional de crítica y ensayo 2016–2017*, Colombia.

14. In cultural studies, "contact zone" describes a space of colonial clashes. The concept was developed by Mary Louise Pratt in 1991 (studying Woaman Poma de Ayala's work). These spaces are where people from different cultures meet and, despite their differences and asymmetrical power relations, forge new relationships. James Cliford (1997) used it to address the power of institutions such as museums and galleries in the construction of collections (archives) and the moral imperative of introducing new voices. Its use has been problematic but relevant since it has allowed the constitution of a new generation of Indigenous and non-Indigenous scholars working in its shadow.

15. In Mignolo and Walsh's *On Decoloniality: Concepts, Analytics, Praxis*, epistemic reconstitution is "to delink from the colonial matrix of power in order to re-link and to re-exist" (227, 229).

16. In 2022 the community in North Carolina decided to buy a piece of land to start what they called Cherán 2.0—Rancho San Francisco de Asís Cherán en Norte Carolina.

17. Indigenous communities convened a great march on October 12, 2016, in support of the accords, giving new meaning to the celebrations of the date. On November 28, 2016, after a new round of negotiations, the agreement was ratified by Colombia's Congress. During the days and nights before the ratification, Uitoto drums from the Amazon, Inga flutes from the Sibundoy Valley, and Afro-Colombian *cantaoras* from the Pacific were heard on the steps of Congress. Finally, at 11:35 p.m. on November 28, 2016, the peace accords were signed.

18. Escobar builds on the work of Marisol de la Cadena (2016), when exploring the possibility of communication across different onto-epistemic formations via *pagos* or *despachos* (same in the Peruvian Andes). The same forms of giving "importance to earth-beings, and in so doing, intensify or improve their being together with it" (94).

Works Cited

Albán-Achinte, A. "Estéticas descoloniales y de re-existencia: Entre memorias y cosmovisiones." *La arquitectura del sentido II: La producción y reproducción en prácticas semiótico discursivas*. Edited by J. Haidar. Escuela Nacional de Antropología, 2011, pp. 87–117.

Allen, Chadwick. *Trans-Indigenous. Methodologies for Global Literary Studies*. U of Minnesota P, 2012.

Belarde-Lewis, M. "No Photography Allowed: Problematic Photographs of Sacred Objects." *Museum Anthropology*, vol. 36, no. 2, 2013, p. 104.

Blalock, Nicole, Jameson D. López, and Elyssa Figari. "Acts of Visual Sovereignty: Photographic Representations of Cultural Objects." *American Indian Culture and Research Journal*, vol. 39, no. 3, 2015, pp. 83–98.

Cadena, Marisol de la. *Earth Beings: Ecologies of Practice across Andean Worlds*. Duke UP, 2016.

Castillo, Jeisson. "About the Artist." *Diálogo*, vol. 19, no. 1, 2019, pp. 135.

Castillo-Gutiérrez, Jeisson. *Portafolio*, 2018.

Chindoy-Chasoy, Tirsa Taira. *Unida entre dos entornos*. Master's thesis, Universidad de Antioquia, 2008.

Escobar, Arturo. *Sentipensar con la tierra: Nuevas lecturas sobre desarrollo, territorio y diferencia*. Universidad Autónoma Latinoamericana, 2014.

Fernández, Carlos Arturo. *Apuntes para una historia del arte contemporáneo en Antioquia*. Gobernación de Antioquia, Colección Autores Antioqueños, 2007.

Ferrari, Simone. "Vilma Almendra y el palabrandar indígena: hacia una integración de saberes desde la Abya Yala." *Integración en la globalización*. Edited by Emilia Perassi and Pablo Guadarrama González. Penguin Random House, 2020, pp. 195–223.

Gómez, Pedro Pablo. *Estéticas fronterizas: Diferencia colonial y opción estética decolonial*. Universidad Distrital Francisco José de Caldas and Universidad Andina Simón Bolívar-Ecuador, 2016.

Jacanamijoy-Tisoy, Benjamín. *Chumbe: Arte Inga*. Ministerio de Gobierno, Dirección General de Asuntos Indígenas, 1993.

———. *El Chumbe Inga. Una forma artística de percepción del mundo*. Ankla Editores, 2017.

———. "Kaugsay suyu yuyay: Lugar, vivir, pensar conceptos de la tradición inga sobre el territorio." *Espacio y territorios: Razón, pasión e imaginarios*. Universidad Nacional de Colombia, 2001, pp. 189–203.

Mignolo, Walter D., and Catherine E. Walsh. *On Decoloniality: Concepts, Analytics, Praxis*. Duke UP, 2018.

Pratt, Mary Louise. "Arts of the Contact Zone." *Profession*, 1991, pp. 33–40.

Quijano, Anibal. "Coloniality and Modernity/Rationality." *Cultural Studies*, vol. 21, no. 2–3, 2007, pp. 168–178.

Ramos, Elvira, and Marisol García. "Notas sobre pesas y medidas en testamentos emitidos en Mérida, Venezuela, en el siglo XVII." *Letras*, vol. 52, no. 83, 2010, pp. 75–101.

Rickard, Jolene. "Cew Ete Haw I Tih: The Bird that Carries Language Back to Another." *Partial Recall: Photographs of Native North America*. Edited by L. Lippard. New Press, 1992, pp. 105–112.

Rodríguez-Muinane, Abel, María Clara van der Hammen, and Carlos Alberto Rodríguez. "Name and Draw: An Exploration of Communicating Traditional Knowledge in the Work of Abel Rodríguez." *Humanities Futures*. Duke UP, 2016. https://humanitiesfutures.org/papers/name-and-draw-an-exploration-of-communicating-traditional-knowledge-in-the-work-of-abel-rodriguez/.

Rojas-Sotelo, Miguel. "Adelante el pasado: Oralidad y visualidad, acto y evento en las prácticas artísticas del mundo indígena contemporáneo." *Revista Kaypunku: Revista de Estudios Interdisciplinarios de Arte y Cultura*, vol. 4, no. 1, 2019, pp. 521–591.

———. *Irrupciones, compresiones, contravenciones: Arte contemporáneo y política cultural en Colombia*. Ediciones Uniandes, 2017.

———. "Soberanía visual en Abya Yala." *Premio Nacional de Crítica y Ensayo de Arte*. Ministerio de Cultura, Universidad de los Andes, *Revista Arteria*, 2018.

Rubio Churay, Brus. "Perfil." *Centro de Antropología Visual del Perú*, 2016. https://www.brusrubio.com/perfil.

Suárez-Guava, Luis A. *El tiempo entre los Inga de Bogotá*. Universidad Nacional, 2003.

Taussig, Michael, *Shamanism, Colonialism, and the Wild Man: A Study in Terror and Healing*. U of Chicago P, 1987.

Tsinhnahjinnie, Hulleah, and H. Lidchi, eds. *Visual Currencies: Native American Photography*. National Museums of Scotland, 2009.

Womack, Craig S. *Red on Red. Native American Literary Separatism*. U of Minnesota P, 1999.

Yllia Miranda, María Eugenia. *Mostrar lo invisible: El viaje del chamán en la pintura indígena amazónica peruana contemporánea*. Universidad Nacional Mayor de San Marcos, 2018.

———. Antropófagos contemporáneos: Paradojas y lógicas visuales en la pintura amazónica contemporánea peruana [Contemporary cannibals: Paradoxes and visual logics in contemporary Peruvian Amazonian painting]. *Arte y antropología: Estudios, encuentros y nuevos horizontes* [Art and anthropology: Studies, meetings and new horizons], edited by Borea G. Pontificia Universidad Católica del Perú, 2017, pp. 387–395.

CHAPTER 2

El camino de una palabra que piensa con el corazón

Mikeas Sánchez
Centro de Lengua y Cultura Zoque y Colectivo Defensoras de Nasakobajk

Violeta Percia
Universidad de Buenos Aires

La poesía contemporánea escrita por autoras o autores indígenas abre una serie de sentidos, experiencias y conocimientos que desestabilizan y descentran los imaginarios eurocéntricos y globalizados; permitiendo, a su vez, correr la mirada etnográfica, aún preponderante en algunos discursos dominantes, donde los cuerpos se consideran como algo que estudiar. En las poéticas zoque, mapuche, diidxazá, kichwa, quechua, guaraní, náhuatl, kamëntšá, mè'phàà, tsotsil, maya k'iche, wayúu, y de las muchas otras naciones preexistentes, los cuerpos tienen su propia voz, palabra y lugares de conocimiento. Las obras en estos idiomas que vienen creciendo en volumen desde la última década del siglo XX, no son ni producciones aisladas ni nuevas, sino parte de un proceso poético que se inscribe en las tradiciones orales y oralituras propias, pues ese es el lugar concreto desde donde hacen su reflexión, legitiman su fuerza de conocimiento –conceptual y visionaria– inscripta en la historia de sus pueblos, en su experiencia colectiva y en la conciencia individual de sus personas sabias. Por este motivo, la poesía se vuelve un territorio privilegiado, ya no para estudiar al otrx desde conceptualizaciones intelectualistas y abstractas que categoricen o avasallen las diferencias, sino para conocer el sentido vivo y real de sus historias, escuchar sus plegarias, sus llamados, sus advertencias, sus profundas enseñanzas. El desafío para la teoría de los Estudios Indígenas y de los Estudios Hispánicos es poder conversar entre lenguas para encontrar palabras que nos ayuden a nombrar modos más respetuosos, sustentables y saludables de pensarnos en una existencia compartida, este trabajo pretende ser un aporte en este sentido.

Respondiendo a este reto, el presente texto se ha concebido desde la conversación considerada como un espacio de pensamiento. Entendiendo que el diálogo consciente, sostenido en el tiempo y en una serie de retribuciones y colaboraciones recíprocas que dan consistencia a la reflexión, puede convertirse en una forma de investigación y en una metodología viable para producir una teoría o una crítica que no se limiten a las fuentes escritas, legitimadas en espacios de circulación y producción intelectuales o académicas pertenecientes solo a una de las culturas en diálogo. Ateniendo a estos emplazamientos, este capítulo se propone como un intercambio abierto en la conversación y como una conceptualización crítica compartida entre Mikeas Sánchez -poeta, maestra, traductora, pensadora, portadora de la visión del mundo cultural y espiritual zoque, y activista en la defensa de su territorio en la región de Chapultenango, Chiapas, México- y Violeta Percia -poeta, documentalista y doctora en Filosofía y Letras por la Universidad de Buenos Aires, donde ha creado el seminario "Poesía contemporánea en lenguas indígenas" para la Carrera de Letras de esa universidad, donde se había ignorado la palabra poética y el pensamiento legítimo de las naciones preexistentes de Argentina y del continente. Buscando inscribirse en aquellas corrientes de investigación que dan relevancia al estatuto original de la poesía no sólo por su valor estético, sino en cuanto forma de conocimiento -que existe e insiste en las fuentes orales, la memoria y la experiencia de los pueblos-, se ha partido de las reflexiones sobre el poemario *Cómo ser un buen salvaje* de Mikeas Sánchez y de su experiencia de autotraducción, dado que se trata de un libro escrito por su autora de manera bilingüe zoque-español. A partir de estas consideraciones, se ha buscado comprender y delimitar un pensamiento de la poesía que la conciba como un lugar de revitalización y reunión de una palabra que piensa con el corazón.

El avance salvaje del mundo

Desde la modernidad occidental, la imagen del "buen salvaje" se utilizó para marcar lo que se pretendía degradar, despreciar y sojuzgar.[1] En el proceso que va de la conquista a la conformación de los Estados nación se sostuvo la idea de que esas culturas a las que se las mira como precarias y vulnerables, debían civilizarse; esto significaba que había que enseñarles los modales para que aprendieran a vivir en sociedad, a vivir la realidad a la manera del extranjero (que bajo esa superioridad impuesta dejaba de ser extranjero para constituirse en autoridad). Estos discursos fueron calando de diferente forma en los distintos países del llamado continente americano, pero aunque con matices de palabras en todos estuvo presente la misma operación de inferiorización de las naciones y pueblos preexistentes. Si en la actualidad se vuelve a hablar de esta historia no es sólo porque estas imágenes han dejado heridas aún vivas, sino también porque siguen formando parte del sentido común del pensamiento hegemonizante.

Según la visión cultural europea y sus dispositivos de colonización -que es la visión que conservan las clases dominantes de los países de América, y una parte mayoritaria de sus sociedades mestizas y blancas-, la imagen del salvaje se construyó, en discursos y prácticas, como el lugar de la inferioridad, de lo atrasado y lo primitivo. Sobre esa construcción fueron legitimadas y profundizadas injusticias que conllevaron acciones de genocidio, violencia, asimilación, políticas de avergonzamiento y despojo de tierras y recursos a lo largo de los distintos territorios.[2] El sociólogo portugués Boaventura de Sousa Santos define este dispositivo colonial como una forma matricial del imperialismo; quiere decir que, para imponerse, el avance colonial necesita construir ese sentido común que permanece intacto "en su capacidad de alimentar el modo en que Occidente se ve a sí mismo y a todo lo que no identifica consigo" (223). Para el pensamiento colonial, el salvaje está marcado desde siempre con una diferencia en función de la cual jamás será considerado ni como igual ni como prójimo, pues no se le considera siquiera plenamente humano. Más aún, queda por fuera del pacto social que está en la base de los Estados modernos, por lo cual no participa del estado de derecho, y no tendrá nunca derechos plenos. De ahí que resulte imposible que la diferencia sea mirada con respeto ya que se utiliza como una medida de la inferioridad en nombre de la cual se expropia al otro de su identidad, cultura, autonomía y territorios.

Contra estos mecanismos que están en la base del racismo, la descalificación, el desprecio y la transformación del otro u otra en objeto o recurso productivo, Mikeas Sánchez opera una crítica poética en su último poemario, *Jujtzye tä wäpä tzamapänh'ajä/Cómo ser un buen salvaje*.[3] Allí realiza una inversión de estos valores coloniales, arraigados todavía hoy en las sociedades dominantes que no quieren perder sus privilegios y que nunca se han arrepentido de sus transgresiones. Así pues, la voz poética de su libro se hunde en el pensamiento zoque –en sus territorios, palabras y sentidos– para retornar haciendo visible la fuerza de una sabiduría mayor que, desde las buenas palabras, los rectos pensamientos y el afecto amoroso hacia el prójimo, conserva conocimientos y experiencias primordiales en la búsqueda de una vida equitativa y en equilibrio. Pero también, se vuelve hacia los afectos y las visiones sensibles de la cultura propia para cargar de actualidad y vitalidad el reconocimiento identitario, continuando una tradición en la palabra que comprende la fuerza de saberse zoque y parte de una cultura antigua.

El poemario de Mikeas es un texto de doble registro, es decir que está escrito a la vez en dos lenguas: zoque y español. De un idioma al otro, en la autotraducción de la propia autora y en esa doble escritura (a dos lenguas) que supone su libro, se producen desbordes de sentidos que permiten cuestionar las ideas y las formas de razonar coloniales. En efecto, entre la versión zoque y la española se advierte en la traducción una primera excedencia semántica o rebalse de significados en lo que refiere, precisamente, al término "salvaje", presente ya en el título. En la versión en español, el libro pone en juego esa connotación que tiene que ver con el "buen salvaje" desde el concepto occidental.[4] Pero en el zoque no existe ese concepto, entonces no es posible traducirlo, ya que no hay nadie a quien haya que civilizar, porque en la cultura zoque todos son iguales: no hay esa diferencia. En la medida en que para esta lengua no existe la palabra salvaje como tal, el término zoque que se utiliza en el poemario para evocar esa idea es "Tzamapänh' ".[5] Sin embargo, esta palabra no refiere a un ser que deba ser civilizado o domesticado, sino que se trata de alguien que conoce la fuerza de la montaña y la resguarda. No es alguien que carezca de lenguaje o de ciencia, por el contrario posee un conocimiento legítimo y preciado.

El Tzamapänh' hace alusión a una historia de tradición oral que cuenta sobre un ser que cuida la montaña, del que se dice, vive en la parte más espesa, más profunda, lejos de las comunidades, alejado de todo.[6] En Copainalá, Chiapas, por ejemplo, se le conoce como el Weya'weyá'. Para esa tradición se trata de un hombre robusto que proporciona fuerzas, que lleva matraca, machete y tecomate lleno de miel, y le gusta fumar puro. Aparece en la tradición oral de distintos municipios zoques con nombres diferentes –Tzama'kanan, Munh'kanan, Tzama'pät, Weya'weya'–, pero es el mismo personaje, alguien que tiene un alma capaz de llevarse bien con todos los animales de la naturaleza. A veces se lo conoce como un ser más espiritual, invisible, que puede hacer perder a la gente. En Chapultenango, el Tzamapänh' es quien protege la montaña, aunque es ambiguo porque no le gusta que nadie se le acerque y puede ser muy agresivo. En la cuestión de la territorialidad es susceptible a enojarse cuando se invade su espacio, entonces puede tener una parte violenta que en realidad es un modo de cuidar el lugar. Como todos los seres ambiguos, el Tzamapänh' es un ser capaz de moverse entre mundos, pero bajo ningún concepto es alguien que necesite una cultura o que tenga una cultura que no vale; para el pensamiento zoque no sólo la diferencia no debe ser colonizada, sino que se acepta, en este caso mostrando a alguien que tiene una función y un lugar específico dentro de la distribución de los poderes del mundo y del territorio. Es decir que si el término "salvaje" remite en español a alguien que queda del otro lado de la humanidad y debe ser domesticado, en zoque, en cambio, el Tzamapänh' refiere a aquel cuya vida en la naturaleza y fuera de la comunidad resguarda los equilibrios de la montaña.

El lugar de la palabra

En "*Tzoko'tzyame*/Pensar con el corazón" –uno de los poemas de *Cómo ser un buen salvaje*– se pregunta "*¿isaj' yanhkasäpya te' tzame?* / ¿A quién le importa ahora la palabra?" (Sánchez 25). Mediante este interrogante el libro denuncia una indiferencia por la palabra que es en realidad –como muestra el poemario– un desdén por la rectitud en el decir, y con ello, por el nombre de las cosas, por la verdad y por los pensamientos en los que florece la existencia. A partir de allí, se evidencia una inversión de sentidos y otra pregunta implícita: ¿cómo pueden las ideas pretendidas como civilizadas reclamarse dueñas de la razón si desprecian el valor de las palabras, si crean un torbellino de confusiones que arrasa con la memoria y los idiomas de la gente? Aquí mismo se instala una diferencia: "Mi abuelo me dijo: / Los zoques somos herederos de la palabra" (Sánchez 25), y apelando a esa instancia oral de transmisión del conocimiento, Mikeas sitúa la herencia zoque en el saber de las palabras que se piensan con el corazón, que se dan como un bien o un tesoro porque permiten recibir, brindar o despedir la vida a su tiempo, con júbilo. El desprecio del mundo actual por las palabras explica entonces el desprecio hacia la cultura zoque y hacia todas las culturas o personas que practican una conciencia del valor de la transmisión de los rectos pensamientos, que nos permiten encontrarnos como personas libres y nos guían, a su vez, en un buen camino para la vida, en un andar afectuoso y amable, comprendiendo la existencia en una dimensión que implica un diálogo permanente con otros.

¿Qué pasa cuando las palabras no alcanzan a ser oídas?[7] ¿Existe acaso un sentimiento más triste que creer que no hay nadie, más allá, para escuchar nuestras plegarias? La otra cara de la desestima hacia las palabras es el menosprecio de la escucha, la desvalorización de la necesidad de escuchar con el corazón (y ser escuchados en) el latido del mundo (ese lugar en el que todos estamos inmersos y somos uno). En la degradación de la palabra se inscribe por tanto la señal de una profunda indiferencia hacia las y los otros; la marca de una falta de empatía y de respeto hacia el sentir de nuestros prójimos. El desprecio de la palabra es entonces también el signo de un orgullo poderoso: el de aquellos que desprecian a los que puedan estar sufriendo sus ofensas; el de aquellos que piensan que no hay nada –más allá de sus deseos– que esté allí para juzgarlos o levantarlos. Son los que piensan con la cabeza, los Nhkirawas (Sánchez 25). Se hace imposible entenderse con ellos porque se aferran a sus propias razones y tienen cerrados tanto los oídos como el corazón.

Mikeas habla en su libro de una palabra sagrada: "Una sola es la sagrada palabra, como una sola es la vida" (Sánchez 12). El sentimiento de la palabra sagrada se liga a la conciencia de que nada perdura en la tierra y de que estamos expuestos a esa fragilidad del tiempo, que vuelve vanidad el exceso y la acumulación de cosas materiales. Sin embargo, frente a la impermanencia y la intempestividad de la historia, lo que se puede heredar a otros sigue siendo la palabra: ella es además un tipo de herencia que, como el agua, llega a todos por igual, es blanda pero fuerte; y bondadosa, pues a todos alcanza.

En la tradición de los antiguos poetas aztecas como Netzahualcóyotl estaba presente esta visión de que estamos en una vida donde nada es permanente, donde nuestra existencia es quebradiza, pero se pensaba que un modo de alcanzar una trascendencia era dejar algo bonito en ese paso fugaz por el mundo.[8] Más aún, aquello que es posible dejar como verdad y valor para otras personas puede ser una palabra: el *in xóchitl in cuícatl*, una flor y un canto.[9] De las flores vienen los frutos; de los cantos, los llamados a levantarse, a celebrar, a andar por buenos caminos, a hallar buenas sendas, a encontrarnos en una voz que nos reúna en común, que nos congregue en una danza que despierta la tierra –en los cantos las voces se elevan–.

En muchos pueblos originarios existe esta conciencia de que la palabra es sanadora en la medida en que se tiene en claro que hay un efecto, no mágico, sino más bien sagrado en las palabras. Si se reflexiona, por ejemplo, sobre aquello que desde la visión mestiza se ha englobado bajo los términos de "brujería" o "hechicería", o se piensa en libros como *Conjuros y ebriedades: cantos de mujeres mayas* de Ambar Past –que recopila antiguos cantos de sanación y protección tsotsiles– puede verse que siempre está implicada la palabra. Estos son apenas algunos ejemplos de los muchos sentidos poéticos que forman parte de los cantos medicinales de curación y del cultivo de una palabra-orante, presentes en las culturas antiguas de Abiayala. Tales expresiones del arte poético oral permiten observar que el poder o la fuerza de las palabras tienen que ver con la intención y con la carga energética (con el aliento, el soplo o el espíritu) que conllevan, o que se depositan en ellas; pues por allí pasa el sentido que se les da a los vocablos, y que estos llevan y trasladan. Una expresión no sólo involucra la fonética, sino la intención de lo que se busca y se abre en ella, de ahí que tenga un efecto.

Para el pueblo zoque, la palabra es muy importante. Desde que son pequeños se les da a los niños y niñas una planta que se llama *wewe'*, la cual crece en la montaña donde está el Tzamapänh'. Esta plantita es como el ave del paraíso pero más grande. Se suele dar a los hijos cuando están chiquitos porque hace un sonido especial: se mueve como acordeón y produce una música. Se dice que al jugar con esa florecita, los pequeños adquieren el don de la palabra. Poder hablar nos da una identidad que no hay que desdeñar ni desaprovechar; significa un don que no debe malgastarse ni usarse en vano. Existen entonces categorizaciones de las palabras: hay palabras hirientes, palabras amorosas, palabras que tienen que ver con distintos contextos. Como decía la madre de Mikeas, alguien que habla con palabra dolorosa es alguien que puede ofender a otro. En la cultura zoque, el don de la palabra se adquiere desde la infancia, sí, pero debe usarse con prudencia, porque las palabras son poderosas armas.

Este pensamiento profundo sobre el modo en que el lenguaje nos conforma y define cobra sentido también en la poesía en cuanto que la palabra tiene ese poder sanador o ese poder hiriente, o reflexivo, de los cuales se habla en la tradición oral. Así pues, la palabra sagrada que se aprende de pequeña, de pequeño, va desarrollándose de diferentes maneras, algunos la cultivan más que otros y llegan a ser grandes oradores o importantes conversadores, con una facilidad para narrar y contar historias; otras u otros pueden ser capaces de usar ese don para la sanación espiritual o física de la gente. Aquel poder que tiene la palabra cada uno lo va desarrollando de acuerdo con el don que se le concede. "La sabiduría es una flor / que pocos pueden resistir / *Te' musoki'uy jäyäre eyari' ompapä' / jinhte' anhke' i'ijs musipä pyäjkinh'tzyowa*'" (Sánchez 92). Cuando hablamos de la palabra, viene un colibrí a la ventana. Nuestros pensamientos son como un colibrí que busca esa flor (esa sabiduría), que permite que el hablar se convierta en palabra sagrada.

La palabra sagrada como tal, *masanh tzame*, se concibe como un don. Es un saber, y muchos lo tienen, en especial los médicos tradicionales como el abuelo de Mikeas, que tenía ese conocimiento de la palabra sagrada que sana. La espiritualidad zoque se practica entre el movimiento danzante del espíritu y el bien de la palabra. Hay que aprender a hacer estas oraciones que tienen un ritmo especial para la curación, que se hacen totalmente en zoque y se practican para curar a los que se espantan o tienen una enfermedad física. Las energías protectoras del río o de las montañas a veces transmiten ese don del hablar. Así, desde el conocimiento zoque, tanto el miedo como la confusión pueden sanarse con una buena palabra, y con la ayuda de fuerzas como la de Nasakopajk o de las plantas que crecen en su seno. Hay palabras que se transmiten y otras que nacen de manera espontánea, que son dadas como una gracia a través del sueño. De ahí que la autoridad de la palabra también venga de la rectitud del corazón de quien obra con humildad, amor, conciencia y respeto. Pero existen asimismo lugares que le dan fuerza y rectitud a la palabra. El territorio zoque es una tierra rica en minerales, con muchos ríos, vegetación y montañas. La madre de Mikeas, aunque era muy católica, siempre comprendió que había otra espiritualidad que tiene que ver con la tierra, decía a sus hijos cuando eran niños que le hablaran a Nasakopajk, y ella siempre le hablaba a la tierra. Ella enseñó que cuando alguien te ofende, te hace sufrir y te causa dolor no se le debe desear mal a esa persona. Ella decía: no desees el mal a quien te daña, pero quita tus sandalias y pon tus pies y tu mano en la tierra, y pídele que te dé fortaleza para resistir ese dolor, y también que sane a esa persona que te está dañando, no le desees nunca el mal. Por Nasakopajk (el gran espíritu de la tierra) pasa todo, pasa la tristeza, la felicidad, el dolor. Todo pasa sobre Nasakopajk porque ha vivido tanto que nos conoce a todos, y nada es nuevo para ella. Una palabra que se eleva a Nasakopajk es una palabra que se vuelve sagrada, porque es el oído de ese Ser que nos cobija con su gran fuerza espiritual –que nos alimenta y nos engendra, que nos recibe cuando nos vamos de este mundo, que nos abriga y nos sostiene cada día– quien se hace depositario de aquella palabra, quien la va a escuchar primero.

Esos puntos energéticos que son la montaña, el volcán, los ríos, tienen su propio pensamiento y nos hablan. La palabra también nos sirve para comunicarnos con ellos. El conocimiento se construye en la lengua a través de muchísimos años y de miles de personas, por eso los idiomas guardan en la memoria la sabiduría de quienes supieron expresar palabras sagradas y se las dejaron a otras y otros. Las y los sabios zoque han dejado a sus hijas e hijos conocimientos que forman parte de este sentido del espíritu, que trae salud y alegría a los cuerpos, que trae vida a la vida que pasa.

La poesía es un corazón que late en la escucha del tiempo. Ese momento de inspiración se siente cuando se escribe poesía desde las voces antiguas que transmitieron las buenas palabras, y que nos han sido heredadas. Al igual que el río que habla. Desde la visión zoque, se considera que ese poder espiritual energético que tiene la naturaleza es su pensamiento mismo, el cual se abre a nuestros sentidos cuando logramos escuchar y comprender lo que nos dice, lo que nos está diciendo. Cuando nos privamos de ese sentido de escuchar lo que hay en torno nuestro nos bloqueamos, al no escuchar se nos bloquea el corazón, se nos ciega la mirada; esto nos hace daño pues no nos permite creer espiritualmente ni liberarnos.

Cuando pensamos en el poder de la palabra y en cómo nace la palabra sagrada, hay que comprender esa conexión con el espacio de la vida, con Nasakopajk, y con las otras y otros sabios que nos están hablando, pero se trata de una conexión genuina, no fingida. En gran parte de la poesía indígena se habla de la naturaleza a un nivel más contemplativo. Mikeas Sánchez tiene poca poesía así, que hable de la naturaleza, pero en su poesía está presente el respeto por esa conexión con las palabras sagradas, y su poesía es tocada por la fuerza de esa verdad que viene del corazón, la verdad de lo que se piensa sin rencores, con una mano en el corazón y con los pies en la tierra. La belleza de esa conexión con el río, de poder escuchar lo que el río siente y quiere hablarnos, de poder hacernos uno con el sufrimiento que está padeciendo a causa nuestra, es parte de la belleza de una poesía que defiende las palabras sagradas. Para escuchar hay que tener el corazón fresco, limpio, ser también misericordiosos y compasivos con el sufrimiento de otros. En la actualidad, los territorios están sufriendo. Nuestras hermanas y hermanos están sufriendo. Y también debemos estar atentos a eso. No ser indiferentes. La palabra poética se enlaza aquí con la defensa del territorio.[10] Es una palabra comprometida con las buenas palabras entendidas como caminos que buscan aclarar el pensamiento de la gente, traer calma y tranquilidad a los corazones, y enseñar modos más saludables y respetuosos de vivir juntos.

En la cultura desarraigada, que viene como un viento que arrasa los suelos de todas las regiones, el valor de la palabra se pierde. Para una sociedad que piensa con la cabeza, la palabra se reduce a su valor significante. Es decir que sólo se mide por su valor de cambio, se ha convertido en una mercancía que seduce, y así se vende y se intercambia.

Conocer las historias y los nombres

Conocer las palabras es también conocer su intención; conocer para qué y cómo fueron usadas por aquellos que supieron nombrar y llamar las cosas. *Cómo ser un buen salvaje* lleva un epígrafe de Juan Guillermo Sánchez Martínez donde se recuerda a uno de los luchadores indígenas asesinados recientemente por la defensa del territorio Yukpa:

> Antes de ser asesinado defendiendo el Perijá
> el cacique Sabino Romero explicó ante las cámaras
> que no bastan los artículos y las sentencias para reclamar las tierras
> si no se conocen las historias y los nombres de los cerros y los ríos. (5)

Dice también Mikeas en su libro que por sus nombres en ore se conoce el mundo. "Todo cuanto existe te pertenece, / conoces el nombre" (Sánchez 65), advierte la voz poética a sus hermanas y hermanos zoques. Conocer los nombres no implica designar, clasificar, marcar o medir las cosas, sino comprender la alteridad de lo que se está nombrando, conocer su raíz, crear una escucha y un afecto entre la palabra y lo que se habla a través suyo.

Existen palabras esenciales del pensamiento zoque que no encuentran traducción en español, o que tienen un sentido más fuerte en ore, pues en la traducción no conectan del todo esa fuerza del corazón y del pensamiento, ni ese conocimiento que viene en la palabra propia. Por ejemplo, *ore' pät* y *ore'yomo* –que remiten a un reconocimiento identitario–, o términos como "Oko'sawa", "Gran Apu' ", "Tuj'sawa" o "Nasakopajk", por mencionar algunos –los cuales no son nombres propios de divinidades o de personajes mitológicos, sino modos de comprender el territorio y los elementos que dominan en él, de conocer sus fuerzas, de entender sus voluntades, y sobre todo, de comunicarse con ellos. Estos nombres quedan sin traducción en los poemas de Mikeas. Son palabras esenciales que hablan de sentidos que están en el pensamiento de las lenguas, que otras lenguas desconocen, motivo por el cual no cuentan con vocablos para nombrarlos. Se trata de nombres que el español no tiene porque no conoce lo que nombran, de ahí que deba aprender a nombrar en las lenguas que sí cuentan con esos conocimientos en la memoria de su gente.

Se trata de problemas de traducción que tienen que ver con la visión de mundo, con la forma de vivir el mundo en el territorio, y con contextos muy diferentes. Al vivir en la ciudad o en otra cultura, te vas formando de acuerdo a lo que vives, a lo que creces. En el caso del mundo zoque hay cuestiones que tienen que ver con el pensamiento que existe en la naturaleza, relacionado sobre todo con Nasakopajk. Se traduce fácil Nasakopajk como "pachamama" y "madre tierra", pero es muy seco decirlo así, porque también es el padre. Es la madre-padre, es doble, *bi*. No es solamente *la*, es también *él*. Se alarga el sentido, pero no puede englobarse en un sólo término donde está la dualidad. Esa dualidad que tiene que ver con la bondad pero también con la maldad y con los pensamientos más bajos que tiene el ser humano, que no están separados. Al hacer las traducciones hay que jugar con las palabras. En el español se puede inventar la metáfora, se puede crear esa imagen a partir de otros términos. Pero en la poesía de Mikeas hay palabras que no se traducen. Es un reto para la versión en español el poder colocar estas palabras porque están fuera de contexto (lo que nombran no pertenece al mundo tal como lo concibe y lo nombra el castellano). Aún más, si esas palabras se las piensa desde el pensamiento occidental no nombran lo que se entiende en zoque, de ahí que no se pueda simplemente poner palabras como naturaleza o madre tierra, ni siquiera río o montaña o viento. Desde el pensamiento occidental, el río no piensa, las montañas no te hablan, los vientos no te escuchan; a los animales hay que domesticarlos, no tienen pensamiento propio, no existe la energía que te acompaña como son los naguales, sino que los animales se tienen de compañía solamente y no se considera que pueden tener una opinión propia. Se trata de cuestiones que son difíciles de traducir y de enseñar porque tienen que ver con la esencia misma de lo que es el ser desde la visión zoque: el ser de una planta, un río, montaña o animal. Son modos de comprender el mundo que mucha gente los concibe porque su cultura es afín, pero la mayoría no los entiende. Entonces leen un poema de un poeta indígena que habla desde estos lugares y les resulta algo muy simple, lo cuestionan como ingenuo, o quizá carente de trabajo intelectual o estético. Pero el problema es que se está nombrando algo que no tiene nombre en esa lengua vehicular y mayoritaria a la que se traduce.

Se observa así que en ocasiones la cultura occidental tiende a minusvalorar la poesía indígena que habla de la naturaleza en estos sentidos, reduciéndola a una clasificación temática en la que se neutraliza la fuerza vital de la ancestralidad y la identidad de sus culturas. Pero este tipo de afirmaciones que provienen de la crítica académica mayoritaria no hacen más que simplificar la potencia de estas poéticas, mostrando que se pronuncian desde una sola cultura, que no han podido tender los puentes de la traducción entre lenguas, y ver lo que se dice en esas palabras intraducibles.

Entonces, traducir (o dejar sin traducción) determinadas palabras son desafíos, pero también posicionamientos de una cultura que se ve minorizada y nunca va a tener la posibilidad de conseguir ese alcance que desde hace muchos años tienen ya las lenguas que son hegemónicas. La traducción debe ser sensible a lo que se dice en un vocablo, mostrar qué está viendo una cultura cuando pronuncia ciertos términos. Comprender esos nombres es abrir sentidos a la percepción, y entrar en espacios de conocimiento distintos.

En la actualidad hay territorios que transitamos, lagos, montañas que perdieron los nombres o fueron olvidados, y se los llama como los designó el colonizador. Son denominaciones que se han pensado con la cabeza y no con el corazón. Se pierde así la fuerza y la posibilidad del diálogo con el territorio, con sus dueños reales, legítimos e invisibles. Se produce como una afasia, como una no-lengua. Nos quedamos todos sin idioma por haber silenciado la lengua de quienes sabían los nombres. Como dice Mikeas, la herida que somos le sangra a quienes la infringen. La herida colonial de las y los que siguen siendo sojuzgados, desplazados, eliminados en la cultura y el territorio, sangra en el vacío de los que andan sin conciencia, sin raíces, sin sentidos; entonces Mikeas dice en zoque: "Somos la herida que te sangra, / Somos la respuesta a tu vacío. / Ven hermano blanco, / te enseñaremos el canto que jamás se olvida. / Ven hermana blanca, / te daremos el secreto de la belleza infinita" (Sánchez 83). Los que están lastimando están en deuda; pero esa deuda les vuelve como un vacío, ya que han perdido el lenguaje para hablar con el entorno y con la fuerza bondadosa de los espíritus que lo habitan.

En *Cómo ser un buen salvaje*, se dice que una frágil raíz no resiste el tiempo (61). Se hace mención así a ese mundo contemporáneo lleno de corrupción, mentiras, engaños, trampas y baratijas. Mundo de mercenarios y ladrones, donde gobiernan los amos de la decadencia, donde se evidencia el real salvajismo del mundo que pierde los nombres y las palabras sagradas. Donde se escucha una música que no tiene alma (Sánchez 77). Vivimos en una modernidad que nos tiene acostumbrados a estilos de vida consumistas, en la que se naturaliza la explotación de los pueblos donde están los recursos, para poder sostener ciertas comodidades que tenemos. Hay que saber de dónde vienen las cosas. Los discursos hegemónicos nos han impedido pensar que cada cosa viene de algún lugar, que alguien la hizo; no hay un pensamiento crítico, no se reflexiona sobre qué implica tener o querer tener todo lo que viene y nos venden. Con las crisis climáticas, el planeta está en mucho peligro. La pandemia lo ha vuelto visible. Nos habla sobre todo del miedo a la muerte. La gente ha sentido cerca la muerte. Como seres humanos somos frágiles, perecederos, esa seguridad que creíamos tener no la tenemos. El pensamiento colonial ha dado a luz una cultura huérfana, que no tiene nombres; un mundo sin principios en el que no hay respeto por los otros.

La poesía de Mikeas construye una fortaleza desde el antiguo pensamiento zoque a través de una mirada sensible y un compromiso presente con la necesidad de conservar una realidad que se mantenga fuerte ante todo ese avance negativo de la cultura salvaje. Así la voz poética le habla a la niña y al niño zoque, y va trayendo esa fuerza del idioma y de las palabras sagradas; va llamando y exhortando a su gente a reconocerse parte de ese pensamiento propio. Se vuelve una palabra convocante, que incluye, que contiene a quien la escucha. Pero luego también convoca a aquellos otros y otras que quizá quieren escuchar, pero se sienten excluidos porque no tienen palabras, porque ya no creen en las palabras, o no creen sólo por la palabra y necesitan la señal de los que vieron y han conocido gracias a ella. La poesía busca no perder la esperanza, encontrar algún punto donde poder tocar a alguien, sacudirlo. La palabra puede curar, transformar, pero también tiene que haber cierta reciprocidad: esa responsabilidad del otro para abrirse a las palabras sagradas. Mientras cada quien no se abra, mientras no lo permita, es difícil. Tiene que existir esa apertura para poder recibir lo que se da. Para tener las buenas palabras, las palabras sagradas, no sólo hay que saber que se heredan, que es posible traducirlas, sino asimismo permitirse recibirlas.

Notas

1. Con la llamada Ilustración europea, la arquitectura de la *humanitas* se construyó a partir de la antinomia con la barbarie, lo salvaje, la monstruosidad y la animalidad –ideas que le han permitido a Europa la esclavización y sojuzgamiento de las naciones invadidas. En este marco, el término "salvaje", o *sauvage* en francés, ha servido para marcar la antinomia del mundo civilizado. Si la noción de bárbaro que utilizaban los griegos señalaba al incivilizado por su falta de *logos* (lo cual significaba en realidad no hablar la lengua griega), la palabra "salvaje" inicia, de modo paralelo, una larga tradición donde la humanidad se concibe en oposición a la naturaleza, instalando una frontera entre humanidad y animalidad. Desde la lógica de la modernidad occidental, las modernas ciencias de la naturaleza y la razón instrumental, la naturaleza debe ser domesticada y puesta al servicio del desarrollo de la cultura (una cultura, la occidental, considerada como universal). El salvaje es entonces el que aún vive del otro lado de la cultura, del lado de lo que hay que domeñar.

2. Sobre las políticas de avergonzamiento como operación colonial remitimos a las reflexiones de la poeta mapuche Liliana Ancalao, "El idioma silenciado": http://www.latinamericanliteraturetoday.org/es/2018/febrero/el-idioma-silenciado-de-liliana-ancalao.

3. Libros ya clásicos del pensamiento propio de Abiayala, como *La revolución india* de Fausto Reinaga o *Si me permiten hablar* de Domitila Chungara han dado testimonio con numerosos ejemplos

del modo en que el término "salvaje" fue utilizado por las oligarquías nacionales y las clases dirigentes para justificar la expropiación, el saqueo y la violencia sobre los mundos indígenas. Actualmente, es posible observar la reapropiación irónica del vocablo, empleado en varias de las poéticas indígenas contemporáneas como herramienta de desenmascaramiento de esa violencia. Tal es el caso de *Stxaj no' anima/Oración salvaje* (2011) del poeta maya q'anjob'al Daniel Caño, o *Soy una maldita salvaje* (*Eukeuan nin matashi-manitu innushkueu/Je suis une maudite sauvagesse*) de la poeta innu An Antane Kapesh. Asimismo puede rastrearse el uso de este término ligado a la noción de "paria", en *Parias zugun* de la poeta mapuche Adriana Paredes Pinda, por mencionar sólo algunos.

4. Si bien el mito del "buen salvaje" constituye un lugar común de la idealización del estado de naturaleza, como estado de inocencia anterior al pecado del *Génesis*, ha tenido una significación funcional en la construcción de esa *humanitas* colonizadora en autores del siglo XVIII como Cartier, Montaigne, Diderot o Rousseau, y más contemporáneamente en otros como Lévi-Strauss. Desde el pensamiento latinoamericano estas ideas han sido denunciadas con ironía por Oswald de Andrade y su teoría de la antropofagia, y retomadas en su crítica de la cultura occidental por el escritor brasileño Haroldo de Campos.

5. "Ore" significa zoque (que es la asignación que se le ha dado a este idioma desde el español). Es decir que ore es el nombre propio y más preciso para referirse al idioma que en español se conoce como zoque. El término "ore" se utiliza tanto para designar la lengua como para significar la idea de palabra.

6. Tanto para la referencia del Tzamapänh' como de otros términos en lengua zoque referidos más abajo, nos hemos basado en las fuentes orales conocidas por Mikeas Sánchez en cuanto hablante y conocedora de su cultura zoque.

7. También el poeta mapuche Elicura Chihuailaf ha señalado la urgencia y la demora permanente de un verdadero diálogo entre culturas y naciones en uno de sus primeros libros, *Recado confidencial a los chilenos*.

8. Véase por ejemplo el poema de Nezahualcóyotl "Yo lo pregunto", en *Ms. Cantares mexicanos*, fol. 17r.

9. Como explica Miguel León-Portilla, en el conocido "Diálogo de flor y canto", los tlamatinime consideraban que "lo único que puede ser verdadero sobre la tierra" son las palabras venidas de la flor y el canto, aludiendo a la expresión *in xóchitl in cuícatl* que forma un difrasismo y puede traducirse como una referencia a las buenas palabras que se dicen con el corazón (León-Portilla 43).

10. La poeta mapuche y machi Adriana Paredes Pinda, desde Wajmapu, habla del sufrimiento de los territorios y de una experiencia poética de cuidado de los mismos, afín a la que cuenta Mikeas Sánchez. Véase además la revista *Diálogo*, vol. 22, no. 1, primavera de 2019, dedicado enteramente a la literatura, el arte y el pensamiento indígena comprometido con el buen vivir y contra el extractivismo.

Obras citadas

Campos, H. de. "Lo concreto barroco". *Galaxias*. La Flauta Mágica, 2010.

Chihuailaf, Elikura. *Recado confidencial a los chilenos*. 1998. LOM, 2015.

León-Portilla, Miguel. *Antigua y nueva palabra*. Taurus Aguilar, 2004.

Paredes Pinda, Adriana. *Riquezas vivas de Lago Ranco VII capitulo Machi Adriana Pinda*. *YouTube*. Web. Accedido el 25 de junio de 2021.

Sánchez, Mikeas. *Cómo ser un buen salvaje: Jujtzye tä wäpä tzamapänh'ajä*. Editorial Universidad de Guadalajara, 2019.

Sánchez Martínez, Juan Guillermo. "Altamar". *Agenda Cultural Alma Máter*, no. 236, diciembre de 2016, https://revistas.udea.edu.co/index.php/almamater/article/view/326593.

Santos, Boaventura de Sousa. *Una epistemología del sur: La reinvención del conocimiento y la emancipación social*. CLACSO-Siglo XXI, 2009.

CHAPTER 3

Hacia una relacionalidad cuir de la tierra: Géneros y sexualidades en Abiayala y Turtle Island

Marco Antonio Huerta Alardín
University of California, Irvine

Tras la emergencia de un marco teórico y metodológico robusto que atiende la intersección entre los estudios sobre la indigeneidad y los estudios de género y sexualidad en las universidades de América del Norte, es preciso considerar cómo este archivo de conocimientos y métodos puede ser utilizado para el estudio y el análisis de los sistemas de género y sexualidad de las naciones indígenas en América Latina.[1] Imaginar un futuro en donde los saberes de las personas indígenas queer del norte global sean accesibles para las personas indígenas cuir del sur global y viceversa, implica comenzar a trascender las fronteras materiales, lingüísticas y culturales entre Norteamérica y Latinoamérica, que no son otra cosa más que un legado colonial europeo de la rivalidad de las potencias europeas que lucharon a muerte entre ellas por dominar el pillaje rapaz del continente. Al transferir el concepto queer al contexto latinoamericano, pero sobre todo al contexto indígena abiayalense, se corre el riesgo de perpetuar esa extracción y de generar aún más destrucción y distorsión epistemológica. Sin embargo, este ejercicio de enfoque transnacional conlleva riesgos importantes, aunque a su vez abre espacios para sostener conversaciones necesarias y facilita la innovación del pensamiento en torno a estos conflictos. Este capítulo ofrece un punto de partida para reflexionar a detalle sobre cuáles son los riesgos que conlleva el soslayar la dinámica del poder entre el conocimiento generado por el Norte y el conocimiento generado por el Sur. Es una oportunidad de valorar la teoría producida hasta el momento y de identificar los matices en la intersección de los vectores del género, la sexualidad y la indigeneidad. Mi convicción es que la incorporación de estas obras a la investigación académica puede ayudar a revisitar nociones sobre colonialismo y género y sexualidad.

La emergencia de un campo: Queer Indigenous Studies

Durante las últimas tres décadas, se ha visto un creciente interés y reconocimiento de las formaciones de género y diferencias sexuales de las naciones indígenas de Norteamérica. Esto se debe en gran parte a los activismos que las personas queer y no-normativas de las comunidades indígenas han generado para crear múltiples maneras de hacer visibles sus luchas. Estas luchas dieron cuenta que era necesaria la generación de un lenguaje común que les permitiera hacerse legibles frente a los ojos del mundo colonial, mas bajo sus propios términos. Había que crear un lenguaje incluyente que describiera las borraduras frecuentes de las personas indígenas-queer.

En principio, era necesario distanciarse de los contingentes LGBTQ occidentales que, desde su fundación, han enfocado su activismo en los derechos de las personas queer sin comprender la urgencia de conmiserarse de las causas de las personas indígenas. Otra instancia que representaba la necesidad de nueva terminología era el caso de las circunstancias extremas que muchos hombres gay nativos experimentaron durante la peor parte de la crisis del SIDA. Cuando querían regresar a sus hogares en las reservaciones para pasar sus últimos años con sus familias antes de morir por complicaciones del VIH, muchos de ellos eran rechazados en sus comunidades porque decían que portaban "la enfermedad de los hombres gays blancos" (Fernandes 146).

Había que nombrar también lo que ha ocurrido con parejas indígenas no-normativas que buscaban unirse legalmente y encontraron que mientras que el Estado nación cuenta con legislación que protege el matrimonio igualitario, en ocasiones este no es el caso de las naciones indígenas. Algunas naciones indígenas no reconocen uniones no-tradicionales bajo el argumento de que no forma parte de sus historias y costumbres (McKie). También era de primer orden contrarrestar la imposición violenta del término "berdache" que lxs primerxs antropólogxs que estudiaron esta intersección impusieron desde su entendimiento occidental. Era necesario además un lenguaje que ayudara a reclamar lo que había antes con relación al entendimiento de la formación y la organización del género y la sexualidad y que podría haber sido olvidado por la comunidad a merced de siglos de colonialidad y modernidad (âpihtawikosisân).

En 1990 se usó por primera vez el término en inglés "Two-Spirit" en la tercera conferencia anual intertribal de gays y lesbianas indígenas en Winnipeg, Canadá, y se refiere a "indígenas norteamericanxs que cumplen uno de los muchos roles de género mixtos que se encuentran tradicionalmente entre múltiples grupos indígenas de estadounidenses nativos y de las primeras naciones canadienses" (Hayes 2).[2] Este término varía en sus usos de cultura en cultura, pero a pesar de ello, se mantienen ciertas similitudes entre quienes suscriben esta identidad. Sin embargo, es importante reconocer que este es un concepto genérico y, como tal, este tipo de terminología es susceptible de soslayar matices relevantes y que no todas las naciones ni todas las personas indígenas escogen usar el término o identificarse de esta forma.

A treinta años del surgimiento de la teoría queer, se celebraba la ampliación de dicha categoría de estudio al incorporar un subcampo de estudio que se ocuparía de asuntos relacionados a la intersección entre indigeneidad y lo queer.[3] Con la publicación del volumen antológico *Queer Indigenous Studies* (2011) y su contraparte literaria *Sovereign Erotics* (2011), estos libros inauguraron oficialmente el campo de los Queer Indigenous Studies con el prestigio de una publicación impresa bajo el auspicio del sello editorial de una universidad estadounidense. Y este no fue un hecho menor, ya que fue la primera vez que un volumen académico se centraba en la intersección de las variaciones sexual y de género y la indigeneidad. El libro representó un esfuerzo por descolonizar las formas en que se produce el conocimiento en torno a los cuerpos racializados y sexualizados. Según lxs editorxs, el libro se guía por la política de la interrupción y la resistencia de la colonialidad del poder imbuida en la representación y en la generación del conocimiento relativo a las personas indígenas-queer para poner el foco en lo que estas personas tienen que decir sobre ellxs mismxs, en sus propios términos (Driskill et al. 4). La reciente aprobación académica, sin embargo, no puede pasar por alto la larga historia de variación sexual y de género al interior de epistemologías indígenas milenarias.

En cambio, resulta contradictorio que la edición de unos libros tan innovadores por su enfoque interseccional, que trasciende y expande los límites de lo que se entiende por conocimiento, parezca de pronto alinearse con el Estado nación para potenciar la separación material, cultural y lingüística entre Norteamérica y Latinoamérica. Estos volúmenes no incluyen información ni reflexiones sobre las naciones indígenas de América Latina y es una ausencia que se manifiesta en el campo como persistente. Poco más de una década después de la publicación de *Queer Indigenous Studies*, al enfrentarme como investigador para crear crítica en torno a la producción cultural de personas indígenas-cuir en Latinoamérica, es evidente que los estudios latinoamericanos presentan un desfase en torno a la apertura interdisciplinaria y a la instrumentación de enfoques interseccionales de investigación respecto de los asuntos del género y la sexualidad en las naciones indígenas.[4] El presente volumen busca trascender y derribar esos obstinados muros que dividen.

Consideraciones transhemisféricas de género y sexualidad desde Turtle Island

Hay algunxs académicxs que intervienen en los estudios latinoamericanos que se caracterizan por pertenecer a naciones indígenas de Norteamérica y cuyos trabajos de investigación apuntan a la creación de herramientas teóricas y metodológicas que permiten pensar la indigeneidad en el continente más allá de las fronteras territoriales, culturales y lingüísticas de los Estados nación. Sus trabajos dan cuenta además de que es posible realizar investigación de manera ética y responsable con una sensibilidad más aguda de frente al complejo entramado racial y cultural de América Latina. Estos trabajos apuntan a la posibilidad de pensar los asuntos de la indigeneidad más allá del Estado nación y ofrecen la oportunidad de crear una coalición que incremente el archivo documental y que abra el panorama a perspectivas de otras latitudes.

Shannon Speed es una profesora e investigadora chickasaw que interviene en los estudios latinoamericanos con el concepto de las "settler capitalist structures" que permite pensar en los Estados nación de América Latina como parte de los *Settler Colonial Studies*. Speed argumenta que los Estados nación latinoamericanos son "settler states" aunque no se les suele analizar de esa forma (Speed 783). Al proponer esta lectura, Speed declara que como chickasaw a ella siempre le ha parecido problemática la división entre las personas indígenas del norte y las del sur (784). Speed argumenta que en América Latina las personas indígenas han sido explotadas corporalmente y desposeídas de sus tierras de la misma forma en que los settler studies describen la explotación y el despojo en Norteamérica. Speed argumenta que creer lo contrario es comprar el cuento del mestizaje u otros proyectos raciales de los Estados nación latinoamericanos.

Speed provee múltiples y significativas instancias de evidencia de las similitudes y coincidencias entre los procesos de colonización del norte y el sur. Entre ellas, indica que si bien los proyectos de racialización conocidos como el mestizaje en Mesoamérica y el blood quantum en Norteamérica difieren, en lo esencial contribuyen al mismo proyecto colonial de asimilación forzada (Speed 787). Pero en cada instancia en donde encuentra estas similitudes Speed se encarga de aclarar que esas generalizaciones no ocurrieron de forma uniforme ni de manera sistematizada a lo largo del continente. Esto es importante porque si bien existen diferencias significativas entre las diversas regiones del continente, también es cierto que el enfoque transnacional de Speed es útil para entender que las "settler capitalist structures" han sido y son una constante en América Latina.

Otro ejemplo de un latinoamericanista de Turtle Island está en el trabajo de Joseph M. Pierce, profesor e investigador cheroqui que hace una reflexión del trabajo teórico que surge del examen de las obras "monstruas" creadas por mujeres trans-latinoamericanas como Susy Shock y Claudia Rodríguez. Pierce observa el contexto histórico y geográfico en el que emergen estas posturas monstruosas que responden a las formas en que el estado-nación se apodera del control de los cuerpos disidentes. Además elabora un entramado histórico de la conceptualización del monstruo en la tradición hispánica que deviene en las estrategias que se encuentran en el corazón de este movimiento estético y político. Pierce define su investigación y centra su interés en cómo artistas trans y travestis desarrollaron una respuesta "monstrua" disruptiva ante la normatividad de género y la creciente cooptación de la disidencia sexual y de género por el Estado y el capital (Pierce, "I Monster" 307).

Pierce rastrea y ubica la tradición de la monstruosidad como parte del legado colonial hispánico y que se ha transformado a través del tiempo para servir distintos propósitos de alteridad y el ordenamiento taxonómico de lo natural. A través de la lectura de los trabajos dramáticos y poéticos de Susy Shock y Claudia Rodríguez, Pierce puede concluir que lo monstruoso de estas artistas implica una renuencia a ceñirse a los parámetros normativos de inclusión multicultural y de ciudadanía sexual neoliberal (308). La lectura de Pierce sobre estos trabajos concluye que la monstruosidad de Shock y Rodríguez cuestiona las maneras en que el cuerpo es entendido con relación a los mecanismos biopolíticos de control. Este análisis provee el contexto necesario para poder comprender la importancia de estas artistas y de sus intervenciones a lo queer desde el sur global que construyen resistencias partiendo desde sus propios cuerpos.

Tanto Speed como Pierce sostienen enfoques teóricos transnacionales en su trabajo de investigación académica, pero la singularidad de su pertenencia a sus naciones indígenas es sin duda un factor que les otorga una mirada más aguda y empática al momento de valorar a sus sujetxs de investigación en Latinoamérica. Su trabajo permite observar modelos de investigación con consideraciones transhemisféricas desde miradas que pertenecen a las naciones indígenas de Turtle Island y que no necesariamente se encuentran imbuidas en el excepcionalismo estadounidense del cual surge la teoría queer (Eng y Puar 2). Estos acercamientos ofrecen modelos metodológicos para comenzar a esbozar consideraciones sobre la indigeneidad cuando se intersecta con la sexualidad y el género en diversas latitudes del continente.

Latinoamérica y la teoría queer

Para comenzar a observar un panorama transhemisférico de la teoría queer y su relación con Latinoamérica, es importante primero establecer que escritores como Néstor Perlongher en Argentina y Pedro Lemebel en Chile ya manifestaban en sus escritos reflexiones sobre la complejidad y la necesidad de comenzar a pensar la variación sexual con conceptos y lenguaje que correspondieran a los contextos latinoamericano e indígena. De esto se encuentra consciente Sayak Valencia, quien señala que los escritos de Perlongher y Lemebel fueron "publicados entre 1980 y 1992, que es el mismo periodo en el que la insurgencia queer como movimiento político y más tarde como taxonomía académica tomaba cuerpo y forma en la geografía estadounidense" (Valencia 31).

Desde esa tensión epistémica hemisférica y con una perspectiva descolonial, Valencia pone énfasis en la necesidad de distanciarse de la teoría queer del norte global a través del gesto de extrañamiento lingüístico que implica el significante castellanizado: cuir. Esta se plantea como "una respuesta directa a las críticas y resistencias [...] que tienen algunos teóric*s tanto latinoamerican*s como estadounidenses a la importación del término *queer* sin considerar sus contextos y trayectorias políticas" (Valencia 35). En esta consideración Valencia asume como necesario que este gesto lingüístico adquiera una dimensión política al articular la representación de un colectivo diverso que no se encuentra representado y que se niega a asimilarse en el sistema de nomenclatura de lo queer. Valencia explica que "*cuir* visibiliza y da voz a unas políticas de supervivencia y alianza" que dirige la mirada hacia el sur en contraofensiva de la imposición de la mirada occidental (34).

Este giro lingüístico de la nomenclatura que fue adoptado mayoritariamente por activistas y artistas de Argentina y Chile implica un esfuerzo por remover no sólo las barreras lingüísticas culturales y materiales entre el norte hegemónico y el sur "g-local", como lo formula Valencia, sino por resistir la mirada lectora y la taxonomía hegemónicas de los textos de la teoría queer.[5] Sayak Valencia explica que es necesario este distanciamiento epistemológico con el fin de visibilizar las asimetrías entre la representación geopolítica de lo queer y lo cuir, y la cooptación por parte del estado neoliberal para crear una ilusión de multiculturalidad y de reconocimiento legal. En este gesto lingüístico, Valencia también observa el potencial de establecer una perspectiva interseccional que apela al uso subversivo del género, la sexualidad y el lenguaje para combatir el racismo, la violencia patriarcal y la destrucción de la naturaleza. Para Valencia lo clave son las múltiples posibilidades de subversión del gesto.

En otro sentido, Héctor Domínguez-Ruvalcaba interviene en el campo de los estudios latinoamericanos y de la teoría queer con su notable concepto de la traducción de lo queer. Domínguez-Ruvalcaba ofrece reflexiones de cómo se podría traducir el concepto queer en los contextos latinoamericanos como parte de la circulación de las ideas entre el norte y el sur globales. El autor hace una serie de análisis de casos en donde le permite hacer una reflexión sobre el tipo de traducción entre culturas que se está llevando a cabo desde lo queer. Domínguez-Ruvalcaba establece las constelaciones de las relaciones entre la producción teórica de las instituciones del norte global, y destaca las investigaciones y disquisiciones que se han realizado en torno a los estudios sobre el género y la sexualidad en Latinoamérica. Domínguez-Ruvalcaba expone su idea del acto político que implica la traducción de lo queer como un método a través del cual se pueden observar los problemas locales al reconocer los márgenes y las opresiones de los cuerpos no-normativos (Domínguez-Ruvalcaba 5).

Domínguez-Ruvalcaba entiende este acto político como uno de reconocimiento e inclusión y desde el inicio declara que en su foco no se encuentra debatir cuál sería la traducción correcta de lo queer, sino liberarlo de cualquier discurso prescriptivo. Sin embargo, Domínguez-Ruvalcaba está consciente de los riesgos que implica esta conversación transnacional y, principalmente, el riesgo que implica el locus de enunciación de la teoría queer con relación a América Latina. A pesar de ello, Domínguez-Ruvalcaba encuentra valor en el "uncanny side of the imperial corpus of knowledge" que representa la producción teórica de las personas queer de razas marginalizadas en el norte global ya que constituye el ala disidente dentro de la metrópolis (10).

En contraste, una de las pensadoras que desde Latinoamérica ha advertido sobre los riesgos de adoptar sin cuestionar los preceptos de la teoría queer norteamericana ha sido la performista chilena conocida como Hija de Perra quien ha descrito los efectos colonizadores de la academia estadounidense. Hija de Perra advertía que "los nuevos saberes del Género se agolpan en nuestros límites territoriales y nos encasillan con nuevas etiquetas [...] hoy en día los del norte nos indican una nueva lectura para comprender lo que ya existía en nuestras tierras" (De Perra 10). Hija de Perra denuncia que la academia norteamericana esencialmente tiene la posición de validar tanto lo queer como lo cuir. Luego procede a rechazar esa etiqueta taxonómica que la mirada del norte la categoriza como queer, ya que es una etiqueta que se le impuso sin su consentimiento. Además describe la confrontación identitaria que la teoría queer le produjo encima de la alienación que ya sostenía por existir y crecer como ella misma en un contexto como el de la dictadura chilena. Esto no lo contempla la teoría queer norteamericana.

Esta disensión de Hija de Perra está presente también en la obra de tantas otras pensadoras latinoamericanas que han no sólo contribuido a estas conversaciones con un conocimiento cimentado en sus experiencias y en sus territorios, sino que han criticado también el tono imperialista y a veces solipsista de los discursos neoliberales del feminismo blanco, los estudios descoloniales y de la teoría queer.[6] La necesidad de situar y contextualizar los temas del género y la sexualidad de América Latina y de asumir una postura frente a las taxonomías del norte global se presenta como la constante hasta ahora en este breve repaso de obras teóricas sobre la indigeneidad, el género y la sexualidad.

Es importante mencionar que el presente capítulo no pretende ser una reflexión exhaustiva ni totalizadora de las diversas tradiciones y genealogías del pensamiento que han abordado la relación asimétrica entre las epistemologías del norte y del sur y la necesidad de explorar la variación y la disidencia sexual en forma transhemisférica. Un ejemplo de ello es el trabajo que llevó a cabo Joseph M. Pierce con otrxs investigadorxs en el número especial de *GLQ* en cuanto al rastreo y la identificación de la historia de las reflexiones en torno a "la circulación de la teoría queer, su privilegiamiento de ciertas lenguas y cuerpos, sus fundamentos epistemológicos y las encarnaciones a través de las cuales lo cuir ha sido a la vez una promesa emancipadora y un método de subyugación para los pueblos de Abya Yala/ América Latina" (Pierce et al., "Introduction" 321).[7] En este número especial de *GLQ*, como en este capítulo, lxs autorxs interrogan las circunstancias de desigualdad que gobiernan el pensamiento teórico y la producción del conocimiento y su relación con la colonialidad (322). A continuación, consideraré dos ejemplos recientes que proponen metodologías que potencialmente reducirían la brecha artificial entre los estudios sobre indigeneidad y sexualidad del norte y del sur.

Hacia una relacionalidad de la tierra

La denominación neoliberal de la teoría queer queda articulada cabalmente por David L. Eng y Jasbir K. Puar. Explican que el campo de la teoría queer está fundado en el excepcionalismo norteamericano y en el ideal liberal de adquirir o ampliar los derechos de las personas queer. Lo que se encuentra obviado en esta premisa es que la única condición para acceder al empoderamiento y beneficiarse con los nuevos derechos en los marcos legislativos del Estado nación como el matrimonio igualitario, la adopción homoparental o la despenalización de la sodomía, es la asimilación total como ciudadanx del estado neoliberal. ¿En dónde deja esto a las culturas indígenas que durante siglos han resistido la asimilación? ¿Cómo forzar a los cuerpos trans dentro de un régimen biopolítico de control a cambio de leyes que no garantizan su derecho básico a existir? Si bien la "subjectless critique" ha operado en favor de ayudar al entendimiento de algunos asuntos relacionados con el género y la sexualidad, esta teoría también tiene unas limitaciones importantes, especialmente al pretender otorgarle cualidades de universalidad. Los ensayos incluidos en este número especial de *Social Text* editado por Eng y Puar formulan alternativas para superar esas limitaciones e ir más allá (a la izquierda) de lo que se conoce como teoría queer hasta ese momento.

La académica chickasaw Jodi A. Byrd escribe sobre la importancia de verdaderamente centrar los saberes y las vidas indígenas queer junto con la contextualización apropiada del territorio en donde éstos emergen. Byrd observa una discontinuidad ontológica entre lo queer de los Indigenous Studies y lo queer de la teoría queer. Byrd argumenta que es posible resarcir esa brecha y unirlos a través del concepto de la tierra, o articulado en inglés "ground". Declara: "Ground—as land, as base, as territory, as wellness, and as center—persists as a guiding principle for decolonization, but it also becomes the locating authorization for claims, for meaning, for rightness, and for identity, subjectless or not" (Byrd 107). Es por esta razón que es indispensable tomar en cuenta el territorio al momento de analizar la organización del género y la sexualidad al interior de naciones indígenas.

Byrd ofrece un principio metodológico que corporiza ese grounding en el cuerpo de las personas indígenas de forma similar al modo en que la teoría queer comenzó a ocuparse de los cuerpos de razas marginalizadas y de los cuerpos trans. Este grounding se convierte entonces en una manera de centrar lo que ha sido arrebatado, borrado y asesinado por el colonialismo. Byrd argumenta que es a través de esta relación con la tierra que los cuerpos indígenas representan la tierra, representan los sistemas de organización sociopolítica indígenas y activan procesos de descolonización. Esta operación de grounding es necesaria para entender a cabalidad la manera en que las naciones indígenas se organizan con relación a la normatividad del género y la sexualidad. Así, la contribución de Byrd se convierte en un instrumento relevante para comprender la "grounded normativity" y la "grounded relationality" en cada instancia.

Byrd comparte un enfoque que es necesario para pensar las normatividades y la relacionalidad que guardan las naciones y las comunidades indígenas en función de la organización del género y la sexualidad sobre un territorio determinado. De igual forma, con este enfoque se pueden producir reflexiones más profundas sobre los papeles de la variación sexual y de género en las múltiples dimensiones de las cosmovisiones de las comunidades indígenas. Byrd misma asume que aún tiene trabajo por hacer "to consider how both indigeneity and queerness transform in conversation with and through global souths and beyond the white settler colonies that have so often been the site of critical analysis" (121). Sin embargo, su reflexión sobre la relacionalidad de la tierra representa un buen punto de partida para abrir la conversación hacia los territorios y las naciones del sur global.

Body Land y relacionalidad

Afortunadamente ya existen quienes se encuentran formulando cuestionamientos y argumentos sobre el género y la indigeneidad en América Latina a través de la instrumentación de metodologías basadas en la relacionalidad. Una de ellxs, Isabel Altamirano-Jiménez, se identifica como una feminista binnizá (Altamirano-Jiménez 322) y establece una relación directa entre el extractivismo neocolonial y la violencia de género que afecta especialmente a las mujeres indígenas en la región del istmo de Tehuantepec en Oaxaca. Altamirano-Jiménez emplea el concepto de "body land" para describir cómo la actividad extractivista en el istmo de Tehuantepec afecta corporalmente a las mujeres, particularmente a las mujeres indígenas de la región, y se refleja en problemas de la salud reproductiva, la reorganización de las relaciones de género y el incremento de la violencia de género y cómo estas están cambiando la vida social local (321). Basa parte de su pensamiento en la teoría de "transit of Indianness" de Jodi A. Byrd, útil para pensar en los estados del primer mundo como estados coloniales que se encuentran activamente implicados en los procesos actuales de la ampliación de la extracción de recursos naturales a nivel mundial (322). Altamirano-Jiménez explica que al usar el concepto de "body land" su análisis revela que la relacionalidad es central en el análisis de las luchas indígenas en contra de la desposesión territorial y para entender las luchas de las mujeres indígenas en contra de la violencia de género (322).

Para Altamirano-Jiménez la tierra es una fuente de conocimiento que sostiene las cosmologías de las naciones indígenas del istmo de Tehuantepec. Las relaciones en el istmo de Tehuantepec han sido trastocadas tanto por la colonización europea como por la empresa neoliberal extractivista de los "settler states" de América del Norte. Altamirano-Jiménez argumenta que este abuso de la tierra tiene consecuencias que se reflejan directamente y de la forma más violenta en los cuerpos de las mujeres que se encuentran consternadas por el futuro de sus hijxs ante la desposesión y la destrucción de la tierra. Explica que son cuerpos los que resisten los procesos extractivistas contemporáneos y tal resistencia tiene efectos materiales que tienen consecuencias especialmente virulentas en los cuerpos de las mujeres indígenas. Altamirano-Jiménez concluye que es la labor extractivista la que ha modificado las relaciones con la tierra, con los poderes coloniales y con unxs y otrxs.[8]

De esta forma, Altamirano-Jiménez produce un modelo de análisis transnacional desde su locus enunciativo como parte de la Nación Binnizá y como miembro de la academia norteamericana. Altamirano-Jiménez reformula y crea nuevas herramientas para pensar los problemas de género y las luchas sociales que tienen que enfrentar las mujeres indígenas a lo largo y ancho del continente y que son atribuibles al extractivismo, lo cual se revela por la relación misma de sus cuerpos con la tierra. Altamirano-Jiménez se centra en las mujeres indígenas, pero su intervención promueve la posibilidad del uso del "body land" como análisis para pensar y comprender asuntos de género y sexualidad relacionados con las personas muxe' y las personas nguiu' de la Nación Binnizá en el propio istmo de Tehuantepec.

¿Estudios indígenas cuir?

Este breve repaso sobre diferentes posturas con relación al estado actual de la teoría queer y en particular de lo que se ha entendido como Queer Indigenous Studies ofrece una oportunidad para contemplar este subcampo y a la misma teoría queer como un conocimiento generado con un locus de enunciación geográfico específico con normas y principios relacionales específicos. En el caso de la teoría queer norteamericana, esta debe ser entendida como un constructo colonial moderno neo/liberal que emerge dentro del excepcionalismo estadounidense y como tal muestra insuficiencias y presenta riesgos de violencia epistémica. Sin embargo, a pesar de esa insuficiencia, hay otrxs académicxs que han facilitado la ampliación y la sensibilización de la visión de los estudios latinoamericanos, los settler studies y los estudios de género y sexualidad desde sus propios *loci* enunciativos como ciudadanxs de naciones indígenas norteamericanas. Esta breve reflexión sobre los enfoques teóricos que desde Turtle Island buscan examinar los matices que se ubican en la intersección de la indigeneidad, el género y la sexualidad ha sido una oportunidad para definir los marcos metodológicos necesarios para abordar esta misma intersección, pero en el contexto de América Latina donde la "grounded relationality" es altamente relevante por el número de culturas y los procesos de colonización que fueron desiguales a lo largo del territorio del continente.

Será de primer orden pensar en la "grounded normativity" que describe Byrd en su relacionalidad indígena queer, por ejemplo, al observar que la Nación Binnizá organiza su cultura en torno a sus mujeres y reserva un lugar especial para la variación sexual y de género, a través de la inclusión de las personas muxe' y las personas nguiu' en el corazón de las actividades de la comunidad. El trabajo de lxs pensadorxs que se ha comentado en este ensayo provee herramientas para poder comprender la interconexión entre la forma en que operan las estructuras capitalistas coloniales que persisten en el presente como el extractivismo, el racismo, el sexismo, la organización binaria del género, la transmisoginia, la lesbofobia y la homofobia y los efectos que tienen sobre los cuerpos de las personas indígenas, según ilustra el concepto de body land que describe Altamirano-Jiménez. Pienso en todas las posibilidades de aplicar este marco metodológico en función de estudiar la tradición literaria de la Nación Binnizá con la instrumentación de estos innovadores conceptos.[9]

Si bien la teoría queer, los estudios latinoamericanos y los estudios nativos presentan riesgos, violencias, borraduras, contradicciones y omisiones importantes, el campo de las investigaciones indígenas queer y los estudios de género en Norteamérica también ofrece hoy una amplia diversidad de marcos teóricos y metodológicos transnacionales que pueden fungir como un punto de partida para los estudios indígenas cuir en Abiayala. Específicamente cuando tantxs pensadorxs han manifestado la necesidad de comenzar a tratar estos asuntos relacionados al género, la sexualidad y la indigeneidad como problemas del colonialismo que como tal ha transformado las relaciones de los pueblos con su gente y sus territorios a lo largo de todo el continente.

Como apunta Pierce en el epílogo de su libro *Argentine Intimacies: Queer Kinship in an Age of Splendor, 1890–1910*, este capítulo pretende contribuir en la expansión del campo de los estudios cuir/queer al centrar la geotemporalidad de las teorías de los nortes globales e interrogar su viabilidad dentro de contextos locales, su traducibilidad, y las dinámicas de poder involucradas en la cuirización de América Latina (271). Los trabajos de lxs autorxs incluidos en este breve repaso histórico y transhemisférico ofrecen un atisbo a la posibilidad de describir las contradicciones y las aperturas en torno al pensamiento de la variación sexual y de género bajo una perspectiva que tome en cuenta los territorios y las materialidades epistemológicas y ontológicas de sus pobladorxs. La ampliación del campo de los estudios cuir al enfocarse en el estudio de la indigeneidad, así como la intersección de los diferentes campos de estudio involucrados en esa expansión, implican el surgimiento de formas innovadoras de entender la realidad de las experiencias ancladas a los cuerpos y sus contextos en Abiayala. Esta expansión posibilita entrar en conversación con las epistemologías de Turtle Island y de otras latitudes del globo, pero en un terreno nivelado al participar como iguales dentro de los diálogos y reflexiones sobre variación sexual, formación de género y colonialidad.

Notas

1. "Turtle Island" es un nombre común que se le ha dado a Norteamérica en el ámbito académico de los estudios nativos. Este nombre surge de la identificación de un mito común entre varias

culturas indígenas, aunque no todas las naciones indígenas reconocen el mito ni la denominación como parte de su cosmovisión.

2. Este término tiene su origen etimológico como una traducción directa del término ojibwe "Niizh manidoowag" que se refiere a un individuo cuyo cuerpo alberga simultáneamente un espíritu masculino y un espíritu femenino (Hayes 2). La cita es traducción del autor.

3. Para efectos de este ensayo se considera este como el subcampo de los estudios de género que ha visto su desarrollo en los últimos cuarenta años en las universidades de los Estados Unidos. Este locus geográfico es relevante en términos del argumento que Ngũgĩ wa Thiong'o esboza sobre la Ilustración y Europa en *Globalectics*. De igual forma, es importante mencionar aquí la estrecha relación de esta crítica con la discusión sobre la abstracción de ontologías que esboza Elizabeth A. Povinelli en *Geontologies*.

4. A la fecha, tanto Andrea Smith como Qwo-Li Driskill, incluidxs en *Queer Indigenous Studies*, enfrentan acusaciones por parte de ciudadanxs de la nación cheroqui que no reconocen a ningunx de lxs dos académicxs como parte de su pueblo. Esto formará parte crucial de la discusión en torno a lo recalcitrante del liberalismo hegemónico de la teoría queer que David L. Eng y Jasbir K. Puar denuncian en *Left of Queer*. Como se explicará más adelante, se opta por el uso de esta hispanización de "*queer*" para designar la variación y la disidencia sexual en los contextos hispanohablantes y distinguirla de los contextos angloparlantes y del norte global.

5. Se refiere a la interrelación compleja entre lo global y lo local. Valencia alude al gesto cuir como un proyecto ético de resistencia geopolítica (35).

6. María Lugones, Rita Laura Segato, Silvia Rivera Cusicanqui, Julieta Paredes Carvajal, Gabriela Cano Ortega, María Josefina Saldaña Portillo, Lourdes Martínez-Echazábal, Yuderkys Espinosa-Miñoso, Aura Cumes Simón, Marlene Wayar, Susy Shock, Claudia Rodríguez, Yásnaya Elena Aguilar Gil, et al.

7. Traducción del autor.

8. Sirva como muestra la violencia contra mujeres ikoots previo a la masacre en la comunidad de San Mateo del Mar en 2020 y la desaparición de numerosxs líderes sociales y ambientales indígenas en años recientes.

9. La tradición impresa del canon literario binnizá tiene sus inicios en el último cuarto del siglo XIX en los círculos intelectuales formados por zapotecos que tuvieron las posibilidades para dejar el istmo y estudiar en la Ciudad de México. A la vuelta del milenio, Natalia Toledo Paz e Irma Pineda Santiago se convirtieron en las primeras mujeres binnizá en publicar un volumen individual de poesía en zapoteco y español. A ellas han seguido otrxs creadorxs muxe' y nguiu' como Víctor Cata, Lukas Avendaño, Gerardo Valdivieso Parada, Yadira del Mar, Elvis Guerra y Paula Ya López cuyos trabajos han sido publicados en zapoteco y en español en años recientes.

Obras citadas

Altamirano-Jiménez, Isabel. "Possessing Land, Wind and Water in the Isthmus of Tehuantepec, Oaxaca". *Australian Feminist Studies*, vol. 35, no. 106, 2020, pp. 321–35.

âpihtawikosisân. "Language, Culture, and Two-Spirit Identity". *Law, Language, Culture*, March 29, 2012, apihtawikosisan.com/2012/03/language-culture-and-two-spirit-identity.

Byrd, Jodi A. "What's Normative Got to Do with It? Toward Indigenous Queer Relationality". *Social Text*, vol. 38, no. 145, 2020, pp.105–123.

De Perra, Hija. "Interpretaciones inmundas de cómo la teoría queer coloniza nuestro contexto sudaca, pobre, aspiracional y tercermundista, perturbando con nuevas construcciones genéricas a los humanos encantados con la heteronorma". *Revista Punto Género*, vol. 4, 2014, pp. 9–16.

Domínguez-Ruvalcaba, Héctor. *Translating the Queer: Body Politics and Transnational Conversations*. Zed Books, 2016.

Driskill, Qwo-Li, et al. *Queer Indigenous Studies: Critical Interventions in Theory, Politics, and Literature.* U of Arizona P, 2011.

——, et al. *Sovereign Erotics: A Collection of Two-Spirit Literature.* U of Arizona P, 2011.

Eng, David L., and Jasbir K. Puar. "Introduction: Left of Queer". *Social Text*, vol. 38, no. 145, 2020, pp. 1–24.

Fernandes, Estevão Rafael. "Homosexualidades indígenas y descolonialidad: Algunas reflexiones a partir de las críticas two-spirit". *Tabula Rasa*, vol. 20, 2014, pp. 135–157.

Hayes, Lenny. *Walking in Two Worlds: Understanding the Two-Spirit & LGBTQ Community.* Minnesota Indian Women's Sexual Assault Coalition & Minnesota Two Spirit Society, 2014.

McKie Brings Plenty, Scott. "Same-Sex Marriage Ordinance Again Dies in Council without Consideration". *Cherokee One Feather/Tsalagi Soquo Ugidahli*, Eastern Band of Cherokee Indians, July 9, 2021, theonefeather.com/2021/07/09/same-sex-marriage-ordinance-again-dies-in-council-without-consideration.

Pierce, Joseph M. *Argentine Intimacies: Queer Kinship in an Age of Splendor, 1890–1910.* SUNY P, 2019.

——. "I Monster: Embodying Trans and Travesti Resistance in Latin America". *Latin American Research Review*, vol. 55, no. 2, 2020, pp. 305–321.

——, et al. "Introduction: Cuir/Queer Américas: Translation, Decoloniality, and the Incommensurable". *GLQ: A Journal of Lesbian and Gay Studies*, vol. 27, no. 3, 2021, pp. 321–327.

Povinelli, Elizabeth A. *Geontologies: A Requiem to Late Liberalism.* Duke UP, 2016.

Speed, Shannon. "Structures of Settler Capitalism in Abya Yala". *American Quarterly*, vol. 69, no. 4, 2017, pp. 783–790.

Valencia, Sayak. "Del queer al cuir: Ostranénie geopolítica y epistémica desde el sur g-local". *Queer y cuir: Políticas de lo irreal.* Edited by Fernando R. Lanuza and Raúl M. Carrasco. Editorial Fontamara, 2015, pp. 19–37.

Wa Thiong'o, Ngũgĩ. *Globalectics: Theory and the Politics of Knowing.* Columbia UP, 2012.

CHAPTER 4

Una conversación cosmoléctica a través de *Cherrufe, la bola de fuego*

Manuel Carrión-Lira
UC San Diego

Antonio Catrileo
UC San Diego

En este ensayo proponemos realizar una yuxtaposición trans-Indígena (Allen) para leer *Cherrufe, la bola de fuego* (2008) de Ruth Mariela Fuentealba Millaguir. La capacidad de yuxtaposición (y no comparación) del prefijo *trans-* "place[s] diverse texts close together across genre and media, aesthetic systems and worldviews, technologies and practices, tribes and nations, the Indigenous-settler binary, and historical periods and geographical regions" (xviii). No hemos buscado cosmogonías indígenas para interpretar mejor, sino que la yuxtaposición nos permite respetar la autonomía y tender puentes de reciprocidad intelectual indígena. Es decir, es una decisión política que transparenta nuestra posicionalidad: escribir desde territorio Kumeyaay ocupado por los Estados Unidos nos empuja a reflexionar sobre nuestra posición actual para comprender y conectarnos con distintas experiencias y conocimientos indígenas a lo largo de Abiayala.

Cherrufe, la bola de fuego (2008) de Ruth Mariela Fuentealba Millaguir es una novela que nos presenta un ordenamiento del tiempo, la memoria y el territorio mapuche conectado a una idea cósmica del movimiento del universo. Nos muestra la indigeneidad mapuche atada a un territorio; y por tanto a la historia colonial del despojo y la traición de los chilenos. De esta manera, buscamos interpretar y leer la novela desde una posición que "refutes the academic tendency to differentiate cosmogony from epistemology" (Chacón 13), lo que implica utilizar categorías de valoración indígena, conceptos y conocimientos autónomos para desentrañar interpretaciones que interpelan al canon literario y la crítica cultural eurocéntricas.

Nuestro objetivo es hacer un puente de diálogo entre los modos de ser/estar propuestos por Adriana Paredes Pinda mediante *epu rume*, entendido como una doble conciencia que refiere a la experiencia intercultural mapuche y con lo que Gloria Chacón propone en *Indigenous Cosmolectics* como un modo de ver a través del *kab'awil* que habilita una doble mirada. De esta manera, es posible recomponer una noción de textualidad indígena que va más allá de la escritura alfabética latina, y por tanto más allá del canon literario que cuestiona la existencia misma de la literatura indígena. Mediante una lectura cosmoléctica de la novela –en conjunto con otros relatos y trabajos críticos– podemos tener acceso a una perspectiva mapuche que entiende el *cherrufe* no como un mito sino como una fuerza vital del cosmos que se expresa en la *mapu* (territorio) y se conecta con la vida humana mediante formas específicas de conocimiento mapuche: el *pewma* (aprendizaje en sueños) y el *perimontu* o *perimontun* (visión).

Cherrufe como texto *raki*

Cherrufe, la bola de fuego es la primera novela mapuche publicada. En esta se conecta el microcosmos cotidiano que vive la comunidad con la coreografía azul de cuerpos celestes que componen el *wenumapu* (mundo de arriba). La mayoría de las textualidades disponibles sobre el *cherrufe* vienen de etnografías antropológicas y análisis disciplinares que analizan este relato como mito. Asimismo, el único artículo que hemos encontrado disponible sobre esta novela es de Iván Carrasco, quien asevera una incompatibilidad entre la tradición de la novela y la enunciación indígena. Carrasco señala que *novela* se refiere al género del discurso global mientras que *mapuche* conlleva una fuerte connotación étnica, lo que para el autor encierra una contradicción o antítesis paradojal, debido a que la "la novela no forma parte de los géneros etnoliterarios ni literarios de la sociedad mapuche, sino de la tradición europea" (31). Esta manera de leer la novela clausura una relación con paradigmas de interpretación indígena y entrega una visión esencialista de las textualidades mapuche como limitadas a la oralidad, descartando toda la producción escritural alfabética mapuche de los últimos siglos. Sostenemos que para comprender la producción cultural y literaria indígena de manera compleja es necesario recuperar/construir otras herramientas de análisis que no sólo respondan a los cánones eurocéntricos que determinan lo que es o no es la escritura. Carrasco entenderá la novela como una forma de resolución de una paradoja entre mundos diferentes, material e ideológico: "se refiere metafóricamente a la condición de los personajes femeninos, que son mestizos, aunque ideológicamente mapuches" (34). Al momento de comentar las presentaciones que los autores y autoridades mapuche hacen del texto, Carrasco se detiene en comentar cómo uno de ellos explica que la autora es nieta del *lonko* (autoridad o líder) Millaguir que empezó las gestiones del parlamento de Koz Koz, último parlamento mapuche registrado en la historia previa a la usurpación. Sin embargo, Carrasco está preocupado y explica que "lo paradojal es que ella es mestiza, como indican sus apellidos. Y que escribe en lugar de cantar o contar oralmente" (35).

En la crítica literaria que hace Carrasco se perpetúa una expectativa de la enunciación indígena atada además a valoraciones corporales que interpretamos como ansiedades coloniales y patriarcales. Al usar la patrilinealidad del apellido como signo de verificación indígena, y al separar el aspecto ideológico del material-corporal, Carrasco imagina una mujer indígena que cumple con un canon antropológico y estático del pasado. Su manera de entender el mestizaje queda claro cuando nos dice que "todos somos mapuches y chilenos, unos más que otros" (Carrasco 36).

Es posible identificar una relación problemática entre los límites de la literatura y la idea de raza en Chile, que niega lo que Héctor Nahuelpan Moreno denomina *zonas grises* donde el mestizaje no clausura la indigeneidad, sino que es considerado como parte constitutiva de la conformación de la historia indígena en Chile: "Las zonas grises de las historias mapuche devienen así en espacios sociales que pueden ser analizados y problematizados. Pero también, en espacios cognitivos que abren perspectivas analíticas que permiten enfatizar en la complejidad que albergan las historias mapuche, y cómo éstas desafían las representaciones reificadas y normativas" (Nahuelpán 13). En este sentido, las limitaciones que nos ofrece Carrasco reflejan la necesidad de tomar otros caminos metodológicos para leer la novela que puedan entender de manera amplia el ser mapuche en relación con la colonialidad, habitando la contradicción.

Al respecto, Carla Llamunao señala que "la necesidad de estudios situados que provengan desde los y las integrantes del propio pueblo mapuche se ha vuelto una urgencia, no con el afán de privar al resto de personas, sino para pensar y repensarnos, desde dentro, como pueblo dinámico" (152). Es vital proponer un constante diálogo con la cosmovisión creando y desafiando la misma idea de tradición: "¿Qué bases epistémicas sustentan aquellos análisis? ¿Qué elementos cruzan e influencian las lecturas e interpretaciones de las producciones mapuche?" (152). Consideramos importante poder analizar la novela *Cherrufe, la bola de fuego* como una textualidad que está en diálogo con la cosmovisión mapuche como un marco metodológico que nos permita analizar el conocimiento transgeneracional y relacional sobre el *cherrufe* como un cuerpo que transita en distintos mundos articulando formas de ver y de ser/estar que desafían el canon porque precisamente posee vínculos críticos con este.

El rol de la *machi* (autoridad político-espiritual) tiene la capacidad de transitar por distintos mundos para propiciar la medicina para la comunidad. Son las *machi* quienes entregan la apertura para entender otros modos de ser que van más allá del entendimiento humano. Adriana Paredes Pinda es una *machi*, poeta y académica que tiene un vasto trabajo comunal en territorio mapuche-williche, además de varios libros de poesía publicados. Ella ha reivindicado el concepto de *epu rume* para referirse a la doble capacidad y doble conciencia que se ve reflejada en la literatura mapuche, que "genera un texto 'epu rume zugun', texto con dos corazones, con dos pensamientos, con dos lenguas" (Paredes Pinda 12). Esta manera de aproximarse nos ofrece un entendimiento más complejo de la literatura mapuche que nos permite interpretar la novela *Cherrufe* como una práctica contemporánea para relatar la memoria de la comunidad donde "la comprensión del rakizuam mapuche puede ayudar a sanar una que otra herida de la modernidad, en los ámbitos de la palabra y el pensamiento, no por un afán etnocentrista, sino en un anhelo de restaurar, restituir e hilar aquello que sí tenemos en común" (6). Recupera del *epu rume* una capacidad movilizadora que critica el esencialismo con el que se ha leído la literatura mapuche.

La doble conciencia que propone Paredes Pinda no silencia la colonialidad como parte constitutiva de la historia mapuche contemporánea, asumiendo sus mismas contradicciones y tensiones con el estado chileno o argentino. Ella reflexiona sobre el mismo mestizaje como parte de esta historia de desgarro colonial, que ha tenido la capacidad de ir variando en el tiempo y espacio. Proponemos ingresar a la novela desde esta metodología generativa que incluye el mismo pensamiento mapuche para desde ahí dialogar con otras textualidades *cherrufe*, viajando y conectando mundos. Paredes Pinda nombra a esta particularidad de formas que viajan de un lugar a otro como parte de un pensamiento que es transitorio y migrante, haciendo referencia a las aves como mensajeras y que pueden ser puentes de comunicación entre los mundos de arriba y abajo. Propone la categoría de texto *raki* como un "tipo de texto poético, capaz de volar en círculos como la bandurria, y acercarse a una comprensión mapuche de su misma existencia, como texto desdoblado, en el desdoblamiento ancestral de verse a sí mismo y encontrarse con su propio ser" (11–12). Nos regala esta otra manera de comprender la posicionalidad de la autora de la novela como una escritora *champurria*, es decir, que reconoce en su experiencia de mestizaje una potencia para narrar la historia mapuche de su propia comunidad y territorio a través del conocimiento intergeneracional sobre/con el *cherrufe*. Esta idea del pensamiento *raki* "reconoce su carencia y desde allí se configura y encarna su sentido existencial en el mundo contemporáneo" (9). La carencia es consecuencia del despojo colonial y se manifiesta en un tipo de pensamiento que ella nombra como *wechante*, es decir, hace alusión a la ausencia de sol, la austeridad, la mezquindad, la avaricia, el empobrecimiento, el desplazamiento que muchas personas mapuche han vivido en los últimos siglos. Al reconocer estos destellos de memorias borroneadas, Mariella Fuentealba Millaguir moviliza esas hebras de memoria en torno al *cherrufe* para darles nueva vida en su narración.

Cherrufe bajo la doble mirada

La propuesta cosmoléctica de Chacón abre nuestra noción de escritura alfabética para así tomar en cuenta textualidades indígenas como los textiles, la cerámica, la oralidad y los sueños. Todas estas podrían ser consideradas por Paredes Pinda como distintas maneras en que se pueden expresar los textos *raki*. Pues la escritura no se bajó de los barcos de los colonizadores, sino que siempre ha existido en las sociedades indígenas de Abiayala. Por otro lado, la cosmoléctica nos permite dejar de reducir la producción cultural y literaria indígena contemporánea bajo la rúbrica binaria de tradición/modernidad, oralidad/escritura, occidental/no-occidental; pues la cosmoléctica "allows writers to challenge the idea that 'the 16th-century collapse of the Amerindian world left the colonized subjects without the possibility of producing critical thinking'" (13), y finalmente la cosmoléctica "counters the sociological imagination that indigenous (thesis) and European roots (antithesis) produce a mestizo synthesis, or, in José Vasconcelos's work, the culmination in the cosmic race where Indians and blacks eventually disappear" (13).

La cosmoléctica en Mesoamérica no solo se resiste a la dialéctica que reproduce la estructura amo-esclavo, sino que incluye un cuarto elemento propio de la filosofía mesoamericana, se trata del "*kab'awil*, a vision that duplicates" (Chacón 13). Esta visión que duplica se relaciona con la propia experiencia indígena de la colonización, como una estrategia para negociar que no funciona con el exclusivo *o*, sino con el aditivo *y*. Esta visión doble, o que doblemente ve, se trata de una forma de hacer mundo que algunas comunidades indígenas han elaborado para prevalecer con autonomía y soberanía cultural, pero también soberanía territorial que hace frente a las continuidades coloniales en las instituciones, las expresiones de colonialidad en el saber o a la prevalencia del colonialismo interno como administración político-jurídica del territorio. Nuestro interés es hacer un puente de diálogo cosmoléctico *raki*: conectar ambas formas dobles, tanto de ver (*kab'awil*) así como de ser/estar (*epu rume*).

Según Chacón, *kab'awil* habilita el método "double gaze to literary exegesis" (19), concepto teórico que además de venir de una tradición indígena mesoamericana precolonial, nos sirve para nombrar la "entremedio-eidad" (*in-betweenness*) que se necesita para criticar "assimilationist projects, nation-state history, sexism within indigenous communities and progressive political parties" (20). La duplicidad *kab'awil/epu rume* nos entrega una crítica de la colonialidad, pero también una mirada afirmativa de la indigeneidad situada, pues ambas son capaces de construir una genealogía epistemológica con una noción temporal que se extiende más allá de la época colonial, implicando en ese conocimiento una metodología de resistencia, adaptación y florecimiento indígena aún viva. Específicamente el cuarto elemento del *kab'awil* nos permite observar la contradicción sin la expectativa de la síntesis. Es un esfuerzo por mantener dos o más visiones presentes, reconociendo la tensión política y epistémica que dibuja esta distancia entre experiencia indígena y experiencia no-indígena. Por otro lado, *epu rume* emerge específicamente como una doble posición ontológica propia del mundo mapuche: la experiencia del mestizaje como algo múltiple e inacabado y que habita en dos lenguas (español y mapuzungun) y dos corazones (chileno y mapuche). Como señala el poeta mapuche Bernardo Colipán en el prólogo de la novela: "*Cherrufe* va a precisar una zona intermedia, fronteriza en donde se funden los tiempos del fogón o de la memoria y el tiempo cotidiano o histórico" (17). La yuxtaposición trans-Indígena (Allen) que emerge gracias a estos dos métodos/formas nos permite navegar esta duplicidad como una múltiple. Es un horizonte para evitar el esencialismo y etnocentrismo en nuestra lectura, y es evidencia de un diálogo cosmoléctico. Desde aquí, la novela *Cherrufe* se entiende como la negociación de los distintos mundos que habitan en el territorio de Panguipulli siguiendo a las aves que constituyen la bandada de relacionalidad *raki* que dibuja la bola de fuego.

Leer la novela desde la herramienta de la doble mirada implica poner atención a su estructura narrativa y en los capítulos no como dos versiones –en mapuzungun y luego en español–, sino que implica habitar la sociedad mapuche contemporánea desde la metodología *raki*, que va y viene. No hay traducción literal, sino dos miradas o aproximaciones posibles, esa doble mirada no nos muestra una síntesis de mestizaje indigenizado, sino de una persona indígena que habita en un mundo indígena y también en uno chileno, y que puede moverse entre ambos. Nos detendremos en ciertos conceptos mapuche que permiten esta doble valencia, y que de alguna manera articulan una noción de parentesco (*kinship*) trans-Indígena entre la doble mirada de *kab'awil*, y los dos corazones (*epu rume*) que palpitan a través del vuelo *raki*.

La novela nos presenta una textualidad que no separa planos ontológicos ni temporales para las distintas generaciones de mapuche que articulan las acciones, sino que nos muestra diferentes mundos/tiempos simultáneos mediante el conocimiento asociado a los *pewma* (sueños donde se aprende). Como señalan algunas y algunos pensadores mapuche, el "*pewma* es acto de ver en el estado de sueño, *perimontu* es el acto de visualizar un *ngen* o dueño-guardián" (Pichinao 20), "el *perimuntun* es una visión no explicitada que uno ve, pero no está seguro, en el *pewma* se ve manifestada, es decir, que yo hice tal cosa o que casi lo hice" (Ñanculef 145). Existe convergencia en entender el *pewma* como un espacio articulado por la visión y otros sentidos, y lo que sucede en el *pewma* tiene el estatuto de acción. El *perimontu* o *perimontun* sería cuando se tiene acceso a una visión no tan clara fuera del mundo de los sueños, como ver un *ngen*, que se asocia a manifestaciones visuales y sensoriales de una fuerza espiritual que corresponde a un territorio.

Al comienzo de la novela estamos sumergiéndonos en un recuerdo, un sueño, una memoria que conocemos a través de un *pewma*. Cuando Charito despierta luego de haberse conectado con la historia de sus antepasados, le comenta a su abuela lo que ha visto:

> –¿Qué pasa Charito?– susurró la mami.
> –Tuve un sueño muy extraño mami, y tengo miedo.
> –Cuéntame, dime que pasó.
> –No sé bien mami, vi rukas, mujeres llorando, un hombre muerto, una gran bola de fuego.
> –¿Qué dices? ¿¡Bola de fuego!?
> –Sí, mami, fue todo tan extraño, tengo mucho miedo. (32)

La abuela toma como un hecho lo que pasó en el sueño. No se trata de una interpretación mediante sistemas de símbolos o arquetipos, sino de un mensaje concreto de advertencia fruto de una experiencia concreta de conocimiento entregado de forma transgeneracional a través del *pewma*. De inmediato, luego de comentar este *pewma*, la bola de fuego se materializa fuera del mundo de los sueños. El abuelo Queche llega cubierto de sangre, conectando el asesinato de su antepasado revivido en el *pewma* con el altercado con un chileno del presente. Altercado que además ocurre debido a la negación por parte del abuelo a vender un pedazo de su territorio. Desde este momento la novela va a tejer el tiempo de los antepasados al interior del mundo onírico de las mujeres herederas del *pewma*. Emerge una memoria transgeneracional a través del relato, que tiene también una doble mirada: puesta en la recuperación de la memoria –reviviendo la historia de la usurpación–, pero también en el florecimiento de la espiritualidad y forma de vivir mapuche en la ceremonia y éxtasis como una forma de recuperar territorio. La doble mirada, onírico-real del *pewma*, anima los dos corazones de la experiencia intercultural de las mujeres de la novela, habilitando vínculos comunicativos que saltan generaciones, que conectan antepasados en tiempos diferentes permitiendo incluso navegar el futuro mediante la ceremonia.

El *pewma* y *perimontun* resultan importantes de comprender puesto que son formas de conocimiento mapuche mediante las cuales el *cherrufe* se comunica y aparece para la familia Millaguir, conectando así la historia de la traición chilena, como un palimpsesto de usurpaciones y robos territoriales que se acumulan en el reino de los sueños de la familia situada en Panguipulli. La bola de fuego en términos concretos opera como un designio de muerte o tragedia: "Antonia reconoció al cherrufe, como la señal de alguna tragedia, su madre le había transmitido en su niñez la historia del gran cacique Catriel que protegía a su familia luego de la muerte" (25); "esa Bola de Fuego era la última señal y la definitiva para saber que su amado Millaguir debía seguir a sus antepasados, al lugar de los espíritus, al *wenumapu*, la tierra de arriba" (26). El *cherrufe* emerge en la novela cuando colapsan las temporalidades, cuando se dinamiza el relato y cuando de alguna manera la agencia y capacidad de acción es reclamada por las indígenas de la novela, en específico en la forma de una negación ante la transgresión.

La duplicidad múltiple del cherrufe

La novela *Cherrufe* de Fuentealba Millaguir es una de las tantas versiones que existen de los relatos sobre el *cherrufe* que se cuentan en todo Wallmapu (territorio mapuche). Algunas de estas otras versiones han sido narradas por el archivo colonial de algunos viajeros y por la antropología cultural. También existen versiones que se cuentan de generación en generación en algunas comunidades mapuche que nos presentan otras interpretaciones del *cherrufe*.

Identificamos al menos tres narrativas que se diferencian, pero que se yuxtaponen, mostrando relaciones con la novela. La primera tiene relación con el *cherrufe* entendido como un ser viviente que es parte del *itrofilmongen* (biodiversidad o todas las vidas en relación) y que se enfoca en el futuro de la comunidad. En el libro *Wenumapu* de Gabriel Pozo Menares y Margarita Canio encontramos algunos relatos que consideran al *cherrufe* como un designio. Eugenio Millaqueo de la comunidad Kurümawiza (agosto de 2008) señala que una vez que alguien en la comunidad recibe una premonición sobre el paso de un *cherrufe*, "llega mucho la sequía, por ahí se merma el agua, quedan hasta los animales sin tomar agua, quedan las personas sin agua" (125). Este cambio se manifiesta como una transgresión del *itrofilmongen* (biodiversidad) y que les previene de posibles periodos de escasez. Por lo que la comunidad se organiza y prepara para el paso del *cherrufe*. Surge de este modo una preocupación por el bienestar comunal y de las futuras generaciones. El *cherrufe* es respetado porque les advierte de los cambios que pueden ocurrir en el futuro.

Una segunda versión sobre el *cherrufe* tiene relación con su capacidad transformadora y que presenta su ambivalencia entre la antropomorfia y antropofagia. Al respecto Marta Parra de la comunidad Llamüko (septiembre de 2008) cuenta una historia que trata de una anciana que habita en un volcán, madre de cuatro hijos: *Antü* (Sol), *Küyen* (Luna), *Wüñellfe* (Lucero del Amanecer) y, uno de los más temibles, el *Cherrufe*. Aquí la interpretación es unánime respecto al *cherrufe*: "la casa donde cayó el Cherüfe, seguro que alguien fallecerá" (127). Pero también el *cherrufe* es el hermano que lleva diariamente la comida al volcán, y esta comida es carne humana. Similarmente Domingo Colicoy nos comparte su versión del relato que puede ser comprendido como un relato de creación, donde explica que "la tierra era una gran casa, de piedra … *cherrufe* vigila y limpia la casa todas las noches, recoge las cosas que ya no sirven. Él se alimenta de carne humana, pero elimina a las personas que no se portan bien […] El *Cherrufe* así elige" (2).

En ambas versiones se presenta la doble valencia entre la vida y la muerte, no obstante, *cherrufe* es personificado y humanizado, se presenta como un ser que posee hambre y también tiene agencia. Según Rodolfo Casamiquela, la etimología de *cherrufe* es "el que extermina con fuego", "el aniquilador" (188). La investigadora Graciela Hernández señala también que "este ente mítico es definido como un aerolito, una bola de fuego, y también como un monstruo antropomorfo; es decir, no hay criterios unánimes para definirlo sino diferentes versiones que acentúan un aspecto u otro" (154). El *cherrufe* emerge para ocupar el espacio que conecta la antropomorfia con la antropofagia, articulando así una doble figura ontológica: una roca cósmica como signo de mal augurio y un ser de fuego consumidor de carne humana, y que además puede ocupar ambas posiciones indistintamente, moverse de lo humano a lo no-humano, de lo cósmico a lo terrenal. Si bien la cualidad de antropofagia no está abordada en la novela como tal, la antropomorfia emerge en la bola de fuego como signo del malestar o amenaza contra la comunidad. Es en específico la capacidad de anuncio/agencia sobre la vida y la muerte, la que está presente de forma más clara en la novela: "Esa Bola de Fuego era la última señal y la definitiva para saber que su amado Millaguir debía seguir a sus antepasados, a lugar de los espíritus" (26). De la misma manera el sueño de Charito conecta con la premonición y advertencia sobre la vida de su abuelo (32).

Por último, identificamos algunas versiones del *cherrufe* que tienen relación con la fuerza mineral y cósmica que posee como una piedra de poder y que hace un vínculo con el pueblo mapuche para darles fuerza en la guerra contra los españoles (y posteriormente contra el Estado nación chileno y argentino respectivamente). Félix Outes señala que el *cherrufe* es un monstruo y cometa a la vez, "y estas dos caras del mismo se encontraban representadas en una placa grabada procedente de Chimpay –provincia de Río Negro–, a la que consideró 'la materialización del cherufe araucano'" (Outes citado en Hernández 156). Chimpay es la provincia donde el cacique Manuel Namuncurá (hijo del cacique Juan Calfucurá) resistió a la Campaña del Desierto durante fines del siglo XIX. Esta placa es un vestigio de la resistencia y lucha mapuche contra el avance del colonialismo argentino, y el *cherrufe* emerge como una interrupción a las continuidades coloniales:

> Los guerreros que podían vencer a los blancos eran aquellos que sabían manejar la piedra cherufe, "su arte" les permitía utilizar a su favor esta piedra y vencer aún en condiciones adversas. Esta habilidad de los guerreros ranqueles tiene un antecedente célebre, nada menos que en Calfucurá, ya que el líder del cacicato salinero poseía una piedra cherufe. Instalado en la Pampa, este cacique, de origen cordillerano debía sus éxitos militares a las bondades de esta piedra. (20)

Este éxito militar indica un tipo de relación particular entre mineralidad y humanidad, o más bien la relación entre una roca –pedazo de tierra– y la agencia mapuche. El *cherrufe* así metaforiza la reciprocidad entre comunidad y territorio. Si la piedra da poder al cacique, es porque tienen una relación estrecha. Esto indica que la capacidad de elección del *cherrufe* no solo está activa en su versión antropomórfica, sino que en su forma de piedra, también posee las mismas potencialidades. El *cherrufe* emerge aquí como una forma de defensa anticolonial epistémica y bélica contra la usurpación, presentando su doble valencia como piedra de poder militar y vestigio de resistencia. La novela de Fuentealba Millaguir presenta esta capacidad mineral y activa del *cherrufe* asociada a la memoria transgeneracional. Antes de despedirse para pelear contra los usurpadores de su territorio, el Lonko Catriel lleva a su comunidad al lago Panguipulli y les dice: "venid todos los días a ver esta piedra que les señalo, esa gran mole junto al lago, si algo me llegara a suceder, ahí tendrán la señala que ya no volverá mi cuerpo a vuestro lado" (43). En la batalla, el Lonko es capturado, amarrado, torturado, humillado y quemado junto a un tronco, sin embargo, los usurpadores "no sabían que el püllü [espíritu] del gran Lonko viviría para siempre entre nosotros", precisamente porque "Catriel quedó prendido a su tierra" (45). Cuando la comunidad vuelve al lago en busca de la piedra, se dan cuenta que esta "se había volteado, y sobre ella un gran *león* [puma] yacía muerto, con los ojos abiertos como mirándolas, incluso llegaron a pensar que estaba vivo. Levantaron sus miradas al cielo [...] pues ya sabían que habían perdido a su hermano, y que se había transformado en un 'Espíritu de León' (Panguipulli)" (45–46). Finalmente, una gran bola de fuego cruzó el cielo, "el espíritu del Lonko viajó para llegar a sus tierras que defendió hasta morir" (46). De esta manera la capacidad mineral del *cherrufe* se materializa en la tierra, en la roca; y en específico en la relación entre territorio y memoria mapuche. El espíritu del Lonko guerrero y su reclamo territorial se manifiesta en la relación entre el nombre del territorio, la historia del despojo y la vinculación con el *itrofilmongen*: tanto animales, árboles, minerales y humanos en equilibrio. Esta conexión múltiple hace del *cherrufe* una "señal de alerta" (46) se constituye como una forma de conocimiento propia de la comunidad, que honra la memoria, relacionalidad y reciprocidad territorial-humana.

Palabras finales: Cherrufe como una yuxtaposición generativa indígena

Hemos intentado trazar una relación trans-Indígena mediante este ensayo, articulando una relacionalidad más allá de los límites de los Estados nación y desafiando una lectura etnocentrista. Yuxtaponer ambas dimensiones dobles, del *kab'awil* y de *epu rume*, nos permitió utilizar modos-de-ver mesoamericanos para ahondar en modos-de-estar mapuche como un diálogo generativo que posibilita desplegar múltiples interpretaciones que incluso pueden habitar la contradicción. La crítica de Iván Carrasco sobre la novela *Cherrufe* muestra los límites que el proyecto del mestizaje chileno traza al considerar la indigeneidad como monolítica. Optamos por buscar otros modos de comprender la indigeneidad más allá del mismo reconocimiento del Estado chileno y que tienen relación con las propias nociones que el pensamiento mapuche tiene de sí mismo, como una práctica de autodeterminación basada en un conocimiento y prácticas culturales de larga data, que poseen un vínculo con la colonialidad, pero que no se quedan clausurados debido a esto.

Entendemos así nuestro tránsito y lugar como un *raki* que permite reflexionar sobre el tránsito sur, centro y norte, materializando nuestra experiencia indígena y migrante como lugar de enunciación. Y desde esta posición nuestro deseo fue construir un espacio de reciprocidad, donde distintas cosmolécticas se vinculan recíprocamente mediante una doble mirada que devuelve algo no por medio de la deuda, sino por la búsqueda y mantenimiento del equilibrio. Creemos que este modo de entablar yuxtaposiciones intelectuales y críticas, puede extenderse más allá de los límites del etnocentrismo, abriéndose a pensar los vínculos con textualidades no indígenas que son fundamentales para comprender las diversas experiencias y comunidades que habitan Abiayala. Esta forma de entablar yuxtaposiciones cosmolécticas se puede vincular con la producción escritural afrodescendiente, así como con la escritura realizada por migrantes e incluso con la literatura nacional. Yuxtaponer puede ayudarnos a darle sentido a los vínculos específicos que estas textualidades poseen con sus comunidades y así posibilitar relaciones sin necesitar de la síntesis o de la resolución de una contradicción.

Obras citadas

Allen, Chadwick. *Trans-Indigenous: Methodologies for Global Native Literary Studies.* U of Minnesota P, 2012.

Carrasco, Iván. "Cherruve… ¿Primera novela mapuche?…". *Lengua y Literatura Mapuche,* no. 14, 2010, pp. 27–36.

Casamiquela, Rodolfo. "Posibles raíces patagónicas en creencias araucanas III: El mito del cherrufe". *Cuadernos del Sur,* vol. 15, 1983, pp. 187–214.

Chacón, Gloria Elizabeth. *Indigenous Cosmolectics: Kab'awil and the Making of Maya and Zapotec Literatures.* U of North Carolina P, 2018.

Colicoy, Domingo. *Los vegetales en el mapuche kimvn.* 2009. Web: https://www.mapunet.org/documentos/mapuches/vegetales.pdf

Fuentealba Millaguir, Ruth Mariela. *Cherrufe, la bola de fuego.* Corporación Nacional de Desarrollo Indígena, 2008.

Hernández, Graciela. "En tiempos del malón: Testimonios indígenas sobre la Conquista del desierto". *Memoria Americana,* no. 14, 2006, pp.139–166.

Llamunao, Carla. "Lectura/escritura Champurria: Un posicionamiento metodológico para el estudio de poesía mapuche". *Documentos Lingüísticos y Literarios,* no. 39, 2020, pp.151–164.

Nahuelpan Moreno, Héctor. "Las 'zonas grises' de las historias mapuche". *Revista de Historia Social y las Mentalidades,* vol. 17, no. 1, 2014, pp. 11–33.

Ñanculef, Juan et al. *El conocimiento: Ese cántaro quebrado. Taller de epistemologías indígenas y académicas.* Universidad de Chile, 2016.

Paredes Pinda, Adriana. "Epu Rume Zugu Rakizuam: Desgarro y florecimiento. La poesía mapuche entre lenguas". Tesis doctoral, Universidad Austral de Chile, Valdivia, 2013.

Pichinao, Jimena. "Todavía sigo siendo mapuche en otros espacios territoriales: Mapuchewkülekan kake Fütal mapu mew". Universidad Estatal de Campinas, Instituto de Filosofía y Ciencias Humanas, 2012.

Pozo Menares, Gabriel y Margarita Canio. *Wenumapu: Astronomía y cosmología mapuche.* Ocho Libros Editores, 2013.

CHAPTER 5

Desde el corazón de la cultura: Filosofía, investigación académica y racionalidad poética de las naciones amerindias de la Amazonía

Pedro Favaron
Pontificia Universidad Católica del Perú

El presente ensayo propone la necesidad de acercarnos al estudio de los pueblos indígenas desde metodologías propias basadas en las propias epistemologías y ontologías indígenas. Sin dejar de lado el rigor etnográfico y los innegables aportes antropológicos, se postula como más fecundo trabajar abiertos a la racionalidad afectiva de los sabios de las naciones amerindias, realizando estilos de investigación y de redacción que no distorsionen el talante narrativo y poético en el que se expresan los saberes ancestrales. Para llevar a cabo esta propuesta desde los Estudios Hispánicos, resulta ineludible, por un lado, desmontar el eurocentrismo hegemónico; así mismo, resultará beneficioso establecer un diálogo con los académicos e intelectuales de las primeras naciones de Norteamérica, quienes han dado los primeros pasos para alcanzar una libertad metodológica y filosófica. Debido a que la mayoría de este material no ha sido traducido al castellano, quienes recorremos los caminos entre el Norte y el Sur de América tenemos el potencial de enlazar estos campos de estudios, adquiriendo así una relevancia política y democratizadora del saber al interior del ámbito académico hispánico. Este texto se acompañará con algunas pinturas y dibujos de la artista shipibo-konibo Chonon Bensho, generando un diálogo entre la palabra escrita y el arte para enriquecer el aporte etnográfico-creativo, y la propuesta filosófica y reflexiva que se anhela compartir con los lectores.

Un asunto fundamental a la hora de pensar nuestras prácticas de investigación al interior de las ciencias sociales y de las humanidades, es no perder de vista que somos humanos aprendiendo de otros humanos. Reflexionamos sobre prácticas que muchas veces nos incluyen e interpelan. Aunque la búsqueda de la objetividad ha guiado buena parte de las disciplinas académicas, tal intento resulta muchas veces algo demasiado artificial. Ningún investigador está libre de cierto marco paradigmático que condicione sus investigaciones y, por supuesto, sus resultados. La desmedida pretensión de alzarnos por encima de todo condicionamiento cultural no es posible ni deseable. Pienso, en cambio, que un tema de investigación académica podrá franquear el estrecho marco de los especialistas e interesar a un público más amplio, si escribimos y pensamos desde un punto de vista personal, apelando a un residuo anímico que se deje sorprender por la belleza del mundo y de las culturas a las que nos aproximamos. Nuestros campos de estudios no solo nos deben parecer estimulantes desde lo intelectual; es mejor si también conmueven las fibras íntimas de nuestro corazón. Cuando el conocimiento se divorcia de la respuesta estética y anímica, del asombro y del latido, pierde vitalidad y fuerza.

Cuando nos exponemos a otras culturas, es nuestra misma vida la que se transforma. Resulta ingenuo pensarnos inmunes a los pensamientos de quienes nos acogen y nos enseñan de sí mismos y de sus herencias. En lo personal, mi vida y mi pensamiento forman una unidad orgánica; mi búsqueda de los saberes ancestrales[1] de los pueblos indígenas ha respondido a una necesidad íntima y espiritual. Mi sensibilidad entera se ha renovado en el encuentro con estos saberes. Casi desde que empecé a caminar con los pueblos indígenas, he intentado realizar investigaciones y reflexionar filosóficamente desde el afecto, nutrido de la convivencia prolongada con los sabios de las comunidades amerindias y llevando a cabo una inmersión en las culturas indígenas, en la cotidianeidad de las comunidades y en los saberes ancestrales. Al graduarme de los estudios de doctorado en la Université de Montréal, dejé Canadá (en dónde viví por mis años de estudios) y me asenté en la Amazonía peruana; y en la Comunidad Nativa Santa Clara de Yarinacocha, del pueblo shipibo-konibo, conocí a Chonon Bensho, quien es mi esposa. Desde entonces, pasé diez años viviendo en el territorio shipibo. Soy miembro por afinidad matrimonial de una familia que ha practicado la medicina tradicional desde un tiempo indescifrable, de generación en generación. Esta convivencia y parentesco, si bien me ha hecho perder (al menos en cierto grado) la "distancia científica", me ha permitido familiarizarme con el idioma, relacionarme afectivamente con el pueblo y acceder a un flujo de sabidurías que solo se revelan al interior del estar-en-común: he sido instruido en conocimientos que los sabios solo dicen a quienes aman, a quienes son parte de su familia, y que se transmiten de forma exclusiva de padres a hijos, de abuelos a nietos, de tíos a sobrinos. Yo realizo buena parte de mi investigación etnográfica junto a mi esposa, y mis reflexiones se despliegan nutridas de nuestras conversaciones; de la misma manera, su arte bebe de estas investigaciones y de mis pensamientos. Es por eso que acompaño este artículo con sus trabajos artísticos, para dar cuenta de este diálogo íntimo, en el que nuestras creaciones y voces se complementan.

Al formar parte de una red indígena de parentesco y afinidad, he re-aprendido a pensar con el corazón. En la lengua shipiba, la palabra "shinan" es polisémica y connota pensar, sentir, imaginar y anhelar; y, como entre otros pueblos amazónicos, se suele considerar que el pensamiento nace del corazón (jointi). Se trataría, por lo tanto, de la expresión de una racionalidad afectiva y cardiaca: como toda dinámica racional, nuestros pensamientos (non shinabo) son capaces de planificar, de prever, de cuantificar y de tomar decisiones en base a una evaluación de los posibles peligros y beneficios de cada acción; sin embargo, a diferencia de los postulados cartesianos de la modernidad hegemónica, la razón no es concebida como algo autónomo, sino que todo ejercicio de racionalidad, en un sentido indígena, es

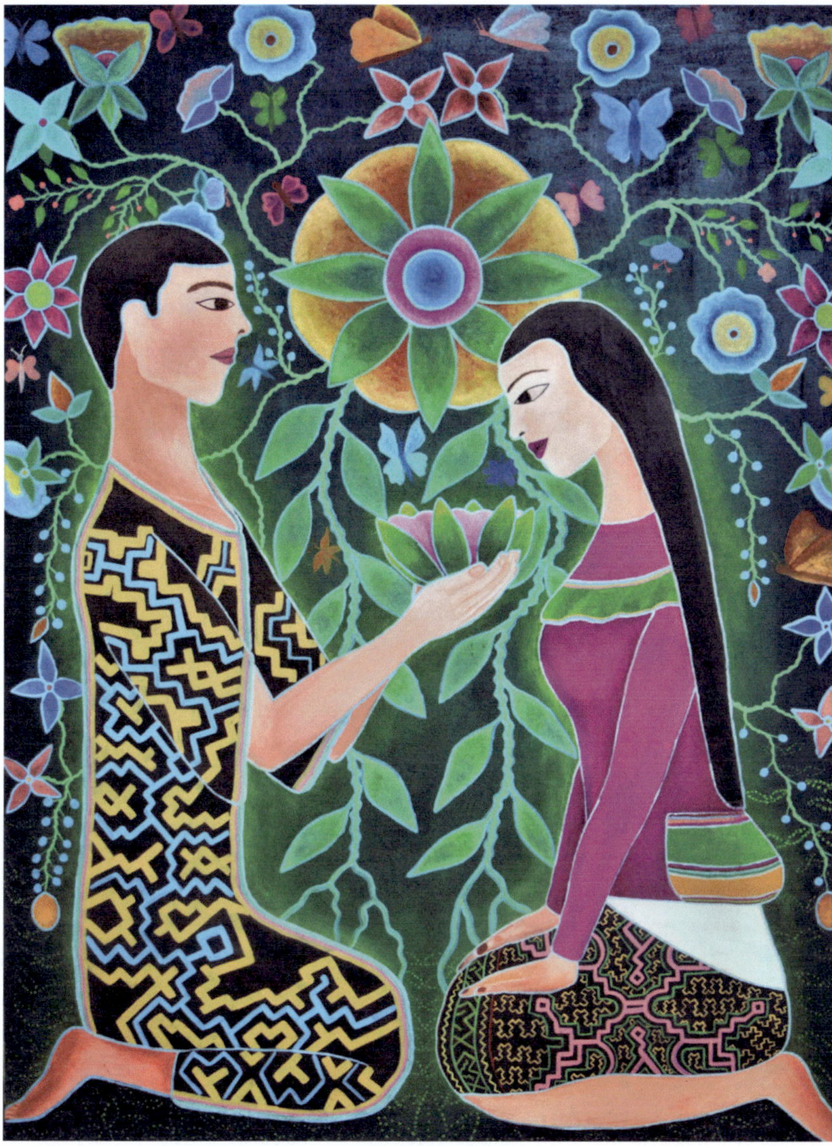

Figure 1. Chonon Bensho, *Inin Nete*, óleo sobre lienzo, 150 × 90 cm.
Inin Nete significa "mundo aromático", y este es uno de los aspectos fundamentales de la medicina tradicional del pueblo shipibo-konibo. El Inin Nete da cuenta de una fuerza perfumada que brota desde el mundo espiritual de la medicina y que es la base de la curación de los pacientes. Los Dueños espirituales de la medicina son siempre seres perfumados que emanan un olor semejante al de las flores y al de las plantas aromáticas; ellos encuentran desagradable el olor de los seres humanos, debido a sus vicios, a sus hábitos nocivos y a su mala alimentación.

indesligable del afecto, de nuestra corporalidad, de nuestros vínculos de parentesco, del legado de los antepasados, del territorio ancestral que nos acoge y nos sustenta, de la intuición visionaria que nos permite vislumbrar los mundos suprasensibles y de una experiencia poética de la existencia. Además, la racionalidad afectiva no pretende conocer al resto de seres vivos y al cosmos desde la separación objetiva, ni busca dominarlos o instrumentalizarlos como si se trataran de meras cosas; sus prácticas epistémicas, por el contrario, se hacen desde la inmersión y de la interacción, reconociendo que el ser humano es parte integral de la red sagrada de la vida, y que todo intento de zanjar una distancia insalvable entre la humanidad y el cosmos es demasiado artificial y potencialmente dañino.

El pensamiento afectivo de los pueblos indígenas, entonces, sabe llenar con empatía, las diferencias físicas y lingüísticas que separan a los diversos seres del cosmos: es desde el propio corazón que se recuerda que todos los seres vivos estamos emparentados, que somos parte de un mismo tejido existencial, que todos compartimos un mismo aliento vital y que es posible aún dialogar entre nosotros, conversar con el Sol, agradecer a la Tierra, pedir permiso a los espíritus guardianes de las montañas. La racionalidad afectiva nos permite romper con el "inanimismo" de la modernidad hegemónica, que es incapaz de percibir la vida y la sensibilidad de los territorios. Desde la inmersión en la vida, dialogando con los ríos y las plantas, los antiguos sabios percibieron el alma de los seres, y se dieron cuenta de que las aves, los árboles e incluso algunas piedras, tienen consciencia y afecto, forman sus propias comunidades y participan de la consciencia. Esto, por supuesto, no puede ser concebido desde el paradigma positivista y un comprensión estrecha del materialismo; es necesario hacerlo desde las perspectivas y epistemologías de los sabios visionarios. No creo que el formar parte de una familia indígena y el haber recordado cómo pensar con los órganos más sensibles de mi cuerpo, sea, bajo ningún aspecto, un demérito de mi propuesta filosófica y académica. Mis afirmaciones y apreciaciones sobre las culturas indígenas, por el contrario, se han hecho más finas, profundas y acertadas. Y veo cada vez con mayor suspicacia las afirmaciones de muchos antropólogos contemporáneos, quienes, claramente, por sus carencias en el manejo de la lengua y su poco tiempo de trabajo de campo, llegan a conclusiones que, al menos hoy, me parecen fruto de una distorsión hermenéutica.

Rompiendo el cerco eurocéntrico: Los estudios indígenas y los estudios hispánicos

Llevé mis estudios doctorales en el Departamento de Lenguas Modernas de la Université de Montréal, una institución académica francófona que es el centro intelectual de una ciudad que ha decidido preservar su diferencia cultural y lingüística en el contexto predominantemente anglófono de Norteamérica. Mi tesis doctoral profundizó acerca de las prácticas medicinales, visionarias, poéticas y narrativas de las naciones de la Amazonía occidental. Mi asesor de tesis fue el Dr. Juan Carlos Godenzzi, un excelso lingüista peruano que supo acoger y orientar mi temperamento libertario y mi sincero afecto por los pueblos indígenas. Bajo su dirección, en ese mismo momento, había un grupo de estudiantes dedicados, en su mayoría, a los Estudios Indígenas. Podría decirse que éramos un grupo de Estudios

Indígenas en un departamento que nos acogió sin la menor duda de la relación fecunda y natural entre los Estudios Hispánicos y los Estudios Indígenas. Sin embargo, esta relación fluida parece más una excepción que una constante. Por lo general, en los departamentos de Estudios Hispánicos se da una primacía a la herencia eurocéntrica y a los paradigmas metodológicos de la modernidad hegemónica. Y esta no es solo una tendencia vigente en los departamentos en Norteamérica, sino que en buena parte de las academias en las que prima la producción intelectual en lengua castellana se evidencia un talante conservador y un orgullo letrado; si bien muchas instituciones universitarias han acogido ideas del progresismo culturalista, metodológicamente no hay mucha apertura a formas de hacer academia ajenas a las establecidas desde el eurocentrismo.

Hay una suerte de moda, no siempre exenta de populismo y oportunismo, por acercarse a los temas indígenas; sin embargo, muchos de los académicos que recién se empiezan a interesar en estos temas, nunca han convivido de forma prolongada con las comunidades indígenas ni han sido educados por el afecto de la pedagogía ancestral. No falta quienes pretenden estudiar las manifestaciones culturales de los pueblos indígenas con sus viejas metodologías y evidencian una seria dificultad para desarrollar concepciones más amplias, libres y porosas de entender lo académico, que puedan acoger los saberes ancestrales con generosidad y apertura. En buena medida, el drama de las propuestas decoloniales es que, si bien denuncian la colonialidad epistémica, rara vez abandonan el andamiaje teórico moderno. Pocos académicos piensan desde el seno de las propias lenguas, sensibilidades, racionalidades y territorios indígenas. Por supuesto que, luego de las fuertes críticas al colonialismo académico en la segunda mitad del siglo XX, las posiciones autoritarias se han moderado, ya que no son políticamente correctas. Sin embargo, muchas veces estas mismas posturas críticas también buscan imponer sobre los pueblos indígenas sus propias ideologías (sean estas marxistas, feministas, psicoanalistas, estructuralistas, deconstructivistas entre otras).[2] Estos métodos, que surgieron de procesos históricos ajenos a los pueblos indígenas, suelen falsear los resultados, cuidando que las conclusiones no entren en contradicción con la ideología del autor. Realizar investigaciones entre pueblos indígenas desde metodologías eurocéntricas resulta bastante prepotente y, definitivamente, no permite escuchar las voces genuinas de los saberes ancestrales.

Dentro del ámbito hispánico, se suele considerar que la potestad en el estudio de los pueblos amerindios corresponde a la antropología, lo cual es bastante problemático. La antropología nació al mismo tiempo que la expansión colonial del siglo XIX y sirvió, en un principio al menos, a los intereses opresivos de los imperios modernos. En muchas ocasiones, los estudios antropológicos han sostenido prejuicios que consideraban a las culturas indígenas como un rezago del pasado, con un mínimo desarrollo intelectual y con concepciones espirituales infantiles. Los miembros de las naciones originarias han sido repetidamente descritos como salvajes y, en algunos casos extremos, como semihumanos.[3] A pesar de las pretensiones de objetividad, buena parte de los textos antropológicos procuraron demostrar lo que se creía saber de antemano: que los pueblos indígenas eran sociedades atrasadas con respecto al paradigma civilizatorio y evolucionista de la modernidad hegemónica, y que los médicos tradicionales eran psicóticos y paranoicos, dominados por lo irracional. No se puede negar, sin embargo, que la misma antropología contemporánea ha sido bastante crítica con sus predecesores. Pero, a pesar de los avances, el intento de generar metodologías de investigación y de redacción basadas en las propias epistemologías y ontologías indígenas suele despertar, desde la antropología, aún mucha resistencia. El ego antropológico se resiste a dejar de lado sus prerrogativas.

El surgimiento de académicos indígenas ha planteado la necesidad de trabajar con metodologías interculturales que respondan de mejor manera a la espiritualidad y pensamiento de estas naciones. Los Estudios Indígenas, entendidos como intentos de hacer academia desde fuera del paradigma de la modernidad hegemónica (aunque en diálogo con ella y, sobre todo, con las vertientes más libertarias al interior de la propia modernidad), buscan abrir campos al interior de las academias para pensar lo indígena desde nuestras propias experiencias y anhelos, nutridos de las maneras ancestrales de entender el conocimiento y la relación con el cosmos. Sin dejar de lado el rigor etnográfico, conviene desmarcarse de la rigidez disciplinar de la antropología, para penetrar en la racionalidad afectiva y poética de las naciones amerindias de una manera más abierta y respetuosa de las enseñanzas ancestrales. Cada contexto cultural nos propone un modo propio de interpretarlo; se trata de tener el silencio interior necesario para dejar que los propios saberes de las naciones originarias nos propongan las rutas adecuadas para penetrar en ellos y para expresarlos de la mejor manera posible. Trabajaríamos, entonces, desde lo que Gabriel Arévalo denomina "el paradigma indígena de investigación".[4] Si los Estudios Hispánicos quieren participar de los cambios paradigmáticos, metodológicos, ontológicos y epistémicos que aportan al mundo académico los saberes indígenas, han de dejarse los apegos y dependencias frente a la modernidad eurocéntrica, y la comprensión misma de lo académico tiene que ensancharse. Se trata de que las sabidurías ancestrales de los pueblos indígenas puedan expresarse en términos académicos con libertad, sin una excesiva necesidad de adaptarse y asimilarse, conservando su propia voz.

Desde los vínculos de afecto: Una academia enraizada al territorio y a la cultura

Los Estudios Hispánicos tienen mucho que beneficiarse del rumbo tomado por los Estudios Indígenas en las universidades de Norteamérica. Debido al eurocentrismo hegemónico entre las élites académicas del ámbito hispánico, yo no hubiera podido imaginar una investigación y una reflexión filosófica en estos términos si no fuera por el hondo encuentro que tuve con las propuestas de académicos provenientes de las naciones originarias de Norteamérica. En primer lugar, durante mi época de estudiante de doctorado en Montreal, realicé varios viajes para visitar a distintos sabios indígenas, quienes me acogieron con amistad, y participé en múltiples ceremonias que tocaron las fibras más íntimas de mi psique y de mi espíritu. En segundo lugar, he establecido diálogos académicos con distintos pensadores indígenas de Norteamérica, que me han permitido sustentar y perfilar mejor mis opciones metodológicas. La conversación entre los diversos intelectuales y sabios indígenas del continente, sin tener que pasar por el filtro legitimador de las instituciones hegemónicas, es necesaria y liberadora. Como la mayoría de este material está en inglés, se trata de textos muy poco conocidos en la América hispánica; de ahí que, quienes tenemos acceso a ellos, debemos acercar estas propuestas a nuestros territorios. Para quien, como yo, se ha asentado en el seno afectivo de una familia indígena, resulta de gran gozo poder leer (o escuchar) a los intelectuales indígenas expresarse en términos propios, realizando investigaciones académicas sin perder su raíz anímica, vibratoria y cultural, sin renunciar a su diferencia y singularidad.

El reto de hacer investigación académica desde un "paradigma indígena de investigación" es doble: no se trata de descartar lo que hemos aprendido de las academias modernas, sino de ser fiel a estas enseñanzas tanto como a las que hemos recibido de las sabidurías ancestrales. Los intelectuales indígenas suelen coincidir en las exigencias éticas que tienen que cumplir las investigaciones que se realizan en los territorios comunales. Al ser parte de una familia indígena, mis trabajos deben responder a las expectativas y presupuestos éticos de mis parientes, honrando, ante todo, al afecto y a la afinidad que nos vincula. ¿Acaso me sería posible analizar las prácticas y discursos de mis propios familiares como si fueran meros objetos de estudio? Las sabidurías indígenas nos hablan, de forma insistente, acerca de la importancia de preservar nuestras relaciones afectivas y de parentesco; sin estos vínculos, desde una perspectiva ancestral, se hace imposible la realización de nuestra individualidad y el desarrollo pleno de nuestras potencialidades. El ser no se realiza de manera autónoma; no somos en soledad, sino que es en relación con nuestros parientes, dialogando con el resto de seres vivos y con los territorios que habitamos, que llegamos a ser plenamente humanos (jonikon). No podemos desechar el afecto que nos vincula con el cosmos, ni el soplo anímico que sustenta a todos los seres. Muchas veces, cuando hacemos investigación cultural entre las naciones originarias, una grabadora e incluso un cuaderno de notas nos separan de nuestro interlocutor. El diálogo necesita abolir las distancias, generar empatía, ennoblecer el cariño. Se trata de mirarnos a los ojos y ver sinceridad en el otro, de vivir con plenitud el vínculo que se da entre mi corazón y el corazón del prójimo. Una misma luz, que viene de los antepasados y del Espíritu, nos alumbra, nos anima y nos brinda sabiduría.

Junto a mi esposa, hemos realizado nuestras investigaciones poco a poco, conversando con nuestros parientes, escuchándolos y recordando, sintiendo cómo el cariño y la sabiduría de sus palabras penetran en nuestros latidos y se hacen parte misma de nuestros cuerpos. Las palabras y consejos de los mayores nos han transmitido una fuerza ineludible. Nuestras investigaciones se basan en el respeto a los guardianes de los saberes ancestrales, sin importar si son personas que carecen de estudios académicos. En su humildad, los ancianos poseen una dignidad que pasa desapercibida para el ojo ilusionado por la utopía del progreso, pero que se percibe con claridad meridiana cuando contemplamos con el corazón. Conviene descartar la prepotencia, aún vigente entre muchos académicos, de considerar superior su saber especializado frente al de los ancianos. Nuestros mayores son verdaderos reservorios de conocimiento; conviene acercarse a ellos con respeto y afecto. Creo que, si bien el dilema de la distancia entre la academia y los sabios ancestrales no se ha resuelto del todo, ya que incluso desde los propios Estudios Indígenas no siempre es posible descartar la soberbia intelectual, es evidente que estos nuevos acercamientos sí han hecho un avance considerable para que podamos escuchar las voces de los ancianos y de los ancestros con mayor consideración. Solo siendo humildes y respetuosos, sin alardear de nuestros estudios, los ancianos nos dirán sus saberes. La base de toda metodología de investigación entre los pueblos indígenas debe ser la humildad, la mutua confianza y la apertura de mente, corazón y espíritu para acoger las voces insondables de los sabios y dejarnos transformar por ellas.

En este sentido, un primer paso para escuchar con respeto a los ancianos ha sido dado por la reivindicación académica del testimonio. Por ejemplo, el libro escrito por el antropólogo francés Bruce Albert junto con el sabio Davi Kopenawa (*A queda do céu: Palavras de um xamã yanomami*), es un extraordinario ejemplo de la profunda sabiduría de la que se puede dar cuenta cuando se abre un espacio para que los pensadores indígenas puedan expresarse y compartir su pensamiento con la humanidad, sin tratar de disciplinar su vocación poética, metafórica y visionaria. Otro ejemplo valioso es el del libro *El bebedor de Yajé*, en el que los nietos de Fernando Payaguaje, sabio airo-pai (secoya), recogen los testimonios de su abuelo. Al tratarse de testimonios de dos médicos visionarios, ambos dan cuenta de las epistemologías y ontologías de la medicina amazónica. Sin embargo, reconociendo la importancia de este tipo de aproximaciones, estos ejercicios no resuelven del todo el problema del eurocentrismo metodológico, puesto que el testimonio suele ser visto por la academia de forma condescendiente como "la palabra de los subalternos" (como se acostumbra decir desde los departamentos de Estudios Hispánicos de Norteamérica). De lo que se trataría, más bien, además de dar voz a los ancianos, es de también permitir que sus saberes penetren en la academia, pongan en duda las certezas metodológicas y confronten los modos hegemónicos en los que se entiende la producción de conocimiento, permitiendo así ensanchar el propio paradigma epistémico y ontológico desde el que parten nuestras investigaciones. Esto no implica cerrarse a los aportes de la modernidad, sino establecer las condiciones necesarias para realizar un diálogo respetuoso y transversal desde una academia indígena. De esta manera, se podría empezar a delinear la posibilidad de realizar una reflexión antropológica y filosófica nutrida de estos saberes, capaz de dar cuenta de los múltiples aportes que pueden dar al pensamiento humano y a la búsqueda de alternativas frente a la crisis de la modernidad.

Este tipo de investigación y reflexión solo la puede realizar quien no tiene apuro y sabe cómo liberarse de la presión que impone un sistema académico competitivo, burocrático y exitista. Conviene permanecer en un estado de reposo y de consagración a la sabiduría ancestral. A mi entender, antes que un mero trabajo académico, se trata de un camino de aprendizaje y de vinculación con las fuentes espirituales de la existencia, que ha de tomarnos toda la vida; una búsqueda verdaderamente filosófica y espiritual, entendiendo a la filosofía, en su acepción original, como una entrega unánime y amorosa al saber. Para poder expresar estos aprendizajes, es necesario desarrollar un pensamiento académico desde la poética indígena. El pensamiento del corazón propicia una racionalidad afectiva que experimenta la existencia empáticamente y que sabe dar cuenta de que la salud y el bienestar de la humanidad, no son aspectos independientes del cuidado y el respeto por el resto de seres vivos y por la totalidad cósmica.

Según ha escrito el académico cheroqui Brian Yazzie Burkhart, el conocimiento indígena es siempre vital, encarna, se hace respiración; y nos ayuda a vivir nuestra vida de forma equilibrada y saludable, habitando la Madre Tierra con belleza y sabiduría. El conocimiento, en estos términos, no puede nunca estar divorciado de la experiencia y de la acción (Yazzie

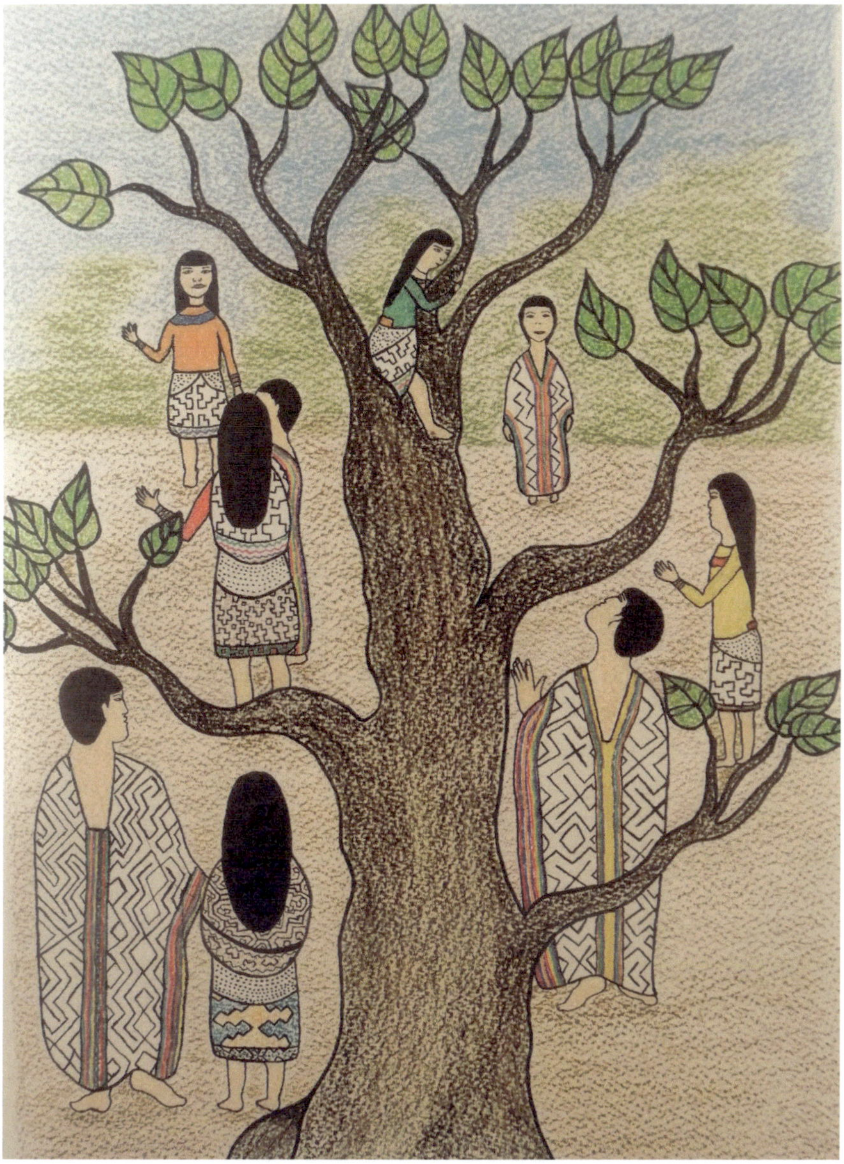

Figure 2. Chonon Bensho, *Jiwi* (árbol medicinal), tinta y lápiz de color sobre cartulina, 36 × 25 cm.

Chonon Bensho desarrolla una obra en la que convergen de manera armónica las técnicas del arte académico con la herencia de los antiguos artistas shipibos. Se trata de un arte indígena moderno e intercultural, vibrante y contemporáneo, pero que al mismo tiempo se eleva a lo trascendente y atemporal mediante un lenguaje simbólico y arquetípico. Sin rechazar los aportes occidentales, la pintura de Chonon se enraíza en los relatos ancestrales del pueblo shipibo-konibo, en las prácticas y plantas de los médicos tradicionales, y en el mundo perfumado de los espíritus Dueños de la medicina.

Burkhart 20–21). Se es una persona sabia en tanto se sabe vivir bien, en armónica convivencia con el resto de seres vivos, y beneficiando a los demás con su saber. Una sabiduría que no tiene implicancias positivas en la vida de los otros, es mezquina y estéril. Inspirados en estas concepciones, las investigaciones y reflexiones realizadas desde el paradigma indígena tendrían que ser un aporte, en primer lugar, a las propias naciones originarias con las que hemos establecido vínculos de afecto y confianza; principalmente, tal vez, se debería contribuir a la formación de nuevos académicos indígenas, facilitándoles un diálogo en el que se puedan sentir acompañados y en el que conseguir sus aspiraciones universitarias no signifique, necesariamente, perder sus raíces culturales y lingüística, ni ocultar sus diferencias reflexivas y espirituales. Pero, así mismo, una reflexión filosófica nutrida de los saberes ancestrales, debe ser también un aporte para toda la humanidad, mostrando formas alternativas de habitar la Tierra y de relacionarnos con los otros seres vivos, que resulten más armónicas y dignificantes.

Pensar con el corazón: La racionalidad poética y narrativa de los pueblos indígenas

La consagración de nuestras vidas a las sendas antiguas y sagradas de la sabiduría indígena demanda que seamos fieles a lo que los abuelos nos enseñaron y protejamos el legado de quienes nos precedieron. Un conocimiento que no aporte claridad, verdad y belleza es de poca importancia. Según ha escrito Anne Waters, académica de la nación seminole, las reflexiones de los pueblos indígenas, por lo general, están orientadas a buscar, mediante una conducta moral, un balance con el orden cósmico y con el resto de seres vivos (103). Mi responsabilidad, como miembro de una red indígena de afectos, es buscar, en el mundo de los antepasados y conversando con los Dueños espirituales de la medicina (jakon nete), la sabiduría necesaria para retomar el equilibrio y el respeto por la vida, y contribuir así al bienestar del conjunto existencial. El ser indígena se reconoce ligado de forma íntima con el resto de seres; y de este reconocimiento surge, de forma espontánea, una ética natural que nos orienta y nos enseña a respetar a los demás. Según ha escrito V. F. Cordova, una académica apache, la primera lección que brinda la pedagogía indígena es que las acciones de cada individuo tienen consecuencias para sí mismo, para sus parientes y para su comunidad, pero también para la red sagrada de la vida (178). La educación ancestral busca que seamos humanos en un sentido legítimo (jakon jonibo), respondiendo a las enseñanzas de los sabios del pasado, siendo capaces de responsabilizarnos por nuestros actos, y que procuremos vivir en balance con el cosmos.

Una reflexión filosófica en base a los saberes ancestrales, precisa de una escritura diferente a la que es hoy habitual en las ciencias sociales: el lenguaje acartonado y destinado solo a los especialistas, asfixia el talante poético y narrativo de los sabios. Es en las narraciones ancestrales que se manifiesta el espíritu filosófico y visionario de los médicos y sabios indígenas. Los relatos de los abuelos traen de forma implícita una innegable dimensión ética. Ciertas acciones dramáticas señalan los principios de vida que garantizan una existencia equilibrada, legítima, propia de la condición humana. Aunque el humor no queda

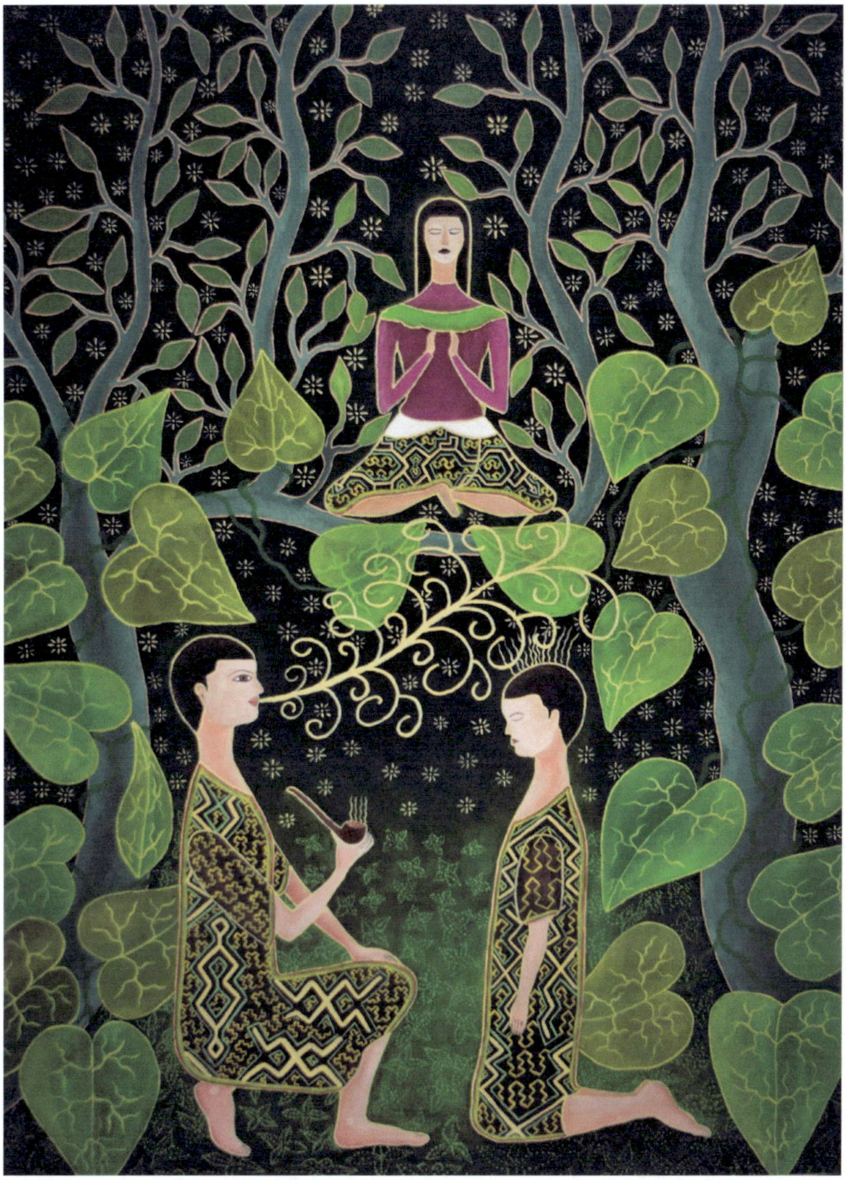

Figure 3. Chonon Bensho, *Rao Nete*, óleo sobre lienzo, 150 × 90 cm.
Rao Nete es una expresión shipiba que significa mundo de la medicina. Este mundo de la medicina hace referencia a una dimensión espiritual con la que el médico Onanya entra en contacto para curar. Es un mundo sutil y luminoso de una alta vibración espiritual, del que emana la fuerza curativa de los cantos medicinales y del soplo del médico. Esta fuerza es capaz de regenerar al ser humano y devolverle la salud. Los espíritus Dueños de este mundo se conocen con el nombre Chaikonibo; son antepasados que viven lejos de la ciudad, en pureza, conservando las antiguas sabidurías.

excluido, se relata ante todo para despertar reflexiones y transmitir conocimientos, los que deberán ponerse en práctica; los conocimientos narrativos nos enseñan, ante todo, a habitar la Tierra con belleza. Además, el lenguaje simbólico de las narraciones puede dar cuenta de aquellas realidades íntimas y espirituales ante las que nada tiene que decir el lenguaje de la lógica moderna y el método científico. El sentido profundo de la vida no puede ser expresado por una lengua técnico sino que solo lo poético y la narrativa arquetípica dan testimonio justo de estas realidades trascendentes y sutiles, fundamentales de la condición humana, de la realidad más honda y cardiaca del ser. Lo poético no pretende agotar los sentidos de las palabras, sino que preserva la multiplicidad expresiva y las posibilidades interpretativas, dando espacio así a una relación más dinámica, vital e intuitiva con el lenguaje. Y es justamente por este sentido de lo poético, que va más allá de lo estrictamente literario, y que no es exclusivo de los pueblos indígenas (sino que, en buena medida, es compartido por diversas culturas), que la poesía puede ser entendida como un medio privilegiado para la traducción de los saberes ancestrales indígenas.

Diversos investigadores se han dedicado al estudio de las narraciones ancestrales de la Amazonía, dando cuenta de su importancia para conocer el pensamiento amerindio. Es conocido el estudio estructuralista sobre los mitos amazónicos de Levi-Strauss, cuya impronta en la antropología de la región es perdurable. Otros ejemplos, entre muchos, son el trabajo de recopilación realizado por André Marcel d'Ans con las narraciones de la nación huni kuin (antiguamente llamados cashinahua), así como el del sacerdote salesiano Siro Pellizaro con narraciones, cantos y testimonios entre los shuar. Así mismo, también existen recopilaciones de narraciones ancestrales realizadas por los propios miembros de los pueblos indígenas. Un ejemplo es el libro *Duik Muun: Universo mítico de los aguarunas*, escrito de forma bilingüe por Aurelio Chumap Lucía, con colaboración del sacerdote jesuita Manuel García-Rendueles. Otro, el libro de relatos shipibos *El origen de la cultura Shipibo-Conibo* (1998), cuya recopilación y traducción estuvo a cargo de la Fundación Cultural Shipibo-Konibo, presidida por Ronon Bari (cuyo nombre castellano es Glorioso Castro Martínez). El valor de estas recopilaciones es inestimable. Sin embargo, aún faltan más estudios académicos que, sin descuidar ni negar los aportes de la antropología y otras disciplinas académicas, realicen una interpretación de estos relatos desde las propias perspectivas indígenas, para así dar cuenta plena de sus contenidos filosóficos. En parte, esta posibilidad orientó mi tesis doctoral *Las visiones y los mundos: Sendas visionarias de la Amazonía occidental.*

Creo que las narraciones ancestrales pueden ser el principal sustento para el desarrollo de una filosofía amerindia que pueda aportar a una nueva conciencia ecológica y poética que nos permita honrar nuestra pertenencia al tejido existencial. Mis parientes me cuentan que los antiguos sabios Meraya, como nuestro abuelo Ranin Bima, permanecían atentos a las voces profundas de la existencia; sabían conversar, mediante sus cantos o en sus sueños, con todos los seres vivos y con todas las substancias. Basados en su ejemplo vital, nuestra reflexión filosófica no puede seguir una ruta sin alma y ajena al corazón, sino que tiene que realizar una antropología que vaya más allá del límite de lo humano, entendiendo que la humanidad no puede ser pensada al margen de sus vínculos con la totalidad de la existencia. Es menester abrir nuestro propio camino en la academia y encontrar maneras propias de legitimar nuestro pensamiento. Para la racionalidad poética y afectiva, el conocimiento

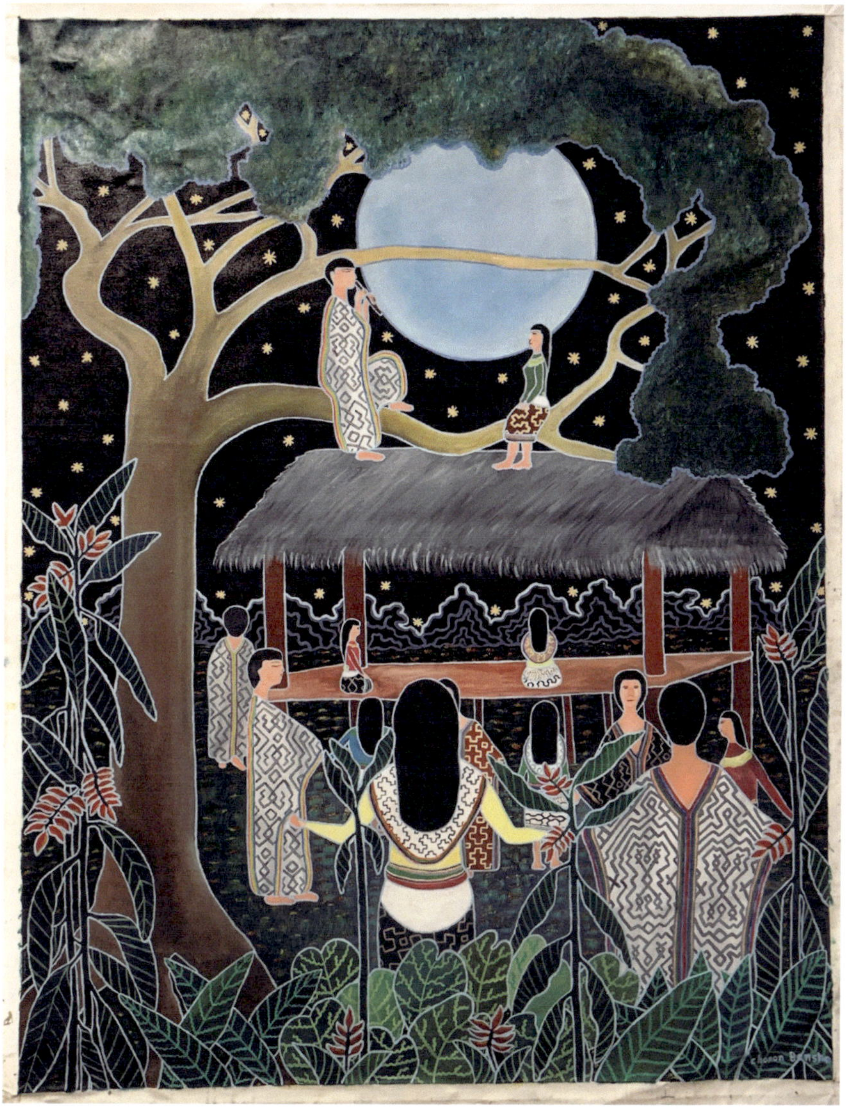

Figure 4. Chonon Bensho, *Ani Xeati* (la fiesta ritual de los antiguos), óleo sobre lienzo, 150 × 120 cm.

Nuestros abuelos contaban que al principio de los tiempos, cuando el mundo era nuevo, los antiguos shipibos se vestían pobremente. Su ropa no tenía nada especial, ninguna belleza, ninguna alegría. Hasta que un día una mujer encontró a una sirena en la orilla de un lago; y esa sirena era una joven hermosa que tenía todo el cuerpo cubierto con diseños kené. La mujer regresó a su casa y dibujó en el suelo de tierra los diseños que había contemplado en el cuerpo de la sirena. Desde entonces, los shipibos bordaron esos diseños en su ropa, los pintaron en sus telas y en las cerámicas, los tallaron en los horcones de sus casas y en los remos de sus canoas.

surge desde nuestra participación y apertura, desde nuestra predisposición a ser interpelados por los seres vivos hasta sentir la presencia de su alma en nuestro propio corazón. Una escritura que responda a los fundamentos epistémicos y ontológicos de los pueblos indígenas ha de tener, a semejanza de las narraciones antiguas, cierta circularidad que permita ver cómo las historias y las enseñanzas se concatenan entre sí. Resulta indeseable seccionar en estancos aislados la comprensión indígena del conocimiento, así como el tratar de llegar a conclusiones demasiado cristalizadas y definitivas. Si queremos responder a las racionalidades indígenas, no podemos separar como disciplinas autónomas a la epistemología, la ontología, la ética, la estética, la espiritualidad, las narraciones, la imaginación, las visiones, los sueños y nuestra propia afectividad.

Todos los aspectos de la vida y del saber pertenecen a una misma rueda de comprensión. Según el pensador maya Carlos Cordero, la perspectiva indígena integra las ciencias, la estética y lo espiritual. En términos similares se ha expresado el filósofo cheroqui Brian Yazzie Burkhart, quien asegura que para los pueblos indígenas ninguno de estos campos puede ser separado ni existe una jerarquía entre ellos. Por eso, afirma, una filosofía en términos indígenas no puede prescindir de la poesía (Yazzie Burkhart 22–23); tampoco hará distinciones rígidas entre lo racional y lo intuitivo, entre concepto y narrativa, entre conocimiento y práctica. Según ha escrito Anne Waters, los relatos de los pueblos indígenas guardan saberes y observaciones científicas, y dan cuenta de las relaciones adecuadas que debemos establecer con los seres vivos y con lo sagrado (103). Mi íntima convicción es que en las narraciones ancestrales se manifiesta el espíritu filosófico y visionario de los sabios antiguos. Como estos saberes no son expresados de forma conceptual ni tratan de forjar un dogma, cada quien debe interpretarlos según sus aptitudes y su hondura iniciática. Los saberes ancestrales son manantiales aún poco explorados que pueden beneficiar a la humanidad y donar formas más saludables de habitar la tierra.

Nuestro abuelo Ranin Bima, por ejemplo, cuando necesitaba el tronco de un árbol de Catahua para hacer canoa, le explicaba al Dueño espiritual (Ibo) de la especie que estaba talando para poder pescar y así nutrir a sus familiares y visitar a los parientes. La palabra poética del abuelo llegaba hasta el Dueño del árbol, quien, debido al respeto y al afecto con el que le había hablado, le daba el permiso para cortarlo. Sin embargo, el abuelo no tenía derecho a cortar más árboles, movido por su codicia. Los antiguos nos enseñaron que el ser humano no puede imponerse sobre el territorio, sino que solo debe depredar lo necesario para subsistir y luego dejar que el bosque recupere su balance. Quienes depredan movidos por sus deseos egoístas son atacados por los Dueños del territorio y caen enfermos. En esta ética de la convivencia podemos hallar inspiración para proponer alternativas y empezar a imaginar un cambio civilizatorio que sepa sintonizarse con el flujo vital del planeta.

A manera de conclusión: Siguiendo los pasos de los antiguos sabios

Mis parientes afirman que los antiguos sabios Meraya (médicos visionarios del pueblo shipibo-konibo) alcanzaban facultades psíquicas y espirituales extraordinarias. Cuentan que podían sumergirse en las aguas y sobrevivir sin necesidad de oxígeno. Cuando emergían, sus cuerpos no se habían mojado. Los Meraya se iban a vivir por semanas, meses e incluso años con los espíritus de los ríos y de los lagos. Sus cuerpos se hacían muy livianos gracias a los procesos iniciáticos, bañándose con plantas y cumpliendo rigurosas abstinencias. Los Meraya soñaban con otros territorios y otros tiempos. Ellos conocían el futuro y sus oráculos eran ciertos. Aprendían a moverse con conciencia y a voluntad por las geografías sutiles. Sus espíritus ascendían al firmamento y se suspendían en la profundidad celeste (naishama). Podían hablar con las aves y recibir sus conocimientos; con los jaguares negros de la noche, para pedirles protección; solicitaban sus propiedades medicinales a las plantas; dominaban, con la fuerza de sus pensamientos, a los dragones ronin que cuidan de los lagos y viven en los remolinos de los ríos. Los jóvenes que querían iniciarse en la medicina se inspiraban en esas narraciones para someterse a las abstinencias del aprendizaje visionario. Los antiguos crecían siendo curados, desde su infancia, por los sabios. Se cuenta que algunas noches los Meraya templaban sus mosquiteros y se metían dentro; luego empezaban a fumar y desaparecían, se iban a otros mundos, de los que traían insondables conocimientos.

Mucho de esto parecerá ficción para el campo letrado. Sin embargo, si se quiere ser respetuoso y entablar un diálogo en igualdad de condiciones con los saberes ancestrales, conviene aceptar que la racionalidad de los pueblos indígenas es diferente al pensamiento hegemónico, pero no por eso inferior. La sabiduría de los Meraya está ligada a los territorios, a la relación simbólica y poética con las realidades sensibles y suprasensibles. Los cantos medicinales dialogan con los elementos fundantes de la existencia. Los Meraya del pasado realizaron un despliegue profundo de las posibilidades espirituales y psíquicas gracias a sus abstinencias iniciáticas, a su concentración y silencio. La sabiduría de los antiguos nos enseña que la humanidad no puede realizarse de forma plena por cuenta propia, sino que es necesario relacionarse con los seres espirituales y con los antepasados. Para llevar a cabo estos desplazamientos visionarios y vincularse con los mundos suprasensibles, los médicos antiguos se purificaban y aprendían de las plantas maestras. La sabiduría de los Meraya considera que las plantas son seres plenamente realizados, que permiten a la humanidad vincularse con realidades trascendentes. Resulta evidente el refinamiento del pensamiento ancestral, así como sus hondas implicancias epistémicas y ontológicas. No puede negarse que los antiguos médicos pensaron filosóficamente la existencia; y que hallaron hondas respuestas acerca del sentido de la vida y de la experiencia humana.

La narrativa poética de los relatos ancestrales no pretende expresar conceptualmente todo el conocimiento de quien los enuncia de una manera cerrada e inmutable. Los relatos posibilitan, más bien, a quienes los escuchan, llegar a sus propias conclusiones; los invitan a encontrar la sabiduría implícita en las historias, desde una perspectiva personal. Las narraciones nos permiten experimentar las vivencias de otras personas, para de esa manera reflexionar acerca de nuestra vida y encontrar un conocimiento que podamos internalizar de forma honda y duradera. La imaginación humana, tal como testimonian los sueños, suele expresarse en términos narrativos e imágenes poéticas, para dar cuenta de lo más profundo del ser y de los múltiples mundos en los que transcurre nuestra existencia (desde los más densos hasta los más sutiles). Estas enseñanzas de los sabios del pasado, aun careciendo de una escritura alfabética, pueden ser un fecundo sustrato que nutra una reflexión filosófica profunda y elevada. La filosofía, en su sentido primordial y amplio, trasciende los límites

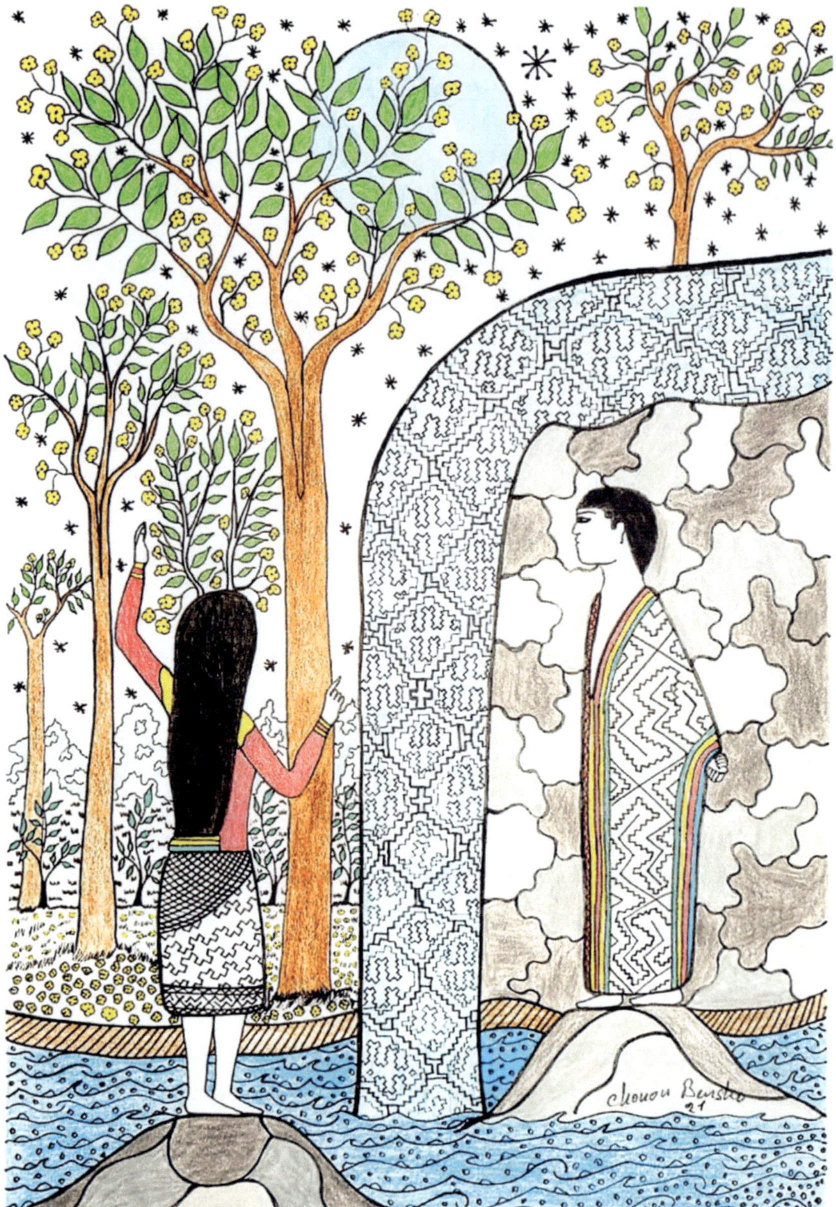

Figure 5. Chonon Bensho, *Inin Paro* (el río aromático de la medicina), tinta y lápiz de color sobre cartulina, 36 × 25 cm.

Para alcanzar el mundo espiritual de los Dueños de la medicina, el médico Onanya debe bañarse con hojas de las plantas noirao, que son hojas perfumadas que cambian el olor del ser humano, purificándolo, impregnándolo de un aroma semejante al olor de las vegetales. La persona que se está preparando, se baña con estas plantas y debe guardar largos periodos de ayunos y abstinencias para transformarse y convertirse en un sabio. El mundo aromático de las plantas noirao purifica todas las impurezas y malos aires del ser humano. Cuando el Onanya logra purificarse, transforma su olor y alcanza este mundo de alta vibración y de belleza impronunciable, aprende lo que se podría denominar, hablando a un nivel arquetípico, los aspectos femeninos de la medicina.

de la domesticación académica; el pensador original habla desde lo poético al corazón de la humanidad y de la vida. Pienso que los Estudios Indígenas abren un resquicio, al interior de las academias, para realizar un pensamiento filosófico que, sin renegar de lo conceptual, pueda también abrirse a lo narrativo, a lo poético y a la potencialidad de lo imaginal. Quienes nos vinculamos a este campo de trabajo y logramos liberarnos de las trabas impuestas por una concepción demasiado estrecha y cristalizada de la disciplina, podemos realizar un pensamiento académico propiamente indígena, que sea a la vez moderno y ancestral, conceptual y poético.

Notas

1. Lo ancestral no debe ser entendido acá desde un prisma historicista y museográfico como un supuesto archivo invariable que provendría de una supuesta "noche de los tiempos"; es una categoría imaginal, de principal importancia cultural y política, en tanto ciertas prácticas adquieren sentido y dignada al ser atribuidas a los antepasados.

2. Para quienes tengan interés en profundizar esta crítica al positivismo marxista y de la izquierda hispánica, les recomiendo la charla del filósofo andino Atawallpa Oviedo Freire, titulada "El Marx que no conoce la izquierda", que se puede visualizar en YouTube (https://www.youtube.com/watch?v=poKgg-RE2mI). Aunque reconoce la importancia de la crítica feminista, la académica maorí Linda Tuhiwai Smith afirma que "en la política de las mujeres indígenas existe una continua resistencia a la forma en la que las feministas occidentales han tratado de definir los asuntos de las mujeres indígenas y de categorizar las posiciones en que deben ser ubicadas estas" (277).

3. Gunther Tessmann, por ejemplo, investigador alemán que escribió el libro *Los hombres sin Dios* (1928), estaba gobernado por un furioso racismo; afirmó que los antiguos shipibo eran "creaturas sin sensibilidad y simiescas". Tessmann se refiere a ellos con el denigrante nombre de chama, apelativo que algunos mestizos de Ucayali siguen usando. El etnógrafo alemán afirmó que los shipibo carecían de toda imaginación, creatividad e inclinación espiritual; dijo, incluso, que entre ellos no existía ninguna "mitología" (véase Tournon 115).

4. "El paradigma indígena de investigación se caracteriza por ser parte de una agenda social y política de decolonización y autodeterminación de los pueblos indígenas que, basada en la cosmovisión y conocimientos indígenas, guía la creación de marcos 'teóricos' y 'metodológicos' de la investigación en donde las prácticas culturales y formas de expresión indígenas tienen una profunda conexión con el investigador, el proceso de investigación y los participantes. Se orienta por un conjunto de valores surgidos de las cosmovisiones indígenas en clave de componente ético en la investigación" (Arévalo 62).

Obras citadas

Arévalo, Gabriel Andrés. "Reportando desde un frente decolonial: La emergencia del paradigma indígena de investigación". *Experiencias, luchas y resistencias en la diversidad y multiplicidad.* Edited by Gabriel Andrés Arévalo and Ingrid Zabaleta Chaustre. Asociación Cultural Mundo Berriak, 2013, pp. 51–78.

Chumap Lucía, Aurelio, and Manuel García-Rendueles. *Duik Muun: Universo mítico de los aguarunas.* Vols. 1 and 2. CAAAP, 1979.

Cordero, Carlos. "A Working and Evolving Definition of Culture". *Canadian Journal of Native Studies*, no. 21, 1995, pp. 28–41.

Cordova, V. F. "Ethics: The We and the I". *American Indian Thought: Philosophical Essays*. Edited by Anne Waters, Blackwell Publishing, 2004, pp.173–181.

D'Ans, André-Marcel. *La verdadera bíblia de los cashinahua: Mitos, leyendas y tradiciones de la selva peruana*. Mosca Azul Editores, 1975.

Favaron, Pedro. *Las visiones y los mundos. Sendas visionarias de la Amazonía occidental*. CAAAP, 2017.

Fundación Cultural Shipibo-Konibo. *Non requenbaon shinan, el origen de la cultura shipibo-konibo*. Arteidea Editores, 1998.

Kopenawa, Davi, and Bruce Albert. *A queda do céu Palavras de um xamã yanomami*. Companhia das Letras, 2010.

Payaguaje, Fernando. *El bebedor de yajé*. Vicariato Apostólico de Aguarico, 1994.

Tournon, Jacques. *La merma mágica: Vida e historia de los shipibo-conibo de Ucayali*. CAAAP, 2002.

Tuhiwai Smith, Linda. *A descolonizar las metodologías: Investigación y pueblos indígenas*. Txalaparta, 2017.

Waters, Anne. "Language Matters: Nondiscrete Nonbinary Dualism". *American Indian Thought: Philosophical Essays*. Edited by Anne Waters, Blackwell Publishing, 2004.

Yazzie Burkhart, Brian. "What Coyote and Thales Can Teach Us: An Outline of American Indian Epistemology". *American Indian Thought: Philosophical Essays*. Edited by Anne Waters, Blackwell Publishing, 2004, pp. 15–26.

PART 2

Reflections on Indigeneity, Translation, Pedagogies, and Epistemologies

CHAPTER 6

Man are' taj utz k'aslemal la': Indigenous Ecologies and the Limits of Cross-Disciplinary Translation

Nathan C. Henne
Loyola University New Orleans

Last semester, in my Latin American Studies class Indigenous Literatures in Translation, one module focused on a series of Maya K'iche' poems that engage cultural differences in thinking about ecology. Just before teaching this latest version of that class, I had been invited to consider teaching a class on Indigenous ecologies that would be cross-listed in Environmental Studies, so I decided to experiment a bit and focus the literature class on trying to identify specific elements of Indigenous ecologies in literary and other cultural "texts" that would appeal to them. I am convinced that students and scholars in the field of Environmental Humanities can benefit from including what have been marginalized Indigenous ways of thinking about our engagement with other realms of ecology around us because these ideas challenge the underlying hierarchies causing the ecological crisis. However, these benefits cannot be realized without first undertaking an aggressive decolonial translation of the original languages to understand the borrowed practices as they exist in the complete epistemological system of the original. That is, by understanding these lifeways from *within* Indigenous cosmovisions we can prevent the colonial practice in Western scientific disciplines of borrowing ideas from other cultures but attempting to splice them onto narrow, culturally biased assumptions that science presents as objective. This chapter shows how these culturally contrived assumptions in translation short-circuit the kind of aggressive and far-reaching ecological thinking that this interdisciplinarity offers in the first place.

Of course, accurate analysis of Indigenous texts can never occur without an acute awareness of translation issues and how the very act of translation threatens to colonize and subsequently derail the reliability of those ecological relations. That challenge becomes even more important when working in a cross-disciplinary context like Environmental Studies.

While Indigenous onto-epistemologies are beginning to have noticeable influence at the fringes of Environmental Studies, most scholars working in the field still do not generally have experience with the broader context of Indigenous onto-epistemologies that take shape in the cradle of language.

I begin with a poem by Humberto Ak'abal (Momostenango, Guatemala) that I taught because it addresses these two aspects of interdisciplinary overlap: first, the poem's central idea dialogues with the field of Environmental Studies on several levels, including underlying notions of ecology that resonate with so-called *buen vivir* Indigenous sets of practices like *utz k'aslemal* and *sumak kawsay*, which I further develop in due course; second, the poem specifically illustrates the colonial complications of translation, especially when Indigenous texts and concepts distilled from them are borrowed across disciplines. "Kotz'i'j" ("Las flores"/"The Flowers") gives us a good place to start to think about both the benefits and complications of incorporating "literary" Indigenous texts in departments other than those that have traditionally handled them.

KOTZ'I'J (by Humberto Ak'abal)	**Las Flores (Spanish)**	**The Flowers (English)**
K'iche' (original)	(Trans: Ak'abal & Miguel Rivera)	(Trans: M. Rivera & Robert Bly)
Ri uxe' ri taq kitz'i'j kuj kitaq ub'ixik chaqe ri ajilanik	Las raíces nos mandan a contar	Roots tell us
—Rumal ri kotz'i'j are ri'—	—por medio de las flores—	—through the flowers—
xa jeri' ri ucholaj ri ulew chupam.	cómo es la tierra por dentro.	what the earth is like on the inside
We ri kotzi'i'j ke chaqijarik'	Y las flores se marchitan,	And the flowers wither,
ke'kamik	se mueren	they die
rumal cho uwächulew	porque acá afuera	because out here
xa jun kisij ri k'aslemal	la vida es una mierda	life is shit

(Downloaded from: https://www.akabal.com/ on 24 sept. 2021)

On the first read, I asked my students to make connections to elements of the sociohistorical context of coloniality in Maya areas that we had discussed and to identify elements of ecology, broadly conceived, as they read Ak'abal's "Kotz'ij" and its translations to English and Spanish. Given the ecological context of the class, my students were quickly able to identify how the voice of the poem speaks from a critical comparative cultural perspective. They talked about how the poem drives at the way Westerners tend to think about beauty in nature (flowers) versus how other cultures might privilege, even aesthetically, the roots that do the work of transfer between the underground and surface worlds. Eventually, the students also made connections with the particular historical context of Guatemala we had handled previously in class. For example, they situated the "out here life is shit" lines in the sociohistorical conditions of coloniality that many K'iche' people, like Ak'abal, have suffered since Contact.

From there, students needed some coaching to get to the underlying cosmovision I wanted to uncover. I asked them to identify how "Kotz'i'j" might represent relationships between humans and the other realms of their shared ecology beyond the aesthetic and historical aspects. That is, the roots tell us something through the flowers: they speak; we listen. This communication may not seem particularly surprising in the poetic context—after all, poets frequently give voice to inanimate things. But what if these voices of ecology are not an artistic flair? What if this two-way communication illustrates a basic way of being in the world, where humans regularly talk to and listen to various realms of the ecology?

Structuralist anthropologists traditionally reduce this cultural characteristic to animism and identify it as a typical element that many Indigenous cultures retain as part of their "religions." What if instead of religion, we think about this communication with the realms of the world around us as a cultural understanding of an ideal ecology where these realms around us have agency *as themselves*, not as "gods?" What if—in spite of the agency these nonhuman realms have—they do not fit into a typical religious hierarchy (gods→humans→other) as structuralist anthropologists traditionally describe it (Henne, Reading 29, 50)?

In traditional Maya K'iche' practice, this listening and speaking with various realms around us in the world is a crucial foundation of *utz k'aslemal,* which, in turn, is not a religious concept.[1] *Utz* translates most directly as "good" and *k'aslemal* as "life," but the phrase means much more than "the good life." For the Kaqchikel (Guatemala) intellectual and activist Aura Cumes:

> [*Utz k'aslemal*] no es solamente un pensamiento, una filosofía o una teoría, es antes que nada una experiencia de vida. Es decir, es a la vez un pensar, un vivir, y un sentir. En tanto es una manera de experimentar la existencia [que] es profundamente espiritual. En esta concepción de la vida se enseña que todo vive: la tierra, las montañas, el agua, las plantas, el sol, la luna, las estrellas, así como todo lo que no vemos pero tiene movimiento. (8)

In short, *utz k'aslemal* refers to a way of being in the world that decenters humans and their perspectives in order to see the interacting realms of the world in a much more interconnected way, both ontologically and epistemologically (Reading 179, Camey 10–1). What the roots say in "Kotz'i'j" is an introduction to *utz k'aslemal* on a few different levels.

Utz k'aslemal functions as the foundation for K'iche' epistemology because it is through that ongoing communication with the realms around us that humans know what the world is and how to be in it. But *utz k'aslemal* clearly also functions on the ontological level because it encompasses much more than human knowledge; it is through *utz k'aslemal* that humans, and these other realms (or the "cosmic community," as Itzamná calls them, or "other than human beings," as Marisol de la Cadena puts it), become what we/they are. And what we/they are—our/their ontology—changes according to our interactions in that shared place. To achieve *utz k'aslemal,* we must be aware of—and participate in—different communication with different realms according to where we are. Our interactions change according to how each place is made up (collective ontology) of the sum of all the interrealm communication unique to that place at that time. This onto-epistemology must remain a fundamental part of *buen vivir* for it to migrate across disciplines effectively.

In the interest of decoloniality, I suggest we think about *utz k'aslemal* as precisely ecological—instead of as animist religion—because the concept has to make sense within the whole K'iche' epistemological context, not within circum-Mediterranean-derived notions of hierarchical religion. That is, our understanding must correspond to the larger questions: How did/do K'iche' people know what the world was/is and should be according to the principle of *utz k'aslemal*? Can we approach the cultural practice of listening and talking to the many realms that participate in the world with us as part of an ecological process of collectively becoming rather than as an animist religious practice?

By extension, can the K'iche' concept of *utz k'aslemal* offer a different point of departure for thinking about the ecology in the context of Environmental Studies? I am convinced that it can. However, we have to work through a few significant complications from an alert decolonial perspective to get there.

While we have begun to understand the mutual communication at the heart of *utz k'aslemal* from a simple close reading of this Ak'abal poem, there's a danger of a deeper erasure if we stop here. For example, a cross-disciplinary attempt to incorporate aspects of Indigenous ecologies from a text like "*Kotz'i'j*" might come to the simple—and quite palatable—conclusion that Indigenous ecologies are based on a more open communication with nature to achieve more harmony. However, we must also take the next, more difficult step and simultaneously engage the radically different ontologies that underlie *utz k'aslemal* and this facile "translation" of it.

For our purposes, this next step means interrogating and displacing the Western ontological category of nature and its accompanying logic in translating Indigenous ecological texts. Put simply, though translators often use the words "nature" and "naturaleza" for various Indigenous American ways of seeing the world and cosmos around us, those words do not capture the same way of understanding and enacting those relationships. Even many Indigenous writers and translators resort to using "nature"/"naturaleza" at some point in their translations of Indigenous *vivir bien*/*buen vivir* phrases even though these concepts are inextricably attached to a long Western cultural and philosophical trajectory. They do so because no efficient ways of adequately signaling the massive differences are available in English or Spanish, and quite simply, the academic tradition and its underlying colonial logic have not historically had the patience to grapple with the inefficient but necessary means to describe these fundamental differences.[2]

Abraham García Hernández—a native K'iche' speaker from the Cantel area who has earned a degree in sociolinguistics from Universidad Mariano Galvez and who has worked for decades as a K'iche' translator on numerous published translations—agrees emphatically that no words in K'iche' translate accurately as either "harmony" or "nature" (personal communication). So how could *utz k'aslemal* mean "living in harmony with nature," as so many texts translate it?[3]

But, astute readers might say, the above translations of Ak'abal's K'iche' poem do not explicitly use the words "nature" or "*naturaleza*." How could this Western concept distort these translations then? I show below how a second level analysis of this poem reveals serious issues of colonial residue arising from translation where the Western concepts of nature *silently* inserts itself. But first we need to take a closer look at the journey of the *buen vivires* into the mainstream in the broader context.

Revealing the *utz k'aslemal* case and ascertaining any such "contamination" from an Indigenous perspective is complicated. First, not much multidisciplinary work has been published from the perspective of K'iche' people on *utz k'aslemal*. The limited published K'iche' sources we have on *utz k'aslemal* come mostly from a social science perspective in the specific, politically charged context that seeks to forge state policy changes. (By contrast, much of what I have discussed so far comes from my informal conversations with Maya friends and colleagues over the years because I am trying to describe *utz k'aslemal* as it exists organically in K'iche' communities rather than as it is currently being marshaled for this specific political purpose.) Second, I am not Maya K'iche', even though I was born in Guatemala and raised in a couple of different Maya K'iche' communities around Maya K'iche' people. Last, it is crucial to learn to recognize and uproot various levels of underlying colonial logic that lie embedded in the historical and intellectual processes of understanding, describing, and translating Indigenous ecological relations like this outside the epistemological systems that produced them.

For these reasons, I now take a detour from Guatemala to the Andes, specifically Bolivia, Ecuador, and Peru. By broadening our geographical scope here, we can take advantage of an opportunity to look at other Indigenous American concepts that productively engage with the K'iche' *utz k'aslemal*. The advantage of taking this detour is that the related concept *sumak kawsay* (Kichwa "living in fullness") has been critically and prolifically handled by Indigenous scholars working from several disciplinary perspectives.

Most important for our comparative ecological purposes, the "animism" and subsequent interrealm communication underlying *utz k'aslemal* are also fundamental to the Andean *sumak kawsay*, to which we now turn. In *sumak kawsay* "hay una vida animada, en el mejor de los sentidos, para la comunicación con el espacio que nos rodea, por eso es que las montañas y los collados tienen vida, el alcor y las rocas hablan y se quejan, el agua y los humedales lloran" (Itzamná 310). In the Pacha (roughly translated as "cosmos") that is the foundation of *sumak kawsay*, "There is no dichotomy between living beings and inert bodies—all have life, and all life is understood as the relation between all parts of the whole" (Solón 2). Thus, the voices of the *kotz'i'j* in the K'iche' poem—as a function of *utz k'aslemal*—represent the voices and agencies of the many other realms that need to be engaged in the *buen vivir* complex of Indigenous practices.

A Comparative Case Study: *Sumak kawsay* and the Andean Constitutions

Recent developments in Ecuador and Bolivia offer an opportunity to look at more than a decade of the academic process of the cross-disciplinary absorption of a couple of Indigenous-Andean ecological terms into the mainstream national dialogue and subsequent policy making. In 2008 and 2009, the Ecuadorian and Bolivian governments radically revised their constitutions expressly to include Indigenous worldviews that had been erased from circles of power for centuries. For the first time, these countries saw the formal inclusion of Indigenous socioecological thinking in fundamental nation-making documents: constitutions. As a result, there has been an explosion of publications in different fields that have tried to take up the so-called *buen vivir* concepts that had newly crossed into the mainstream, a sample of which I handle in this chapter.

Both revised constitutions prominently featured untranslated Indigenous phrases in Indigenous languages (*sumak kawsay/suma qamaña*, among others), which represents a monumental shift in the five-hundred-year colonial history of Latin America. Including Indigenous epistemologies by name seemed to signal a stark departure from the Western development model as the ultimate measure of national success. Although various revolutionary constitutions in Latin America—those of Mexico and Cuba, for example—had certainly been radical in different ways, the traditional Left's ideology in Latin America was still firmly based on the modern concepts of progress and development (Ávila 14). By contrast, these Andean constitutions—by invoking Indigenous practices directly and unapologetically—threatened to radically alter both the domestic and foreign policies of these nations. But did they? We have an opportunity to look at how the practical Indigenous aspects of these terms have held up in the "translation" and intercultural transfer into the mainstream in the decade and a half since the constitutional conventions that inscibed them.

From a decolonial perspective, the issues of translation in transfer across epistemological systems in the Andean nations involve the following questions: Has the invocation of Indigenous terms in these constitutions reflected—in national policies—the wider epistemologies and resulting alternative ecologies these concepts evolve out of? Or have the Indigenous terms been appropriated by hegemonic ideology and affected minimal real change in practice? These cases of *sumak kawsay* (Kichwa) and *suma qamaña* (Aymara) (generally referred to as *el buen vivir*/living well) provide a kind of laboratory to see whether it is possible to incorporate radically different ecological terms into what remains essentially a neoliberal, capitalist, and globalized world system without drowning them in Western logic.

The first step should be to provide any uninitiated readers with a basic springboard definition of *sumak kawsay*, but that is not as simple as it sounds. The very idea of definition as definitive is itself Western and *sumak kawsay* staunchly resists it. The former Bolivian ambassador to the United Nations Pablo Solón warns: "There is no decalogue of VB [vivir bien]; rather, it is a broad, evolving framework. Any attempt to define it in absolute terms would thus stifle its dynamism" (1). Thus, a decolonial reader will take the following with a grain of salt.

In the most basic terms, *sumak kawsay* broadly describes an Andean way of life that, like *utz k'aslemal*, requires taking into account the well-being of all elements that share the cosmos. The related practices enable humans to make decisions that lead to a full, balanced, and sustainable life based on a broad, holistic notion of the cosmos's health (Itzamná 281). For efficiency's sake, I focus mainly on the Kichwa/Quechua version of the term: *sumak kawsay* as generally representative of the Andean region because significant crossover links it closely with the related Aymara (Bolivia) *suma qamaña*.[4] The Aymara activist Fernando Huanacuni Mamani, a key "cosmovision consultant" in the Bolivian Constitutional

Convention, offers very similar translations of the Aymara and Kichwa (spelled "Quechua" in Bolivia and Peru) terms, so I include only the latter for *sumak kawsay*: "*Sumak*: plenitud, sublime, excelente, magnífico, hermoso(a), superior; *Kawsay*: vida, ser estando, estar siendo" (13). His insistence on "fullness" for "sumak" suggests much more of the inherent nuance in the term than the generic, abstract binary "good," which is most commonly used. Unfortunately, most publications on the matter retain the much less precise "good/well," or "bien/buen."

The Quechua intellectual and activist Ollantay Itzamná provides an in-depth and nuanced description in his essay "*Sumaq Kawsay (buen vivir), un estilo de vida subyacente en el mundo andino*." Because the ecological principles in his description apply most directly to our purposes here, I single three out (all shared with *utz k'aslemal*): an intricate interrelatedness or entanglement of all things (on an ontological level), complementary duality at the root of ontology (as opposed to oppositional binaries), and reciprocity as a cosmic ethic (283–286). I focus on the first two in terms of their compatibility with *utz k'aslemal* and my critical analysis of the effectiveness of translation in the process of cultural transfer.

First, let me be clear: overall, the inclusion of these Indigenous concepts (and crucially, the *untranslated* words for them) in founding documents that strive to define a new plurinational character is, in itself, a huge and lasting triumph not just for Andean Indigenous peoples but also for Indigeneity everywhere. The Puruhá (Ecuador) *curandero*, writer, and Indigenous activist Atawallpa Oviedo Freire leaves no doubt as to the overall benefit of the crossover: "What was [most] important [as a result of the inclusion of Indigenous concepts] was that this new-ancient system is now present and active in the dialogue and the debate of the academy and the realpolitik," regardless of any emerging critiques (6, my translation). For Oviedo, the process that the constitutional convention followed generally succeeded in capturing this Indigenous notion. "*El buen vivir* is not an academic invention as some intellectuals have suggested; it's not that someone made up the word and popularized it with certain general concepts; rather they consulted with various community elders [abuelos y abuelas] and asked them what name they would use to reflect the Andean way of life, and the majority agreed on *sumak kawsay*, including those in Ecuador, Bolivia and Perú" (8).

I defer to Oviedo on his overall positive evaluation of the process undertaken in getting *sumak kawsay* into the Ecuadorian constitution. Still, there is another aspect of the translation equation that deserves some attention, too. How have national policies and practices actually changed as a result of these Indigenous phrases as frames? When non-Kichwa-speaking people interpret the practical ramifications of invoking something like *sumak kawsay*, how do they go about translating it and understanding its nuances to make it a political reality in the current world system? In a multilingual society whose laws and legal logic are founded in Indo-European languages and Western history, decolonial translation is crucial to prevent Indigenous terms from being appropriated and subsumed as something other than what they mean in Indigenous cultures.

Looking for the telltale nonhierarchical relationships between humans and the other realms of ecologies in *sumak kawsay* is one specific decolonial strategy that can help determine whether the constitutions retain their Indigenous foundations. Like *utz k'aslemal*, *sumak kawsay* is founded on non-human-centered visions of relationships among different realms in an ecological system—what the Kaqchikel sociologist Aura Cumes (Guatemala) calls a crucial "horizontality" in *utz k'aslemal* (9). If these Indigenous lifeways were going to retain their meaning and dictate state policy, subsequent legislation would reject outright the anthropocentric development paradigm that has driven national policies (as well as the rise of liberalism and humanism) all over the world in the modern era—regardless of whether the economic system leans capitalist or socialist.

In fact, from the perspective of *sumak kawsay*, the supposed opposition between the two political ideologies—capitalism and socialism—that had squared off in proxy all over the Americas for decades was a mirage because both are driven by the same anthropocentric development paradigm (Oviedo 23–24). By contrast, as a cornerstone of the constitution, *sumak kawsay* would legally anchor a radically different, biocentric logic when crafting national policy on such issues as resource extraction.

One of the architects of the *sumak kawsay* sections of the Ecuadorian constitution, the economist Alberto Acosta, though not Indigenous himself, steadfastly insisted on including *sumak kawsay* because it would loudly signal Ecuador's departure from Harry Truman's post–World War II notion of development as the end-all measure of success, which has fundamentally dictated Latin American politics ever since (155). For Acosta, the inclusion of *sumak kawsay* in the Ecuadorian constitution would signal the need to abandon the development paradigm as a foundation and search for other ways of shaping national policy and measuring outcomes.

Of course, for a meaningful *sumak kawsay* to have a profound effect on policy, several disciplines would first have to be able to "translate" the Kichwa term into a comprehensible notion in their own disciplinary contexts, but those translated notions would still need to retain their Kichwa heart. Could that happen in a world system still fundamentally linked to the development paradigm? Could this translation preserve, for example, the associated underlying Indigenous epistemology of fuzzy ontologies (that result from the first two of Itzamná's ecological principles above) in a meaningful way when the scientific mandate demands precise demarcation? This would be no small feat because *sumak kawsay* not only directly challenges the basic assumptions of Western civilization and interrupts its liberal, humanist trajectory but also undercuts the clear ontological separations of the scientific process.

On the other hand, looking for answers to the above questions from a totally idealistic perspective would also be a mistake. Unlike in traditional Western thought, in Indigenous ontoepistemologies, contradictions can fruitfully coexist because Indigenous cosmovisions tend not to be totalizing (Mignolo "Idea," xvii–xviii; Beling and Vanhulst 34). Besides, significant transformation of the *sumak kawsay* concept was always inevitable in the multidisciplinary process of "translation" over the few decades since Indigenous terms and concepts have worked their way into mainstream consciousness. Still, some semblance of Indigenous fundamentals must survive meaningfully.

Certainly the Ecuadorian constitution uses blatantly Western concepts right from the beginning to describe *sumak kawsay*: "Decidimos construir una nueva forma de convivencia ciudadana, en diversidad y armonía con la naturaleza, para alcanzar el buen vivir, el *sumak kawsay*" (8). As I show in due course, "la naturaleza" is a Western construction that undercuts any understanding of *sumak kawsay*. Yet the Ecuadorian constitution actually offers "naturaleza" as an equivalent for Pacha Mama in the third line of its preamble, which Westernizes the notion from the outset.[5]

Furthermore, a close reading of the resulting Ecuadorian constitution reveals development as a core principle. In fact, one of the mentions of *sumak kawsay* is in a section titled "Régimen de Desarrollo" (105). Oviedo concludes that so-called sustainable development positions such as "green development," "green capitalism," and "market environmentalism," which invoke *sumak kawsay*, actually continue prioritizing resource extraction for export as the basis for the nation's economy (170–173). Similarly, Itzamná concludes that development always ends up being predatory regardless of the sheep's clothing it comes dressed in (302).

In 2014, six years after the Ecuadorian constitution was legally ratified, Antonio Hidalgo-Capitán and Ana Cubillo-Guevara describe the concept of *buen vivir* as it coalesced in the mainstream after this inevitable process of translation and consequent acculturation as follows: "Es un concepto que se conforma así como un collage postmoderno de concepciones indígenas, campesinas, sindicalistas, cooperativistas, solidarias, feministas, pacifistas, ecologistas, socialistas, teólogo-liberacionistas, descolonialistas, etc." (29). To many Indigenous critics, the most immediately disruptive result of this postmodern "collageization" of all these diverse sources has been that the nonhuman members of the cosmic community have been completely secularized and thus stripped of their consciousness, personality, and subjectivity, which is fundamentally incompatible with the Indigenous heart of the concept. Because these elements of the consciousness of everything are indispensable, these critics insist on using the term *sumak kawsay* (or *suma qamaña*)—instead of the Spanish "equivalent" of *el buen vivir*—to signal the difference. Using the Spanish term would fail to resist that *el buen vivir* "ha sido despojado de la dimensión espiritual que tiene el *sumak kawsay*... y ha sido además aderezado con aportaciones occidentales que nada tienen que ver con las culturas ancestrales" (Oviedo 28, 174–176). Oviedo's choice of the term "spirituality" is less than ideal because it tends to imply the mistaken notion that *sumak kawsay* fits in the category of "religion," but he is not using the word "spirituality" in the sense that the elements of the universe are "gods." He means it in the sense of consciousness, subjectivity, and personality.

Perhaps we can overcome these misleading implications of "spiritual" in translation here by following the Peruvian decolonial anthropologist Marisol de la Cadena's lead in a number of ways. First, we can avoid assumptions about spirituality in *buen vivir* practices by characterizing the relationships between people and these other-than-human beings as kinship rather than spirituality (Uncommoning, 37). Rivers and mountains, for example, are "our brothers," which affords them a heightened subjectivity in English without invoking Western spirituality. Second, de la Cadena goes on to make a crucial distinction about modern Indigenous worldviews, which can "make reference to *both* a piece of land under the jurisdiction of the Peruvian state *and* an entity that emerges through the Awajun Wampis' [eastern Peru] practices of life that may, for example, make people the relatives of rivers" at the same time (Uncommoning, 37, original italics). This ability to hold two distinct ontological views of the same thing at the same time distinguishes this Indigenous cosmovision from the totalizing Western view that can accept only one of the two because of strict epistemological limitations.

The resulting consciousness of all things—and the subsequent subjectivity it authorizes—is indispensable to *sumak kawsay* because it centers the nonhierarchical and interrealm communication at the heart of the epistemological process and refuses the oppositional duality at the heart of Western logic. The problem with this part of the "translation" is that this consciousness and subjectivity flies in the face of both dominant religion and science.

Monotheism Invalidates *Sumak Kawsay*

Oviedo (35–6) and Itzamná (289) identify the rise of monotheism (roughly two millennia ago) as the crucial historical crossroads in the sense of other cultures around the world moving away from philosophies that loosely correlated with *sumak kawsay*. When monotheistic traditions removed God/the Divine from the material earth and made it something abstract, two fundamental things changed: first, listening and speaking to the realms of the earth became sacrilege, which severed the intimate relationships between humans and the other realms of the cosmos; second, all non-human elements of the cosmos were relegated to a hierarchically inferior level below God (on the top) and humans (below God, but above all else).

Essentially, humans were removed from the "cosmic community," which eventually led to the culturally determined concept of nature as "that which humans move through, but are not a part of" (and, to be clear, I am extrapolating beyond Itzamná and Oviedo). By contrast, Itzamná describes the relationship among the realms in Andean thinking as "interdependent" (293), which can be seen as horizontal, refusing permanent hierarchy like the one underlying the category "religion." The Judeo-Christian God made humans in his image and imbued them with immortal souls—thus separating them from nature (and effectively making the concept of nature come into being). Leaders in the first millennium in these areas replicated God's reasoning and crafted and justified policies from an increasingly anthropocentric perspective. The biocentric foundation of any *sumak kawsay*–type practices—which rely on nonhierarchical, multiple-path communication among all the realms in ecology (Itzamná's cosmic community)—could not survive this shift in those places in the world.

When monotheism set humans on a level above the other realms of the cosmic community, another important consequence in the ecological context followed. It created stark ontological separation—both between humans and the other realms with which they constantly exchange and between the human individual (Self) and the other humans around her. Both of these changes were based on an emerging logic of binary opposition: human/nonhuman (Nature); and Me (Self)/not Me. This logic of binary opposition completely repudiates what Itzamná calls the holistic and cyclic logic underlying Andean notions of *sumak kawsay* (282). These oppositional (and ontological) binaries do not have any place in Andean ways of understanding human relationships with the world around us (Cadena, *Earth Beings* 206) either in terms of "natural" or "religious" relationships (as the academy might separate them). *Utz k'aslemal* shares this disdain for clear ontological separation (Camey 11).

Ontology of Separation Incompatible with *Sumak Kawsay*

In the Age of Reason, science picked up and further intensified a similar ontology of separation. The primary objective of science is the accurate and objective description of the separate elements of the cosmos. It, too, relies on binary opposition thinking to create precisely delineable separation among different ontological beings who inhabit a shared environment. By contrast, an important similarity common to both concepts before us—*sumak kawsay* and *utz k'aslemal*—is an insistence on the underlying interconnectedness of all things to the extent that they cannot be violently separated ontologically—even conceptually to a certain extent—despite the analytical advantages such a definitive separation has brought in the evolution of Western scientific knowledge. Cumes summarizes that aspect of utz k'aslemal this way: "Todo está interconectado, interrelacionado, es complementario e interdependiente, de modo que el deterioro de algo desencadena la descomposición de todo" (8).

Early in her career, Barbara Tedlock called these fuzzy divisions in Mesoamerican Indigenous cosmovisions "dialectical or complementary dualism" (44). In the Andean region, however, Oviedo categorically rejects the term "dialectical" in this context because, in its Western use, the oppositions cannot continue to coexist but must be resolved (19–22). In Indigenous thought, complementary oppositions cannot ever be separated (into thesis and antithesis, for example) because they bleed over into each other ontologically. Nature does not make sense as a concept for this same reason. Ultimately, these Indigenous ecologies do not divide between what is and is not nature, which would be necessary for the concept to make any sense; if everything that exists is part of nature, then the term has no meaning.[6]

Itzamná explains the radical ontological difference of this non-nature: "In Andean philosophy, separate substances don't exist; neither do absolute ontologies" (283). Further, "todos los opuestos se encuentran y coexisten en un permanente proceso de complementariedad que tiende siempre hacia el equilibrio." I have called this feature in K'iche' thinking a diffused ontology (*Reading* 169) and this pervasive interrelatedness denies Western ontological separation. We must recognize it as key in the realization of living in fullness.

Whose Indigeneity? Who Is Indigenous?

It is important to acknowledge that there are many different ways of being Indigenous in the world and my privileging the views of committed activists like Itzamná and Oviedo risks essentializing Indigeneity. Many Indigenous people have adopted their way of being "Indigenous" to the particular realities of the many different places to which they have relocated. Nonetheless, their different perspectives must not be marginalized as not Indigenous enough, even though the process of constitutionalization tends to do just that in Western legal terms. For example, "The term 'original people' [in the Bolivian Constitution] affirms and recognizes but at the same time obscures and excludes the large majority of the Aymara- and Qhichwa-speaking population of the subtropics, the mining centers, the cities, and the indigenous commercial networks of the internal and black markets" (Rivera Cusicanqui 54).

Their Indigeneity, so to speak, has inevitably changed from when they lived in their places "of origin." But, to ignore these emerging, complicated—while certainly still Indigenous—subjectivities that respond to their new environments (among a myriad of other shifting factors around them) is dangerously naïve and perpetuates coloniality. Trying to home in on "the Indigenous" in this way "denies the contemporaneity of these populations and excludes them from the struggles of modernity . . . ensnaring them in indigenist stereotypes of the noble savage and as guardians of nature[, which] refers us to a past imagined as quiet, static, and archaic" (53).[7] No singular Indigeneity has ever remained stable and unchanging as its people have come into contact with other cultures and places, whether that contact was with other Indigenous cultures or with Western cultures, whether in pre- or post-Contact times.

What is more, many of the people who make up the thousands of Indigenous cultures in the Americas behave according to fundamental aspects of a development paradigm themselves. As Itzamná puts it: "La gran mayoría de indígenas articulados en los cerca de 5 mil pueblos en el planeta estamos habitados por el antropocentrismo, por tanto denominamos y dominamos a la Madre Tierra como naturaleza (cosa inerte, sin conciencia), y la maltratamos como cualquier cristiano, musulmán o judío que tiene a su Creador en lejano cielo y concibe a la materia como cárcel y enemigo del sublime espíritu" (294). It is undeniable that millions of Indigenous people are pursuing their daily lives in many ways that align with the principles of modernity. No doubt, most Indigenous people I know in Guatemala would be, if forced to choose, de facto pro-development and will say that a primary goal of theirs is that their children have more (using standard development measures) than they did or do. The reasons for these "conversions" are complicated (and beyond my scope), but Itzamná singles out education, religious indoctrination, and mass media disinformation (294). These major tools that build cultural hegemony significantly complicate the task of preserving meaningful elements of Indigenous ecologies in the translation of *sumak kawsay* and of leaving out the distorting Western principles that threaten to colonize our understanding.[8]

Nonetheless, Peruvian Quechua poet Hugo Carrillo Cavero concludes positively that, in spite of centuries of colonization that "supuso la imposición cultural, relegando el idioma y el conjunto de valores, creencias y costumbres tradicionales; en una palabra, el sistema de vida andino, a algo que debía ser erradicado de raíz, [...] el mundo andino supo salvaguardar su idioma y gran parte de su forma de entender la vida, que hoy emerge con frescura intacta después de siglos de opresión" (305). Although there are many ways of being Indigenous in the world, we have a tool in the poetics of Indigenous languages that lets us glimpse key elements of how specific practices in the world resonated in cultures in previous eras. The survival of Indigenous languages in the Andes was crucial. Now, can *sumak kawsay*, in fact "emerge with freshness intact after centuries of oppression" even through the perils of translation?

Decolonial Translation: ~~Nature~~

The key to any relevant notions of *sumak kawsay* and *utz k'aslemal* being able to "emerge with freshness after centuries of oppression" to bring to bear on the current ecological crisis—despite all the complications I have identified—comes down to decolonial translation. Many terms that make explaining difficult concepts more expedient in English and Spanish also introduce hidden aspects of colonial logic into the emerging idea in the receiving languages. As Linda Tuhiwai Smith points out, even those scholars who speak Indigenous languages as first languages can unconsciously introduce colonial logic in translation because they are so necessarily immersed in the default language and logic of the academy (2). As Carrillo puts it, all translation has in some ways been "opacada por el ruido y los deseos estridentes de la modernidad" (294) because the "white noise" is hidden in the logic of the terms routinely used in translation.

The term that best illustrates this problem of translation in the work of almost everyone writing on the *buen vivir* complex is the Spanish "naturaleza" or the English "nature." A few writers—Beling and Vanhulst, for example—dedicate some time to the complications of using a term like "nature" to describe *sumak kawsay*, but they do not go far enough. Most continue to use this complicating term after some critical handling, as though something called "nature" actually existed in the world. Certainly nothing like "nature" has any place in *utz k'aslemal*. Nature is a Western-derived concept that begins to take central importance as a cultural way of understanding the world that grows directly out of the rise of monotheism and later the Scientific Revolution, traced here through Oviedo and Itzamná.[9] Nature could come into being only when God was conceptually removed from the material world and became an abstract ontological entity, hierarchically superior to everything in the world. The subsequent hierarchical split between the second two terms in the God/humans/nature triad that completes the birth of nature happened when the Judeo-Christian God created humans in his image (which showed his preference for humans over all other things in the world), imbued them with souls, and gave Adam the authority to name all the things in nature.

In the following centuries, the Age of Reason in Europe may have expelled God from the triad, but it solidified the concept of nature because it kept humans separate from—and superior to—nature due to their rationality (rather than their likeness to God and possession of souls). The intense classification processes of science took this concept even further from the ontological inseparableness underlying *sumak kawsay*. Taken together, these historical trajectories have constructed nature by drawing clean ontological separations between different beings, which directly contradicts the notion underlying *sumak kawsay* and *utz k'aslemal*.

Sociologists have used the related Quechua concept *ayllu* to refer to the traditional social unit of Andean life. However, *ayllu*, too, incorporates much more than its human participants. According to Marisol de la Cadena, *ayllu* is not a collection of individual entities. Entities simply do not exist outside of the relationships with all the other realms around them in a mutually constituting relationship (*Earth Beings* 101–4). By contrast, it is clear that the concept of nature needs discrete prior entities to come into being in a way that is incompatible with *ayllu*.

This implicit hierarchy and stark separation of the Western intellectual trajectory goes loudly unspoken in any use of the term "nature"/"naturaleza." Yet Oviedo goes on repeating "naturaleza" in explaining the various relationships that *sumak kawsay* handles. Unlike

Oviedo, Itzamná seems to make a significant and consistent effort not to resort to "naturaleza." At one point he specifically—though parenthetically—defines "naturaleza" as "(cosa inerte, sin conciencia)" (294) to signal the problem with the term in the context of sumak kawsay.

People trained or working in the Western academy either tend to assume a kind of equivalence or simply resort to using "naturaleza" for reasons of expediency in certain contexts. For example, even Ulises Zevallos-Aguilar, whose work on Andean poets is decidedly decolonial, describes a regional variant of *sumak kawsay* (*allin kawsay*) as a system in which "los seres humanos deben vivir en equilibrio con la naturaleza (flora, fauna, tierra). Reconocen que son huéspedes de ella" (330). Although he parenthetically substitutes "flora, fauna, tierra" to describe *allin kawsay*, positioning humans as guests of something called "naturaleza" inadvertently introduces too many of the assumptions I outline here and ultimately Westernizes modern readers' understanding of *allin kawsay*. Others scholars include "nature" much more carelessly and frequently. For example, Acosta's prolific and important writing on the subject of *sumak kawsay* repeatedly and uncritically relies on the concept of naturaleza.

In short, the concept of nature inherently introduces three elements that directly contradict *sumak kawsay*: an absolute ontological separation, a human-centered ordering, and a permanent hierarchy among the realms. However, this is not to say that a dialogue between these contrasting positions cannot happen. Juan G. Sánchez Martínez lays that out as the primary challenge before us: "Hoy, el desafío es facilitar un diálogo intercultural entre mentalidades opuestas" (396). Beling and Vanhulst insist that what *sumak kawsay* actually is today "arises out of a combination of (1) the ethical principles of ancient Andean-Amazonian cultures, (2) the contributions of contemporary critical intellectuals, and (3) from an incipient assimilation of both these sources by the political sphere" (31). For them, this combination not only is inevitable but also should be accepted pragmatically. "Unless [*Sumak Kawsay*] is to remain confined to anti-modern islets, it necessarily requires undergoing a dialectical process of transformation whereby it is rendered amenable to dialogue with modern discourses—that is, discourses built on modern cognitive/cultural categories. The individual human subject, for example, is a non-entity in the Quichua [*sic*] worldview, which does not conceive of the idea of 'being' other than in relational terms. It seems safe to assume that this aspect of *Sumak Kawsay* could never permeate modern societies" (34).

But Beling and Vanhulst pick up the key Aymara principle of *ch'ixi* that could signal a way forward. Under *ch'ixi*, "two binary opponents can constructively engage with each other to yield a higher instance, a space of mediation where tensions can be fully developed (rather than melted into some form of unity or homogeneity). The result is thus not a synthesis, but a restless 'cultural magma,' an incandescent breeding ground for cultural creativity" (Beling and Vanhulst 34).

I agree that this space in Andean thought—where a contrasting idea can exist alongside its negation without either one defeating the other—describes a similar characteristic in K'iche' that I have called "a poetics of the uncertain" (Cartography 26–27). But where does this leave us in terms of nature and *sumak kawsay/utz k'aslemal*? Does it mean that we have to allow nature—its inherent hierarchies and its ruthless desubjectivization of the cosmic community—to dictate the parameters and shades of these Indigenous concepts?

I do not think so at all. Critical and decolonial translation practices must carefully screen how Indigenous terms are represented in the receiving languages; only then can that coexistence in tension happen. The first step is as simple as a staunch refusal to use the words "nature"/"naturaleza" as translated equivalents.

Put simply, when we fail to push back on the concept of nature, Indigenous epistemologies are left on the doorstep while detached concepts are ushered into the mainstream and appropriated. In my research, I have singled out the inclusion of nature in the associated literature as the most invasive in terms of undermining alternative Indigenous ecologies in translation to the mainstream.[10] Now, I want to turn back to Guatemala—to *utz k'aslemal* and to Ak'abal's poem—to show a specific example of how translation can create this problem.

Where Is Nature Hiding in Translation in "Kotz'i'j?"

Ak'abal's poem served initially to present the aspect of interrealm communication in *utz k'aslemal* from a K'iche' poet's point of view. Now that we have shored up our understanding of the related *buen vivir* concepts throughout the Andes, we can apply the lessons learned there about the ensuing complications of translation to our close reading of this poem and then zoom back out to political applications in Guatemala. How might translation of specific words and ideas in the poem occlude underlying K'iche' epistemologies in the transfer to the discipline of Environmental Humanities? After all, issues of translation from Indigenous languages become exponentially more fraught in disciplines that do not specialize in critical issues of language. Mixing in culturally derived concepts like nature means that the ways other cultures construct (often imperceptibly) the world tumble through those cracks and fail to shape the world correspondingly in translation.

Neither translation of "Kotz'i'j" specifically includes the word "nature" or "naturaleza," but both translations rely on key elements that subtly encourage readers to assume equivalence in that regard. Two specific differences in poetics show how Indigenous ways of thinking about human relations with other realms in our ecosystems are occluded by basic assumptions readers associate with nature, even when the word "nature" itself doesn't appear.

The pairing that gives "Kotz'i'j" its fundamental poetic balance in the Spanish and English translations is deceiving. In translation, this pair of phrases (in lines 4 and 7) appears as an oppositional binary that seems to structure the poem on a corresponding opposition in nature. The English and Spanish translations counter line 4's "por dentro"/"on the inside" with line 7's "acá afuera"/"out here" to provide the poem's culturally enlightening surprise punch. It inverts the value of the visible beauty of nature to human eyes "out here" and replaces it with the dark, colorless, but nutrient-providing and crucial elements of underground ecology "on the inside" that do not get photographed or eulogized.

However, two important elements of the poetics (and resulting worldview) of the original K'iche' slip out in both of these translations, and these omissions impact the resulting way of thinking about our relationship with ecology. First, in the original K'iche', the comparison is not strictly oppositional; line 4 gives us *upam*—literally "its [the earth's] stomach"—and line 7 balances that with *uwachulew*—literally "its face, the earth." Stomach and face are certainly distinct parts of the body, but their differences are not purely oppositional like the abstract binary pairing in/out that the Spanish and English translations substitute for this pair. This abstract in/out binary reflects the fundamental binary implicit in both Christian and liberal/humanist orderings of the world I trace in this essay that divide the human world (as either "chosen" or rational, respectively) and the rest of the physical world into a neat binary. The in/out abstract binaries of these translations reinforce the resulting Western idea of nature as a fundamental part of the environment through which humans move, but of which they are not a part.

As I have shown, this Western notion of nature—inherently based on a clear human/nonhuman binary separation—does not exist, either in the world or in traditional Indigenous ecologies. K'iche' ecologies imagine/construct the sum total of the relationships among all the realms of ecosystems very differently as a basis for cosmovision. Replacing the earth's "stomach" and "its face" with an abstract in/out poetics subtly implies that both Ak'abal's poem and the cosmovision it reflects, in fact, fall in line with Western notions of a binary-based nature.

While the poetics of Ak'abal's "Kotz'i'j" also balances around a comparison of difference, in the K'iche' "its stomach" versus "its face" is complementary in that, for example, the face passes food to the stomach. That difference does not ground on a binary oppositional as "in here" versus "out there" does. Inserting such an oppositional binary in translation and ignoring the complementary part of the relationship between its "face" and "stomach" functionally performs epistemicide and allows Western students, academics, and politicians to feel like they are including Indigenous visions of the world. Actually, the imported binary fundamentally distorts the character of that ontological vision of the elements in the world around us.[11]

But the complication in the translation of Kotz'i'j goes beyond the oppositional binary character it imports and the erasure of the complementary and fuzzy boundaries between realms in Indigenous thought it ignores. Replacing these two concrete body parts with an abstract binary opposition also erases the body of the earth that grounds so many Indigenous characterizations of the world in all kinds of oral and written texts (like *Popol Wuj*).[12]

This tendency in K'iche' and other Maya poetics—to talk about the Earth as a body—fundamentally reflects *utz k'aslemal* because it shapes a real kinship between humans and the earth and deeply affects our engagement with the other realms of the world. If the body of the world has the characteristics of the human bodies we suffer in so acutely, our relationships to it are framed by this kinship of continual loss and suffering in the process of renewal and growth. Amputating the specific body parts of the world in Ak'abal's K'iche' ignores a basic ecological ordering principle in it that should effectively undercut traditional Western understanding of nature. When Indigenous ideas come across to the mainstream, whether in the academy or in other institutions, they must not be dissolved piecemeal within the universal paradigm that the West imagines—if they are, epistemicide occurs.

But the need for decolonial translation goes beyond poetry in Guatemala, too; the decidedly political leap that we saw in the Andean nations is underway here now, too. *Utz k'aslemal* is currently being bandied about in the CODECA (Comité de Desarrollo Campesino) protest movements that are demanding a thorough revision of the still virulently colonial Guatemala Constitution. However, given that the "D" in CODECA stands for "desarrollo" (development), I remain skeptical that the translation of *utz k'aslemal* into the mainstream can retain those crucial elements laid out here any more than it has in the Andes. My close K'iche' friend and frequent collaborator Abraham García Hernández is more optimistic than I am. He is certain that *utz k'aslemal* can introduce alternative ecological thinking into political reality in Guatemala, an alternative ecology that did not emerge in public discourse as a result of the sterile—and peripheral, it turns out—legal documents produced in the peace process in 1995–1996 (Acuerdo sobre identidad y derechos de los pueblos indígenas, or AIDPI, and the Peace Accords, of which AIDPI forms a part) that had promised to include Indigenous traditional practice meaningfully in describing the fundamentally plurinational character of Guatemala.

However, the Andean comparative case above does not bode well. The Aymara intellectual Pedro Portugal Mollinedo has called the whole notion of *suma qamaña* as it has emerged in Bolivian national rhetoric "poppycock and wasted time." In 2014, Beling and Vanhulst concluded, "Among scholars concerned with BV, there is large consensus about the fact that Ecuador and Bolivia, the breeding grounds of the Buen vivir discourse, increasingly resemble textbook illustrations of neoextractive economic agendas [and] are currently rather following a pathway of economic development that reinforces well-worn (neo)extractivist practices (mainly oil exploitation but also large-scale mining)" (36). Their overall conclusion is less negative in terms of the wider effects of the introduction of *sumak kawsay* into mainstream thinking and debate. "Buen vivir has begun to gain resonance on a global scale and to influence various groups and social movements that are looking for viable alternatives to the discourse of development based on economic rationality and the Modern-European ideal of progress" (36). Perhaps there is hope that *utz k'aslemal* can further this momentum in its political application in Guatemala in the near future. However, as the traditional academic custodians of Indigenous literatures, we have an important role in translating and reading Indigenous literature in ways that break the grip of colonial logic and introduce whole Indigenous ecologies instead of just catchy phrases into political and interdisciplinary applications.

Notes

1. In June 2022, I spoke with a group of practicing Kaqchikel *ajq'iija* (daykeepers) at the Oxlajuj Aj conference in Sacatepequez, Guatemala, who debated among themselves whether the specific name "utz k'aslemal," now used to refer to this set of practices, was actually a late and comprehensive adoption in Guatemalan Mayan languages that capitalized on the wider dissemination of the *buen vivir* names in the Andean languages (addressed in due course). This is a distinct possibility since the first published mention (precisely as "utz k'aslemal") I can find in Guatemala only dates from 1999, although the variant phrase "utzilaj kaslem" appears once in Ximenez's eighteenth-century copy of the sixteenth-century alphabetic Popol Wuj. However, these Kaqchikel *ajq'iija* are adamant that the pervasive set of practices we are talking about, to which we now refer to by *utz k'aslemal*, has

fundamentally centered different Maya groups' participation in/with the cosmos for many multiple generations.

2. Some very important exceptions to this traditional bent in anthropology and sociology have emerged in the past few decades. See, e.g., Eduardo Viveiros de Castro (e.g., *Metafísicas caníbales*), Marisol de la Cadena (e.g., *Earth Beings*), and Boaventura de Sousa Santos (e.g., *Epistemologies of the South*). I am finding these contributions, which all center on decolonial understanding of radically different ontologies, immensely valuable in this line of inquiry. My related book project on *utz k'aslemal* gives me the space to engage their profound contributions extensively.

3. In 1996 Dennis Tedlock was the first to publish about the absence of a word in K'iche' that correlates to "nature" (222).

4. Aníbal Quijano provides the most complete summary of the many related concepts that go by different names in different languages in the Andean world (2014, 847).

5. While spelled "Pachamama" in some cultures, in the Ecuadorian constitution it is rendered as two distinct terms.

6. Again, this is why there is no word in K'iche' that translates to "nature."

7. See Waldmüller (19–20) for how problems of translation directly relate to the wider problems of essentializing Indigenous knowledge that have persistently challenged anthropological treatments of "lo andino" from within the *indianismo/indigenismo* movements.

8. For a complete analysis of the "developmentalization" of Indigenous people in Guatemala, see Nicholas Copeland.

9. Josef Estermann traces the early Greek roots of the idea of nature/naturaleza but argues that it is only in the context of monotheism that the concept really consolidates as we know it today (187–188).

10. I more thoroughly identify the colonial roots of "nature" in the context of the Indigenous *nawal* in chapter 5 of my *Reading Popol Wuj*. Of course, radical Western philosophers and ecocritics, like Isabelle Stengers, Donna Haraway, and Timothy Morton, have traced the Western origins of the construction/enactment of "nature." John Law and Marianne Lien's "Denaturalizing Nature" looks carefully at the constructed oppositional binary at the heart of the concept.

11. Identifying issues of translation to Spanish in Ak'abal's poetry is delicate because Ak'abal—like most Indigenous authors—often translated his own poems to Spanish out of necessity. This self-translation practice introduces several complications and conflicting agencies to consider, which Tiffany Creegan-Miller traces in detail, employing Arturo Arias's useful notion of "transcreation" (106–108).

12. For example, the cosmology of *Popol Wuj*—the "oldest book in the Americas"—builds its description of the emergence of the earth on an array of body-part words, including the exact two terms that Ak'abal uses here (*upam* and *uwachulew*). For a review of the broader resonance of the earth as body in Mesoamerican cultures, see my *Reading Popol Wuj* (79–90).

Works Cited

Acosta, Alberto. "Los buenos convivires: Filosofías sin filósofos, prácticas sin teorías." *Estudios Críticos Del Desarrollo*, vol. 7, no. 12 (2017), pp. 153–192.

Ak'abal, Humberto. "Kotz'i'j." *Humberto Ak'abal: K'iche' (Mayan) Poet*. 2015. Web. Accessed on 24 September 2021.

Ávila Romero, Luis Enrique. *Alternativas al colapso socioambiental desde América Latina*. Bielefeld UP, 2021.

Beling, Adrian, and Julien Vanhulst. "Buen Vivir: New Wine in Old Wineskins?" In *Alternautas: (Re) Searching Development: The Abya Yala Chapter*. Vol. 1. December 2014. Accessed on 14 June 2021. http://www.alternautas.net/publications-1/2016/2/18/2014-vol-1-issue-1.

Cadena, Marisol de la. *Earth Beings: Ecologies of Practice across Andean Worlds*. Duke UP, 2015.

———. "Uncommoning Nature: Stories from the Anthropo-Not-Seen." In *Anthropos and the Material*. Edited by Penny Harvey, Christian Krohn-Hansen, and Knut G. Nustad. Duke UP, 2019, pp. 35–38.

Camey Huz, Licerio. *El buen vivir y la defensa del territorio en pueblos indígenas de Guatemala*. FLACSO Guatemala, 2014.

Carrillo Cavero, Hugo. "Trenzando cantos: Las dificultades del diálogo intercultural." In *Muyurina y el presente profundo: Poéticas andino-amazónicas*. Edited by Juan Sánchez Martínez and Freddy Roncalla. Hawansuyo-Pacarina, 2019, pp. 305–328.

Copeland, Nicholas. *The Democracy Development Machine: Neoliberalism, Radical Pessimism, and Authoritarian Populism in Mayan Guatemala*. Cornell UP, 2020.

Cumes, Aura. "Prologo" in *El UtzlliiJ K'aslemal El Raxnaqull K'aslemal "EI Buen Vivir" de los Pueblos de Guatemala*. Confluencia Nuevo Baktun, 2014.

de Sousa Santos, Boaventura. *Epistemologies of the South: Justice against Epistemicide*. Paradigm, 2014.

Estermann, Josef. *Filosofía Andina: Sabiduría indígena para un mundo nuevo*. ISEAT, 2006.

Henne, Nathan C. "A Cartography of the Uncertain: The Maya Textual Exile." *Cartographies of Exile: A New Spatial Literacy*. Edited by Karen Elizabeth Bishop. Routledge, 2016, pp 25–43.

———. *Reading Popol Wuj: A Decolonial Guide*. U of Arizona P, 2020.

Hidalgo-Capitán, Luis, and Ana Patricia Cubillo-Guevara. "Seis debates abiertos sobre el *sumak kawsay*." *Íconos: Revista de Ciencias Sociales*, no. 48, 2014, pp. 25–40.

Huanacuni Mamani, Fernando. *Buen Vivir/Vivir Bien: Filosofía, políticas, estrategias, y experiencias regionales andinas*. Coordinadora Andina de Organizaciones Indígenas, 2010.

Itzamná, Ollantay. "Sumaq Kawsay (Buen Vivir), un estilo de vida subyacente en el mundo." *Muyurina y el presente profundo: Poeticas andino-amazónicas*. Edited by Juan Sánchez Martínez and Freddy Roncalla. Hawansuyo-Pacarina, 2019, pp. 281–303.

Law, John, and Marianne Lien. "Denaturalizing Nature." In *A World of Many Worlds*. Edited by Marisol de la Cadena and Mario Blaser. Duke UP, 2018, pp. 131–171.

Miller, Tiffany D. Creegan. *The Maya Art of Speaking Writing: Remediating Indigenous Orality in the Digital Age*. U of Arizona P, 2022.

Oviedo Freire, Atawallpa. *Buen Vivir (Sumak Kawsay): "Tercer Estado", alter-nativa al capitalismo y al socialismo*. Sumak Editores, 2017.

Portugal Mollinedo, Pedro. "Suma Qamaña, Poppycock, and Wasted Time." In *Latin American and Caribbean Ethnic Studies*, vol. 12, no. 2, 2017, pp. 177–187.

Quijano, Anibal. "'Bien vivir:' entre el "desarrollo" y la des/colonialidad del poder." *Cuestiones y horizontes: De la dependencia histórico-estructural a la colonialidad/descolonialidad del poder*. CLACSO, 2014, pp. 847–859.

Rivera Cusicanqui, S. *Ch'ixinakax Utxiwa: On Practices and Discourses of Decolonisation*. Polity, 2020.

Sánchez Martínez, Juan G. "Un tinkuy entre el tiempo y el espacio: Mni wiconi (el agua es vida)". *Muyurina y el presente profundo: Poeticas andino-amazónicas*. Edited by Juan Sánchez Martínez, and Freddy Roncalla. Hawansuyo-Pacarina, 2019, pp. 389–401.

Solón, Pablo. "Vivir Bien: Old Cosmovisions and New Paradigms" *Great Transition Initiative* (February 2018). greattransition.org/publication/vivir-bien. Accessed 7 July 2023.

Tedlock, Barbara. *Time and the Highland Maya*. Rev. ed., U of New Mexico P, 1992.

Tedlock, Dennis. *Popol Vuh: The Definitive Edition of the Mayan Book of the Dawn of Life and the Glories of Gods and Kings*. Touchstone, 1996.

Tovar, Marcela, and Miriam Chavajay. *Más allá de la Costumbre: Cosmos, orden y equilibrio: El derecho del pueblo Maya de Guatemala*. SAQB'ICHIL-COPMAGUA, 2000.

Tuhiwai Smith, Linda. *Decolonizing Methodologies: Research and Indigenous Peoples*. 2nd ed. Otago UP, 2012.

Viveiros de Castro, Eduardo. *Metafísicas caníbales: Líneas de antropología postestructural.* Translated by Stella Mastrangelo. Katz Editores, 2010.

Waldmüller, Johannes. "Human Rights Indicators as 'Development 2.0'?" *Alternautas: (Re)Searching Development: The Abya Yala Chapter. Vol.1, Issue 1, pp 76-87.* December 2014. www.alternautas.net/publications-1/2016/2/18/2014-vol-1-issue-1. Accessed 7 July 2023.

Zevallos-Aguilar, Ulises Juan. "Poesía quechua peruana última y buen vivir (2010–2015)." *Muyurina y el presente profundo: Poéticas andino-amazónicas.* Edited by Juan Sánchez Martínez and Freddy Roncalla. Hawansuyo-Pacarina, 2019, pp. 329–342.

CHAPTER 7

Castellanización y mantenimiento de la diferencia radical en la poesía y canto quechuas

Ulises Juan Zevallos-Aguilar
Ohio State University

La enseñanza de la producción cultural de los pueblos indígenas de Abiayala se está convirtiendo en una necesidad en las universidades norteamericanas. A varios departamentos de español se les ha dado la responsabilidad de dar cuenta de su diversidad cultural y lingüística. En sus reformas curriculares han ido de la inclusión de temas amerindios en cursos panorámicos, a la creación de cursos enfocados en sus literaturas y artes plásticas y visuales. Este capítulo presenta un caso de enseñanza de poesía quechua peruana (escrita y cantada) en el departamento de español de la Ohio State University con el fin de lograr tres objetivos: primero, comprender la diversidad de la cultura latinoamericana expresada en el uso del español y varias lenguas amerindias con sus propias variaciones y registros lingüísticos; segundo, hacer ver la castellanización del quechua en la historia; y, por último, mostrar el mantenimiento de la diferencia radical de las culturas indígenas expresadas en sus idiomas. En otros términos, este ensayo, desde la perspectiva de un profesor de aula, demuestra cómo la enseñanza de poesía y canción en quechua ayuda a los estudiantes a entender la existencia, por un lado, de una cultura quechua que interactúa y se contamina con el español mutuamente desde el siglo XVI. Por otro lado, los estudiantes aprenden que la cultura quechua contemporánea todavía mantiene una diferencia radical. Su ontología, epistemología y cosmología, son intraducibles lingüísticamente por la existencia de diferencias sintácticas, fonéticas, fonológicas y semánticas entre el quechua y el español, pero son inteligibles a través de la traducción cultural.

Challwaschallay (1970) del Conjunto Condemayta: Diferencia radical e intraducibilidad lingüística

En clase presento tanto la poesía como el canto en quechua. Comienzo con el huayno, el mayor género musical que se produce y escucha en el Perú. "Challwaschallay" (Mi amorcito) es un huayno tan antiguo que no se sabe a ciencia cierta quién es su autor. Está escrito en quechua cuzqueño rural de la familia del quechua II.[1] Tiene una calidad poética muy superior a la de huaynos contemporáneos. En sus letras se cuenta la historia de un amor no correspondido. Una amante hace una búsqueda incesante de su amado que no se da cuenta de ser objeto de amor o no quiere iniciar la relación amorosa. Más bien está buscando a otra mujer. Para expresar estos sentimientos se utiliza la metáfora amorosa quechua del pez (*challwa*).

Este huayno es uno de los más emblemáticos del repertorio del Conjunto Condemayta. Este grupo musical integrado por Saturnino Pulla Jiménez y María Tintaya Rayo fue creado en 1970 en la ciudad del Cuzco. Sus seguidores consideran que el grupo es practicante del huayno tradicional. A pesar de que "Challwaschallay" no es de su propia creación, sus audiencias, incluidos varios músicos, creen que fue compuesta por el grupo de Pulla Jiménez. El único dato verificable es que se trata de un huayno cusqueño de la provincia de Quispicanchis. Probablemente fue creado tomando como base un *harawi* precolombino. La canción destaca porque mantiene la metáfora amorosa "challwaschallay". Se la ha traducido al español como "mi amorcito". Pero, su estudio nos introduce a la especificidad de la cultura quechua. Contrasta con metáforas castellanas o inglesas amorosas y coincide con lenguas nórdicas.[2] Para los aymaras y quechuas los peces tienen carácter sagrado y mítico. Gamaliel Churata en *El pez de oro* (1957) y Odi Gonzales en su poemario *Tunupa* (2002), cuando recrean mitos andinos sobre peces y sirenas, hacen visibles su ontología relacional entre seres humanos y seres acuáticos. La especificidad empieza en el carácter aglutinante del idioma quechua. En la metáfora "challwaschallay", para crear sentido a una raíz (*challwa*) se le añaden varios sufijos para crear densidad semántica. El sufijo *-cha* significa pequeño, querido. El sufijo *-llay* mío o mía con énfasis. En español se podría traducir como "miísimo" o "miísima". En suma, el sustantivo *challwa* tiene el significado de un amante muy querido, pero es inasible, escurridizo, resbaladizo, como el pez que se quiere atrapar con las manos desnudas. Al mismo tiempo, está significando el brillo, belleza y persistencia de un pez andino que nada contra la corriente en el río de la vida. En otro nivel de significación, este huayno gatilla la nostalgia por un mundo perdido. Por la introducción de la trucha y la contaminación ambiental producida por la actividad minera, muchas especies nativas de peces se han extinguido. Literalmente, hay muchos ríos y riachuelos muertos en los Andes por los relaves mineros.

Sin embargo, cuando se hace un análisis del lenguaje del huayno "Challwaschallay", se ve que también tiene muchos vocablos en quechuañol: *wiltarimuy*, viene de vuelta o volver; *gusturaqchus*, que deriva de gusto, gustar. Por último, este dialecto del quechua ha incorporado el sustantivo loma. Por cierto, el quechua tiene sus propios verbos que dan cuenta de las acciones y sustantivos referidos: *kutiy* es volver; gustar es *misk'ichikuy*; loma es *moqo*. En breve, en las letras de este huayno tradicional coexisten rasgos específicos de la cultura quechua y hay evidencia de su castellanización.

"Chachaschay" (1991) de Uchpa: Cambios del quechua en la historia.

Uchpa (ceniza) es una banda, en actividad desde 1991, que canta canciones en quechua con música de *rock* y *blues*. Fredy Ortiz, el cantante y compositor de la banda, es consciente de los procesos que llevaron a la creación de sus distintos tipos de canciones (Joo, "El quechua suena en rock"). "Chachaschay" es la pieza musical más vista y escuchada de la banda en conciertos y YouTube. Es la canción que los ha identificado como grupo. La incluyen en la mayoría de los programas de sus giras. Es una canción muy conocida de la familia de huaynos populares de los departamentos de Apurímac, Ayacucho y Huancavelica que han recreado. Ortiz ha señalado que la canción original es un "huayno de chacra" que la escuchó en Ocobamba, Apurímac, pueblo donde nació y vivió su primera infancia. Manifiesta que él ha sido un mero transcriptor de una canción cantada en quechua chanka que también pertenece a la familia del quechua II.

La denominación de "Chachaschay" como un "huayno de chacra" tiene por lo menos dos sentidos. Es un huayno que alegra y contrarresta el cansancio mientras los labradores quechuas están trabajando la tierra. Por tanto, es una pieza musical cantada por los sectores sociales más bajos de los pobladores andinos. Según la clasificación de las canciones en quechua de los hermanos Montoya, los huaynos de chacra equivalen a las canciones de "indios" que se diferencian de las canciones "señoriales" en varios niveles. En sus palabras "en el caso de los Indios [...] la improvisación es la norma. De un carnaval a otro, de un año a otro, la memoria frágil guarda un motivo que vuelve a ser tratado para encajar dentro de los límites impuestos por la melodía. Mujeres y hombres parten de un recuerdo y lo completan y lo enriquecen. Nada es fijo y definitivo" (*Urqukunapa Yawarnin*, 18). Las declaraciones de varios intérpretes de música andina confirman la aseveración de los hermanos Montoya cuando la reclaman como huayno de sus lugares de origen: pueblos de los departamentos de Ayacucho, Cusco y Huancavelica. Los cambios y las transformaciones de las canciones son evidentes.

Las diferentes versiones que se han podido encontrar del huayno en los archivos nos permite hacer un análisis diacrónico. Sin lugar a dudas, el huayno no es originario de Ocobamba, Apurímac. El primer registro de "Chachaschay" se encuentra en los *Huaynos del Cusco* (1981) de Gabriel y Gloria Escobar.[3] Según la información proporcionada por los antropólogos, la versión que consignaron en su recopilación pertenece al cantante Embajador de Quiquijana (Efraín Cuba).[4] El etnomusicólogo Josafat Roel Pineda fue el encargado de registrar la versión cantada por el músico cusqueño en 1957. Existe otra versión más tardía recogida por José María Arguedas en 1962 en Huancavelica. La transcripción de Roel Pineda la voy a estudiar para ver los cambios y las transformaciones que se han dado en la versión de Uchpa después de treinta y cuatro años.

En este tipo de estudio de "Chachaschay", lo primero que salta a la vista son las distintas representaciones ortográficas del quechua. Continúa un debate irresuelto entre un grupo de profesores de quechua y estudiosos académicos de la lengua con ideologías lingüísticas diferentes. Para los primeros el quechua tiene las cinco vocales del castellano y cierto número de consonantes. Para los segundos el quechua tiene solamente tres vocales y otro número de consonantes. En la transcripción de la versión del Embajador de Quiquijana se utilizan las cinco vocales del español y uso de consonantes que no están transcritas de manera correcta desde una perspectiva lingüística. La transcripción de Ortiz sigue los dictámenes de la ciencia del lenguaje. Escribe con tres vocales y utiliza los signos de la fonética internacional.

El tema de "Chachaschay" es clásico, en el sentido que atañe a los seres humanos de todas las épocas y latitudes. La versión del Embajador de Quiquijana trata de la confusión de amor y deseo en una relación heterosexual. En la canción un amante masculino quiere asegurar el amor e interés de su amada otorgando regalos. En esta canción el obsequio es un anillo de oro que demuestra la seriedad de sus intenciones. Por eso el amante pregunta si los padres de la amada ya saben de su existencia. Con este obsequio el amante también busca la aceptación de los padres de la mujer. Involucra a la familia en su relación amorosa. El valor material del anillo es evidencia de su solvencia económica y lo convierte en el yerno perfecto. En la siguiente estrofa la canción cambia de tema. El huayno recrea la ansiedad masculina. El amante próspero, a pesar de que está cumpliendo todo el protocolo amoroso, tiene sus dudas sobre la efectividad de los regalos para conseguir el amor de su amada. Su inseguridad la aminora con una concepción machista de la relación de pareja.[5] Declara que no le importa mucho el amor de esta mujer, sino que solo quiere satisfacer su deseo. Indirectamente, considera a su amada como pueblerina y simple. Añade que tiene a la mano mujeres más sofisticadas en las ciudades grandes de Arequipa y Lima. Al final de la canción asegura que su fuerza masculina va a permitir la posesión del cuerpo de la amada. Hace una comparación, típica del huayno popular, de su relación de pareja con una escena de caza de una ternera emprendida por un zorro. Cuando se la coteja con la versión de Uchpa los cambios son evidentes. Esta última tiene menos versos y es más repetitiva. Los versos se han reducido a menos de la mitad y se ha perdido parte del contenido que le daba más profundidad a la representación de una situación amorosa en la versión del Embajador de Quiquijana.

La vigencia de "Chachaschay" se debe también a su calidad poética. En esta pieza musical se encuentran los dispositivos propios del huayno tradicional en quechua. Bruce Mannheim (1986) y Jean Phillipe Husson (1993) coinciden en señalar que "los pares semánticos" o el "paralelismo semántico" es el dispositivo poético más importante de la poesía quechua. Mannheim apunta que "los huaynos son un tipo de danza, rítmicamente regulados y estróficamente organizados. Los textos de las canciones están frecuentemente estructurados en dobletes semánticos apareados. Dos líneas que podrían ser idénticas están unidas con la alternancia de las raíces de dos palabras semánticamente relacionadas" ("Popular song…", 60). Por su parte Husson declara "entre estos procedimientos que nos permiten hablar de arte poético, uno es de tal envergadura que aparece como la marca característica de la poesía quechua; se trata del efecto que denominamos paralelismo semántico, y que consiste en una serie de correspondencias, al nivel de sentido, entre palabras homólogas situadas en secuencias contiguas" ("La poesía quechua prehispánica", 65). En un lenguaje más accesible, Martin Lienhard apunta que el paralelismo semántico se logra con pares gramaticales y léxicos. En su artículo "La cosmología poética en los waynos quechuas tradicionales", ha señalado que "En los textos de los waynos, los paralelismos gramaticales producen una especie de macro-ritmo binario, basado a veces en la simple repetición de un sintagma poético (bis), pero más generalmente en la repetición, con variantes léxicas, de una estructura gramatical" (355). A manera de ejemplo, para ver cómo ocurren los paralelismos semánticos vamos a analizar los cuatro primeros versos de "Chachaschay" del Embajador de Quiquijana.

1 ¿Ñacu mamayki yacanña? cacascay	¿Sabe ya tu madre, muñequita
2 quri anillu qusqaata? Cacascay	del anillo de oro que te di?
3 ¿Ñacu taytayki yacanña cacascay	¿Sabe ya tu padre, muñequita,
4 quri anillu qurasqayta? Cacascay.	del anillo de oro que te puse?

En los cuatro primeros versos se repite la estructura gramatical y se cambian sustantivos y verbos para darle ritmo. Las correspondencias se dan entre el primer verso y el tercero, y el segundo y el cuarto. Entre el primer verso y el tercero el paralelismo semántico ocurre cuando se contrastan los sustantivos "mama" (madre) y "tayta" (padre). Los dos términos son opuestos y complementarios. Esto necesariamente tiene que ocurrir para incluir la concepción de género en la cultura quechua. Martin Lienhard ya lo ha señalado en el análisis de otra canción quechua. A diferencia de las culturas europeas, donde el plural de los progenitores siempre se masculiniza, en el caso de la cultura quechua los géneros de los padres tienen que aparecer. De otra parte, es una muestra de la concepción dual del mundo andino ("La cosmología poética..."). El paralelismo entre el segundo y cuarto verso ocurre en los verbos *qusqaata* (di) y *qurasqayta* (puse). Sus infinitivos son *qoy* (dar) y *churay* (poner). En este se utilizan parónimos que dan cuenta de acciones distintas.

En la versión de Uchpa desaparece *taytay* (padre) y el verbo *qurasqayta* (puse) cuando se eluden los versos tres y cuatro. Del mismo modo para completar el cuarteto se juntan los dos primeros versos de la segunda estrofa. Se tiene como resultado una estrofa de cuatro versos, en vez de dos estrofas con cuatro y tres versos respectivamente: Ñachu mamayki yachanña chachaschay / Quri anillu qusqayta chachaschay / Yachachun yachachun chachaschay / quri anillu qusqayta chachaschay (bis). De la misma manera, en la versión de Uchpa solamente se relata la acción de regalar, pero se eliminan las estrofas sobre la ansiedad masculina. Uchpa para completar las pérdidas de versos y estrofas repite la misma estrofa reemplazando "Chachaschay" con "Trebolchay".

También hay diferencias en el léxico de las dos versiones. Esto se puede explicar por la enunciación de la canción en dos dialectos compatibles del quechua de la región sur. La versión del Embajador de Quiquijana está en quechua cusqueño. La versión de Uchpa está en quechua apurimeño o chanka. En efecto, los léxicos de estas dos variedades del quechua sureño tienen varios préstamos lingüísticos del español, detalle que demuestra su carácter popular y postcolonial. En cuanto a los españolismos, en vez de *istrilla* de la versión del Embajador de Quiquijana se utiliza *lucero* en la versión de Uchpa. También comparten algunos españolismos como *anillu*. Sin embargo, es oportuno observar que el quechua tiene sus propias palabras. Estrella en quechua tiene dos palabras: *ch'aska* y *kkóyllur*,[6] mientras *anillu* es *siwi*. El tema que ha superado el paso del tiempo es el de los regalos para asegurar la continuación de la relación amorosa. No podía ser de otra manera. En un país que desde los años cincuenta ha sido afectado por diversas olas de modernización capitalista, la cosificación de la relación amorosa en la cultura quechua es un hecho consumado. En suma, ha ocurrido un empobrecimiento del contenido y vocabulario del huayno en cuarenta años. La cultura quechua se ha occidentalizado más.

“Vida vidascha” (2004) de Chaska Anka Ninawaman: Castellanización y constatación de varios registros del quechua.

“Vida vidascha” es un poema que pertenece al poemario bilingüe *Ch’askaschay: Poesía en quechua (runasimi)* (2004). La lengua materna de su autora es el quechua y aprendió el castellano en su alfabetización. Los poemas en quechua de *Ch’askaschay* están escritos en quechua popular urbano de la región del Cusco. Es una variación de la familia del quechua II. Las traducciones al castellano fueron hechas por la propia autora.

Anka Ninawaman ha tomado muchas decisiones en su traducción. Ella cree en la estrategia cultural de que para sobrevivir en un lugar hostil hay que cambiar. Pero la transformación no necesariamente conlleva a la desaparición de su primera lengua y cultura. Tampoco aboga por una cultura no contaminada de origen prehispánico. Acepta la abundancia de préstamos lingüísticos del castellano que se hace en el quechua popular urbano. Manifiesta su desazón con las posiciones puristas sobre el quechua que abogan por un quechua inca, puro sin préstamos lingüísticos. Aparte de la diglosia más conocida de español sobre el quechua y otras lenguas amerindias, ella cree que existe otra entre el quechua puro y los quechuas contaminados. Los propulsores del quechua inca, según Anka Ninawaman, quieren continuar la dominación de la mayoría de quechua hablantes y disfrutar de las pocas oportunidades que se les ha dado en general.[7] Por ejemplo, considera legítimo el uso del neologismo “vidascha” porque registra la experiencia urbana del migrante quechua y rechaza el término “Kawsay” que proponen los puristas. Del mismo modo, quechuiza los modismos del español como el de “pasar la vida”. Según Anka Ninawaman, “vidacha configura nuevas imágenes y nuevos códigos simbólicos, transmite no sólo la imagen del joven emigrante que pasa sufrimientos y tristezas en los espacios ciudadanos [*sic*], sino que transmite la actual vivencia de los quechuas que están siendo fuertemente atravesados por el sistema dominante étnico tanto en la ciudad como en la comunidad” (“La producción literaria”, 166). Su reflexión sobre la creación de neologismos la pone en práctica en su creación literaria. Su poema “Vida vidascha / Vida vidita” (166–167) está escrito con un vocabulario de quechuañol (“vidachay”, “vidascha” y “pasaq”), resultado de quinientos años de contacto lingüístico. El poema trata sobre la vida de los quechuas en el mundo contemporáneo que se caracteriza por seguir sufriendo pobreza y hambre. El quechuañol se puede observar a nivel gramático. En la creación del neologismo “vidascha”, la sustantivo en español, vida, ha añadido el sufijo del quechua *-cha* como marcador de cariño. Asimismo se ven cambios semánticos cuando traduce libremente el verbo “muchuy” como “sentir hambre”, aunque su significado en quechua es sufrir. Su propósito fue mostrar que para los quechuas migrantes a la ciudad, como ella, el mayor sufrimiento fue el hambre luego de escapar del escenario de una guerra interna. Los quechuas que eran capturados en el campo, durante el conflicto entre Sendero Luminoso y las fuerzas armadas peruanas entre 1980 y 1992, eran torturados antes de ser asesinados extrajudicialmente. Sin embargo, el yo poético ve con optimismo que seguirán avanzando en la vida. Aumenta un verso en su versión castellana para referirse al hecho de que los quechuas han sobrevivido el genocidio de la guerra interna de los años ochenta. Ellos fueron las principales víctimas de la estrategia de tierra arrasada del ejército y marina peruanos o las masacres de comunidades completas emprendidas por el ejército popular de Sendero Luminoso. En suma, la posición de Anka Ninawaman es aceptar los cambios lingüísticos y culturales ocurridos en su lengua y cultura, reconoce que están en una mala situación económica y social, y sin embargo, considera que pueden construir un futuro mejor.

Para terminar, en la enseñanza de los tres casos se ha visto diversas intensidades de españolización en variedades y registros del quechua. En el análisis del léxico se encuentran muchas palabras en vocablos del quechuañol y traducciones idiomáticas. La españolización voluntaria ha dado lugar al surgimiento de nuevas subjetividades (quechuas urbanos). Los estudiantes se enteran de que existen por lo menos dos ideologías lingüísticas sobre la castellanización. En los debates que tienen lugar sobre el quechua contemporáneo, los optimistas dicen que hay un enriquecimiento y los pesimistas (puristas) señalan su empobrecimiento y posible desaparición. Lo valioso es que estas polémicas nos llevan a ver dialectos y registros de quechuas rurales y urbanos. Por otra parte, los estudiantes aprenden que a pesar de la españolización creciente del quechua por la disglosia existente, la cultura quechua todavía mantiene su diferencia radical o especificidad (metáfora amorosa del pez y el uso de paralelismos semánticos) entendidos a través de la traducción cultural. Entonces, la enseñanza de poesía quechua en un departamento de español ayuda a entender la existencia de procesos culturales complejos donde las lenguas registran cambios que benefician o perjudican a los hablantes de diversas lenguas. La existencia de situaciones disglósicas, en las que intervienen diferencias sociales, económicas y políticas son las que llevan a concebir lenguas y culturas superiores e inferiores. Incluyo en el anexo las canciones completas que han sido estudiadas en este ensayo.

Notas

1. El quechua es una familia de lenguas con rasgos comunes. Los lingüistas las han clasificado en quechua I (quechua central), quechua II (quechua yungay, quechua norteño y quechua sureño)
2. No tengo conocimiento de que los hablantes de castellano e inglés comparen al ser amado con un pez. Las lenguas nórdicas sí poseen metáforas donde el pez representa al ser amado. En el danés es el arenque.
3. Esta versión adolece de varios problemas. La transcripción es bastante arbitraria. No utiliza un alfabeto estandarizado. En una transcripción más especializada, por ejemplo, las palabras mencionadas a continuación tendrían la siguiente escritura. cacasca por chachaschay (mi juguetito); ñacu, por ñachu (ya); quri, por qori (oro), qurasqayta, por churasqaita (poner, puesto); atuhpa, por atoqpa (del zorro); kacarinñacu, por cacharinñachu (ya no la suelta).
4. Efraín Cuba tuvo gran actividad en los años cincuenta y sesenta. Grabó muchos discos y participaba en los programas de los coliseos en Lima. Sus interpretaciones más recordadas son "Valicha" (huayno del Cusco) y "Chofercito de mala suerte" (huayno de Huancayo). Se caracterizaba por vestir y comportarse de manera extravagante. Era perfectamente bilingüe en castellano y quechua. Cantaba en ambas lenguas con el acompañamiento del Conjunto Corimarca de Tinta.
5. Quizás por este carácter machista no fue incluido en la antología de los hermanos Montoya a pesar de su popularidad. En la definición de los parámetros de su selección señalan que van a

excluir los huaynos cholos machistas: "Debemos dejar clara constancia para las lectoras y lectores que hemos excluido de esta antología un conjunto de canciones que descriptivamente se llaman en general 'cholas', profundamente machistas" (11). El significado de "Chachaschay" confirmaría su carácter machista. En castellano significa mi juguetito. Parece que es un antiquísimo del quechua. El *Diccionario kkechuwa-español* (1944) de Jorge A. Lira es el único que traduce "chácha" como "juguete". Aféresis de "achácha" (85). Cuando pregunté a varios hablantes de quechua no tenían una traducción del término. Cuando le preguntaron a Fredy Ortiz sobre el significado respondió que era un arbusto nativo de Apurímac.

6. Según Lira *ch'aska* se traduce como "Lucero, astro brillante, estrella lucera. Venus o planeta el Segundo del sistema solar. Divinidad que se veneraba en el templo del sol o Kkorikáncha" (167). *Kkóyllur* en castellano significa "Estrella; lucero, astro, planeta cuerpo celeste luminoso" (477). Es oportuno anotar que en la versión del Embajador de Quiquijana el uso del españolismo *istrilla* disminuye la poeticidad al referirse a la estrella en general y no al planeta Venus. En cambio, en la versión de Uchpa se la recupera con la palabra española lucero. Pero en ambos casos la pérdida del léxico quechua se evidencia.

7. Anka Ninawaman señala: "El idioma quechua ha sido asimilado por los blancos mestizos como un código simbólico de dominación. Se erigen en doctores y 'seudo eruditos' que se atribuyen hablar el verdadero idioma quechua de los incas, con lo cual terminan descalificando el idioma que utilizan los verdaderos quechuas de hoy en día. Se han autoidentificado con ser los verdaderos portadores del idioma quechua. Y hasta pretenden ser los descendientes de la panaca real inca. Consideran que el resto de la población habla el runa simi, o sea una lengua del pueblo, de la plebe. Se ha construido una supuesta identidad cuzqueña o incásica que en definitiva niega y desconoce a quechua hablantes de origen comunal y de origen urbano" ("La producción literaria", 164).

Obras citadas

Anka Ninawaman, Ch'aska Eugenia. *Poesía en quechua: Ch'askaschay*. Abya Yala, 2004.

———. "La producción literaria en el idioma quechua como una alternativa en el fortalecimiento de la identidad e interculturalidad". *Identidad lingüística de los pueblos indígenas de la región andina*. Edited by Ariruma Kowii and J. A. Fernández Silva, Universidad Andina Simón Bolívar y Abya-Yala and Instituto Ítalo-Latino Americano, 2005, pp. 153–77.

Churata, Gamaliel. *El pez de oro*. Cátedra, 2012.

Escobar, Gabriel, and Gloria Escobar, eds. *Huaynos del Cusco*. Editorial Garcilaso, 1981.

Gonzales, Odi. *Tunupa*. Ediciones el Santo Oficio, 2002.

Husson, Jean-Phillipe. "La poesía quechua prehispánica. Sus reglas, sus categorías, sus temas a través de los poemas transcritos por Waman Puma de Ayala". *Revista de Crítica Literaria Latinoamericana*, no. 37, 1993, pp. 63–85.

Joo, Gaby. "El quechua suena en rock". *Ideele* 146 (2002). Accedido diciembre del 2010. http://www.idl.org.pe/idlrev/revistas/146/pag39.htm

Lienhard, Martin. "La cosmología poética en los waynos quechuas tradicionales". *Cosmología y música en los Andes*. Edited by Max Peter Baumann, Vervuert Verlag and Iberoamericana, 1996, pp. 353–368.

Lira, Jorge A. *Diccionario kkechuwa-español*. Universidad Nacional de Tucumán, 1944.

Mannheim, Bruce. "Popular Song and Popular Grammar, Poetry and Metalenguage". *Word*, vol. 37, no. 1–2, 1986, pp. 45–75.

Montoya, Rodrigo, et al. *La sangre de los cerros. Antología de la poesía quechua que se canta en el Perú: Urqukunapa yawarnin*. Centro Peruano de Estudios Sociales, 1987.

Anexo

Vida vidascha de Chask'a Anka Ninawaman

Vida vidascha
Ay vida vidachay,
qanllas yachanki
nuqaq vidayta
wakcha vidayta,
pi wakchallas
man vida pasaq
mana muchuy yachaq,
wakcha vidallansis
allin Guerra pasaq

sólo tú sabes mi vida
la vida de los runas.
Qué runa no sabe pasar la vida,
qué pobre
no sabe pasar hambre,
sólo nuestra vida de runa
sabe pasar la guerra,
sólo nuestra vida de pobre
es de guerreros ch'askaschas

Challwaschallay del Grupo Condemayta

Mayun mayuntas purishani challwaschallay
manañan tariykiñachu challwaschallay
Astawansi yuyarini challwaschallay challwaschallay
sutiykita yuyarispa challwaschallay challwaschallay

kutirimuy wiltarimuy challwaschallay
killa qhawariq tunpallapis challwaschallay challwaschallay
pitishayki suyashayki challwaschallay
munasqaykin maskhashanki challwaschallay challwaschallay

¿gusturaqchus purishanki
gusturaqchus purishanki
mayun mayunta purichiwaspa
loman lomanta purichiwaspa?

Estoy caminando de río en río, mi amorcito
no logro encontrarte mi amorcito
te recuerdo con demasía mi amorcito
más aún recuerdo tu nombre mi amorcito

regresa, vuelve mi amorcito
aunque sea sólo para ver la luna mi amorcito, mi amorcito
te estoy esperando con ansias mi amorcito
estás buscando a quien amas mi amorcito, mi amorcito

Estás vagando por gusto
Estás vagando por gusto
me estás haciendo caminar de río en río
me estás haciendo caminar de loma en loma.

Si está interesado en conocer a los intérpretes, la música y la pronunciación de las letras puede ver el video en https://www.youtube.com/watch?v=JwHnXCBjrMU.

Chachaschay (1957) del Embajador de Quiquijana

¿Ñacu mamayki yacanña? cacascay	¿Sabe ya tu madre, muñequita
quri anillu qusqaata? Cacascay	del anillo de oro que te di?
¿Ñacu taytayki yacanña cacascay	¿Sabe ya tu padre, muñequita,
quri anillu qurasqayta? Cacascay.	del anillo de oro que te puse?
Yacacun yacacun cacascay	No importa que sepan, muñequita
Aswan allintan qusqayki, cacascay	te daré todavía otro mejor
Aswan mixurtan curasqayki, cacascay.	
¿Silupi istrilla faltancu? Cacascay	¿Acaso faltan estrellas en el cielo?
¿Nuqah munahniy faltancu? Cacascay	¿Acaso falta quién me quiera?
¿Silupi istrilla faltancu? Cacascay	¿Acaso en el cielo faltan las estrellas?
Nuqah munahniy bastanti.	¡Las que quiera son abundantes!
¿Silupi istrilla faltancu? Cacascay	¿Acaso hay estrellas en el cielo?
¿Nuqapah sunquyki kashancu? Cacascay	¿Será para mí tu corazón?
Kacumpas amapas, cacascay	Me quieras o no me quieras
nuqah munahniy faltancu, cacascay.	no faltará quien me quiera, ay.
Arkipapipas kashanmi, cacascay	Hay en Arequipa
Limacapipas kashanmi, cacascay	En Lima también,
Nuqah munahniy ñiñaca	niñas que me quieran
Nuqah waylluhniy niñaca.	niñas que me amen.
Imáyna atuhpa curincá	¿Cómo, qué cría de zorro será
Istrima callata mixuhun	comer terneritas solo quiere?
Huhtan hap'in	¡La coge
Kumpan	la tumba
Dalin	la suena,
P'atan	la muerde,
Kanin	destroza!
Manaca "Ñiñuca, atuhca" nihtinpas	
Manacha "niñucha, atuqcha" niktinpas)	¡Aunque le diga "señorcito"!
Kacarinñacu.	
Kacharinñachu	¡El zorro no la suelta!

Si está interesado en conocer a los intérpretes, la música y la pronunciación de las letras puede ver el video en https://www.youtube.com/watch?v=eFT2nqPaSM4.

Chachaschay (1991) de Fredy Ortiz

Ñachu mamayki yachanña chachaschay	Ya sabe tu mamá chachaschay
Quri anillu qusqayta chachaschay (bis).	Del anillo de oro que te di chachaschay (bis).
Yachachun yachachun chachaschay	Bueno pues que lo sepa chachaschay

quri anillu qusqayta chachaschay (bis).
Cielupi lucero kachkanchu chachaschay
Ñuqa sunquykipi kachkanchu chachaschay (bis).
Kachum pasamapas chachaschay
Ñuqa munaptiy atinin chachaschay (bis).
Ñachu mamayki yachanña, trebolchay
Quri anillu qusqayta, trebolchay (bis)
Yachachun yachachun, trebolchay
Quri anillu qusqayta, trebolchay (bis).

Del anillo que te regalé chachaschay
Está el lucero en el cielo, chachaschay (bis)
¿Estoy yo en tu corazón?
Mira, esté o no esté chachaschay
Yo cuando quiero puedo chachaschay (bis).
Ya lo sabe tu madre, trebolchay
Del anillo de oro que te di, trebolchay (bis)
Bueno pues que lo sepa, trebolchay
Del anillo de oro que te regalé,
trebolchay (bis).

Si está interesado en conocer a los intérpretes, la música y la pronunciación de las letras puede ver el video en https://www.youtube.com/watch?v=-TWUo73eVdg.

CHAPTER 8

Viven hasta ahora, canancamapas causan: El Manuscrito de Huarochirí como puente al futuro

Victor Quiroz Ciriaco
Universidad de California, Berkeley

Estelle Tarica
Universidad de California, Berkeley

Ana Lucía Tello
Universidad de California, Berkeley

El texto ahora conocido como "Manuscrito de Huarochirí" fue compuesto a principios del siglo XVII en la zona de Huarochirí, no muy lejos de la actual ciudad de Lima, Perú. Narra las hazañas de personajes sobrehumanos cuyas historias de amor, astucia, enojo y lucha forman la tierra ancestral, un ambiente de picos nevados y quebradas cálidas que descienden desde las alturas hasta la costa árida del mar en valles y ríos. Aquellos personajes son "huacas", seres otros-que-humanos, progenitores y progenitoras venerados con quienes los humanos de esta zona costeña-andina establecen relaciones de parentesco y reciprocidad.[1] En el texto, conocemos la resistencia de la huaca femenina Cavillaca a ser esposa de la huaca masculina Cuniraya y su transformación en gran piedra del mar (Figura 1), y el nacimiento del pico Pariacaca y su potencia creativa y vencedora, la huaca principal de esa tierra (Figura 2). Aprendemos de las competencias físicas y artísticas de sus hijos Huatyacuri y Tutaykiri para asegurar el reino de su padre, a través de la música, el baile y otras destrezas, y de la libertad sexual ejercida por Chaupiñamca, creadora, mentirosa y guiadora de llamas perdidas. También aprendemos de cómo el recuerdo y la veneración festiva de los y las huacas siguieron en las comunidades de la zona durante la época colonial pese a las campañas de evangelización a que fueron sometidos los pueblos andinos.

Tal como la *Nueva corónica y buen gobierno* (1615), de Guaman Poma de Ayala, y los *Comentarios reales* (1609), del Inca Garcilaso de la Vega, escritos en la misma época, el manuscrito de Huarochirí es un texto de gran riqueza expresiva que es clave para el estudio de las sociedades indígenas andinas y el colonialismo español. Sin embargo, a diferencia de aquellos textos, el manuscrito de Huarochirí pocas veces es estudiado fuera de la

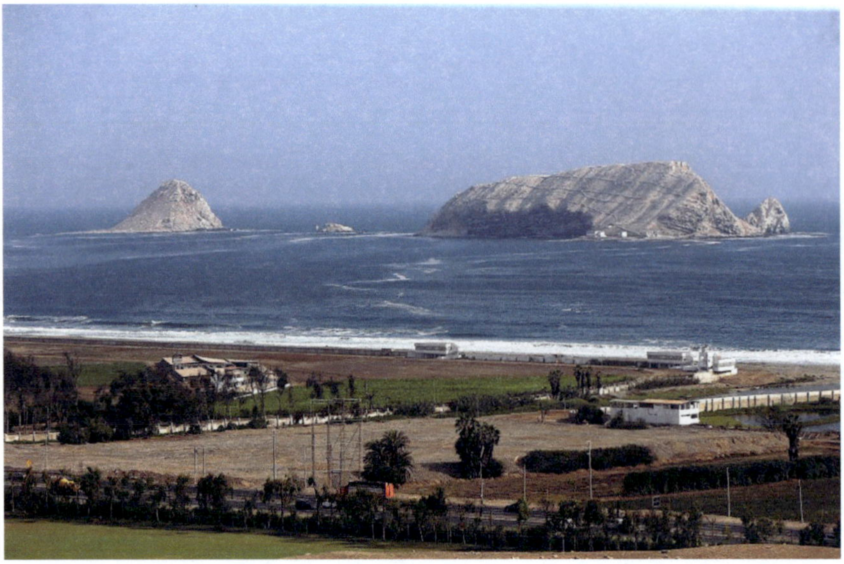

Figura 1. Isla de Cavillaca al frente de Pachacamac. Foto de Yessica Porras.

etnohistoria.[2] Su marginalización en los Estudios Hispánicos obedece a múltiples factores. Quizás el principal sea que está escrito en quechua y la primera traducción completa al español no aparece sino hasta 1966, realizada por José María Arguedas. Pero aún ahora que estamos armados de buenas traducciones al castellano, no solo se trata de incluir este texto en los Estudios Hispánicos, también es necesario prestar atención a las resonancias que emite el texto, las cuales desestabilizan y sobrepasan el proyecto literario hispanoamericano.

En una primera instancia, el manuscrito de Huarochirí demuestra un entretejido de prácticas escriturales con otras formas de inscripción, algunas de las cuales son territoriales. Por ende, el estudio de este texto fortalece un concepto de literatura que va más allá de lo escrito, incluso de lo oral, y pone a la república de letras en contacto con las geografías particulares que animan las formas de inscripción andinas. Asimismo, la revaloración del manuscrito cuestiona el lugar relegado de las literaturas indígenas en el origen de las letras hispanoamericanas para demostrar su vigencia tanto para el presente, cuanto para un futuro proyecto colectivo, cuyos lindes son más vastos que los de la nación moderna. Finalmente, la inclusión del manuscrito de Huarochirí en las clases y los cánones de literaturas hispánicas, motiva un diálogo interdisciplinario entre los Estudios Hispánicos y los Estudios Indígenas, ya que este último campo ofrece marcos interpretativos imprescindibles para profundizar en el conocimiento del texto. Estos marcos ayudan a percibir cómo el autor nativo del manuscrito de Huarochirí dejó constancia de concepciones espacio-temporales y relaciones comunitarias que ofrecen alternativas para repensar nuestro presente críticamente. Con sus relatos, este autor anónimo cumplió con el imperativo de ser un "bueno ancestro", en palabras del crítico Daniel Heath Justice (Nación cheroquí de Oklahoma). Creó un puente al futuro que ha llegado hasta nosotros.

Si bien hay múltiples senderos para acercarse al texto, aquí seguiremos en las líneas abiertas por críticos que trabajan desde las epistemologías indígenas, tales como Justice, Silvia Rivera Cusicanqui y Mishuana Goeman, entre otros. Nos centraremos en la conexión entre la memoria andina inscrita en el manuscrito y los saberes y prácticas indígenas contemporáneas. Los relatos de los y las huacas invitan a concebir el tiempo y el espacio de manera más propicia a la convivencia humana dentro de un entorno que es a la vez social y natural. Para las sociedades andinas, la comunidad comprende no solo el conjunto de personas humanas que comparten un territorio, sino que es un ensamblaje de personajes –*runas* o humanos, *huacas* o deidades y *sallqa* o naturaleza (Rengifo Vásquez 89)– que conforman una comunidad socionatural.

Este acercamiento al texto conlleva además un elemento de análisis feminista, pues pone en el centro el accionar de los personajes femeninos y permite tejer conexiones entre sus actos y el activismo de mujeres indígenas contemporáneas. La valoración de la agencia del sujeto femenino en el texto, así como las relaciones dialógicas entre el sujeto y su comunidad (humana-territorial), evidencian otras formas de ser-estar en el mundo que han sido marginadas por la dominación colonial. Estas modalidades no solo persisten adaptándose a los avatares de la modernidad, sino que revelan otras posibilidades de ser moderno. El documental peruano *Hija de la laguna* (2015) de Ernesto Cabellos Damián da cuenta de ello. Este presenta la lucha de Máxima Acuña Chaupe y las comunidades campesinas de Cajamarca para defender la Laguna Azul de la destrucción que originaría la extracción del oro que yace en su lecho por parte de la minera Yanacocha. La historia es contada desde la perspectiva de Nélida Ayay Chilón, activista ambientalista cajamarquina, quien narra la lucha liderada por Acuña Chaupe desde un discurso indígena ecofeminista.[3] Vejada y difamada por las huestes de la empresa minera Yanacocha, Máxima continúa resistiendo y cuidando la Laguna Azul, la Mamayacu (madre agua, como la llama Nélida). Planteamos que su lucha recodifica y reactiva, en la era contemporánea, la agencia femenina de las piedras guardianas del manuscrito de Huarochirí y revela que es necesario repensar las formas de interacción entre el ser humano y la naturaleza en medio de la catástrofe ecológica contemporánea.

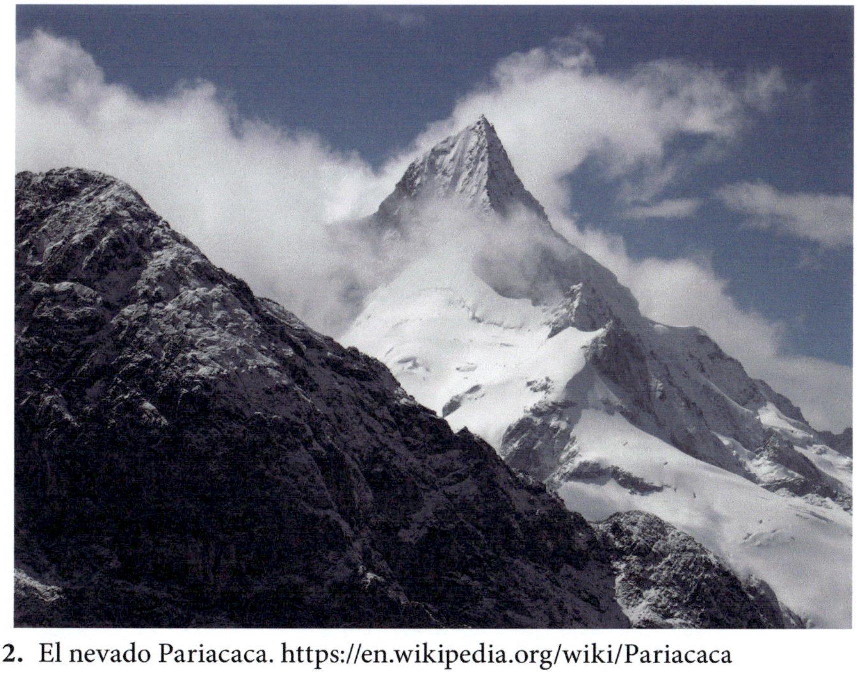

Figura 2. El nevado Pariacaca. https://en.wikipedia.org/wiki/Pariacaca

Proponemos entonces interpretar el manuscrito de acuerdo a categorías y conceptos elaborados por pensadores indígenas contemporáneos, para investigar el complejo posicionamiento de la voz narrativa y resaltar los temas de la complementariedad, la reciprocidad y el rol de la memoria en las luchas indígenas por su autodeterminación. De tal forma, el manuscrito permite tejer nuevos puentes entre los Estudios Hispánicos, los Estudios Indígenas del Norte y el pensamiento indígena en Abiayala.

Contextos coloniales

Al momento de la gestación del manuscrito, cerca de 1598, los españoles habían dominado la zona de Huarochirí durante setenta años. El mundo social del autor habría estado compuesto de un entramado complejo de elementos españoles y andinos. Reducciones, repartimientos y encomiendas se superponían sobre las trazas político-geográficas incaicas y pre-incaicas (Salomon 12–13). La ejecución del inca Túpac Amaru y las epidemias devastadoras del siglo XVI eran un recuerdo vivo (Salomon 14). Además, los huarochiranos habían enfrentado un intenso esfuerzo evangelizador, en quechua, por parte de los jesuitas (Duviols 216). Los cristianos pretendían que los y las huacas eran "ídolos", y que las prácticas de veneración mediante las cuales se aseguraba el buen vivir de los habitantes del lugar, eran "pecados" y "ritos paganos". Los lugareños, por su parte, resistían diariamente tales absurdos, aún cuando habían sido evangelizados al cristianismo.

Tal es la situación en 1597 cuando llega el padre Francisco de Ávila, cuzqueño, para encargarse de la doctrina en la parroquia de San Damián en Huarochirí. Era una provincia relativamente rica y el puesto otorgaba a Ávila beneficios económicos importantes (Acosta 574). Si bien el enriquecimiento del cura a través del trabajo forzado de "indios" era lo normal, parece que Ávila se excedió. El archivo eclesiástico da testimonios de los abusos que habría cometido contra sus parroquianos. Lo acusan repetidas veces y por ello es encarcelado un tiempo en 1607 (Duviols 216–18). Será por vengarse contra sus acusadores,

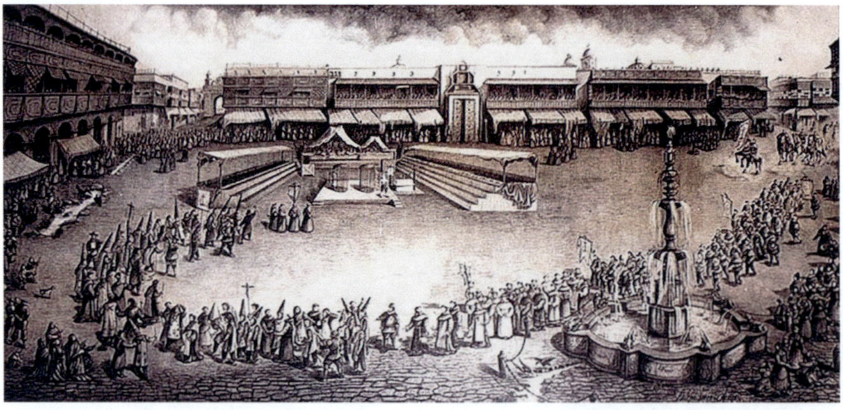

Figura 3. Ejemplo de un Auto de fe, Lima, siglo XVII. Autor desconocido. Museo de la Inquisición, Lima. https://commons.wikimedia.org/wiki/File:Auto_de_fe_Lima.jpg

probablemente, que Ávila emprende en 1608 una brutal campaña de extirpación de los y las huacas del área. En 1609 organiza un auto de fe en Lima donde quema diversos objetos venerados, incluso *mallquis*, los cuerpos preservados de los antepasados, que eran huacas de gran poder (Duviols 221) (Figura 3). La campaña siguió durante varios años, elogiada por las autoridades eclesiásticas y causando gran destrucción. Los pueblos afectados no cesaron de protestar por el despojo.

El manuscrito emerge justo antes de esa campaña. Fue escrito alfabéticamente en un quechua parecido al idioma que los españoles llamaron "lengua general del Perú". Sus autores hablaban probablemente el aru como primera lengua (Salomon 30–31). No se sabe el origen exacto del texto, aunque se conoce que fue concebido y compuesto como libro (Salomon 2). Es probable que haya sido redactado a pedido de Ávila para que él pudiera demostrar ante sus superiores la vigencia de los modos de vida andina que los españoles consideraban "diabólicos", para así atentar contra la credibilidad de sus acusadores. Sin embargo, su autor no era español ni criollo, sino una persona de los lugares mencionados en el texto mismo –un "indio", de acuerdo al hablar despectivo que se impuso durante la colonia (el autor del libro utiliza ese término solo una vez). Por

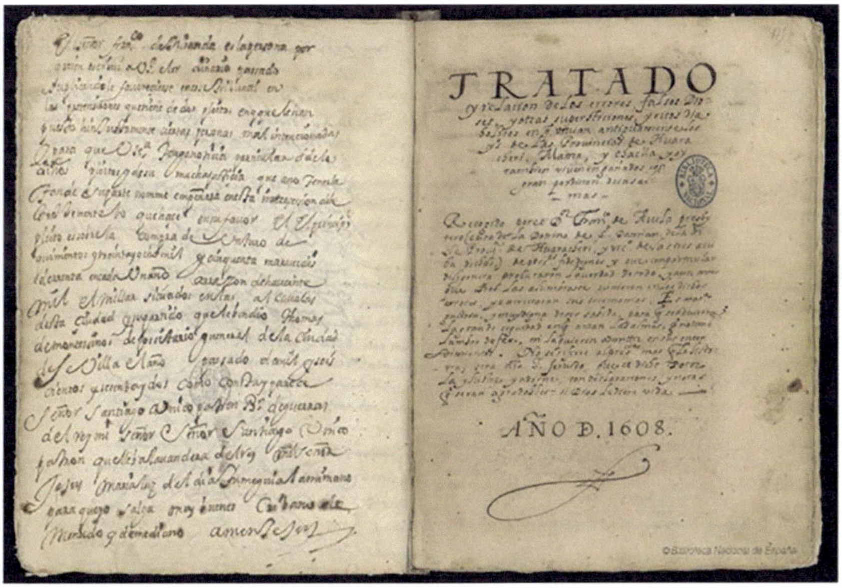

Figura 4. Avila, Francisco de. *Tratado y relación de los errores, falsos dioses y otras supersticiones y ritos diabólicos, en que vivían antiguamente los indios de las provincias de Huaracheri, Mama y Challa, y hoy también viven engañados, con gran perdición de sus almas; recogido por el Dr. Francisco de Ávila, presbítero (cura de la dicha provincia de Huacheri y vicario de las tres arriba dichas). Año de 1608.* En *Papeles varios sobre los indios Incas, Huarochiris y otras antigüedades del Perú* [Manuscrito]. Madrid, Biblioteca Nacional de España, MSS/3169, fol. 115r. Imagen procedente de los fondos de la Biblioteca Nacional de España. http://bdh-rd.bne.es/viewer.vm?id=0000087346&page=1

ende, varios proyectos ideológicos coexisten en el texto. Por un lado, tenemos la intención general de "conocer para controlar" (clave para la empresa colonial) y el propósito específico de Ávila de probar "idolatrías" para desacreditar a "indios". Por otro lado, encontramos el deseo indígena de registrar y reconceptualizar la memoria andina en el marco de la sociedad colonial (Salomon 2), así como el proyecto de negociación de los que recién se habían convertido en "indios", como estrategia de supervivencia en el sistema dominante.

Miradas ch'ixi

¿Cómo conceptualizar el complejo posicionamiento por parte del autor del manuscrito de Huarochirí? La cuestión de si el autor era indio o mestizo, si su voz representa una perspectiva auténticamente indígena o contaminada ya por la cristianización, surge entre los estudiantes de nuestras clases cuando hemos enseñado el texto.[4] La verdad es que nos parece una aproximación de limitado interés. Tales nombres son ficciones encubridoras, emblemas tomados de un repertorio identitario colonial que es de poco alcance explicativo a la hora de entender la perspectiva narrativa del relato. Por tal razón, preferimos abordar el manuscrito a partir de lo "ch'ixi," un concepto elaborado por la socióloga y activista boliviana Silvia Rivera Cusicanqui.[5]

Ch'ixi significa "abigarrado" o "manchado" en aymara. Designa un tipo de tonalidad gris que a la distancia se ve gris, pero observado de cerca es posible distinguir "manchas blancas y negras entreveradas" (Rivera Cusicanqui, *Un mundo* 79). Rivera Cusicanqui lo toma como herramienta teórica para dar cuenta de un encuentro de opuestos que no aspira a la fusión conciliadora, sino que más bien mantiene las tensiones existentes entre ambos polos. Para ella, lo ch'ixi implica "una activa recombinación de mundos opuestos y significantes contradictorios, que forma un tejido en la frontera misma de aquellos polos antagónicos. La vitalidad de este proceso recombinatorio ensancha esta frontera, la convierte en una trama y en un tejido intermedio, *taypi*: arena de antagonismos y seducciones" (Rivera Cusicanqui, *Principio* 5). Rivera Cusicanqui lo concibe "no sólo como zona de contacto, sino como zona de fricción" (*Un mundo* 83). A diferencia de los conceptos de lo "mestizo" o "híbrido", lo ch'ixi no puede ser usado para un proyecto de integración nacional, pues se (re)crea dentro de la multiplicidad, la indeterminación y la contradicción. Es una perspectiva que activa el mundo, no tanto una identidad. Rivera Cusicanqui propone el *Nueva corónica y buen gobierno*, de Guaman Poma de Ayala, como ejemplo de una mirada ch'ixi. De acuerdo con ella, lo ch'ixi se manifiesta sobre todo en la yuxtaposición del texto y la imagen: mientras términos como "bárbaro" o "salvaje" aparecen en el texto para referirse a los contemporáneos "indios" de Guaman Poma, los dibujos son más bien articulaciones de nociones indígenas, por ejemplo, el caso del calendario ritual (*Sociología* 175–178) (Figura 5). A través del texto es posible reconocer un entretejido de prácticas y creencias indígenas con comportamientos y valores introducidos por el colonialismo (Rivera Cusicanqui, *Sociología* 248).

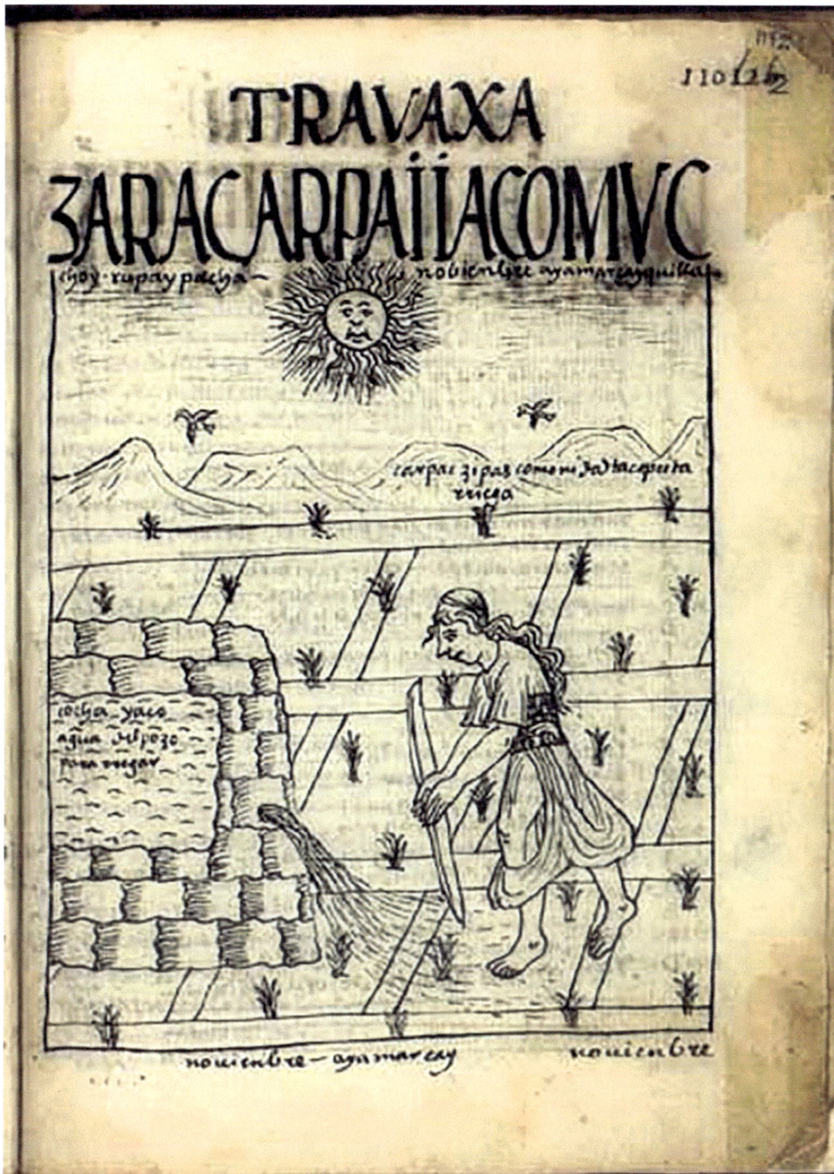

Figura 5. Guamán Poma de Ayala. "Dibujo 396. Noviembre: tiempo de regar el maíz, de escasez de agua, tiempo de calor; Aya Marqay Killa, mes de llevar difuntos". En *Nueva crónica y buen gobierno* (1615). Copenhague, Det Kongelige Bibliotek, 1162 [1172]. Imagen procedente de los fondos de la Det Kongelige Bibliotek. http://www5.kb.dk/permalink/2006/poma/1172/es/text/

Similarmente, estimamos que el manuscrito de Huarochirí es una instancia de mirada ch'ixi. Esta la podemos apreciar en cómo el narrador del manuscrito se aproxima a la cuestión de la escritura. En el prefacio, el narrador se lamenta de que, dada la ausencia de escritura en las sociedades andinas prehispánicas, no haya llegado a sus días suficiente información sobre la vida de estas:

Si los indios de la antigüedad hubieran sabido escribir, *la vida de todos ellos, en todas partes, no se habría perdido.* Se tendrían también noticias de ellos como existen sobre los españoles y sus jefes; aparecerían sus imágenes. (primera página del Manuscrito; las cursivas son nuestras) (Figura 6)

Runa yn.o ñiscap Machoncuna ñaupa pacha quillacacta yachanman carca chayca hinantin causascancunapas manan canacamapas chincaycuc hinacho canman himanam viracochappas sinchi cascanpas canancama ricurin hinatacmi canman.[6]

Sin embargo, a lo largo del texto él mismo advierte la pervivencia de estas prácticas y conocimientos en pleno siglo XVII: "Y aún ahora" / "cunapipas" (capítulo 9), "Y así, de este modo, viven hasta hoy" / "ynatac canan camapas causancu" (capítulo 7). De esta manera, el narrador reconoce que la ausencia de escritura no constituye un impedimento para que la memoria y el conocimiento sean transmitidos, pues estos están inscritos en los mismos cuerpos y prácticas de los miembros de la comunidad. Valoriza ambos, el archivo y el repertorio, entendido el primero como materiales –textos, mapas y otros objetos– que trascienden la distancia espacial y temporal, y el segundo como prácticas y conocimientos inscritos en los cuerpos que por lo general son considerados efímeros (D. Taylor 19–20).

En el manuscrito, es posible encontrar ejemplos de este repertorio grabado en los cuerpos en los bailes y cantos celebrados en honor a las huacas (capítulo 9). El paisaje contiene historias que se recuerdan a través de relatos y otras prácticas colectivas, tal como la historia de la piedra en que se transforma el Amaru durante el enfrentamiento entre los huacas Pariacaca y Huallallo Carhuincho (capítulo 16). Entonces, si bien el narrador del manuscrito valora la escritura porque la asocia a la permanencia, sus páginas revelan la importancia que le concede al repertorio como un sistema para almacenar y transmitir prácticas y nociones que no son estáticas, sino que constantemente se están recreando. De hecho, la misma diferencia entre archivo y repertorio queda atenuada a través del manuscrito, porque revela hasta qué punto una inscripción permanente, tal como una transformación geológica (p. ej.,

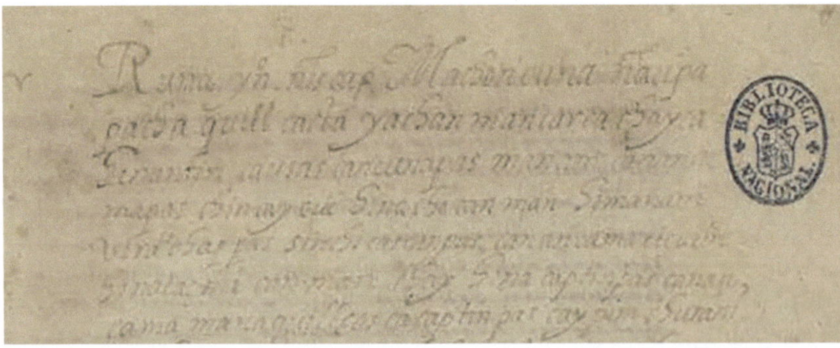

Figura 6. *Runa ynº niscap Machoncuna naripapacha quill casta yachan mancarca Chayca…* En *Papeles varios sobre los indios Incas, Huarochiris y otras antigüedades del Perú* [Manuscrito]. Madrid, Cristóbal de Molina et al. Biblioteca Nacional de España, MSS/3169, fol. 64r. Imagen procedente de los fondos de la Biblioteca Nacional de España. http://bdh-rd.bne.es/viewer.vm?id=0000087346&page=1

la aparición de una piedra), depende del repertorio para convertirse en historia. El narrador del manuscrito es consciente de que las historias de las comunidades huarochiranas no solo están grabadas en las páginas que escribe, sino también en el paisaje y los propios cuerpos de los comuneros.

Probablemente el tejido ch'ixi del manuscrito se observa más claramente en los apartados sobre la fiesta. Por un lado, para el narrador del manuscrito, la fiesta representa la continuidad de conductas pecaminosas, asociadas a la bebida y la sexualidad desenfrenada, pero por otro, la fiesta es una de las manifestaciones más evidentes del vitalismo de las sociedades andinas. Es precisamente en las descripciones detalladas de las fiestas donde irrumpe una episteme ajena a la lógica colonial. En la fiesta coexisten la desmesura y la redistribución ritual, que no pertenecen al orden racional del capital, y las lógicas de la acumulación y el prestigio individual (*Principio* 15). Además, la fiesta adelanta nociones como la complementariedad (que se retomará más adelante), de ahí que sea un momento propicio para renovar las relaciones entre los comuneros mismos, y entre estos y los seres-otros-que-humanos con que conviven.

El narrador condena que la celebración de la fiesta sea una oportunidad para adorar a huacas en lugar de al dios cristiano (capítulo 9). Del mismo modo, a veces critica el consumo de alcohol que se produce en el contexto de la fiesta. El narrador despoja a la bebida de su carácter ritual –es decir, desconoce su rol en el (re)establecimiento de lazos entre los miembros de la comunidad, humanos y seres-otros-que-humanos– para presentarla más bien en términos de exceso y decadencia (capítulo 21). De acuerdo con la antropóloga Catherine Allen, la chicha es usada en celebraciones comunales para sellar pactos entre quienes conforman el *ayllu* y entre estos como totalidad y los lugares sagrados (122), que "son experimentados como una sociedad paralela de personalidades animadas y poderosas" (17).[7]

Sin embargo, en otros pasajes, el narrador muestra una actitud hacia tales prácticas que bordea con la admiración. Por ejemplo, la descripción de la fiesta en honor a Chaupiñamca cierra con esta frase: "Y cuando cantaban y bailaban esta danza, *comenzaba la maduración del mundo*. Todas estas cosas hacían en esa pascua (de Chaupiñamca)" / "taquiptintacsi ancha pucoy pachapas carcan caycunactam canan chay pascuanpi rurar cancu" (capítulo 10; las cursivas son nuestras). El narrador reconoce la capacidad de la fiesta de intervenir en el mundo, de hacer el mundo andar. Es decir, los cantos y los bailes no son meros elementos decorativos o conductas pecaminosas, sino que cumplen un rol fundamental en los ciclos de la vida.

Concebir la perspectiva del manuscrito como una voz o mirada ch'ixi evita caer en idealizaciones de los textos indígenas o en romantizaciones de las prácticas incontaminadas de los grupos andinos. Sería tendencioso invisibilizar las tácticas de adaptación de los indígenas huarochiranos del siglo XVII en aras de presentar una imagen pura del sustrato indígena del manuscrito que resiste en el tiempo. Producido en el contexto de extirpación de idolatrías, en el manuscrito se entretejen la condena de prácticas y creencias prehispánicas con la admiración ante la supervivencia de la cosmovisión indígena pese a los continuos procesos de ocupación y colonización. De tal forma, la mirada del narrador del manuscrito se revela como una mirada ch'ixi, tramando la intersección de diversas perspectivas hacia el sistema de conocimientos y prácticas que fue condenado por los extirpadores de idolatrías.

Reciprocidad y complementariedad

Entender el enunciado ch'ixi del manuscrito nos ayuda a concebir los procesos dinámicos y creativos de resistencia y adaptación de los autores del texto. Lo ch'ixi es por ende un concepto para la interpretación del pasado colonial y la pervivencia del colonialismo. Ilumina la situación histórica de los pueblos indígenas en la época posterior a la conquista, cómo retoman su pasado en medio del catastrófico escenario colonial del siglo XVI para proyectarse a sí mismos en el futuro.

Aparte de la mirada del narrador del texto, es importante entender qué nos enseñan los relatos mismos, las lecciones que ofrecen en cuanto a la convivencia entre diversos tipos de personas, humanas y otras-que-humanas. El crítico Daniel Heath Justice propone interpretar las literaturas indígenas en torno a cuatro preguntas matrices: ¿Cómo aprendemos a ser humanos? ¿Cómo nos comportamos como buenos parientes? ¿Cómo nos convertimos en buenos ancestros? ¿Cómo aprendemos a convivir juntos? (28). Estas preguntas son sumamente valiosas para orientar una interpretación del manuscrito de Huarochirí.

El texto adelanta conceptos de convivencia complementaria y recíproca que circulan en el pensamiento indígena tanto del norte como del sur, tal como podemos apreciar en el análisis de Leah Sneider desde una perspectiva pan-indígena de Norteamérica, sobre los aportes de los estudios de género indígenas. La complementariedad de género se define como responsabilidades comunales delineadas a partir del género, entendido este como relacional y no como esencial o predeterminado (Sneider 63–64). La complementariedad probablemente sea el concepto indígena que irrumpe con más fuerza en las páginas del manuscrito. Sneider señala que la complementariedad reúne "conceptos de responsabilidad y relación en el mantenimiento del equilibrio social o comunal" (63). En otras palabras, la complementariedad es un entramado de "relaciones responsables, recíprocas y respetuosas" dentro y entre las comunidades, y entre estas y su entorno ambiental.[8]

En el texto, estas "relaciones responsables, recíprocas y respetuosas" pueden observarse en múltiples relatos, tanto entre los personajes huacas así como entre estos y los habitantes humanos. Por ejemplo, varios relatos representan la construcción de canales de riego, piezas claves en la sofisticada tecnología andina. Estos canales son el fruto de la cooperación entre comunidades de distintos pisos ecológicos, pero también entre humanos y huacas. El autor relata la historia de cómo Pariacaca convierte un pequeño acueducto en "una acequia ancha, con mucha agua" / "astauan haton yachispa", con la participación de los animales. Lo hace a pedidos de la huaca Chuquisuso para que los *runas* que la veneran puedan regar sus tierras (capítulo 6). En el siguiente capítulo, los habitantes de Cupara se organizan para limpiar la acequia y le ofrecen a Chuquisuso chicha, *ticti*, cuyes y llamas en agradecimiento por el agua (capítulo 7).[9] También entre las mismas huacas hay relaciones de complementariedad generadora. Pariacaca ayuda a Chuquisuso porque quiere acostarse con ella. La unión sexual entre estas huacas, una masculina y otra femenina, da origen a un gran acueducto.[10]

Cabe apuntar que la complementariedad no implica relaciones exentas de tensiones o conflictos. En el manuscrito, existen ejemplos de encuentros violentos, no solo entre los personajes huacas principales, como Pariacaca y Huallallo Carhuincho, sino entre las diversas entidades que cohabitan el mundo: las piedras que se golpean unas contra otras y así forman morteros y batanes (capítulo 4) o el árbol llamado Pullao que entabla una lucha con la montaña de nombre Huicho hasta desplazarla al mar (capítulo 5). El equilibrio dentro de la comunidad y entre las comunidades se está reconstruyendo constantemente. El manuscrito muestra esos choques como generadores, tal como ocurre con los elementos del paisaje, cuyas interacciones constantemente (re)crean la topografía y (re)definen las relaciones con los otros miembros de la comunidad.

Un elemento clave de estas interacciones es la petrificación, cuando un personaje huaca se transforma en piedra.[11] En el caso de los relatos en torno a la creación de obras de riego, la piedra queda como un ente protector de la acequia con quien la comunidad establece vínculos de reciprocidad por medio de rituales y ofrendas cada año. Así se enlaza un elemento natural del paisaje (la piedra) con un elemento social del espacio (el acueducto) a través de prácticas memorísticas corporales. Tales relatos iluminan las relaciones de reciprocidad entre los seres humanos y las entidades del paisaje, y modelan relaciones sociales y socionaturales equilibradas.

Tiempo y memoria

Algunos relatos del manuscrito narran hechos del pasado reciente, como cuando los incas establecieron su dominio en la zona y reconocen la fuerza de los y las huacas locales. La mayoría, sin embargo, trata eventos del pasado lejano, "en tiempos antiguos" / "ñaupa pacha" (capítulo 8). Aún así, los episodios guardan una vigencia absolutamente directa con la época de su autor o autores, pues explican cómo actuar para venerar a los y las huacas y reconocer sus obras generadoras de la vida. Refuerzan la importancia de la memoria colectiva para renovar los vínculos socionaturales de la comunidad. La memoria es clave para asegurar la pervivencia humana, refrán repetido a lo largo del texto.

Esto problematiza una visión lineal del tiempo. Los y las huacas no solo son recordadas u homenajeadas cada año, sino que estas existen-persisten en un flujo temporal que conecta sincrónicamente distintas eras.[12] Esta coexistencia multitemporal se aprecia de muchos modos en el manuscrito; por ejemplo, cuando el narrador no puede precisar si una huaca preexiste a otra (capítulo 14). De modo similar, esta perspectiva temporal surge cuando se diluyen las fronteras entre un pasado más lejano y un pasado más reciente. Por ejemplo, Pariacaca y Macahuisa, huacas "muy antiguas" o "de los tiempos del mito", actúan en el mismo período histórico que el inca Túpac Inca Yupanqui (capítulo 23). Asimismo, Cuniraya Huiracocha, una de las huacas fundacionales de la región de Huarochirí, se encuentra con el inca Huayna Capac (capítulo 14). Esta visión temporal desestabiliza la concepción de un tiempo constituido por una secuencia progresiva de eventos. Así, "el viento del progreso" (Benjamin 257–258) no arrasa con los elementos del pasado (la piedra y los rituales).

Esta coexistencia entre diferentes temporalidades se aprecia en la articulación de las celebraciones rituales con las labores de mantenimiento de los sistemas de irrigación de las comunidades huarochiranas que continúan hasta nuestros días. Los trabajos de mejoramiento de los acueductos o lagunas del área a la que se refiere el manuscrito (obras que implican el uso de máquinas e instrumentos modernos) no colisionan con las prácticas antiguas.[13] Los flujos capitalistas del aparato estatal interactúan con los símbolos (la piedra) y las prácticas comunitarias (la memoria oral, la limpieza ritual) que persisten en el tiempo. No son procesos excluyentes desde la perspectiva de la comunidad.

La propiedad de tierras brinda otro ejemplo de cómo esta tensión temporal presente en el manuscrito se encarna en las sociedades andinas. Desde una perspectiva histórico-lineal y desde un marxismo unidireccional-determinista, el avance de la propiedad privada tendría que ir eliminando progresivamente la noción de "propiedad colectiva" en tanto que "remanente premoderno".[14] En el caso de las comunidades andinas, como las de la zona de Huarochirí, esto no ha ocurrido. Un caso representativo es el de la comunidad de Quinti, donde la propiedad privada convive con la propiedad comunal.[15] Esta convivencia se expresa a veces conflictivamente o a veces a modo de retroalimentación, como cuando los miembros de la comunidad emplean sus títulos de propiedad particulares para unirse colectivamente en una disputa legal por el control de tierras contra otra comunidad o contra una empresa, por ejemplo.

Asimismo, dicha convivencia se actualiza en la relación escritura/oralidad, dado que la documentación legal (escrita) puede enfrentarse o integrarse al uso de la memoria oral huarochirana (inscritas en el manuscrito) como táctica para validar la posesión de los territorios de la zona. Estas formas de vinculación entre una memoria escrita y una memoria oral retroalimentan o cuestionan discursos legales, políticos o económicos de administración territorial estatal o privada según las necesidades del enunciador nativo. Todo ello dialoga con los postulados de diversos pensadores indígenas contemporáneos del norte y del sur que subrayan la importancia de la memoria colectiva indígena como factor clave en la construcción territorial.[16]

En *Mark My Words: Native Women Mapping Our Nations*, Mishuana Goeman, de la Nación Indígena Tonawanda Band of Seneca, sostiene que las narrativas indígenas proponen espacialidades alternativas que cuestionan la organización colonial/imperial de la tierra, los cuerpos y los paisajes. Siguiendo a la geógrafa feminista Doreen Massey, Goeman invita a pensar en el espacio no como una superficie sobre la cual se actúa, sino como el producto de interrelaciones en constante (re)construcción y la simultaneidad de historias (5–6). Precisamente, entre las comunidades que habitan Huarochirí hoy, el espacio es también concebido a partir de una simultaneidad de historias, tanto las historias de los "tiempos antiguos" / "ñaupa pacha" como las historias de la época del autor o autores del manuscrito, o historias de tiempos más recientes. Por consiguiente, en la cosmovisión comunitaria, no rige un sistema donde los elementos-prácticas se borran definitivamente porque nuevos componentes (modernos) los desplazan. Más bien, de forma ch'ixi, los elementos del pasado y los contemporáneos mantienen una interacción, del mismo modo que las piedras guardianas y las comunidades huarochiranas del presente.[17] Es importante no perder de vista estos aspectos para no violentar epistémicamente los saberes comunitarios que se encarnan en sus textos y en sus prácticas sociales.

Este diálogo entre el manuscrito de Huarochirí y el texto de Goeman y otros textos desde los Estudios Indígenas permite resaltar con mayor claridad hasta qué punto es insuficiente un acercamiento al texto desde la literatura peruana, un marco que coloca el texto en un pasado desaparecido e impone una idea nacional de la tierra. Como apunta Goeman, la relación de las comunidades indígenas con la tierra no es fija ni inmutable (28), sino que incorpora y entreteje nuevas formas de experimentar el tiempo y el espacio, tal como lo muestran los relatos creados por las comunidades huarochiranas.

Conclusión

Estas lecturas del manuscrito permiten situar las instancias de potencial resistencia indígena en el texto de manera más consistente. Es necesario observar con cuidado cada estrato del texto. Volviendo al tema de la piedra, por ejemplo, notemos que los evangelizadores vieron en los relatos sobre petrificaciones una vía para introducir mensajes católicos (la conversión de la mujer de Lot en estatua de sal, por ejemplo). Sin embargo, el manuscrito

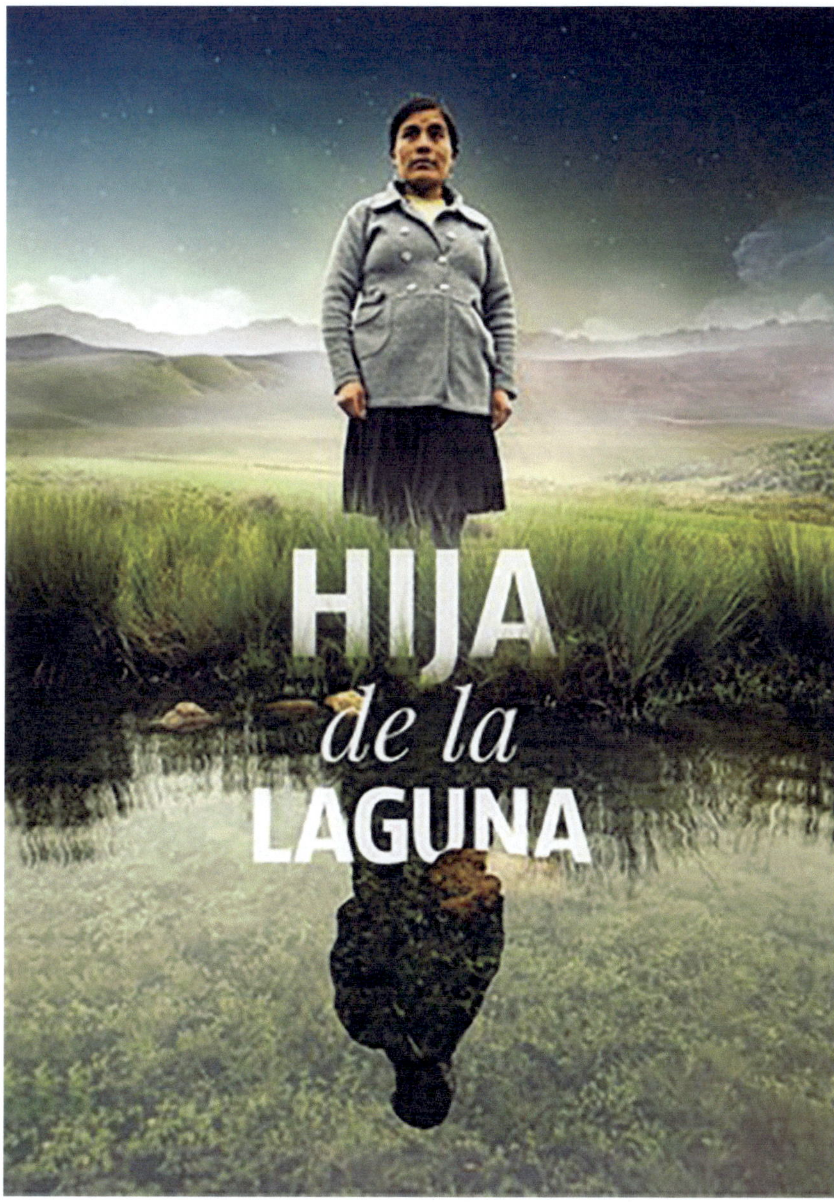

Figura 7. Póster de la película *Hija de la laguna* (2015), del director Ernesto Cabellos Damián, sobre el trabajo activista de Máxima Acuña Chaupe y Nélida Ayay Chilón.

constantemente incrusta líneas de fuga que desestabilizan y hacen estallar esta directriz colonizadora. Al respecto, destacan los relatos de huacas femeninas donde queda claro o se infiere que ellas desean petrificarse para ser guardianas de la laguna luego de haber tenido relaciones sexuales con una huaca masculina. En casos como este, la agencia femenina desestabiliza sentidos católicos como "pecado" o "castigo" donde la petrificación funcionaría para punir el acto sexual.[18] Esta desestabilización permanece como potencial disruptivo en el tiempo y se activa en los rituales de limpieza de la acequia y en las ofrendas a la piedra guardiana. El culto a la huaca Chuquisuso sigue funcionando como un contrapeso simbólico frente al control católico sobre los cuerpos de las mujeres. En este sentido, la codificación y re-apropiaciones de la piedra guardiana emulan la configuración y usos del manuscrito: ambos son palimpsestos de voces e intenciones desplegadas desde un entramado sociocultural marcado por la experiencia colonial. La historia de luchadoras contemporáneas como Máxima Acuña Chaupe y Nélida Ayay Chilón, retratadas en la película *Hija de la laguna*, retroalimenta los relatos de las huacas femeninas que protegen las lagunas o acueductos de Huarochirí (Figura 7). Su lucha en el presente ilumina hasta qué punto el manuscrito de Huarochirí contiene relatos que son "buena medicina", en palabras de Justice, porque "nos recuerdan quiénes somos y a dónde vamos, como individuos y también en relación con quienes compartimos este mundo. Estas historias nos recuerdan sobre las relaciones que hacen una buena forma de vivir" (Justice 6).

Incorporar el manuscrito de Huarochirí a los Estudios Hispánicos, atentos a cómo nos enseña a recordar para renovar, nos obliga a pensar más allá del historicismo y el patrimonialismo que dominan las historias literarias nacionales y latinoamericanas.[19] Permite tejer conexiones con el pensar de otros pueblos indígenas, de Abiayala o más allá, para confrontar los retos del momento actual. La voz narrativa del autor y sus relatos sobre los y las huacas construyen temporalidades y cartografías que cuestionan las historias y geografías dominantes y que se vinculan con las luchas de autodefensa de los pueblos indígenas. Leído desde la perspectiva de esas luchas, el manuscrito de Huarochirí puede considerarse "parte de nuestro resurgimiento cultural, político y familiar, y de nuestros continuos esfuerzos para mantener nuestros derechos y responsabilidades en estas tierras en disputa" (Justice 6). Esperamos que el acercamiento al manuscrito de Huarochirí en el presente contribuya a fortalecer ese resurgimiento.

Notas

1. A partir del texto mismo es posible deducir mucho sobre qué es una huaca. Para perspectivas desde la investigación académica, ver los ensayos en Bray, ed., y Castro-Klarén y Millones, eds. Sobre los seres-otros-que-humanos o seres-de-la-tierra, ver De la Cadena; Allen.
2. Sobre el manuscrito de Huarochirí desde la etnohistoria, véase G. Taylor; Ortiz Rescaniere (*La pareja*); Salomon.
3. José Carlos Díaz examina las estrategias de representación del uso del discurso indígena en el documental, así como sus articulaciones con el feminismo, la ecocrítica y el marxismo.
4. Sobre la polémica en torno a la autoría del manuscrito, véase G. Taylor.
5. Nuestro acercamiento al manuscrito a partir del concepto aymara ch'ixi puede entenderse como complemento al acercamiento que ofrece José Yáñez del Pozo a partir del concepto quechua

yanantin, otra manera de hablar del sistema de relaciones de oposición y complementariedad que recorre el texto. Véase Yáñez del Pozo.

6. Optamos por identificar el capítulo donde se encuentra el texto citado del manuscrito de Huarochirí, en vez de la página, para facilitar la tarea de aquellos lectores que disponen de otra edición o versión del texto original. La versión que aquí usamos es *Dioses y hombres de Huarochirí*, traducida por José María Arguedas.

7. Todas las traducciones al español de los textos críticos son de nuestra autoría.

8. Sobre la complementariedad de género en el contexto andino, ver Platt.

9. El *ticti* es la espuma que se forma en la superficie de la chicha cuando ésta empieza a hervir.

10. Sobre las relaciones entre la petrificación y el tema amoroso en el manuscrito véase Rubina y el reciente trabajo de Ballón, ambos desde una perspectiva semiótica.

11. Sobre la piedra como materia, ver Dean.

12. Sobre lo que Silvia Rivera Cusicanqui denomina "simultaneidad de tiempos heterogéneos" o "tiempos mixtos", véase *Un mundo ch'ixi es posible* (76).

13. Sobre la interacción entre las festividades y las labores de construcción o mantenimiento de acueductos en la zona de Huarochirí, véase Ráez.

14. Sobre este tema ver Cotler.

15. Ver Ortiz Rescaniere, "Unas imágenes".

16. La persistencia de los relatos recogidos en el manuscrito se aprecia en trabajos de inicios del siglo XXI, como *Hijas de Cavillaca* (2002).

17. Para desarrollar este aspecto véase el artículo de Lecaros. Ella ha explorado cómo algunas formas de organización sociopolítica de las sociedades huarochiranas de fines del siglo XX se articulan con patrones de pensamiento indígena inscritos en el manuscrito, especialmente la interacción entre un sistema cuatripartito y un elemento excluido (4+1). Por su parte, Gabriela Sternfeld encuentra similitudes entre el asambleísmo de las comunidades andinas contemporáneas y las reuniones de huacas en el manuscrito.

18. Véase el artículo de Pacheco para un análisis más elaborado de este aspecto. Sobre las relaciones amorosas en el manuscrito véase también Ortiz Rescaniere *La pareja*.

19. La idea del "patrimonialismo nacional" como desposesión de los bienes indígenas tangibles e intangibles, viene de Chacón (17).

Obras citadas

Acosta, Antonio. "Estudio biográfico sobre Francisco de Avila". Edited by G. Taylor. *Ritos y tradiciones*, pp. 551–616.

Allen, Catherine. *The Hold Life Has: Coca and Cultural Identity in an Andean Community.* Smithsonian Institution, 2002.

Ballón Aguirre, Enrique. "Variaciones sobre un tema etnoliterario: El motivo 'seducción' en el *Manuscrito de Huarochirí*". *Texto! Textes et cultures*, vol. 26, no. 1, 2021, pp. 1–32.

Benjamin, Walter. *Illuminations*. Edited with an introduction by Hannah Arendt. Translated by Harry Zohn. Schocken Books, 1969.

Bray, Tamara, ed. *The Archaeology of Wak'as: Explorations of the Sacred in the Pre-Columbian Andes.* UP of Colorado, 2015.

Cabellos Damián, Ernesto, dir. *Hija de la laguna*. Perú, 2015.

Castro-Klarén, Sara y Luis Millones, eds. *El retorno de las huacas: Estudios y documentos sobre el Taki Onqoy, siglo XVI*. Instituto de Estudios Peruanos, 1990.

Chacón, Gloria. *Indigenous Cosmolectics: Kab'awil and the Making of Maya and Zapotec Literatures.* U of North Carolina P, 2018.

Cotler, Julio. *Los cambios en la propiedad, la comunidad y la familia en San Lorenzo de Quinti.* Instituto de Etnología y Arqueología, 1959.

Dean, Carolyn. *A Culture of Stone: Inca Perspectives on Rock.* Duke UP, 2010.

De la Cadena, Marisol. *Earth Beings: Ecologies of Practice across Andean Worlds.* Duke UP, 2015.

Díaz, José Carlos. "Paraíso y resistencia: La lucha ecomarxista y ecofeminista contra el extractivismo en *Hija de la laguna* (2015) de Ernesto Cabellos". *LL Journal*, vol. 13, no. 1, 2018, pp. 1–15.

Dioses y hombres de Huarochirí (edición bilingüe). Translated by José María Arguedas, introduction by Luis Millones y Hiroyasu Tomoeda. Universidad Antonio Ruiz de Montoya, 2009.

Duviols, Pierre. "Estudio biobibliográfico: Francisco de Ávila, extirpador de idolatrías". *Dioses y hombres de Huarochirí*, 215–228.

Goeman, Mishuana. *Mark My Words: Native Women Mapping Our Nations.* U of Minnesota P, 2013.

Justice, Daniel Heath. *Why Indigenous Literatures Matter.* Wilfrid Laurier UP, 2018.

Lecaros Terry, Ana Teresa. "La organización social de Huarochirí". *Anthropológica*, vol. 14, no. 14, 1996, pp. 288–299.

Ortiz Rescaniere, Alejandro. *La pareja y el mito: Estudios sobre las concepciones de la persona y de la pareja en los Andes.* Fondo Editorial de la Pontificia Universidad Católica del Perú, 2001.

———. "Unas imágenes del tiempo". *Anthropologica*, vol. 13, no. 13, 1995, pp. 141–166.

Pacheco Medrano, Karina. "Piedra de la muerte, piedra de la eternidad. Los seres petrificados en la mitología prehispánica". *Ecos de Huarochirí: Tras la huella de lo indígena en el Perú.* Edited by Gonzalo Portocarrero, Fondo Editorial de la Pontificia Universidad Católica del Perú, Tarea Asociación Gráfica Educativa, 2018, pp. 83–94.

Platt, Tristan. "Mirrors and Maize: The Concept of *Yanantin* Among the Macha of Bolivia." *Anthropological History of Andean Politics.* Edited by John V. Murra, Nathan Wachtel, and Jacques Revel. Cambridge University Press, 1986, pp. 228–259.

Ráez, Manuel. *Dioses de las quebradas: Fiestas y rituales en la sierra alta de Lima.* Pontificia Universidad Católica del Perú, Instituto Riva-Agüero y Centro de Etnomusicología Andina, 2005.

Rengifo Vásquez, Grimaldo. "The Ayllu". *The Spirit of Regeneration. Andean Cultures Confronting Western Notions of Development.* Edited by Frédérique Apffel-Marglin, Zed Books, 1998, pp. 89–123.

Rivera Cusicanqui, Silvia. *Sociología de la imagen: Miradas ch'ixi desde la historia andina.* Tinta Limón, 2015.

———. *Un mundo ch'ixi es posible.* Tinta Limón, 2018.

Rivera Cusicanqui, Silvia, y El Colectivo. *Principio Potosí Reverso.* Departamento de Actividades Editoriales del MNCARS, 2010.

Rubina, Celia. "La petrificación en el Manuscrito de Huarochirí". *Mester*, vol. 21, no. 2, 1992, pp. 71–82.

Salomon, Frank. "Introductory Essay: The Huarochirí Manuscript". *The Huarochirí Manuscript: A Testament of Ancient and Colonial Andean Religion.* Translation from the Quechua by Frank Salomon and George L. Urioste. U of Texas P, 1991, pp. 1–24.

Sneider, Leah. "Complementary Relationships: A Review of Indigenous Gender Studies". *Indigenous Men and Masculinities: Legacies, Identities, Regeneration.* Edited by Robert Alexander Innes and Kim Anderson, U of Manitoba P, 2015, pp. 62–79.

Sternfeld, Gabriela. "Asambleas, negociaciones y autoridades locales en las tradiciones orales del *Manuscrito de Huarochirí*". *Revista Andina* 39, 2004, pp. 75–101.

Taylor, Diana. *The Archive and the Repertoire: Performing Cultural Memory in the Americas.* Duke UP, 2003.

Taylor, Gerald. "Introducción". *Ritos y tradiciones de Huarochirí. Ed. bilingüe quechua normalizado-castellano.* Editado por Gérald Taylor, Instituto Francés de Estudios Andinos, 2008, pp. 9–20.

Yáñez del Pozo, José. *Yanantin: La filosofía dialógica intercultural del Manuscrito de Huarochirí.* Abya-Yala, 2002.

CHAPTER 9

Diálogos hispanos sobre video y cine indígena en América del Norte

Oswaldo A. Lara Orozco
Universidad Nacional Autónoma de México

Esta investigación hace una revisión sistemática de literatura crítica en español sobre estudios de video y cine indígena en América del Norte. Tiene el objetivo de dar a conocer qué se ha escrito en el mundo académico en esta lengua sobre el video y el cine indígena, en esta región, en los últimos años.[1] A pesar de que México ha sido relacionado históricamente con la producción latinoamericana de video y cine indígena -y se ha identificado en esa tradición de estudios-,[2] hay una veta de investigación poco explorada sobre los estudios en lengua hispana acerca de su relación con la producción de video y cine indígena de la región geográfica y política de América del Norte, a la cual pertenece. En ese sentido, este trabajo pretende contribuir a ese vacío y aportar lo que se ha escrito en español sobre las producciones mexicanas, canadienses y estadounidenses de video y cine indígena. Pretendo responder a las siguientes preguntas: ¿existe una tradición de estudios en español sobre video y cine indígena en América del Norte? También, ¿quién realiza esos estudios, en dónde y qué perspectiva domina más, la indígena o la no indígena? El capítulo también sugiere la contribución de las obras audiovisuales a las prácticas decoloniales y a los estudios indígenas.

Para responder estas preguntas, en las siguientes páginas presento un panorama de la emergencia del paradigma indígena de investigación, misma que nos servirá para comprender, posteriormente, la proliferación de obras audiovisuales realizadas por pueblos originarios en América del Norte en los últimos años. El paradigma indígena también nos ayudará a sugerir la contribución de los videos y películas aquí mencionadas a las prácticas decoloniales y a los estudios indígenas. En segundo lugar, analizo los estudios sobre video y cine indígena en esta región y los agrupo en las siguientes temáticas: a) apropiación de medios y tecnologías; b) empleo del video y el cine en la investigación social y antropológica; c) definiciones; y d) textos que analizan videos y películas. A través de esta selección de trabajos se muestra cuáles han sido las recientes preocupaciones sobre el video y el cine indígena, tanto de realizadoras y realizadores como por parte de la academia. Los resultados también dan cuenta de instituciones y actores clave en los esfuerzos de realización del cine indígena, así como de los lugares de mayor producción. Por último, si bien no es un reto de estas páginas, para una futura investigación es pertinente preguntarnos de qué manera dialogarían estos trabajos en español con los estudios sobre el video y el cine indígena de América del Norte escritos en inglés y en francés, con la finalidad de observar un panorama más amplio de estos estudios, así como de conocer semejanzas y diferencias entre esas diversas visiones.

Nota metodológica

Mis fuentes documentales sobre los estudios de video y cine indígena en América del Norte son artículos académicos escritos principalmente en español. Considerando que la pandemia de COVID-19 en el mundo potenció la ya antes consolidada investigación académica en medios digitales, se privilegió el empleo de artículos, no de libros. Inicialmente, las búsquedas arrojaron más de tres mil quinientos resultados, de los cuales el 97 por ciento no correspondían con el objetivo de la investigación.[3] Solamente un 3 por ciento de los textos se relacionaban con los criterios específicos; no obstante, una revisión posterior y más detallada -de los casi cien trabajos recabados- nos obligó emplear solamente poco menos de treinta, que catalogamos como los resultados de la exploración.[4]

En todo este proceso, se identificó que, con base en los criterios de búsqueda, quedaron fuera autoras y autores que han sido clave en la discusión de este campo, tales como Gabriela Zamorano y Claudia Magallanes Blanco -pero en la región de América Latina- o como Byrt Wammack Weber y Freya Schiwy, quienes han escrito sobre cine de comunidades mexicanas migrantes en Estados Unidos y sobre la mirada decolonizada del video indígena en México y América Latina, pero en lengua inglesa. Es decir, quedaron fuera quienes han escrito primordialmente sobre América Latina, porque no es la región de mi interés; y en inglés, porque en estas páginas privilegio los textos en español. Lo anterior, ya que, como se puede constatar, hay una amplia gama de estudios sobre video y cine indígena en la región de América Latina, en español e inglés, y es un campo en el que poco puedo aportar; en segundo lugar, porque esta investigación -realizada desde México- busca girar la perspectiva y aportar al conocimiento general sobre video y cine indígena, pero en otra región (América del Norte) y en otra lengua (el español) para equilibrar la producción general de conocimiento en este campo.

Emergencia del paradigma indígena de investigación

En las últimas décadas han acontecido una serie de procesos que dan cuenta del crecimiento de la influencia de la perspectiva indígena en el imaginario social, y en el campo académico en particular, el paradigma indígena de investigación.[5] Sobre esta perspectiva indígena, Gabriel Arévalo sostiene que el tránsito

> de los cursos de antropología indigenista y sus investigaciones sobre "nativos" hacia la creación de universidades indígenas, diplomados, seminarios, publicaciones e investigaciones agenciadas por indígenas son un reflejo de la tendencia, como lo demuestra también el creciente número de grupos de trabajo indígenas conformados por profesores y estudiantes que desde la cosmovisión de sus pueblos desarrollan procesos educativos y de investigación. (52)

El paradigma indígena de investigación ha transitado por varias etapas, que inician en las décadas de los sesenta y setenta. La primera y la segunda etapa corresponden con el crecimiento de investigadoras e investigadores indígenas en instituciones académicas y con el hecho de que los estándares occidentales en investigación, nada relacionados con su procedencia, les llevaba a emplear estas metodologías para ser aceptados y no rechazados. En la tercera etapa, con un marcado acento en la decolonización y la indigenización de las metodologías, un trabajo clave es la crítica que hace Linda Tuhiwai Smith en 1999, en su libro "Decolonizing Methodologies: Research and Indigenous Peoples", al papel cómplice que la ciencia racional de occidente jugó para legitimar, por un lado, la desacreditación al sistema de conocimientos, los valores y las creencias de los pueblos originarios en el mundo,[6] así como el sometimiento y objetivación que estos pueblos han sufrido en el largo, y aún vigente, proceso de colonización. Por ello, para la autora es imprescindible una perspectiva decolonial, que gire la educación y la investigación hacia las preocupaciones y visiones de los pueblos originarios. Así, tal "proceso de decolonización es una propuesta que hace un llamado a transformar las relaciones de poder en un proceso creativo que [...] busca hacer lugar a los intereses propios de los pueblos indígenas" (Arévalo 58). En la cuarta y actual etapa, en las universidades y "el tejido institucional se crearon seminarios, programas, semilleros de investigación, centros de investigación e investigaciones basadas en el conocimiento ancestral que favorecieron la proyección del paradigma indígena de investigación" (62).

El paradigma indígena de investigación no pretende desechar la tradición racional occidental de la investigación, ni hacer a un lado a sus disciplinas. Como señalan Walter Mignolo y Rolando Vázquez, aunque las disciplinas escolaricen y hagan expertos a los cuerpos en disciplinas canónicas "dirigidas en su práctica a reproducir el privilegio epistémico de la modernidad eurocentrada", por otro lado, se trata de "reorientar el uso de esos conocimientos, ya no para reproducir el orden moderno-colonial, sino para denunciarlo" (Mignolo y Vázquez 494). Reorientando esos conocimientos hacia el proyecto de la decolonialidad, "la pregunta es cómo usar las disciplinas para avanzar proyectos decoloniales y no cómo usar la decolonialidad para avanzar proyectos disciplinarios" (496).

Mignolo y Vázquez se preguntan cuál es el rol de la estética en la colonialidad del saber y la colonialidad del ser. Sobre ello, Adolfo Albán señala que los colonos representaron (primero en la literatura y después en la fotografía) a "los otros", los colonizados, a imagen y semejanza de su retina y pincel hegemónicos, y ello llevó a los pueblos colonizados a una imposibilidad de representarse a sí mismos. El blanco europeo le dio color a las tinieblas de los pueblos originarios exóticos del mundo: silenciadas, relegadas y supeditadas a las narrativas (de la exactitud) que occidente les construyó. Así, "las producciones de las comunidades étnicas estuvieron a la saga de las tendencias de los movimientos, corrientes de pensamiento y de los circuitos de mercado que se consolidan en torno al arte" (Albán 446).

A principios del siglo XX el dominio colonial ya había logrado el control estético de los pueblos indígenas, y el cine, que había iniciado rodaje en 1895, también contribuyó a modelar tanto las identidades nacionales como a cimentar el imperialismo. De acuerdo con Shohat y Stam, "dentro del discurso colonialista, las metáforas, los tropos y los motivos alegóricos desempeñaron un papel primordial a la hora de configurar la superioridad europea" (151). Siguiendo con los mismos autores, las exageraciones esquemáticas de representación en las que incurría el cine de Hollywood construyeron una serie de tropos de "los otros",[7] entre ellos los indígenas: pintarles de rojo la piel a las y los actores, la animalización, ser representados como cuerpo y no como mente, como materia prima y no como elaboración o actividad mental, la infantilización, vestirles con poca ropa, la vida de los europeos al centro y la vida no europea en la periferia. Lo anterior evidencia la necesidad de trascender la mirada hegemónica sobre los pueblos indígenas y la búsqueda de una mirada propia, decolonizada.

Por último, el paradigma indígena de investigación se consolidó en paralelo a las luchas políticas de los pueblos originarios en el mundo a partir de la década de los setenta y a la visibilización de sus necesidades, dando como resultado la firma de la "Declaración de Naciones Unidas sobre los Derechos de los Pueblos Indígenas" (2007).[8]

En ese sentido, sin hacer un análisis de contenido y textual de las obras audiovisuales mencionadas en la literatura que a continuación se revisa, en las reflexiones finales se sugerirá cuál es su aporte al hacer decolonial. Como señala Adolfo Albán, las contra-narrativas indígenas son una forma en que estos pueblos enfrentan la colonialidad del ser, reconociéndose y afirmándose en sus particularidades culturales. Y estas páginas sostienen que los textos que hablan de dichas contra-narrativas, son el medio a través del cual los videos y películas indígenas también se pueden visibilizar, por ello la importancia de su difusión en español en la región de América del Norte; y de la pertinencia de una investigación como quitar la esta, para robustecer la literatura hispánica sobre aquellas obras.

Revisión de la literatura

En general, las investigaciones hablan de diversos temas.[9] Para los pueblos originarios del mundo es preciso apropiarse de medios de comunicación y tecnologías audiovisuales con el objetivo, entre muchos otros, de representar su identidad, sin la visión colonizada de los medios hegemónicos. También, a través de estos textos se observa que existe la necesidad de definir términos como video indígena, cine indígena y cine etnográfico y/o antropológico. Otros trabajos dan cuenta del recorrido que ha tenido el empleo de estos medios en la antropología y en la investigación social. Asimismo, convendrá revisar los textos que han analizado, desde distintos enfoques, videos y películas indígenas, documentales o de ficción. Finalmente, parafraseando a Mignolo y Vázquez, en su trabajo "Pedagogía y (de)colonialidad", en las siguientes páginas será importante preguntarse cómo los pueblos originarios han empleado el cine y el video para avanzar proyectos decoloniales.

Reprogramando medios: De la capacitación a la apropiación

En este primer bloque tenemos textos que abordan variadas experiencias de apropiación de medios y tecnologías audiovisuales, así como de experiencias de capacitación que han ayudado a los pueblos originarios a representar sus identidades. Tal vez uno de los ejercicios icónicos de efímera apropiación fue el de Sol Worth, John Adair y Richard Chalfen, en 1966, quienes capacitaron a navajos (diné), en Estados Unidos, en el empleo de cámaras de 16 mm. Sin embargo, ese ejercicio en Estados Unidos, como sugiere Carolina Soler en su texto "Media-médium: Entre la etnografía y el cine comunitario":

> No dejó de ser un hecho aislado sin un desarrollo inmediato posterior. En Latinoamérica, en cambio, el uso del video por parte de indígenas surgió como un movimiento social y asumió en muchos casos una posición política crítica, con miras a la autodeterminación y a la revitalización cultural; bajo la denominación "video indígena" se formó una importante corriente en torno a la realización audiovisual a lo largo del continente americano. (182)

Este pasaje de transferencia de medios destaca el desarrollo de esa tradición en América Latina, pero no en América del Norte en ese momento.

También tenemos el aporte de Axel Köhler, "Nuestros antepasados no tenían cámaras: El video como machete y otros retos de la video-producción indígena en Chiapas, México", que busca abonar a la comprensión de la práctica del video indígena en Chiapas, por parte de organizaciones de base y organizaciones no gubernamentales (ONG), dentro del particular contexto político y social que se vive en el estado. Para comprender dicho ejercicio, Köhler rastrea los esfuerzos que tuvo la televisión estatal, en el año 2000, para que las lenguas indígenas fueran escuchadas a través de noticiarios y emitió noticias en lenguas tzeltal, tzotzil y tojolabal. Otro aspecto a favor del ejercicio de videoastas es que la tecnología del video es más accesible que el cine,[10] por ello, desde los noventa se convirtió en un medio atractivo. Otro esfuerzo, como respuesta a las demandas del EZLN, fue la creación del Centro Estatal de Lenguas, Arte y Literatura Indígena (CELALI), en 1997, y su departamento de medios audiovisuales, para promover y difundir la cultura indígena. Por último, el caso de Kinoki-lumal, una organización apoyada desde Austria por el colectivo europeo Kinoki, que capacitó a indígenas de Ocosingo y Oxchuc, Chiapas, y Guatemala sobre cómo realizar proyectos de cine y video de manera sustentable. Köhler concluye que quizá los esfuerzos de organizaciones civiles han tenido más compromiso con las actividades videográficas de las comunidades del estado que los que emprendió el Instituto Nacional Indigenista (INI).

Por su parte, Erika Cusi Wortham, en su trabajo "Más allá de la hibridad: Los medios televisivos y la producción de identidades indígenas en Oaxaca, México", comparte la experiencia del proyecto de Transferencia de Medios Audiovisuales (TMA) a organizaciones y comunidades indígenas –que impulsó el INI en 1989– y la de Radio y Video Tamix en el municipio mixe de Tamazulápam del Espíritu Santo, Oaxaca, en 1992.[11] De acuerdo con la autora, ambos representaron un verdadero activismo cultural, además de auténticas propuestas audiovisuales indígenas. La autora concluye que el video indígena es más una práctica social que se construye como su identidad cultural "a través de prácticas y relaciones sociales complejas y propone una posición particular, parcial y siempre política" (46).

En su texto "Estéticas enraizadas: Aproximaciones al video indígena en América Latina", Amalia Córdova hace un recorrido por los diferentes esfuerzos y experiencias de la realización de videos indígenas en América Latina, particularmente en México. Destaca que el video indígena ha contribuido a documentar la memoria de los pueblos originarios, a pesar de las dificultades políticas por las que transitan las y los realizadores. Aunque no existe necesariamente un hilo unificador que sostenga a estas obras, concluye que "en gran medida se mantienen unidos por un enfoque similar en el hacer del trabajo audiovisual, realizado desde una perspectiva conjunta, comunitaria e indígena" (102).

Sobre apropiación de medios, también tenemos el texto "Una mirada al cine indígena: Autorrepresentación y el derecho a los medios audiovisuales", de José Luis Reza, quien aboga por la necesidad de la apropiación de los medios de comunicación, por parte de los pueblos originarios, para obtener mayor visibilidad y defender su existencia. Enfatiza que a través del empleo de estas tecnologías los pueblos indígenas pasan de ser "objetos etnográficos" a ser cineastas y videoastas que comparten su visión al exterior. A pesar de no gozar de grandes presupuestos de producción y tener recursos técnicos y tecnológicos limitados, su objetivo es conservar, difundir y comunicar lo que ocurre en sus comunidades, más que el entretenimiento y la obtención de ganancias inmediatas. Como medios de difusión, destacan dos canadienses: Canadian Filmmakers Distribution Centre e Isuma Production. Finalmente, concluye que lo más importante es que los pueblos luchen por el libre acceso a los medios audiovisuales y la libre difusión de sus trabajos, así como la inclusión democrática de cineastas indígenas.

Por su parte, Alexandra Halkin nos recuerda la importancia de los medios de comunicación en la visibilización que tuvo en la sociedad internacional la lucha indígena zapatista. Su trabajo, "Fuera de la óptica indígena: Zapatistas y videístas autónomos", es una reseña de su experiencia, entre 1995 y 2006, trabajando con las comunidades indígenas zapatistas y como fundadora de Chiapas Media Project/Promedios (CMP/Promedios). Desde su fundación en 1998, CMP/Promedios fue una organización binacional (México-Estados Unidos) que contribuyó con la producción de decenas de videos realizados por indígenas, para su difusión internacional y para consumo interno. Además de cursos de capacitación a indígenas de diversas comunidades en México (con capacitadores nacionales e incluso indígenas), también organizó intercambios entre estudiantes estadounidenses, del Street Level Youth Media, de Chicago, y estudiantes indígenas del Chiapas Youth Media Project. Algunos videos se hablaron en español y otros en lenguas mayas. Actualmente, el sitio de internet del proyecto informa que CMP/Promedios es conocida como Promedios de Comunicación Comunitaria, con base en San Cristóbal de Las Casas, Chiapas.

Por último, "De la soberanía visual a la comunicación intercultural: Apuntes para una historia del cine y video indígena en México y América Latina" de Alberto Cuevas Martínez trata de algunos esfuerzos que se han hecho, en varios países, para capacitar a comunidades indígenas en el manejo de equipo audiovisual para la producción de videos indígenas. Destaca el proyecto de TMA a organizaciones y comunidades indígenas, que ya comentamos, y el caso canadiense de Wapikoni Mobile, surgido en 2004, en la provincia de Quebec.

Este proyecto trabaja con comunidades de las Primeras Naciones de la provincia francófona y de Labrador; en él participan el Consejo de la Nación Atikamekw y el Consejo de la Juventud de las Primeras Naciones de Quebec y Labrador. Wapikoni Mobile busca que las y los jóvenes se expresen a través del video y la música; para ello, les capacita en el manejo de herramientas audiovisuales y así contribuye a una interacción entre ellos y también más allá de sus comunidades. Con un enfoque educativo, el proyecto ha logrado más de "2000 inversiones en talleres de creación y producción de video y música, realizando cerca de 360 grabaciones musicales y 450 cortometrajes, algunos traducidos en varios idiomas" (117). El autor señala que la soberanía visual se logra con el empoderamiento tecnológico y el acceso a medios de comunicación masiva.

El empleo del video y el cine en la antropología y la investigación social: ¿Nuevos lenguajes?

El segundo bloque de textos se refiere en general al uso de tecnologías como el cine y el video en la investigación social y antropológica, y sugiere la construcción de una narrativa postcolonial o, mejor dicho, un nuevo lenguaje y la creación de la antropología visual a partir de la utilización de cámaras para el registro de imágenes.

En su texto "Cine etnográfico: Tecnología, práctica y teoría antropológica", Paul Henley enfatiza la importancia de la tecnología y las entonces nuevas cámaras digitales para hacer antropología, a inicios de este siglo en el que todo está dominado por la imagen. No obstante, desde los inicios del cine (1895), las cámaras se utilizaron como instrumentos del trabajo antropológico:[12] la cámara significó para el antropólogo lo que el telescopio y el microscopio para el científico de ciencias naturales, aunque no pretendiera necesariamente hacer documentales, sino solamente registrar imágenes como modo de descripción etnográfica. El autor resuelve que, pese a que el cine etnográfico es un modo de descripción de datos, nunca reemplazará el texto en el trabajo antropológico, pero sí puede emplearse en conjunción con aquel. En el mismo sentido, en "Por una antropología de la mirada: Etnografía, representación y construcción de datos audiovisuales", Elisenda Ardèvol destaca el potencial de la mediación de la cámara, la fotografía o el film, en la obtención de datos etnográficos en la investigación antropológica, que derivan en antropología visual.

En la misma ruta, Sergio Úbeda sostiene que de la confluencia entre el cine como arte y la antropología como ciencia resulta la antropología visual, que tiene como objetivo narrar y profundizar sobre las culturas humanas y su representación. En "Límites y posibilidades de la práctica del cine etnográfico desde la antropología visual", Úbeda señala que el medio audiovisual tiene la valía de ser un recurso significativo en el trabajo etnográfico para convertirse en un producto cultural y a la vez en recurso metodológico para la investigación social. El autor es optimista al señalar que la antropología visual debe aportar en la forma en que las culturas abordan, en el cine, tanto la representación de las alteridades como las autorrepresentaciones de las mismas.

Otro trabajo es el de Fermín Ledesma Domínguez, "Video indígena y comunicación política cultural: Análisis del caso Chiapas", que trata del empleo del video como recurso de comunicación política cultural en Chiapas, México, por parte de jóvenes. El texto da cuenta de tres fases del empleo del video indígena en Chiapas. La primera (en los setenta), a cargo del INI, se caracterizó por trabajos de antropólogos y/o cineastas que retrataban tradiciones y costumbres de comunidades indígenas pasivas. La segunda corresponde con el proyecto TMA a organizaciones y comunidades indígenas, del que ya hemos hablado y que buscó una autorrepresentación de las comunidades, aunque, a su juicio, no siempre ocurrió una representación alejada de la visión colonizadora y, desafortunadamente, las comunidades no tuvieron mucha incidencia en la definición de las narrativas visuales y en sus contenidos. En la tercera etapa, que tomó fuerza con la irrupción del EZLN en 1994, se da una auténtica apropiación de la tecnología y una mayor incidencia en la decisión de contenidos y narrativas audiovisuales "como recurso de comunicación política y cultural, marcada por una tendencia hacia el videoactivismo" (6).

Finalmente, en "La construcción de la identidad étnica a través de la lente cinematográfica. Una ruptura narrativa en la era global", Alfonso Muñoz Güemes enfatiza en la construcción de un nuevo lenguaje audiovisual y cinematográfico por parte de los pueblos originarios, a la que denomina narrativa postcolonial y que abre camino a una nueva literatura visual, hecha desde un espacio no hegemónico y en respuesta a la imagen estereotipada, y colonial, que de esos pueblos han hecho las y los realizadores no indígenas. Desde un enfoque que el autor considera muy personal, señala que el inicio de esa nueva narrativa postcolonial se da con el documental *Tejiendo Mar y Viento* (Lupone & Palafox, 1987),[13] que identifica como un paradigma etnográfico y al que denomina el metarrelato cultural del nuevo sujeto de conocimiento, porque el ejercicio de Teófila Palafox, coautora del trabajo, encarna

> el momento en el que por primera vez una mujer indígena toma la cámara y crea su propia mirada, pasa de ser objeto de la lente indiscreta de un cineasta externo, a ser ella sujeto cognoscente que se empodera y rompe con el meta relato del antropólogo masculino externo a la comunidad, que crea su visión del mundo indígena. (Muñoz 17)

El autor señala, con optimismo, que el proyecto de TMA a organizaciones y comunidades indígenas contribuyó a la creación de ese nuevo lenguaje cinematográfico.

En busca de definiciones

Con la intención de clarificar el entendimiento de las producciones audiovisuales indígenas, las y los siguientes autores comparten una serie de definiciones de términos como video indígena, cine etnográfico, antropología visual y video comunitario y colaborativo.

Tomando en cuenta que las definiciones se construyen a partir de características comunes, Köhler dice que es claro que existe una categoría de "video indígena" porque existen festivales de video indígena en América. Luego entonces, los festivales presentan películas con características comunes. Parafraseando a Steven Leuthold, Köhler afirma que una característica de estos videos es que "hay una estética indígena propia que es independiente de la tradición occidental [y] su particularidad radica en que es producto de identidades colectivas [o procesos interculturales] con ligas profundas con la tierra y el lugar" (Köhler 1).

En la entrevista que Christian León le hace a Gabriela Zamorano, académica del Colegio de Michoacán, curadora y difusora de video indígena latinoamericano, en su texto "Video indígena: Un diálogo sobre temáticas y lenguajes diversos", Zamorano considera que las definiciones de video indígena están llenas de tensiones:

> Mucho de lo que me he encontrado como video indígena tiene que ver con esta práctica de apropiación de las tecnologías por parte de gente que pertenece a comunidades u organizaciones indígenas y que, en muchos casos, tiene una línea de trabajo más política. Pero el hecho de ser indígena y hacer películas no significa hacer video indígena. Y bueno, también encuentro otros que dicen que no tiene que llamarse indígena. Podemos llamarlo comunitario. (León 20)

Esa es una de las tensiones de las que habla: es importante tratar de hacer las cosas de manera colectiva, pero también cuentan las voces individuales y la voz del artista. Otra tensión es la relación con las y los espectadores: videoastas indígenas haciendo trabajos que se ajusten a los cánones y formatos de festivales, cuando los tiempos y las formas en las comunidades son otros. Finalmente, concibe al video indígena más como proceso que como proyecto, más como algo inacabado, que se va moldeando, que como algo definido.

Por su parte, Antonio Zirión Pérez se enfoca en los alcances de la triada documental colaborativo, cine etnográfico y antropología visual en su texto "Miradas cómplices: Cine etnográfico, estrategias colaborativas y antropología visual aplicada". Sin pretender tratar cuestiones conceptuales profundas, Zirión entiende

> el documental colaborativo como una forma de etnografía experimental o una metodología alternativa para la investigación antropológica, muy propicia para explorar nuevas realidades sociales y culturas en transformación. [...] La noción de colaboración también comprende, a nuestro entender, una forma distinta de organizar el trabajo de realización, una estructura más flexible y horizontal que rompe con las jerarquías rígidas de la producción cinematográfica. (57)

El autor señala que los casos de cine colaborativo emergieron en Norteamérica,[14] por ser una región propensa a la innovación tecnológica, no obstante, en otras regiones del mundo se ha experimentado una mayor evolución de este cine.

Por último, Argelia González Hurtado, en su trabajo "Narrando la diáspora indígena a través de la cámara de Yolanda Cruz", sugiere que "se puede considerar como medio indígena a todo producto mediático que ha sido conceptualizado o producido por grupos o autores indígenas" (89). Tratando de ser más minuciosa, la autora nos dice que

> las producciones mediáticas indígenas deben estar enraizadas estética y culturalmente en la comunidad al representar relaciones sociales dentro de estas [...]; estas relaciones deben de ser representadas con un punto de vista desde dentro de la cultura [...]; o bien los realizadores

> deben estar física y culturalmente enraizados en la comunidad, aunque las producciones sigan las convenciones estéticas hegemónicas. (89)

También aporta que, en el caso de México, la definición de cine indígena ha estado muy relacionada con un estilo de producción apoyado por el Estado, específicamente desde el proyecto de TMA a organizaciones y comunidades indígenas (1989), dejando fuera aquellos trabajos producidos de manera independiente y colaborativa.

Textos que analizan corpus de películas

Por último, en este apartado hablaremos de textos que analizan películas y videos indígenas, ya sea que hayan sido realizados por habitantes de los pueblos originarios o por no indígenas. Entre estos, se comparten experiencias de realización comunitaria sobre la pesca, la práctica del tejido como recurso para contar historias, la migración, las danzas tradicionales, la recuperación de la memoria y la denuncia de injusticias.

Empezamos con Gemma Orobitg Canal y la entrevista a la realizadora Abenaki-canadiense Alanis Obomsawin en su texto "Cine, memoria y resistencia indígena en Canadá". El texto aborda su trayectoria y experiencias de dos documentales clave en su carrera. El primero es *Richard Cardinal*, que produjo cambios en las leyes canadienses sobre las escuelas de acogida, en la provincia de Alberta. El trágico caso de Richard Cardinal, un niño indígena que nunca pudo saber quiénes eran sus padres, cambió las leyes de la provincia: a partir de su historia, las y los niños indígenas, y no indígenas, tuvieron el derecho a saber de sus familias e incluso recibieron apoyos del gobierno para encontrarlas. El segundo documental, *Kanehsatake: 270 Years of Resistance*, aborda la historia de los setenta y ocho días de conflicto entre la nación Mohawk, en el pueblo de Kanehsatake, cerca de Montreal, y la policía y el ejército canadiense, por la defensa de sus territorios que el gobierno planeaba expropiar para la ampliación de un campo de Golf. Aunque la negociación sobre la propiedad de los territorios continuaba hasta 2002, Obomsawin comenta que el campamento que los indígenas hicieron durante el conflicto, al final les dio la victoria, porque la ampliación del campo de Golf no se realizó. La cineasta canadiense concluye que el cine documental es el medio más poderoso para dar a conocer injusticias, y que su labor como documentalista y activista obedece precisamente a ello, denunciar las injusticias que padecen las y los indígenas en su país.

Por otro lado, en "Video indígena y comunicación política cultural: Análisis del caso Chiapas", Fermín Ledesma habla de los trabajos de cuatro jóvenes indígenas zoques de Chiapas: Saúl Kak, Fortino Domínguez, Samuel Ávila y José Cordero. Estos son *Pan y Circo* (Kak 2015), que trata de las prácticas de los partidos políticos en Chiapas y las manifestaciones de campesinos en defensa del territorio zoque; *Viceversa* (Domínguez 2007) aborda los problemas de desplazamiento generados por la erupción del volcán Chichonal en 1982; *Te Tzitzunh Kotzajk 30 años después* (Ávila 2012), que muestra la cosmovisión de los pueblos zoques, sus tradiciones orales y espacios sagrados; y finalmente, *Las huellas de un volcán*

(Cordero 2010), que trata de la memoria colectiva y los problemas ambientales que produjo la erupción del volcán Chichonal.

Por su parte, el trabajo de Aleksandra Jablonska, "La disputa por las identidades étnicas en el cine mexicano contemporáneo", se enfoca en las representaciones de las identidades indígenas en una película de ficción, *Cochochi* (Cárdenas y Guzmán 2009), y dos documentales, *Eco de la montaña* (Echeverría 2014) e *Istmeño, tiempo de rebeldía* (Dell'Umbria 2015). De acuerdo con la autora, en ellas se ha incluido a los propios indígenas y a la naturaleza, esta última como parte misma del mundo indígena. Los trabajos han desfolklorizado la visión fragmentada que de ellos tiene la mirada colonizadora, ofreciendo un panorama de conjunto de todos los elementos que conforman su cultura, su vida espiritual, sus hábitos, sus formas de ejercer el poder y la resistencia, expresada en la defensa de sus territorios. En *Istmeño, tiempo de rebeldía*, la identidad se refleja en sus formas de vida, su organización, creencias, en la ausencia de propiedad privada y la práctica del trabajo sin remuneración en beneficio de todos (el tequio). Sobre *Cochochi*, nos dice que es una cinta diferente porque es protagonizada por los mismos rarámuris, hablan en su lengua, se filma en exteriores y se aprecia la geografía de la comunidad, las tomas son largas con planos generales y el transcurrir lento del tiempo en la vida rural. Jablonska concluye que en esas películas el discurso sobre las identidades étnicas es un tanto distinto a los esfuerzos que hizo anteriormente el INI y el proyecto de TMA a organizaciones y comunidades indígenas; la representación respetó el discurso indígena y mostró sus distintas dimensiones: la visual más allá de la verbal, y la mítica y simbólica más allá de la racional.

Mariana Rivera García realizó una investigación sobre el tejido como narrativa, con comunidades de mujeres tejedoras en México y Colombia, y que comparte en su texto "Tejer y resistir: Etnografías audiovisuales y narrativas textiles". El acervo son cinco etnografías audiovisuales,[15] como ella les llama, y cuya metodología nos permite comprender el fenómeno textil para narrar historias de violencia, desapariciones y desplazamiento que grupos de mujeres han vivido en sus comunidades. El tejido, como actividad colectiva, solidaria y de resistencia, les ha permitido contar aquellas escenas que les son difícil de expresar a través de las palabras, al tiempo que las ha empoderado como medio de resiliencia. En México, trabajó con grupos de la Costa Chica en Guerrero. La autora reflexiona que los cortometrajes le permitieron replantearse "el tema de la mirada, la observación y los sentidos; ha significado también nuevos retos para la etnografía, la metodología y la construcción de conocimientos compartidos" (158). Destaca que uno de los aportes de su investigación fue la vinculación entre grupos de mujeres tejedoras tanto de México como de Colombia. Finalmente, en torno al acto de representación, comenta que "el proceso documental [...] deja ver muy claramente cómo se teje la relación entre el realizador y las personas, se puede descifrar el grado de involucramiento, la honestidad de la estructura y forma narrativa, la elección del tono en el que se narra, así como las imágenes y testimonios" (159).

En "Investigación colaborativa y decolonización metodológica con cámaras de video", Juan Carlos Sandoval Rivera nos habla de una investigación en la que empleó cámaras de video para documentar la pesca tradicional de mujeres en una comunidad indígena de Zaragoza, Veracruz, México. El texto refleja su metodología colaborativa en la realización del documental, desde la publicación de la convocatoria, el diseño, la producción, la post-producción y la difusión del video. El autor realizó un curso-taller con las diez personas que respondieron a la convocatoria, "sobre saberes locales, técnicas de investigación, lenguaje cinematográfico, video participativo y edición de video" (169). El grupo afinó las temáticas del documental y sus responsabilidades en toda la producción. El resultado fue el documental participativo: *Los herederos de Achaneh* (de autoría colectiva 2013), que aborda la pesca tradicional, su transformación y leyendas, en la comunidad indígena de Zaragoza, Veracruz, desde la perspectiva de las y los jóvenes.

Finalmente, Argelia González Hurtado nos habla de los trabajos de la cineasta chatina Yolanda Cruz, en "Narrando la diáspora indígena a través de la cámara de Yolanda Cruz". La cineasta oaxaqueña es una realizadora independiente, particularmente de trabajos sobre la diáspora indígena en Estados Unidos. El primero de ellos, *Guenati'zá: The Ones Who Comes to Visit* (Cruz 2004), es un cortometraje documental que cuenta la historia del viaje de retorno temporal de Ulises García y su familia a su pueblo natal en Oaxaca. Yolanda Cruz es invitada a este viaje por la familia García y el cortometraje muestra la interacción entre la familia y su comunidad de origen. De esta manera, "se entrelazan las voces de los migrantes, los locales, los jóvenes, los viejos, las mujeres y, desde luego, la de la cineasta" (González 90). El segundo es *Sueños Binacionales / Binational Dreams* (Cruz 2005), documental de treinta minutos que habla de la migración de mixtecos y chatinos hacia Estados Unidos; así como de los lazos que estos grupos mantienen con sus comunidades de origen. González finaliza diciendo que los trabajos de Cruz coinciden con las preocupaciones de más cineastas indígenas: la identidad y la representación. En estos documentales queda de manifiesto "que el ser, pensarse e imaginarse indígena se entrecruza con el ser, pensarse e imaginarse: mujer, hombre, activista, mexicano, americano, oaxaqueño, mixteco, migrante, videasta, o artista" (97).

Reflexiones finales

En estas páginas se ha llevado a cabo una revisión de literatura hispánica sobre estudios de video y cine indígena en América del Norte, y se ha privilegiado el empleo de artículos, más que de libros; como producto de una investigación académica en medios digitales en tiempos de la pandemia de COVID-19. Los textos seleccionados fueron agrupados en cuatro categorías. En general, las experiencias de apropiación de medios audiovisuales por parte de pueblos originarios han ocurrido tanto en México como en Estados Unidos y Canadá. No obstante, cabe mencionar que solamente una tercera parte de los textos señalan experiencias de producción de video y cine indígena en Canadá y Estados Unidos; las otras dos terceras partes se centran en obras audiovisuales y/o experiencias de México. Por otro lado, salvo los dos documentales que se citan de la directora Abenaki canadiense, Alanis Obomsawin (de 1986 y 1993), la mayoría (diez) de las obras audiovisuales que apuntan los textos son entre los años 2011 y 2020; y sólo cinco entre 2000 y 2010.

Si hablamos del origen de los textos que componen el corpus de esta investigación, y siguiendo con las preguntas que se plantearon al inicio de estas páginas, no se puede sostener que exista una tradición de estudios en español sobre el video y cine indígena en América del Norte, es decir, escrita en conjunto por investigadoras e investigadores de los tres países de esta región. Es más preciso y entendible, por razones lingüísticas, que esa tradición sea mexicana, porque los textos publicados por revistas mexicanas representan poco más de la tercera parte del total (de casi treinta textos). En segundo lugar, están aquellos publicados en algunos países de América Latina, principalmente en Ecuador, Chile y Colombia; finalmente, otros menos son de revistas españolas y estadounidenses.

Es decir, en nuestro corpus, las miradas académicas que se dirigen hacia el video y el cine indígena en América del Norte provienen predominantemente de México y de algunos países de América Latina; también, el objeto de esas miradas son experiencias de producción de cine y video indígena en México, aunque no siempre auspiciadas con recursos públicos y por instancias gubernamentales: como lo demuestran los casos del colectivo austriaco Kinoki, en Chiapas, y de la organización méxico-estadounidense Chiapas Media Project/ Promedios. La ausencia de textos en español provenientes de Canadá y de los Estados Unidos no significa un desinterés académico en esos países sobre este tema; ya se había apuntado que, sobre ello, hay una tradición de textos en inglés, principalmente provenientes de los Estados Unidos; no obstante, dicha literatura no es objeto de esta investigación.

Otro aspecto a destacar en este trabajo son una serie de características del video y el cine indígena, que se pueden leer entrelíneas: si hablamos de métodos, formatos de producción y estilos, es un cine heterogéneo y horizontal; está más preocupado por un sujeto colectivo que por un sujeto individual; importan mucho las historias de comunidades; puede emplear las lenguas originarias como una poderosa herramienta de resistencia política; está enraizado al territorio, al lugar, a la comunidad y a las costumbres de donde proviene, por diversas que estas sean; por último, puede realizarse en colaboración intercultural, pero privilegiando las preocupaciones de las comunidades.

Sabemos que construir una definición sobre video y cine indígena es tarea compleja –tanto como son diversos los pueblos donde se ejercen estas prácticas–, sin embargo, hemos observado que en este tipo de video y de cine domina una visión que les define como una serie de trabajos, hechos o no por indígenas, que comunican lo que ocurre en sus comunidades; que rescatan su memoria colectiva; que buscan una mayor participación e inclusión democrática en los medios, para representarse como lo que son: mujeres, hombres, niñas y niños, migrantes, activistas, artistas, pescadoras, estudiantes y comunidades con su propia lengua y su particular cosmovisión, a través de la cual resisten de manera colectiva.

Finalmente, considero que la contribución de las obras audiovisuales a las prácticas decoloniales y a los estudios indígenas se observa a través de que estas obras privilegian temas como la defensa de los territorios y recursos; la visibilización de desplazamientos por problemas ambientales; la participación y el liderazgo femenino tanto en la toma de decisiones como en la vida económica de las comunidades; la defensa de tradiciones culturales, orales y espacios sagrados; la preservación de sus distintas lenguas; así como la resistencia política y el derecho a su organización. A través de estas contranarrativas, se ha posicionado la perspectiva indígena en el imaginario social, alejada de la objetivación que la ciencia y la estética colonial han ejercido sobre estos pueblos.

Esta investigación ha demostrado, también, la necesidad que los pueblos originarios tienen de trascender la mirada hegemónica que sobre ellas y ellos se ha construido, de subvertir las relaciones de poder y de representarse a imagen y semejanza de los objetivos del proyecto decolonial: la resistencia, la soberanía visual, la autodeterminación, la autonomía, el reconocimiento, la autoconstrucción, la afirmación cultural y el rechazo a los estereotipos. ¿Cómo lograrlo? No es necesario desechar las herramientas y las tecnologías occidentales que posibilitan la realización del video y del cine, basta con emplearlas para denunciar que todo aquello que hacen es político, porque son personas colonizadas y desposeídas, tanto de territorios, de sus formas de vida y hasta de sus propias imágenes.

Notas

1. Por cuestiones de espacio no pretendo hacer análisis de contenido o de audiencia de las obras audiovisuales aquí mencionadas, de ello se encargan las y los autores citados, quienes son de diversas latitudes, incluida la región de América del Norte.

2. La relación se entiende por razones culturales y de lenguaje; no obstante, existen innumerables estudios sobre la relación del video y el cine indígena mexicano con los demás países latinoamericanos; y además escritos en distintas lenguas.

3. Los títulos contenían palabras y términos que los alejaban de mi objetivo y los acercaban más a América Latina: Brasil, Colombia, Argentina, Bolivia, Ecuador, Chile, mapuche, Video nas Aldeias, América del Sur, aymara, amazonia, andino; entre muchas otras. También, estaban escritos en portugués o en inglés; eran catálogos de festivales de cine; trataban sobre una gran variedad de temas: resistencia, videoarte, videojuegos o videos musicales; pero referidos sólo a América Latina.

4. En este caso, sí se referían a la región de América del Norte, pero no abordaban el cine indígena en particular de ninguno de los tres países; o hablaban de antropología visual, en términos teóricos, basándose en autores europeos; o hacían recorridos a una historia del cine sin mencionar nada sobre cine indígena; o hablaban de cine indígena pero de otras regiones; o de la cinematografía estadounidense, pero desde una perspectiva de sistema-mundo y dominación.

5. Gabriel Arévalo (2013) señala que algunas y algunos autores han posicionado el debate desde los círculos académicos del mundo angloparlante (principalmente de Australia, Nueva Zelanda y Canadá), de los pueblos Sami, Cree, Mäorí, Cree-Metis, Bantú, Hawai y Quandamooka.

6. En otro pasaje de su trabajo, Arévalo (2013) recuerda que "el mito moderno ha creado la visión de que solo la ciencia occidental ha producido un saber válido y útil para los seres humanos. [...] El ego científico llevó a formular que sólo bajo los saberes y métodos occidentales se podría conocer de manera cierta la realidad. Sin embargo, como ya es evidente, los demás humanos no han sido idiotas, crearon saberes, sistematizaron procesos cognitivos, produjeron soluciones racionales a sus problemas, implementaron procesos de enseñanza y construyeron estructuras de saber y hacer, de vital importancia para su supervivencia y sostenibilidad en el tiempo" (60).

7. Para hablar de otros ejemplos de la misma región, es justo decir que esas falsas representaciones también ocurrieron en Canadá y en México. En el primer caso, destaca el documental etnográfico *Saving the Sagas* (Barbeau 1928), en el que, de acuerdo con Christopher Gittings (2002), pobladores de la nación Nisga'a, del Norte de la Columbia Británica, son representados sin capacidad de agencia, porque son los blancos de la National Gallery los únicos capaces de recuperar el patrimonio musical de aquellos, según el autor. Por otro lado, en México también vale la pena revisar el caso de actrices y actores blancos que representaban a indígenas, en películas como *María Candelaria* (1943), *Maclovia* (1948) y *Tizoc* (1957), por sólo mencionar algunos casos de falsa representación.

8. El proceso que implicó la realización y firma de esta Declaración llevó más de veinte años. Vale la pena mencionar que, en relación con este capítulo, son importantes los artículos del 11 al 16, que tratan del derecho a la libre práctica de sus tradiciones y culturas, a la libre manifestación y práctica de sus tradiciones espirituales y religiosas, a la transmisión de sus historias, idiomas y tradiciones orales, al control de sus sistemas e instituciones docentes para impartir educación en sus

propios idiomas, a la diversidad de sus culturas y a establecer sus propios medios de información en sus propios idiomas.

9. Cabe señalar que en adelante se habla de textos que mencionan obras audiovisuales y que la selección de dichas obras obedece a la tarea de cada autor. Solamente menciono las obras audiovisuales que ellas y ellos traen a colación. Por lo tanto, no existe, de parte del autor de este capítulo, ningún criterio de selección de obras audiovisuales. Por cuestiones de espacio no ha sido posible incluir algunos otros textos de autores ya referidos en esta revisión, entre los que recomiendo: "Hacía una re-conceptualización de las prácticas audiovisuales indígenas", de Christian León; "Una mirada crítica a la difusión televisiva del video indígena", de Axel Köhler; y, "La construcción de las identidades en el documental indígena", de Aleksandra Jablonska.

10. El soporte físico del cine es la cinta de película de 35mm., que es más costosa que el soporte de la cinta de video o de las cámaras digitales de video.

11. Como señala Köhler (2007), TV Tamix fue fundada por "participantes del proyecto Transferencia de Medios Audiovisuales [... y] formó la organización Radio y Video Tamix [...] En noviembre [de 1992] aprovecharon la existencia de un transmisor abandonado en su comunidad por IMEVISIÓN [...] para salir al aire [en el municipio] los sábados a las cuatro de la tarde, interrumpiendo la señal de TV Azteca" (187). Después de una serie de conflictos con las autoridades de la comunidad, la estación dejó de transmitir en 1997, retomando actividades un año después, para suspender definitivamente sus transmisiones en el año 2000.

12. El autor comenta que en 1898, Alfred Haddon filmó por cuatro minutos a un grupo de hombres con máscaras en una danza que significaba una ceremonia de iniciación, en un archipiélago cerca de Queensland y Nueva Guinea. Esos ejercicios, dice Henley, no pretendían hacer un documental, sino solamente un registro de imágenes como modo de descripción etnográfica.

13. El distintivo de narrativa postcolonial, por parte de Muñoz Güemes, se debe a que él considera a esa narrativa como una ruptura con la imagen sobre lo indígena creada por agentes externos y no indígenas, y que el autor identifica como una mirada colonial. Entonces, de acuerdo con la visión de Muñoz Güemes, es postcolonial "ya que son los mismos miembros del grupo étnico [...] quienes escogen ciertos elementos técnicos para crear un estilo narrativo propio. Eso conlleva a que ellos mismos también seleccionan las temáticas que abordan, creando sus historias o guiones narrativos con base a los intereses culturales que su propia cosmovisión les sugiere. En este sentido, podemos decir que esta manera de usar la técnica de cine y video les ha permitido crear un nuevo estilo narrativo, buscando sus propios argumentos para el guion o relato" (Muñoz 4).

14. En su trabajo, Antonio Zirión se refiere particularmente a Estados Unidos y Canadá como Norteamérica.

15. Los trabajos a los que se refiere la autora son: *Tejer para no olvidar* (2012), *Escribiendo sobre el telar* (2013), *Telares sonoros* (2014), *Re-tejiendo nuestro taller* (2016) y *El hilo de la memoria* (2015). Las ligas para ver los videos se encuentran en el artículo referido.

Obras citadas

Albán Achinté, Adolfo. "Pedagogías de la Re-existencia. Artistas indígenas y afrocolombianos". *Pedagogías decoloniales. Prácticas insurgentes de resistir, (re)existir y (re)vivir.* Vol. I. Abya-Yala. 2013.

Ardèvol, Elisenda. "Por una antropología de la mirada: Etnografía, representación y construcción de datos audiovisuales". *Disparidades. Revista De Antropología*, vol. 53, no. 2, 1998, pp. 217-240.

Arévalo Robles, G.A. "Reportando desde un frente decolonial: La emergencia del paradigma indígena de investigación". *Luchas, experiencias y resistencia en la diversidad y la multiplicidad. Cuadernos de trabajo*, no. 2, 2013, pp. 51-78.

Córdova, Amalia. "Estéticas enraizadas: aproximaciones al video indígena en América Latina". *Comunicación y Medios*, no. 24, 2011, pp. 81-107.

Cuevas Martínez, Alberto. "De la soberanía visual a la comunicación intercultural: Apuntes para una historia del cine y video indígena en México y América Latina". *Itinerarios de formación e investigación en Ciencias Sociales en América Latina y el Caribe*, CLACSO-CESMECA, 2018, pp. 110-120.

Cusi Wortham, Erica. "Más allá de la hibridad: Los medios televisivos y la producción de identidades indígenas en Oaxaca, México". *Liminar: Estudios Sociales y Humanísticos*, vol. 3, no. 2, 2005, pp. 34-47.

Gittings, Christopher. *Canadian National Cinema. Ideology, Difference and Representation.* Routledge. 2002.

González Hurtado, Argelia. "Narrando la diáspora indígena a través de la cámara de Yolanda Cruz". *Visitas al Patio*, vol.14, no. 2, 2020, pp. 86-99.

Halkin, Alexandra. "Fuera de la óptica Indígena: Zapatistas y Videístas Autónomos". *Revista Chilena de Antropología Visual*, no. 7, 2016, pp. 71-96.

Henley, Paul. "Cine etnográfico: Tecnología, práctica y teoría antropológica". *Desacatos*, no. 8, 2001, pp. 17-36.

Jablonska, Aleksandra. "La disputa por las identidades étnicas en el cine mexicano contemporáneo". *Catedral Tomada: Revista de Crítica Literaria Latinoamericana*, vol. 5, no. 9, 2017, pp. 220-252.

Köhler, Axel. "Nuestros antepasados no tenían cámaras: El video como machete y otros retos de la video-producción indígena en Chiapas, México". *Revista Chilena de Antropología Visual*, no. 4, 2004, pp. 391-406.

Ledesma Domínguez, Fermín. "Video indígena y comunicación política cultural. Análisis del caso Chiapas". *Revista Mexicana de Comunicac*ión, vol. 1, no. 140, 2017.

León, Christian. "Video indígena: Un diálogo sobre temáticas y lenguajes diversos". *Chasqui: Revista Latinoamericana de Comunicación*, no. 120, 2012, pp. 19-22.

Mignolo, Walter y Rolando Vázquez. "Pedagogía y (de)colonialidad". *Pedagogías decoloniales. Prácticas insurgentes de resistir, (re)existir y (re)vivir.* Vol II. Abya-Yala. 2017.

Muñoz Güemes, Alfonso. "La construcción de la identidad étnica a través de la lente cinematográfica: Una ruptura narrativa en la era global". *Saskab: Revista de discusiones filosóficas desde acá*, vol. 12, 2018.

Orobitg Canal, Gemma. "Cine, memoria y resistencia indígena en Canadá: Entrevista a Alanis Obomsawin". *Quaderns de l'Institut Català d'Antropologia*, nos. 17-18, 2002, pp. 121-133.

Reza, José Luis. "Una mirada al cine indígena: Autorrepresentación y el derecho a los medios audiovisuales". *Cinémas d'Amerique latine*, no. 21, 2013, pp. 122-129.

Rivera García, Mariana Xochiquétzal. "Tejer y resistir: Etnografías audiovisuales y narrativas textiles". *Universitas Revista de Ciencias Sociales y Humanas*, no. 27, 2017, pp. 139-160.

Sandoval Rivera, Juan Carlos A. "Investigación colaborativa y decolonización metodológica con cámaras de video". *Universitas Revista de Ciencias Sociales y Humanas*, no. 27, 2017, pp. 161-177.

Shohat, Ella y Robert Stam. *Multiculturalismo, cine y medios de comunicación: Crítica del pensamiento eurocéntrico.* Paidós. 2002.

Smith, Linda Tuhiwai. *Decolonizing Methodologies: Research and Indigenous Peoples.* Zed Books and University of Otago Press. 1999.

Soler, Carolina. "Media-médium: Entre la etnografía y el cine comunitario". *Universitas Revista de Ciencias Sociales y Humanas*, no. 27, 2017, pp. 179-194.

Úbeda Álvarez, Sergio. "Límites y posibilidades de la práctica del cine etnográfico desde la antropología visual". *Revista de Humanidades*, no. 28, 2016, pp. 197-216.

Zirión Pérez, Antonio. "Miradas cómplices: Cine etnográfico, estrategias colaborativas y antropología visual aplicada" *Iztapalapa: Revista de Ciencias Sociales y Humanidades*, 36, no. 78, 2015, pp. 45-70.

Obras recomendadas

Jablonska, Aleksandra. "La construcción de las identidades en el 'documental indígena'". *De Raíz Diversa*, vol. 2, no. 3, 2015, pp. 63-89.

Köhler, Axel. "Una mirada crítica a la difusión televisiva del video indígena". *Anuario CESMECA 2007*, 2008, pp. 175-199.

León, Christian. "Hacía una re-conceptualización de las prácticas audiovisuales indígenas". *Comunicación y sociedades en movimiento: la revolución sí está sucediendo.* Editado por Paula Restrepo, Juan Carlos Valencia y Claudio Maldonado Rivera, CIESPAL, 2017, pp. 61-87.

Obras audiovisuales mencionadas en el texto

Cochochi (Cárdenas y Guzmán 2009)
Eco de la montaña (Echeverría 2014)
El hilo de la memoria (Rivera 2015)
Escribiendo sobre el telar (Rivera 2013)
Guenati'zá: The Ones Who Comes to Visit (Cruz 2004)
Istmeño, tiempo de rebeldía (Dell'Umbria 2015)
Kanehsatake: 270 Years of Resistance (Obomsawin 1993)
Las huellas de un volcán (Cordero 2010)
Los herederos de Achaneh (autoría colectiva 2013)
Pan y Circo (Kak 2015)
*Re-tejiendo nuestro tall*er (Rivera 2016)
Richard Cardinal (Obomsawin 1986)
Sueños Binacionales / Binational Dreams (Cruz 2005)
Tejer para no olvidar (Rivera 2012)
Telares sonoros (Rivera 2014)
Te Tzitzunh Kotzajk 30 años después (Ávila 2012)
Viceversa (Domínguez 2007)

CHAPTER 10

"We *Are* the Canon": On Reconceptualizing Hispanic Studies from Indigenous Studies

Rita M. Palacios (Guatemala-born refugee settler)
Conestoga College

Juan A. Castillo Cocom (Maya, sometimes)
Universidad Intercultural Maya de Quintana Roo

Paul M. Worley (settler)
Appalachian State University

From the Wallmapu to Standing Rock, Indigenous voices have become increasingly prominent in global resistance movements. Although we join this chorus of Indigenous and non-Indigenous academics, scholars, and activists, we are wary that this chapter risks falling into a tired "diversity and inclusion" paradigm, with institutions and disciplines giving lip service to Indigenous Peoples and catchphrases such as "decolonization" without rethinking how they function or impact the lives of Indigenous Peoples. Decolonization in this context affixes historical players to specific roles, one of them being the Indigenous subject as a victim of the state. K'iche' scholar Emil Keme reminds us that Indigenous people inhabited this region long before settlers imposed the notion of Latin America, suggesting that the "Americas must die" in the sense that Indigenous people must move away from the "affective and political affiliation" that ties them to Latin America and instead look to their "own cultural and civilizational project" (53). Far from denying that the state—be it in Mexico, the United States, or Canada—has implemented policies and enacted violence that directly target Indigenous Peoples, what we must become aware of is the academic exercise of theorizing a type of decolonization that removes all agency and power from Indigenous Peoples.

Written in three voices, this chapter explores the relationship between Indigenous and Hispanic Studies as disciplines that, despite their separate trajectories and formations in the North American academy, in many ways have intertwined histories. We suggest that scholars and educators endeavor to not so much "Indigenize" Hispanic Studies but recognize that, without Indigenous Studies, there is no Hispanic Studies. We then provide concrete examples of how to proceed in terms of reorienting the discipline. Indeed, whether we are discussing Columbus's diaries, the works of Bartolomé de Las Casas, or the history produced by Diego de Landa, the earliest works of Hispanic Studies in Abiayala are proto-ethnographic texts that seek to understand an Indigenous "other" for a non-Indigenous reader. Founded on mestizaje, contemporary nationalisms simply update paternalistic gestures of "speaking for" without admitting Indigenous Peoples into nation-states as full citizens. Rather than incorporating Indigenous Studies into the existing paradigms of Hispanic Studies, we argue that Indigenous Studies is foundational to the very notion of Hispanic Studies, and that to incorporate Indigenous voices in our classrooms, disciplines, or institutions, we must begin by interrogating the very roots from which these structures have grown.

Who Studies What, Why, and How?

What would disciplines based on the dominant cultures in the so-called Americas be without the waves of invasion, colonization, and imperial conflict unleashed in the wake of Columbus's stumbling upon islands in the Caribbean? Would Spanish, the language signaled by the term "Hispanic," even be spoken here? It may go without saying that the whole notion of Hispanic Studies in Abiayala as we now know it would not even exist without the events of October 1492. As described by Walter Mignolo in *The Idea of Latin America*, the histories of settlers in this territory are more than simple happenings insofar as they installed an entire regime of knowledge to which the Argentinian scholar refers as Occidentalism. Mignolo's understanding of the consequences of this way of perceiving and then constructing the world bear directly on our arguments here:

> Western people have disciplines and Eastern people have cultures to be studied by Western disciplines. The West was, and still is, the only geo-historical location that is both part of the classification of the world *and the only perspective that has the privilege of possessing dominant categories of thoughts from which and where the rest of the world can be described, classified, understood, and "improved."* (36; italics in original)

Notions of "lo hispano" look quite different depending on whether or not one is in Canada, the United States, México, Argentina, or Spain, and one could argue that the name of the discipline "Hispanic Studies" is outdated given that, as Catherine Davies has pointed out, the discipline took root in Britain and the USA in the early twentieth century, with a primary interest in medieval and Golden Age peninsular studies (1). At the same time, we must understand the role of Spanish, both "as a colonized language within the US and as a colonial language in the hemisphere," as Sarah Dowling notes (26).

And yet regardless of location, Hispanic Studies would seem to have roots in the Iberian Peninsula that were grafted on to or transplanted to the Américas around five hundred years ago, with the hemisphere's Indigenous Peoples being understood as being among the passive objects of active Euro-Western knowledge. Like "American Studies," which in a US context almost never includes the Américas or "Mexican Studies," "Hispanic Studies" thus emerges as one of the dominant categories for describing, classifying, understanding, and "improving," as signaled by Mignolo. As such, we can connect this disciplinary impulse with Maori scholar Linda Tuhiwai Smith's comments about academic writing insofar as it "privileges sets of texts, views about the history of an idea, what issues count as significant," such that "by engaging in the same process uncritically, we too can render indigenous writers invisible or unimportant while reinforcing the validity of other writers" (36). Put another way, by privileging "Hispanic," a designation with European cultural and linguistic roots, is there a way to avoid marginalizing or outright invisibilizing Indigenous Peoples? To further complicate matters, Indigenous Literary Studies as an area of study that focuses on Abiayala is created and sustained by Western academia. Though Indigenous Peoples have lived in the region for millennia and have always found ways to express themselves creatively, their cultural production is only said to start with the Spanish invasion. As Aura Cumes (Kaqchikel) points out, "Existimos como indios sólo a partir del momento colonial" (Cumes and Aguilar Gil). In other words, when the Western academy turns to the exclusive study of texts (literary, historical, philosophical, scientific, to name a few) from the region, only what appears in Latin script is typically considered relevant, thereby erasing most of the knowledge produced by Indigenous people and subsuming parts of it to the service of Western knowledge.

In *Confronting Our Canons: Spanish and Latin American Studies in the 21st Century*, Joan L. Brown reviews graduate reading lists in Hispanic and Latin American Studies programs in the United States and notes that the only preinvasion Indigenous literature included is that "saved" by priests, ignoring Indigenous resistance and survival of more than five hundred years, not to mention the rich cultural production that has existed alongside, and perhaps despite, Western notions of literature: "The core canon contained no literature in any autochthonous dialect, despite their documented existence. Thanks largely to the dedication of Spanish priests, our inheritance of native literature from Hispanic America includes preserved precolonial works" (148). Silvia Rivera Cusicanqui critiques the practice of centering Western "discovery" and "recovery" as it refers to decolonial studies specifically but applies across disciplines, in which hierarchies are re-created and codified language put into place so that the original thinkers (as well as the nuances of their intellectual production) are cast aside and any real commitment and action forgotten:

> Sin alterar para nada la relación de fuerzas en los "palacios" del Imperio, los estudios culturales de las universidades norteamericanas han adoptado las ideas de los estudios de la subalternidad y han lanzado debates en América Latina, creando una jerga, un aparato conceptual y formas de referencia y contrarreferencia que han alejado la disquisición académica de los compromisos y diálogos con las fuerzas sociales insurgentes. (58)

Taking into account what Hispanic Studies means and the place of Indigenous Studies in the academy, when the question relating to the ways in which Indigenous Studies can enrich the former's inquiry arises, we, as scholars, students, and readers of literature, must beware of reinstating the status quo and further marginalizing Indigenous voices.

A host of issues arise when we consider the role of government policy in rethinking education to better reflect changing attitudes and the demands of Indigenous Peoples themselves. From our respective experiences and practices in the places where we live and work (Quintana Roo, North Carolina, and Ontario), one shared concern is the prevalence of performative gestures, which are often disguised as apologies and presented in policy form, leaving little room for dialogue and for real, significant change. Mexico's intercultural universities, for example, adhere to their mission to serve Indigenous communities; however, the Secretaría de Educación Pública pushes for a standardized "classic" curriculum that aligns with other higher education institutions and responds to the needs of industry. In Canada, formal calls for reconciliation address changes to the educational system (Truth and Reconciliation Commission of Canada), and the adoption of a curriculum across the disciplines has been swift but nonetheless critiqued by Indigenous Studies scholars who see the need for structural change rather than mere inclusion (Gaudry and Lorenz 220; Tuck and Yang 10). Over the past two decades, many of the policies that deal with Indigenous education enacted in Mexico, the United States, or Canada form part of the state's conciliatory efforts, a recognition of the harm done and the need for reparation. At the core of these efforts, and inherent in the idea of reconciliation, is the notion of apology, one of the drivers in the efforts to update curricula across disciplines. As we discussed drafts of this chapter, Castillo Cocom pointed out that the concept of apology is not wholly compatible with Yucatec Maya thought around issues of guilt, forgiveness, and fault. So, we must ask ourselves: What does it mean to call for a reconciliation that relies on an apology according to the terms set out by the perpetrator? In other words, how can reconciliation truly take hold if the apology does not consider the injured party's own understanding of the act of apologizing? In fact, we could go so far as suggesting that the apology offered by the state, with its origins in Judeo-Christian tradition, establishes a zero-sum game by which the perpetrator gains and holds a moral high ground in their admission of injury while the question of morality is transferred to the injured party, who must then accept the apology or risk their own morality. In some ways, forgiveness "is thought of as an ethical demand" of the repentant upon the victim, and in such a formulation the victim has a duty to forgive (Gormley 28).

We would like to suggest here that in the case of Hispanic Studies, we need to look at other notions of fault and forgiveness that align with Indigenous thought and practice. For example, according to Kaqchikel visual artist Ángel Poyón, in his community a fault is always accompanied by redress and reparative action; much more than a transaction where an apology is issued and forgiveness granted, it consists of a process, determined by the impact of the injury, in which both parties participate, and the perpetrator is held responsible to an entire community, not just the injured party. In some cases, a sense of shame or wrongdoing is forever attached to the fault so that it may never be repeated.[1] Under this light, and from the perspective of Hispanic Studies, the mere inclusion of Indigenous voices would be akin to a simple apology that reinforces the roles of perpetrator and victim (i.e., the Western academy and Indigenous voices). Instead, we propose that we move toward actual redress and reparation, not with the intent of effacing the fault but of recognizing it and paving a better way forward that changes the terms of engagement.

While reconciliation is indeed important, when led by the state and introduced by institutions, its implementation may leave much to be desired because, after all, the state often does not seek actual change but only its assured perpetuity. As with the inclusion of Indigenous Studies into the Hispanic Studies curriculum, the terms reside in the hands of those who shape it by including and excluding texts, themes, and authors. In many cases, texts written before or during the invasion (precolonial and colonial texts) and before the past two or three decades are presented as "dead texts" by long-dead authors that require no actual engagement with living Indigenous Peoples. Indigenous Studies requires the field of Hispanic Studies to engage fully and ethically with the awareness that the work that we do in the classroom and in our research does have profound and lasting effects on living peoples. Rather than perpetuate ideas that erase entire communities, overlook important achievements that take place beyond the written word and outside of Western norms, center non-Indigenous values, and selectively represent Indigenous voices, we must create space mindfully and change those terms of engagement.

Toward Alternatives

This chapter's title comes from the declaration of Muskogee Creek and Cherokee scholar Craig S. Womack that "tribal literatures are not some branch waiting to be grafted onto the main trunk. Tribal literatures are the *tree*, the oldest literatures in the Americas, the most American of American literatures. We *are* the canon" (italics in original, 6–7). That is, Indigenous literatures and Indigenous cultures in general are not passive objects that one can simply add to a syllabus or a reading list without in some way dealing with the fact that these precede settler societies in these lands by millennia. How can disciplinary formations like Hispanic Studies be inclusive of or dialogue with Indigenous Studies, particularly when, in many ways, such disciplinary formations were and are formed to justify and/or ignore the violence of settler colonialism? Remember, for example, the problematic positions of two Mexican thinkers who, in many ways, remain central to the discipline, José Vasconcelos and Alfonso Reyes. While he is a champion of mestizaje, in *La raza cósmica* Vasconcelos states matter-of-factly: "El indio no tiene otra puerta hacia el porvenir que la puerta de la cultura moderna, ni otro camino que el camino ya desbrozado de la civilización latina" (56). Of course, this statement pales in comparison to the opinions expressed in his *Breve historia de México*, where he writes: "Nada destruyó España [en la Conquista], porque nada existía digno de conservarse cuando ella llegó a estas tierras" (17). He refers to the K'iche' Maya *Popol Wuj* as a "colección de divagaciones ineptas…incomprensible ya para las razas degeneradas que reemplazaron a los no muy capaces que crearon los monumentos" (17). Perhaps more appreciative of Indigenous cultures, in the essay "Visión de Anáhuac (1519)," Reyes all but denies the existence of Indigenous Peoples in the Twentieth Century when he states, "Si esa tradición nos fuere ajena, está como quiera en nuestras manos, y sólo nosotros disponemos de ella" (30).

The contrast here between Womack, Vasconcelos, and Reyes is as telling as it is productive. Settlers must unlearn much of what they think they know about culture, history, and life in Abiayala. With regard to disciplines like Hispanic Studies, we would do well to keep in mind that Indigenous people often do not see themselves reflected in or interpolated by the discipline's frames, canons, institutions, and celebrated figures. Remember, for example, that the K'iche' poet Humberto Ak'abal, one of the hemisphere's foremost Indigenous writers, rejected Guatemala's most prestigious literary award, the Miguel Ángel Asturias Prize, explicitly because, although it was named after a man who won the Nobel Prize, that same man had written a master's thesis entitled "El problema social del indio." In interviews, the K'iche' poet explained that he simply would not accept an award named in honor of someone who had produced such racist scholarship. These difficulties, of course, go well beyond the impact of literary awards and cultural symbols. The Wahpetunwan Dakota scholar Waziyatawin (Angela Cavender Wilson) describes an early experience that she had at an academic conference in which a non-Indigenous senior scholar dismissed her position that, "because Indigenous people have other means of validating [their] historical record, historians should not subject [their] oral traditions to the same historical verification process as they would documentary evidence from their own written tradition" (78). As she goes on to point out, this dehumanization results in a "racist school curriculum" that contributes to high dropout rates among Indigenous youth (79–80). In other words, what may seem like superficial academic quarrels have very real consequences for Indigenous Peoples when their education frames them from racist settler perspectives.

How, then, might settler scholars engage with Indigenous scholars and their scholarship and ultimately collaborate in shaping a way forward? Although it may go without saying, many Indigenous-centered intercultural projects advocate that nation-states and their citizens reshape themselves so that there is true equality among Peoples, languages, and cultures. In a 1997 declaration, México's Escritores en Lenguas Indígenas states explicitly:

> La diversidad es nuestro proyecto. Por ello, pensamos que no puede haber igualdad mientras nuestras lenguas y culturas sigan subordinadas; no puede haber verdad mientras se siga negando nuestra existencia, no puede haber razón mientras no comprendamos que la diversidad es riqueza, no puede haber equidad mientras se privilegia una cultura y se someta a las otras (153).

In other words, the group does not seek to reinstall colonial hierarchies with Indigenous Peoples now positioned on top. Rather, true diversity means an end to such hierarchies and the regimes of inclusion they entail. Elsewhere, one of the group's members, the Nahua poet Natalio Hernández, takes these notions of equality several steps further when he suggests that, in a multiethnic and plurilingual society like México, "La sociedad hispanohablante tiene que aprender los idiomas de su región" (67). In many ways, a truly multilingual education system like the one suggested by Hernández would serve as a counterpoint to the ongoing failures of bilingual education throughout Abiayala. In his criticisms of Guatemala's education system, the Kaqchikel scholar Waqi' Q'anil (Demetrio Cojtí Cuxil) finds that, at present, the asymmetries between Maya languages and Spanish are simply reproduced: Maya speakers stop speaking their languages, whereas for Spanish speakers, speaking a Maya language simply becomes another language they can speak (38). That is, at present and despite best intentions, in a society where Spanish remains the dominant settler language, superficial bilingualism may in fact reinforce the ongoing marginalization of Indigenous languages. Setting herself apart from her contemporaries and coming from a much-needed intersectional lens, Aura Cumes sees the need for an entirely different model given that we risk recreating the same structures and repeating the same shortcomings of the modern nation-state:

> I do not agree with the idea of Plurinational States or the creation of Indigenous nationalisms, if what they do is repeat the bad habits of European nationalisms, many of them involving ethnocide and genocide. I am more in favor of an autonomy based on other, more suitable logics. Still, contemporary colonial-patriarchal Nation-States use their tremendous power to forbid these autonomies, and in the best of cases most accept the idea of "inclusion," a lethal trap for the existence of Indigenous, as this is [a] starting point for extending the Western, capitalistic, colonial and patriarchal ways of life. (Cumes)

Again, these movements are neither exclusive nor essentializing, and they interpolate settler participation. Stressing the importance of settler-Indigenous solidarity, in his article "For Abiayala to Live, the Americas Must Die: Towards a Transhemispheric Indigeneity," the K'iche' scholar Emil Keme states that, "by proposing Abiayala as *our* locus of political enunciation, I am not suggesting a civilizational project that is exclusive to Indigenous Peoples. In our movement toward emancipation, there have been many non-Indigenous sisters and brothers who have walked with us" (52). As Keme suggests, this shift in locus is not a mere discursive move but one that implies thought and action as we move toward the ultimate realization of a more just, egalitarian society. Decolonizing a syllabus or classroom is not enough, as settlers must come to understand how they relate to issues of land tenure, the environment, and the lives of Indigenous Peoples past, present, and future. In rethinking the relationship between Hispanic Studies and Indigenous Studies, we offer the following opportunities:

First, in the words of Castillo Cocom, who, in our discussion of alternatives and other ways forward, proposed: "En la queja misma está la propuesta." In other words, Hispanic Studies must be re-theorized from the ground up. As long as the Iberian roots of Hispanic Studies and its attendant canons are the accepted beginnings of the discipline, Indigenous Studies will remain in a secondary, lesser position. It is important to note that the latter is not a discipline in the traditional sense but a field of study integrated by many disciplines and methodologies. While this important feature presents many challenges, it also provides many opportunities: Hispanic Studies can learn and grow from the emerging and transformative field of inquiry that is Indigenous Studies. The nonhierarchical intertwining of the two will, in many ways, mark the beginnings of a new discipline. Put another way and in more general terms, Sami scholar Rauna Kuokkanen suggests:

> It is up to the academy to do its homework and address its own ignorance so that it will be able to recognize and give an unconditional welcome to indigenous peoples' worldviews

> and philosophies. But before the academy can recognize the gift of indigenous epistemes, it will have to profoundly transform itself; it will not be enough merely to include indigenous epistemologies (i.e., indigenous systems of knowledge or ways of knowing) in pedagogies and curricula. First and foremost, the academy will have to acknowledge that it is founded on very limited conceptions of knowledge and the world. Because of this constrained perception, the academy cannot grasp or even hear views that are grounded in other epistemic conventions. (2–3)

It would be naive to ignore the role that institutions play in shaping or promoting academic disciplines; the call issued by Indigenous scholars is not circumscribed to disciplinary parameters, but it is stridently political, recognizing the need for actual, deep decolonization. Elizabeth Cook-Lynn, speaking from a US context, sees in Indigenous Studies an impetus to "expose the lies of the self-serving colonial academic institutions of America, bolster the rights and obligation to disobedience, and resist the tyranny of the US fantasies concerning history and justice and morality" (16).

Second, moving beyond Hispanic Studies will have important consequences for disciplines such as American Studies and Canadian Studies and how they understand Indigenous Studies as well. Can these disciplines move beyond their emphasis on settler colonialism as the originary moment of these particular settler nation states? What happens if we were to retheorize these areas from the land on which they originate instead of European colonialism?

Third, Hispanic Studies must be hemispheric and tilt away from the European nationalisms that currently tend to define it. Whether we are discussing the colonial period or immigration in the twenty-first century, in many ways Hispanic Studies already acknowledges the insufficiency of national models of belonging. In the context of Indigenous Studies, and particularly within the context of Indigenous Peoples whose territories crisscross the artificial borders of current nation-states, these models are even more problematic.

Fourth, the discipline must be multilingual, and scholars must engage Indigenous languages by learning them alongside Indigenous Peoples. Can the term "Hispanic" in Hispanic Studies be resignified in such a way that it is inclusive of the numerous Indigenous languages that have been, are, and will continue to be spoken throughout the hemisphere? Given that language has been heavily implicated in nationhood since the nineteenth century and remains a limit of national belonging, it would seem doubtful. It would also be glib to suggest that all Indigenous Peoples see Spanish as an imposed language; there are many Indigenous authors whose mother tongue is indeed Spanish. Rather, what we suggest is understanding Spanish as one of a multitude of languages within the discipline of Hispanic Studies.

Fifth, the discipline must be multiscriptural. The bibliography on Indigenous writing systems in the so-called Americas is immense and yet, as formulated in the oft-cited statement by the kamëntsá poet Hugo Jamioy, "No sólo Colombia es un país analfabeta de lo indígena sino que podríamos decir que casi toda América es un continente analfabeta de lo indígena" (quoted in Rocha Vivas, *Palabras* 63–64).[2] Channeling Jamioy, how do settlers understand cultural production in the context of what Colombian scholar Miguel Rocha

Vivas has termed their "reverse illiteracy" (*Palabras*, 64)? Writers such as the Mi'kmaq artist and author Michelle Sylliboy, with her *Kiskajeyi—I Am Ready: A Hermeneutic Exploration of Mi'kmaq Komqwejwi'kaskl Poetry* (2019), and the Kaqchikel artist and author Negma Coy, in *Kikotem: Historias, cuentos, poesía kaqchikel* (2019), directly interrogate the assumption that Latin script is the only writing system in the Americas and speak to the vitality of efforts to continue using Indigenous writing systems.

Sixth, the discipline must understand how it relates to land. As Tuck and Yang point out in the title of their foundational article, "Decolonization Is Not a Metaphor," many "decolonial critiques" fall well short of actual decolonization insofar as they fail to address land rights, sovereignty, or even the work of actual Indigenous Peoples in the Americas (2–3). In this context, how does the acknowledgment that our institutions are on Indigenous lands change how and what we teach? Despite their stated political commitments, institutions in the US and Canada remain hostile to BIPOC scholars, while those in Latin America remain similarly hostile to Indigenous and Afro-descendant scholars. How might those of us who are settlers take action so that our institutions hire more Indigenous scholars and in turn make these institutions places where Indigenous scholars can thrive once they are hired? In turn, how can our institutions be more responsible to the communities on whose land we work and live as guests? Beyond "inclusivity," how does such an understanding lead settlers to better collaborate with members of Indigenous communities, whether these are academics or not, in the production of knowledge? How might such production in turn be used to support Indigenous land claims, whether we are talking about the Water Protectors in the United States and Canada, the Tren Maya in México, or Mapuche land struggles in Argentina and Chile?

Conclusion

In calling for a new discipline, or at least a Hispanic Studies that openly acknowledges and problematizes its Eurocentric, settler-colonial framework, we seek to rethink what we do, as scholars, recasting in new terms the what, how, why, and for whom. We cannot simply include Indigenous texts in our classes without also assuring that our institutions admit, support, and graduate more Indigenous students. We must not proclaim our institutional land acknowledgments without also hiring and retaining more Indigenous scholars and better collaborating with Indigenous communities. The Euro-Western knowledge systems in which we work cannot be updated to accommodate Womack's notion that Indigenous literatures, cultures, and Peoples were here first and are therefore "canonical" in this territory. As we have maintained, in this sense, the "inclusion" of Indigenous Studies within Hispanic Studies curricula begins by recognizing that the latter is in a secondary position to the former and should lead to new and different understandings of everything, from history to relationships with the land. Decentering settler ways of knowing and disciplinary knowledges is but a necessary first step. We have much work to do, but we are hopeful because we are initiating these difficult conversations, reflecting on our practices (as settlers, academics, allies, and so on), rethinking our approaches, and establishing multiple dialogues across disciplines, beyond academe, and through borders. Our work as researchers and educators will be better because we are taking on this responsibility, but more importantly, we are committing to improving our relationships with the people whose land we inhabit, actively engaging and centering Indigenous voices in Abiayala.

Notes

1. Ángel Poyón in discussion with Palacios, June 2021.

2. The bibliography on this subject is immense and varied, and a thorough exploration of this topic lies beyond the limits of this paper. With the usual caveats, the reader might refer to the following, all of which are included in our chapter's bibliography: Hill Boone and Mignolo; Rocha Vivas, *Mingas*; Worley and Palacios; González.

Works Cited

Brown, Joan L. *Confronting Our Canons: Spanish and Latin American Studies in the 21st Century.* Bucknell, 2010.

Cavender Wilson, Angela (Waziyatawin). "Reclaiming Our Humanity: Decolonization and the Recovery of Indigenous Knowledge." *Indigenizing the Academy, Transforming Scholarship and Empowering Communities.* Edited by Devon Abbott Mihesuah and Angela Cavendar Wilson. U of Nebraska P, 2004, pp. 69–87.

Cojtí Cuxil, Waqi' Q'anil Demetrio. *Tijonïk pa Ka'i' Na'oj pa Ka'i' Tzijob'al/Descolonización y Educación Bilingüe.* Maya wuj, 2015.

Cook-Lynn, Elizabeth. "American Indian Studies: An Overview." *Wicazo Sa Review,* vol. 14, no. 2, 1999, pp. 14–24.

Coy, Negma. *Kikotem: Historias, cuentos, poesía kaqchikel.* Cholsamaj, 2019.

Cumes, Aura. Interview by María Íñigo Clavo. "Conversation with Aura Cumes on Maya Epistemology, Postcolonial Theory and the Struggle for Identity." Translated by Lola García Abarca. *Re-visiones,* vol. 7, 2017.

Cumes, Aura, and Yasnayá Aguilar Gil. "Las mujeres indígenas: Defensoras de la vida y los territorios, hacia un pensamiento descolonial." Igualdad de género UNAM. May 27, 2021. https://www.facebook.com/igualdadUNAM

Davies, Catherine. "What Is 'Hispanic Studies'?" *The Companion to Hispanic Studies.* Edited by Catherine Davies, Routledge, 2014, pp. 1–12.

Dowling, Sarah. *Translingual Poetics: Writing Personhood under Settler Colonialism.* U of Iowa P, 2018.

Escritores en Lenguas Indígenas. "Declaración de los escritores en lenguas indígenas en torno a la diversidad étnica, lingüística, y cultural de México." *El despertar de nuestras lenguas/Queman tlachixque totlahtolhuan,* by Natalio Hernández. FCE, 2002.

Gaudry, Adam, and Danielle Lorenz. "Indigenization as Inclusion, Reconciliation, and Decolonization: Navigating the Different Visions for Indigenizing the Canadian Academy." *Alternative: An International Journal of Indigenous Peoples,* vol. 14, no. 3, 2018, pp. 218–227.

González, Gaspar Pedro. *Kotz'ib': Nuestra literatura maya.* Yax Te' Press, 1997.

Gormley, Steven. "The Impossible Demand of Forgiveness." *International Journal of Philosophical Studies,* vol. 22, no. 1, 2014, pp. 27–48.

Hernández, Natalio. *In tlahtoli, in ohtli/La palabra el camino: Memoria y destino de los pueblos indígenas.* Plaza y Valdés, 1998.

Hill Boone, Elizabeth, and Walter D. Mignolo, eds. *Writing without Words: Alternative Literacies in Mesoamerica and the Andes.* Duke UP, 1994.

Keme, Emil. "For Abiayala to Live, the Americas Must Die: Towards a Transhemispheric Indigeneity." *NAIS, vol.* 5, no. 1, 2018, pp. 42–65.

Kuokkanen, Rauna. *Reshaping the University: Responsibility, Indigenous Epistemes, and the Logic of the Gift.* UBC Press, 2011.

Mignolo, Walter. *The Idea of Latin America.* Blackwell Publishing, 2005.

Reyes, Alfonso. *Visión de Anáhuac y otros ensayos.* FCE, 1983.

Rivera Cusicanqui, Silvia. *Ch'ixinakax utxiwa: Una reflexión sobre prácticas y discursos descolonizadores.* Tinta y Limón, 2010.

Rocha Vivas, Miguel. *Mingas de la Palabra: Textualidades oralitegráficas y visiones de cabeza en las oraliteraturas y literaturas indígenas contemporáneas.* Fondo Editorial Casa de las Américas, 2016.

———. *Palabras mayores, palabras vivas: Tradiciones mítico-literarias y escritores indígenas en Colombia.* Taurus, 2010.

Smith, Linda Tuhiwai. *Decolonizing Methodologies: Research and Indigenous Peoples.* Zed Books, 1999.

Sylliboy, Michelle. *Kiskajeyi-I Am Ready: A Hermeneutic Exploration of Mi'kmaq Komqwejwi'kaskl Poetry.* Rebel Mountain Press, 2019.

Truth and Reconciliation Commission of Canada. *Truth and Reconciliation Commission of Canada: Calls to Action.* Truth and Reconciliation Commission of Canada, 2015.

Tuck, Eve, and K. Wayne Yang. "Decolonization Is Not a Metaphor." *Decolonization: Indigeneity, Education & Society,* vol. 1, no. 1, 2012, pp. 1–40.

Vasconcelos, José. *Breve historia de México.* Cía. Editorial Continental, 1956.

———. *La raza cósmica/The Cosmic Race: A Bilingual Edition.* Johns Hopkins UP, 1997.

Womack, Craig S. *Red on Red: Native American Literary Separatism.* U of Minnesota P, 1999.

Worley, Paul M., and Rita M. Palacios. *Unwriting Maya Literature: Ts'íib as Recorded Knowledge.* U of Arizona P, 2019.

PART 3

Indigenous Lands, Competing Found/(n)ational Narratives, and Governance

CHAPTER 11

Huacas y lugares sagrados como poética indígena

Fredy A. Roncalla
Hawansuyo

Si la literatura latinoamericana es un extenso corpus en constante redefinición, no es aventurado sostener que abreva de fuentes europeas tanto en sus idiomas –español y portugués– como en sus mitos fundacionales, que suelen ser grecolatinos y judeocristianos, de tal modo que las indígenas son consideradas "otra" literatura. Explorando lugares y objetos sagrados peruanos que suelen llamarse huacas,[1] y su presencia en la literatura peruana, sostenemos que la relación entre las poéticas indígenas y latinoamericanas es más cercana, a tal punto que la literatura escrita en el Perú se origina en el encuentro / desencuentro entre la escritura y la poética de las huacas. Una breve mirada a varios momentos históricos y autores peruanos nos llevará a plantear la obsolescencia de la categoría "otra literatura" peruana a favor de una espacialidad más horizontal entre las varias normas literarias peruanas ahora acogidas por la poética monumental y ancestral de las huacas, como es el caso del evento "La huaca es poesía".

La Huaca Mateo Salado es un complejo arqueológico prehispánico cerca del centro de Lima. Desde 2013, es escenario de un evento denominado "La huaca es poesía", que convoca autores de varias normas literarias del Perú y Latinoamérica. A la pregunta sobre lo poético de las huacas en el nombre del evento, este trabajo plantea que las huacas son *pakarina* (fuente principal) de las literaturas peruanas. La Huaca Mateo Salado es parte de una red de complejos arqueológicos que han sobrevivido la expansión de Lima, ciudad letrada poblada por Puruchuco, San Marcos, Garagay, Mangomarca, Juliana, Puente Piedra, además de Pachacamac, el gran oráculo. Hacia el norte del Perú se pueden nombrar Caral, Chán Chán, la Huaca de la Luna, Batán Grande, Huaca Rajada-Sipán y otros. En la costa sur quedan vestigios Chincha, Paracas y Nazca. Salvando diferencias, estos sitios son construcciones monumentales de barro y argamasa. Walther Maradiegue, en su manuscrito "Poética del barro: Ruinas andinas", ha estudiado una poética del barro y del desierto diferente de la lítica, que a su vez permitió al indigenismo imaginar la nación a partir de la piedra andina: "analizo el poemario *Visiones de Chán Chán*, escrito por el poeta peruano

José Eulogio Garrido en 1927, como un caso peculiar de poesía andina sobre ruinas construidas en base a adobes de barro y arcilla. Al alejarse de lo que denominó una fijación de la historia intelectual andina por la piedra, este poemario cuestiona el paradigma que asociaba 'Indigeneidad' con lo lítico" (Maradiegue).

En la poesía escrita peruana la huaca costera ha sido aludida en poemas sueltos y libros orgánicos por varios autores. Valgan algunos ejemplos. En *La casa de cartón* de Martín Adán (1928) hay varias alusiones a huacas en los campos de Barranco a Lima; y Bethoven Medina (2012) escribe el poemario *Ulises y Taykamano en Altamar* abrevando de fuentes míticas paralelas. Tanto en *Travesía moche* (2018) como en *Lambayeque evocadora: Espacio y poesía* (2021) el grupo Tetrálogos registra en poemas, planos e imágenes el influjo de las poéticas ancestrales peruanas en la literatura. Esto sin considerar publicaciones recientes cuya enumeración iría más allá de los límites de este breve ensayo

Aquí permítaseme detenerme un poco en el poeta, escultor y pintor vanguardista Jorge Eduardo Eielson, que luego de varios poemarios poblando la página con versos diáfanos y vanguardistas, llega a un momento que busca salirse de ella: quemarla, hacerle huecos, anudarla y enterrarla, desmoronando su sentido. La sección "Papel" de la antología *Poesía reunida* (1976) de Eielson culmina un proceso de varias entregas en que el poeta va minando el rol de la palabra en el papel y el rol del papel mismo, como sucede en "papel pisoteado", "papel higiénico", "papel blanco con cinco palabras", entre otros ejemplos. Eielson se acerca, con sus versiones escultóricas del quipu,[2] a las tradiciones indígenas donde no hay página en blanco ni vacío absoluto. Ahí no caben ni la falsa disyuntiva entre el ser y la nada, ni la crítica de la razón cartesiana por la parecida camisa de fuerza del surrealismo y el psicoanálisis. Más acá se extiende el desierto lleno de signos, pallares, huacos, quipus, acequias, huacas, y tejidos dejados por los ancestros que el poeta integra en su obra. Una parecida cercanía con el arte indígena la tiene también la poeta, *performer* y activista chilena Cecilia Vicuña, que ha incluido cerámica, tejidos, quipus y textos de Guamán Poma en *The Oxford Book of Latin American Poetry.*

Otra propuesta escritural enraizada en las tradiciones indígenas es aquella que Juan Ramírez Ruiz propone en *Las armas molidas* como escritura *hanan* o alfagramática.[3] Hanan es un término quechua que significa arriba o superior, y es uno de los componentes de la poética espacial que interactúa con *kay* (aquí) y *ukun* (adentro). La hanan sería entonces una escritura superior compuesta por alfagramas (término de Ramírez Ruiz) que el poeta propone a partir de su estudio de las tradiciones sígnicas originarias del Perú. Fundado por los poetas Jorge Pimentel y Juan Ramírez Ruiz, el movimiento poético Hora Zero propuso, en la década de los setenta, renovar la poesía peruana a partir del "poema integral", que incluiría toda la realidad peruana para cambiarla a partir del lenguaje. Las huellas y el camino que siguió Ramírez Ruiz para intentar un cambio radical en el lenguaje poético tuvieron precedentes en el seminal libro *La otra literatura peruana* de Edmundo Bendezú. Si bien se puede discutir lo apropiado de ver como "otras" a la literaturas originarias, Bendezú registra su origen desde antes de los incas hasta cuando varias formas originarias de poetizar se van perdiendo al momento de las crónicas coloniales. Ve huellas y archihuellas poéticas en Garcilaso, Betanzos y Santa Cruz Pachacuti Yamqui, y signa a Manco Capaq como poeta capaz de dialogar con las huacas, cosa que a la Biblia no le fue posible en la masacre de Cajamarca, cuando un cura le dijo al inca Atahualpa que el libro le hablaría. Tal huella estaría presente en las *Armas molidas*, donde el poeta, tras signar frejoles pintados, aríbalos, quipus y tokapus como capítulos iniciales de su travesía, hace un recorrido espacio temporal *hanan-kay-ukun* en busca de la escritura alfagramática, hanan, que es signario ancestral y clave para liberarse de la opresiva gramática colonial del conquistador. Esto inspirado por el dibujo del cosmos de Pachacuti Yanqui y por lo que entiende como libro tikuna, aymara, quechua y shipibo a partir de textualidades no alfabéticas ancladas en la oralidad y las poéticas del paisaje, cerámica, tejido, sonido, color y cuerpo. El poeta que camina el desierto con su camisa blanca ni delante ni detrás de nadie presagia las rutas del viaje: agua, fuego, aire y tierra, como propone Juan Guillermo Sánchez (2016) al hablar de los nativo-migrantes de las poéticas indígenas.

Visto esto, se puede sostener que en las extraviadas huellas y archihuellas, la pakarina del texto literario peruano viene de una pugna entre religión católica y huacas, como se verá brevemente. Alrededor de 1565 el cura Cristóbal Albornoz persiguió el mal llamado Taki Onqoy o "enfermedad del canto". Derrotada la religión solar inca, los cultos locales focalizados en las huacas son reactivados mediante el taki por Juan Choqne, para expulsar al dios invasor. Taki es una palabra quechua que designa canto, o cantar. Pero al momento de la conquista y la colonia, lejos de ser simple acto acústico, significa también baile comunal y ofrenda ritual. Su *performance* periódica asegura la continuidad de la cultura y es un vehículo de comunicación con los entes divinos, sean estos huacas, apus o actuales santos. Definido así, el taki es elemento central de la continuidad espiritual y cultural de los pueblos andinos. Proceso curativo del mal colonial, que había destruido el cuerpo social y sagrado, el Taki Onqoy fue un movimiento radical de resistencia a partir del cuerpo cuya poética y *performance*, al igual que el *Ghost Dance*, se expresó en canto y danza.

En el principio fue el taki y no la escritura. Para la iglesia esto era inaceptable, y llamó enfermedad a un movimiento que no lo fue. Nombrar desde el poder colonial es ejercer violencia. Nunca hubo idolatría en el Perú, pero los curas vieron cultos y ritos locales como tal. Entonces persiguieron y destruyeron objetos y lugares sagrados reverenciados como huacas, reprimieron a Juan Choqne, y designaron como enfermedad al taki, que antes como ahora es curativo, regenerador y cohesionador del tejido social indígena. Albornoz contó con la ayuda de un joven Guamán Poma que décadas después, distanciado del cura cronista Martín Murúa, escribió la *Nueva corónica y buen gobierno* (c. 1615) para erigirse en uno de los padres de la literatura peruana. Un texto que pese a su oposición a las huacas, defiende el taki (que es siempre sagrado) y despliega ordenamientos espaciales hanan/urin y arriba/abajo en la página, sujetándose a la poética espacial andina. Poesía concreta con cuatrocientos dibujos del padre del diseño gráfico, el cómic y la yuxtaposición de códigos quechuas y castellanos. Si a Juan Choqne y Guamán Poma los separa religión y escritura, los une la denuncia anticolonial.

Ya antes, al emprender la represión de los cultos locales, Albornóz inicia una inversión colonial donde lo que es de adentro pasa a ser concebido como de afuera, de tal modo que *ayllu*, cultura y pueblos originarios son el "otro". Esto se ha mantenido en estudios utopistas de la historia y el uso del psicoanálisis para condenar a Juan Choqne y el Taki Onqoy como regresión al cuerpo. Pero como posibilidad antisistémica, esta rebelión ha sido inspiración poética. Si *Las armas molidas* empiezan con varios dibujos de Guamán Poma como capítulos iniciales, Juan Choqne es un héroe del canto central. En el libro poema *Taki Onqoy* de Enrique Verástegui (1993), Juan Choqne dirige huelgas a la vez que dialoga con Mariátegui y mayo de 1968. En *El Canto del ruiseñor* de Nilo Tomaylla (2005), el héroe recupera una máscara sagrada robada por un traficante de Lima ayudado por dos jóvenes mujeres, en alusión a Juan Choqne y dos jóvenes que le acompañaban en los ritos del Taki Onqoy. Y en el arte popular o artesanía, han aparecido esculturas de madera enterrada que aluden a Pachacamac y otros seres míticos trabajados a partir de la memoria arquetípica. Lo mismo en joyería, donde pequeños ídolos de bronce representan el tumi, *illas*, lunas, soles, y figuras complementarias masculino / femenino. Tumi es una figura Moche que representa un cuchillo ritual, mientras *illa* es una figura asociada al rayo y el viaje.[4] Estas figuras masculino y femenino representan la dualidad complementaria subyacente a las culturas originarias peruanas y del continente. Y si desde la frontera Mercedes Sosa dedica una canción a Taki Onqoy como símbolo libertario, su continuidad se manifiesta en los danzantes de tijera y la fiesta dentro de las comunidades y pueblos migrantes para los cuales música, danza, canto y vestimenta son materia de la que estamos hechos, como diría José María Arguedas. Antes la música y baile del taki celebraban a las huacas, ahora fiestas patronales y peregrinaciones festejan santos donde antes hubo una huaca.

Décadas después de Juan Choqne, Francisco de Ávila, cura de Huarochirí, iniciaría una segunda persecución religiosa, que la historiografía de la ciudad letrada, manteniendo la epistemología de antiguos curas represores, designa como "extirpación de idolatrías". Según Guamán Poma, que ya había terminado la *Nueva Corónica* y se dirigía a Lima, Ávila acusaba a los pobladores de idolatría para saquear sus recursos y hacer puntos con la jerarquía católica. En este contexto emerge otro padre de la literatura peruana: el redactor quechua, que Gerald Taylor (1987) ha llamado Tomás en *Ritos y tradiciones de Huarochirí del siglo XVII*.[5] Se trata de un ciclo mítico completo. En torno a las huacas Pariaqaqa, Huatyacuri, Chawpiñanca, Huallallo Carhuincho, Cavillaca, entre otras, se cuentan mitos de héroes creadores que luego se convierten en piedras huaca. Me voy a detener superficialmente en algunas instancias de este ciclo sólo comparable al *Popol Vuh*.

Pariaqaqa es una huaca andina relacionada con Pachacamac, oráculo y mega huaca costera, que los curas querían equiparar al dios único. Cavillaca es embarazada por Cuniraya Wiracocha mediante una pepa de lúcuma y huye hacia el mar en Pachacamac. Parte de los atributos de Pachacamac es su asociación a Wiracocha o dios creador, y al Señor de los Milagros. Si el Señor de los Milagros usa el morado de las religiones yorubas africanas como símbolo prevalente, a lo largo y ancho de la historia espiritual peruana hay amplia adaptabilidad de las huacas a nuevos contextos religiosos. No regirse por el monoteísmo les da amplitud: eran multiculturales por naturaleza. Incluso la distribución espacial de las huacas / lugares suele determinar la ubicación de iglesias y sistemas de cruces y cargos en diversos pueblos.

El diálogo de Huaticuri con dos zorros aparece en la novela *El zorro de arriba y el zorro de abajo* que José María Arguedas (1971) escribe sobre Chimbote. Ahí zorros / huacas marcan un mapa identitario que ha salido de la página y ha vuelto a territorios andinos y de la costa. Los zorros son marcadores culturales que empiezan en Huarochirí y tras la novela de

Arguedas tienen ecos en poesía, narrativa y estudios sociales. Por ejemplo, es común referirse a escritores y migrantes andinos como zorros de arriba.

Al estudiar el *Manuscrito de Huarochirí* desde la teoría del paisaje, y ver que los curas no erradicaron del todo a las huacas, Rebecca Carte sostiene que ello se debe a que los nombres de las huacas, que permeaban todo el paisaje (*landscape*), eran una suerte de escritura que los curas no podían leer. Por otro lado, Manuel Burga, en una parte poco considerada de su libro sobre la supuesta utopía andina, ilustra cómo huacas y takis determinan el calendario festivo de los santos y patronos. No otra cosa son el Señor de Huanca, La Virgen de Copacabana, Mamacha Cocharcas, Taytacha Qoyllur Rit'i, entre otros. Los paisajes acústicos, físicos y sagrados son subyacentes a todos los espacios andinos, amazónicos y costeros. No hay lugar sin nombre cargado de historia y herencia arquetípica. El espacio y sus huacas son poesía concreta tanto en los Andes como en las cuatro direcciones del Abiayala.

Paralelo al *Manuscrito de Huarochirí*, a fines del siglo XVI e inicios del XVII cuando el Inca Garcilaso, Pachacuti Yamqui, Góngora, Cervantes y Shakespeare daban su legado a la literatura universal, Guamán Poma concluye su *Primer nueva corónica y buen gobierno* y viaja a pie de Sondondo a Lima para instruir e informar al rey acerca de la barbarie colonial. Del sur al norte, tratando de remontar la espacialidad colonial, el mundo se ve al revés. Con una prosa chapu chapu, mezcla de quechua, castellano y otros idiomas, la *Nueva corónica* es tal vez el libro más estudiado e importante de la literatura peruana. Aquí cabe repasar sólo unos aspectos espaciales. De aquel joven que ayudó a un cura en la represión a Juan Choqne, queda un largo capítulo condenatorio de las huacas y "yerronias"; pero los ordenamientos espaciales de la página escrita y el dibujo funcionan de acuerdo a posicionamientos que, como sabemos, son determinados por la poética o escritura espacial que la cultura inscribe en el paisaje a través de las huacas. Varios de sus dibujos ilustran la fiesta y el taki, en especial uno en el que una llama enseña un canto, y otro en que unas sirenas hacen lo mismo desde un cerro / huaca. No es casual que Guamán Poma defienda una y otra vez el taki. Si desde el monismo la oposición entre Guamán Poma y Juan Choqne es tajante e irreconciliable, desde la complementariedad *yanantin* hay mayor fluidez. Yanantin es una palabra quechua que indica pares opuestos y complementarios que son claves para el funcionamiento social y simbólico: femenino/masculino, arriba/abajo, adentro/afuera. Sin el yanantin la poética espacial no sería posible. Son parte de una unidad mayor. Si Guamán Poma defiende e ilustra el taki en la escritura, Juan Choqne lo hace con el cuerpo y el baile. Guamán Poma es el primer poeta (escritural) concreto del Perú. Se ve en sus dibujos y en su escritura a mano. El cuidado con que traza cada palabra, las diferencias en tamaño de letra, la combinación de subtítulos en las viñetas, sus parlamentos, apuntes al margen de la página y otros elementos paratextuales, dan al texto un miski (sabor dulce) que se pierde cuando se le lee en edición impresa y anotada, y mucho peor en castellano normalizado. Aparte de ello, Guamán Poma es el primer escritor en usar las categorías hanan, kay y ukun que varios siglos después son fundamento de las epistemologías andinas del sur.

En este mismo periodo aparecen el Inca Garcilaso y Juan de Santa Cruz Pachacuti Yamqui. Ya en el exilio, el Inca Garcilaso (1943) trabajó los *Comentarios reales de los Incas* a partir de sus recuerdos de infancia y algunas fuentes escritas. Siguiendo relatos maternos propone varias definiciones de las huacas, que tenían sacralidad polisémica. Una de ellas refiere a objetos o presencias que podían ser sumamente bellos o feos. Es decir portadores de un atractivo sublime, casi en términos de Bataille (1988), pero perfectamente manejables dentro de la cultura. Los *Comentarios reales* influyeron en la rebelión de Túpac Amaru y han sido materia de recientes congresos interdisciplinarios.

Por su parte, el dibujo del universo que presenta Pachacuti Yamqui (1993) ha sido clave en entender la espacialidad de Guamán Poma y los pares masculino/femenino, arriba/abajo, izquierda/derecha en los estudios andinos. En poesía, es la pieza fundamental, el archi-símbolo matriz que Juan Ramírez Ruiz busca y plasma en el alfabeto hanan o alfagramático de *Las armas molidas*. Pachacuti Yamqui tiene además un pasaje acerca del dios serpiente o Amaru, divinidad que ha permeado la historia peruana. Por otro lado, la vaca del conquistador se convierte en la waka andina,[6] ganado de valles y altura asociado al Amaru, al cual se le hace fiestas de herranza, con waka takis (canciones del ganado) e invocación a los Apus para protección y fertilidad.

Vista la influencia de las huacas en los padres de la literatura peruana, hay que señalar que mientras en la costa éstas son restos arqueológicos casi siempre ceremoniales, en los Andes, las huacas han sido resemantizadas como Apus, Pakarinas, Illas y Huamanis (Huamanis y Apus son términos intercambiables). Su sacralidad se ha mantenido a cargo de los guardianes kamasqa en el taki, [7] el gesto ritual y varias poéticas espaciales que empiezan a plasmarse en las literaturas indígenas, y también en escritores canónicos que retoman estas fuentes unas veces con honestidad, y otras como apropiación simbólica. Entre estas transformaciones semánticas y actanciales son de notar las narrativas sobre santos patronos de los pueblos. En *Atando santos: Origen e identidad en la tradición oral* (2018), libro fascinante que cuenta cómo ciertos santos de Moquegua, al sur del Perú, aparecen en un lugar y no siempre se quedan en el santuario que el pueblo les ha construido, Teresa Torres Calisaya propone que esta narrativa debe ser parte del corpus literario nacional. Nada más acertado para replantear la jerarquía literaria más allá de las hegemonías capitalinas y grafocéntricas de la ciudad letrada, que apoyadas en la escritura y el español han pasado, tras un largo proceso de discriminación y jerarquización, a ocupar un lugar central.

Por su parte, ya sea en alusiones a la naturaleza, el espacio, la Pachamama, Apus, Huamanis, zorros y cóndores, la literatura ha mantenido un diálogo fructífero con huacas, Apus y entidades sagradas. Abundan ejemplos de creación y crítica literaria reciente. No es coincidencia que Julio Noriega estudie la literatura quechua y el tecnotexto en *Caminan los Apus*; que Edwin Chillce nos hable del territorio y la cultura como poéticas en el trabajo de Hugo Carrillo, Carlos Huamán y Dida Aguirre; que Alison Krögel preste especial atención a varias poetas mujeres en su libro *Musuq Illa*, nombrado en alusión a un objeto sagrado; y que la editorial en lengua indígena más importante, Pakarina Ediciones, tenga nombre de huaca. Por otro lado, las últimas décadas han sido testigo de la emergencia de poéticas indígenas provenientes de varias culturas originarias del continente que comparten una relación fundante con el territorio, su simbolismo y sus mitos de origen, ya sea en Standing Rock, el desierto Apache, el Wallmapu Mapuche, las fuentes de agua en Colombia, o los bosques amazónicos, para citar algunos ejemplos.

Desde 2013, "La huaca es poesía" ha albergado varias lecturas literarias peruanas, con la inclusión reciente de eventos dedicados a las literaturas indígenas, como charlas y recitales de poesía quechua, amazónica y en mapudungun. La poética concreta del espacio monumental alberga aquella de la escritura y apuntan a borrar de una vez por todas anti-poéticas de hegemonía, exclusión cultural, social y sobre todo humana del quehacer artístico y cultural.

De vuelta al centro.

La Huaca es poesía

Notas

1. Huacas o wakas en la costa peruana suelen ser construcciones prehispánicas, generalmente ceremoniales, mientras que en la cordillera andina remiten a lugares y objetos sagrados.
2. El quipu, es un sistema de notación y resguardo de memoria usado por los antiguos peruanos mediante nudos y cuerdas de diversos colores. En sus *performances* y esculturas Eielson retoma los nudos de los quipus.
3. Hanan es un término quechua que significa arriba o superior, y es uno de los componentes de la poética espacial que interactúa con *kay* (aquí) y *ukun* (adentro). La hanan sería entonces una escritura superior compuesta por alfagramas (término de JRR) que el poeta propone a partir de su estudio de las tradiciones sígnicas originarias del Perú.
4. Ver *Mosoq Illa: Poética del hawari en runasimi* de Alison Krögel.
5. Un estudio más detallado sobre el Manuscrito y sus proyecciones actuales se hace en el capítulo "Viven hasta ahora, canancamapas causan: El Manuscrito de Huarochirí como puente al futuro" de este volumen, redactado por Victor Quiroz Ciriaco, Estelle Tarica y Ana Lucia Tello.
6. Según Juan Guillermo Sánchez, *waka* es nombre del ganado vacuno en la lengua cherokee, influencia del castellano "vaca" en el *tsalagi* (comunicación personal).
7. Encargados de la memoria de las huacas (según el poeta y músico quechuahablante Hugo Carrillo, comunicación personal).

Obras citadas

Adán, Martín. *La casa de cartón*. PEISA, 1974.

Arguedas, José María. *El zorro de arriba y el zorro de abajo*. Editorial Losada, 1971.

Bataille, Georges. *The Accursed Share*. Zone Books, 1988.

Bendezú, Edmundo. *La otra literatura peruana*. Fondo de Cultura Económica, 1986.

Burga, Manuel. *Nacimiento de una utopía: Muerte y resurrección de los Incas*. Fondo Editorial, 2005.

Carte, Rebecca. "Los paisajes vivos como texto: Las topografías sagradas de Huarochirí". *Hawansuyo.wordpress.com*, 4 de mayo de 2023.

Chillce, Edwin. *La poética chanka en tres poemarios*. Editorial Horizonte, 2020.

Eielson, Jorge Eduardo. *Poesía escrita*. Instituto Nacional de Cultura, 1976.

Garcilaso de la Vega, Inca. *Comentarios reales de los Incas*. Emecé Editores, 1943.

Guamán Poma de Ayala, Felipe. *Nueva corónica y buen gobierno*. Institut d'Ethologie, 1936.

Krögel, Alison. *Musuq illa: Poética del harawi en runa simi (2000–2020)*. Pakarina Ediciones, 2021.

Maradiegue, Walther. "Poética del barro: Ruinas andinas". Unpublished manuscript, 2020.

Noriega Bernuy, Julio. *Caminan los apus: Escritura andina en migración*. Pakarina Ediciones, 2012.

———. *Poesía quechua en el Perú*. 2d ed. Pakarina Ediciones, 2016.

Ramírez Ruiz, Juan. *Las armas molidas*. Arteidea Editores, 1996.

Sánchez Martínez, Juan Guillermo. "Coordenadas nativo-migrantes". *Diálogo,* vol. 19, no. 1 2016, pp. 3–4.

Santa Cruz Pachacuti Yamqui Salcamayhua, Joan de. *Relación de antigüedades de este reyno del Pirú*. Instituto Francés de Estudios Andinos, CBC, 1993.

Taylor, Gerald. *Ritos y tradiciones de Huarochirí del siglo XVII*. IEP / Campodónico Ediciones, 1987.

Tomaylla, Nilo. *El canto del ruiseñor: El retorno del ñaupa machu*. Albatros, 2005.

Toro, Eldi, Tania Temoche, Patricia del Valle, and Nora Curiosny. *Lambayeque evocadora: Espacio y poesía*. Tetrálogos, Municipalidad Provincial de Lambayeque, 2021.

———. *Travesía Moche*. Tetrálogos, 2018.

Torres Calizaya, Teresa. *Atando santos: Origen e identidad en la tradición oral*. Pakarina Ediciones, 2018.

Verástegui, Enrique. *Taki onqoy*. Lluvia Editores, 1993.

Vicuña, Cecilia, and David Grossman. *The Oxford Book of Latin American Poetry*. Oxford UP, 2010.

CHAPTER 12

Iddisig, un poco más allá: Dule Poetic Gatherings

Sue Patricia Haglund (Dule)
University of Hawai'i at Mānoa

> *La literatura oral en el pueblo kuna es su misma vitalidad. Todas las luchas que ha librado el pueblo kuna han surgido de su mismo lenguaje-vivencia.*
>
> *Oral literature in the Kuna Nation is its very vitality. All the struggles that the Kuna Nation have fought have arisen from their own language-experience.*
>
> —Aiban Wagua, "Las huellas de la palabra," *La Prensa 1995*

"Poets govern Gunayala" is a fitting, rhythmic description of Dule governance and society, as expressively observed by the Nicaraguan poet Ernesto Cardenal (Colman).[1] After his brief visit to Dule society, Cardenal's observation referred to the *saglas* (or Dule social-spiritual administrative chiefs) as poets. That is to say, poets are the leaders, and their songs are interpretative politics. Dule oral tradition still exists and thrives in Panama. As a Dule woman and scholar, I am making clear that Dule oratory is a thriving language praxis of the autonomous nation of Gunayala, of my people, and of my genealogy. Our oratory is an unbroken, existing practice, and it supersedes Western written texts. To share a little background relating to Dule oratory, we must look to the practice of oratory in the Dule gathering house. In an *onmaggednega* (a Dule gathering house), for example, the *sagla* (the first chief) sings to the community at large, while the *abinsaed* (the second chief) sings in response to the sagla's narrative, and the *argar* (the third chief) interprets and imparts all of the songs' metaphors voicing and decoding these to the rest of the community in vernacular language (Colman; Howe, *The Kuna* 31–50). In all of these songs, the chiefs, from the sagla to the argar, inform and develop the imagination of Dule governance. Further, the saglas display and possess profound historical knowledge and exceptional poetic talent (Colman). And it is for this reason that observers, like Ernesto Cardenal, often describe them as poet-rulers.

Dule governance, in every communal context, comprises multiple leaders and includes medical practitioners and cultural specialists. Each governing entity articulates and fuses together the practices of politics and aesthetics within a single, collective body (Haglund 58). One can neither divide nor compartmentalize the collectivity of Dule artful-political practices and way of life into separate, distinctive systems (Haglund 58). Instead, it is from the entwinement of Dule poetry and governance where we find interweaving layers upon layers of interpretative networks singing with each other and to each other while interpreting each other's songs. The purpose of discussing the correlation between governance and contemporary poetry is to demonstrate continuity and cultural permanence in different contexts. In this chapter, I examine the works of two Dule poets: Aiban Wagua's "Civiliza mi corazón, mamá" (Civilize my heart, mama) and Manipiniktikiya Abadio Green's "Tinaja" (Clay Jar).

Dule poetry centralizes and interprets the way politics manifest an aesthetic governance of Dule lifeworlds and epistemologies. In fact, Dule poetry is an ontological extension that narrates the Dule relationship with Nabgwana (Mother Earth) as a balanced partnership where the Dule view their/our role as being part of the universe but not the center of it (Iguanape). It transmits an evolutionary connection with important events in Dule (hi)stories, such as the 1925 Dule Revolution (which is discussed later in this chapter), while invoking to return to songs and stories of Babigala (which is a network of Dule narratives and histories addressing their existence, the role of a Dule in the universe, as well as addressing a community's social and moral practices). As such, the poems of Aiban Wagua and Manipiniktikiya Abadio Green offer connectivity to and empowerment within Duleness and Dule history by reflecting on the relational bond of humans, land, and Nature. Their poems exemplify philosophical identity and cosmological expression in different poetic forms: the spoken word and written art.

These contemporary Dule poets make use of the Spanish language in their works, which in turn enable their poems to be accessible to a broader audience. Green's and Wagua's usage of the Spanish language in their poetry demonstrates versatility in their existence in two worlds: the Dule and Panama. Here a reader (Dule and non-Dule alike) is invited to understand the essence of being Dule through the poets' perspective and descriptive words as they (re)tell Dule (hi)stories and the ways of life in urban and rural settings. The act of writing allows Dule poets to keep and sustain the culture and tradition not by replacing oral tradition but by broadening oratory to an additional format: the printed text. Writing is an avenue and is an extension of Dule oratory in which the words are active agents that display an ontological practice to represent Dule presence and culture on paper.

In establishing the works of these Dule poets as active agents within everyday Panama, this chapter reveals how the evolution and perpetuation of oratory and written poetry visibly exemplify the metamorphosis of Dule society, culture, and politics. Oral tradition and poetry equally share common experiences while expressing an insurgence of cultural permanence. There is a dual role importance of oratory and written discourse. The roles of Indigenous oratory and Western written text (with)in Indigenous communities/nations are poetically politicized because both forms of discourse create outlets for a people, like the Dule, to persist within the larger, non-Indigenous space(s), continuing to practice their culture, way of life, tradition, language, and history. The addition of utilizing Western written discourse creates an annex to this verbal artistry. Further, they are political and function as a mechanism for communication in order to express directed actions of resistance against injustices committed by a hegemonic group over another.

Even though these Dule poets write in the Spanish language, they still challenge existing perspectives of the Dule represented in outsider narratives and interpretations that tend to perceive the Dule and their writings through foreign, Eurocentric, ethnographic lenses with regard to the political and social spheres and, as such, present ontological biases that deny the Dule any authentic political and artistic actualities. The opinions asserted within both historical and contemporary analyses by non-Dule scholars reproduce these biases. For example, James Howe, an American anthropologist, states Dule writers "seem caught in the contradiction between the written and spoken word" (*Chiefs* 246). By this, Howe claims that Dule authors like Abadio Green (2004) try "to resolve this contradiction through denial, by asserting that 'the writing of indigenous peoples is life,' that is, that oral and written are one and the same" (Howe, *Chiefs* 246). It is important to recognize and note that Howe, as a non-Dule scholar, made valuable contributions to Dule research and studies. However, it is also imperative to critique some of these interpretations when applied to the literary genre. Howe's understanding of Dule writers and their literature is a paradox. Even though he claims there is a contradiction, *there is no contradiction between orality and printed text*. These two systems of communication complement and extend the range and communicative ability of each other.

While insightful in many ways, these perspectives and accounts need to be qualified in order to produce more complete histories of the Dule specifically and of Panama overall. As Chickasaw scholar Jodi Byrd points out, "The problem with hegemony is that one never does have to think about it, and all too often, Native scholars and authors are left with the task of confronting the unthinking hegemonies that continue to shape academic knowledges about indigenous peoples" (83). In the academic realm, where studies of Indigenous peoples are labeled and categorized, often by non-Indigenous peoples, it is imperative to set up a practical intervention of resistance that protects Indigenous peoples and nations from being labeled and cataloged as specimens contained by Western academic structures and knowledges. A nonviolent resistance to academic compartmentalization creates empowerment and independence for Indigenous authors and thinkers from the realm of Western academia that, oddly enough, always finds a way to define them. One mode, for example, mentioned by Byrd through the works of Crow Creek Lakota poet and scholar Elizabeth Cook-Lynn, is the necessity and importance to "restructure Native studies to reflect the intellectual sovereignty of Native nations and to resist the fetishization of political independence by academic hobbyists, tourists, and the writers of fiction and memoir" (83). In the case of the Dule, the peoples' own literary works (which are currently absent from academic discussions) have to be included in Indigenous Studies, as well as Indigenous Abiayala literature.

The lack of recognition given to Dule literature in Panama itself, and also elsewhere in Abiayala, places and categorizes Dule existence in Western academia through the myopic and limited studies of sociological, anthropological, and ethnological frameworks. In fact, non-Dule anthropologists, for example, have obscured significant aspects of Dule culture and existence in Panama. Works from prior amateur anthropologists, such as José Reverte's 1968 work *Literatura oral de los indios cunas* embraced Dule oratory to the extent that it "merited stylistic analysis" (Howe, *Chiefs* 192). Yet Reverte carelessly interprets Dule knowledges and stories with "European rhetoric, folklore theory, a priori assumptions, guesswork, and displays of erudition" (Howe, *Chiefs* 192). Reverte embraces the value of studying Dule oral poetry and stories—but only to skew them with misinterpretations that were non-Dule; also, this outsider interpretation reasserts a Western-centric position on Indigenous peoples like the Dule, insisting that their knowledge and practices were limited and primitive (Howe, *Chiefs* 193). For this reason, I look to the works of Manipiniktikiya Abadio Green and Aiban Wagua to dismantle these Eurocentric misinterpretations.

Aiban Wagua's Poem: "Civiliza mi corazón, mamá"

In "Civiliza mi corazón, mamá," Dule poet and scholar Aiban Wagua references Dule-specific narratives and names as a way to distinguish Dule culture from Panamanian culture (*Kaaubi* 110–112). In Panama, Wagua has published numerous literary works, such as poetry, books, and essays. Some of his titles, just to name a few, include *Kaaubi*, *Gabsus*, *Babgan Soge*, and *En defensa de la vida y su armonía*. Returning to Wagua's poem, there are a variety of elements of Dule culture, medicinal practices, and stories illustrated in the poem. The rhythmic tone of the poem elucidates angst, sensitivity, pain, loss, disconnect, and yearning for connection to a cultural identity. As Raúl Leis points out, Wagua's poem speaks to a profound pain that was so great that the Dule man forgot his name (2).

"Civiliza mi corazón, mamá" opens with the speaker crying out to his mother for comfort. The speaker calls on the variety of mother figures one finds in Dule culture: Nana (the Great Mother), Gabayai (Ibeler's mother), a cry to Nabgwana (Mother Earth) as well as one's biological mother. Wagua writes:

Vengo muy pobre, mamá	I am very poor, mama
recoge mi hatillo de ropa sudada	pick up my bundle of sweaty clothes
y mira que no queda nada en la calabaza	and see that there is nothing left in
de la chicha fresca	the fresh chicha gourd
que se llevó tu adolescente unas lunas atrás.	that your teenager took a few moons ago.
Heme aquí, mamá	Here I am, mama
tu pequeño cazador apiñando lanzas,	your little hunter piling up the lances,
desamado y asustado	as I feel unloved and scared
con una hamaca proletaria mal enrollada.	with a poorly rolled up proletarian hammock.
Vengo lastimado, mamá	I come hurt, mama
he mamado los pechos de Kueloyai	I suckled the breasts of Kueloyai
y entre tanta arma ajena	and among so many foreign weapons
perdí hasta mi nombre	I even lost my name (my trans.; *Kaaubi* 110)

The mother figure in Dule culture is "everything," and the woman is represented and depicted through molas (Dule women's traditional dress), therapeutic songs, Babigala and ecological surroundings (Colman). The repetitious usage of "mamá" calls attention to the speaker's layered profundity of pain and disconnection (Wagua, *Kaaubi* 110–112). At the same time, it is calling attention to the similarly layered longing for solace (Wagua, *Kaaubi* 110–112). The above stanzas display myriad emotions, detailed and layered on top of each other. Similar to the layers of a mola, their adjectival phrases describe the feeling of emptiness that a Dule may experience when one is separated from his/her spiritual-cultural communities and/or is confined to an unrecognizable place. This is reflected in Wagua's choice of words: "very poor," "sweaty clothes," "unloved and scared," "poorly rolled," "hurt" and "lost" (Wagua, *Kaaubi* 110). These expressions simultaneously isolate and integrate the speaker's emotional process relating to Dule history and community.

Furthermore, the thread of connectivity is displayed when Wagua refers to "fresh chicha," "proletarian hammock," and "Kueloyai" (*Kaaubi* 110). Chicha is a fermented cane liquor. It is a vital traditional drink in a Dule girl's puberty ceremony. Symbolically, this drink fortifies and connects the speaker to his/her Dule communal practices, as will be discussed in Manipiniktikiya Abadio Green's "Tinaja." The difference, however, is the emotion behind the expressive usage of chicha. In "Tinaja," the liquor is an empowerment to invoke historical memory and present-day solidarity. However, contrary to that is the way in which the drink is noted in "Civiliza mi corazón, mamá" as a lamentable longing for what is missed. The chicha mediates a reconnection to culture, to family, to the mother figure, to self, that is otherwise inaccessible where the speaker currently resides.

Wagua does not specify the current whereabouts of the speaker. Nevertheless, the phrases "proletarian hammock" and "Kueloyai" imply that the speaker is a Dule who lives in the city—away from the community and outside of Gunayala. While the speaker lives in an urban area, their living experience in this unfamiliar place is one of deception—Kueloyai—as the speaker cries, "I suckled the breasts of Kueloyai" (*Kaaubi* 110). In the Dule origin story of Ibeler and his siblings, Muu Gweloyai or Kueloyai (mother of the toads) raises the orphaned Dule siblings, and Muu Gweloyai tells them she is their mother (Wagua, *Así lo vi* 22–35). Ibeler and his siblings find out from animal allies that Muu Gweloyai's son killed the siblings' mother, Gabayai (Wagua, *Así lo vi* 22–35). After realizing this deception, Ibeler and his siblings find their way back home and set out to battle Gweloyai, Biler, and their allies for the injustices and death of their mother (Wagua, *Así lo vi* 35). In doing so, Ibeler justifies his actions: "Muu Gweloyai me mintió, me robó la mamá, y mi deber fue defenderme" ("Grandmother Gweloyai lied to me, she stole my mother from me, and my duty was to defend myself"; my trans.; Wagua, *Así lo vi* 35). Gweloyai represents deception in unfamiliar places and symbolizes a different way of life in an urban area that steals, separates, and disconnects a Dule's identity, a Dule's living expression and cultural practice. She embodies the perils of emptiness and loss of culture.

Thus, the speaker cries to the mother for salvation. The speaker is isolated from their culture and home. They feel the asphyxiation of Western society, lamenting:

Mamá, susúrrame palabras que perdonan,	Mama, whisper words of forgiveness,
vuelve a civilizar este corazón mío	recivilize this heart of mine
y haz de él una barricada	and make a barricade of it
porque alguien debe quedarse en casa:	because someone has to stay home:
ya suena estridente el tambor de la escuela	the drums already sound shrilling and loud
y han callado tu suara, tu koke, tu kangi.	and have silenced your suara, your koke, your kangi (my trans.; *Kaaubi* 112).

As the speaker asks for forgiveness and calls on the remembrance of Dule culture, rites, musical instruments, and curing chants, there is a slow reconnection to his past, identity, and home. As a result, the reclamation of Dule medicinal practice, culture, and identity is revealed in the recitation of Dulegaya phrases.

For example, the poet calls out myriad phrases that reference different medicines, using words that reflect medicinal practices, language, and practitioners. Wagua provides the reader with a glossary of specific terms: *inaduledi* (medicine man specializing in curing and plants), *akuanusa* (smooth stone used in Dule therapy), and *siguanala* (clay brazier) (*De la tinaja* 35). In terms of medicinal culture, Wagua names *akebir'uala* (medicinal shrub), *suara*, *koke*, *kangi* (musical instruments used in Dule culture), *Tad Ibe* and *Ibelele* (names of the same being who represent freedom, goodness and value) and *usuyae* (the agouti [a type of rodent related to guinea pigs] dance) (Wagua, *De la tinaja* 35). Lastly, Wagua mentions Kueloyai (mother of the frogs in Dule stories) (*De la tinaja* 35). Aiban Wagua utilizes all these Dule sources, especially those of everyday life and medicinal practice, to metaphorically express both content and stories of absence and presence, of invisibility and visibility, and of isolation and returning to community.

Following Ibeler's story in which the siblings confront Kueloyai and return to their proper home, the speaker also must confront his/her own pain and return home. As Dule artist and storyteller José Colman points out: "Porque a los indígenas se nos acusan de ser salvajes, de no entender nada, de ser ignorante, y entonces lo cual no es así. Porque la cultura occidental si no entiende, si no aprende y si no convive con la cultura indígena; nunca va a entender [de lo] que [hay] dentro de la cultura guna" ("Because they accuse Indians of being savages, of understanding nothing, of being ignorant, which is not so. Because Western culture does not understand, if they do not learn by actually living with the Indigenous culture, they will never understand Guna culture"; my trans.; Colman). If a Dule does not confront the real danger of cultural annihilation, then cultural return would be difficult and challenging, but not impossible, to attain.

Manipiniktikiya Abadio Green's Poem: "Tinaja"

I now turn to "Tinaja," a poem by Dule poet, activist, and philosopher Manipiniktikiya Abadio Green who resides in Colombia. This is a short poem about warriors, war, resistance, and continued existence. In this poem, Green uses imagery to symbolize both place and historical events in Dule culture that bind the Dule as a people and society together. He poetically calls into existence the Dule history of resistance as told by the elders, a history against the process of assimilation into Panamanian society:

que la tinaja tiene vida	tinaja has life
que la tinaja representa	tinaja represents
la resistencia de nuestro pueblo.	the resistance of our people (my trans.; Green 26).

The "tinaja" is an earthenware jar. This pottery symbolizes the earth. It is a material made of the land; thus, from its origin, the tinaja is transformed from clay to a jar. The pottery itself is in a new form of life. It is created from small particles of the earth to become an object used for everyday tasks, such as food preparation. In a greater essence, the tinaja also becomes a place of resistance for the Dule—because, like the Dule themselves, the strength of the tinaja brings forth the *strength* of the people who resist the invasion and complete assimilation into the culture of the West.

Dule resistance, although it is briefly described in the poem, is largely symbolic for the poet. It demonstrates how a people and nation come together to fortify themselves, like in the tinaja, from outside invasion. In the armed resistance of the 1925 Dule revolution, the Dule warriors (*urigan*) fought against Panamanian colonial police forces (Tice 61–62). While Dule men took up weapons for the protection and preservation of traditions and culture, Dule women rose up by wearing their traditional mola dress (even though it was banned in the early 1900s by Panamanian colonial police) in order to express their full resistance to assimilation to the Panamanian society (Tice 62). After every battle, the *urigan* must complete a process for community reintegration. The isolation and purification rituals are ways to refocus and reintegrate the *urigan* back into Dule society (Howe, *A People* 272). The *urigan's* isolation cleanses and protects a Dule's spirit or *burba*, but also the community's *burba* (Howe, *A People* 272).

These warriors, in Dulegaya, are described as *uri* (singular form for warrior) or *urigan* (plural form for warriors), *macheret urwed* (man who fights), and *ome urwed* (woman who fights) (my trans.; Colman; Martínez Owen). In addition, by mentioning resistance "La resistencia de nuestro pueblo," most Dule would instinctively understand that Manipiniktikiya Abadio Green is referring to or calling to the reading mind, all of this history of resistance as told and retold by Dule leaders and linked to Dule nation's memory (Green 26).

The short line "La resistencia de nuestro pueblo" is very significant as it indirectly makes reference to a history of war and Dule warrior(s) (Green 26). Despite the importance of Dule warrior history, non-Dule scholars like Kanien'kehaka scholar Taiaiake Alfred, *slight* this history of resistance and rely on their own misapplied interpretation of Dule words. Most significant is the notation of Dule warriors, *urigan*. The Dule understanding of what defines a warrior, thus, contradicts Alfred's interpretation of Dule vocabulary. He states "For the Kuna: there is no literal equivalent for the English term [warrior]…and the closest approximation is *napa-sapgued*, meaning 'One who protects or guards the land, or nature'" (Alfred 80). He further claims the Dule lacked a term for "warriors" in their own language (Alfred 80). To clarify his position, Alfred continues, "To get at this notion beyond my own people's cultural heritage, I asked a number of people from different nations to tell me what the *warrior* word was in their own language" (80). In his endnotes, Alfred explains that the term for warrior in Dulegaya was provided by Anishinaabe scholar Brock Pitawanakwat, who speaks Spanish, but not Dulegaya (Alfred 100).

I draw out Alfred's usage of the Dule term for warrior in order to demonstrate the perils of lexical misrepresentation. Unintentionally, this misrepresentation takes away and discounts the Dule *urigan* (warrior) history, which, in turn, makes them indistinguishable. Additionally, the misapplication of the Dule word for warrior, both during and after translation, does not fully consider the complexity and nuance needed to fully describe a people and language. The Dule are a prime example of a people whose culture is still intact; they exercise the right of self-determination, and oral tradition continues to be an integral practice in their communities. The example of *urigan* makes clear that certain ideas assumed and/or applied to Dule and Dule culture by non-Dules place limitations upon how others may view Dule people, culture, and history.

This outsider-driven misrepresentation and misinterpretation is problematic even when done by other Indigenous scholars. The unwanted, problematic viewpoints overlook all interactions and history the Dule had and continue to have with other persons who reside in Panama and those who reside outside the country's territorial borders. These groups include other Indigenous peoples of Panama, as well as settlers from Jamaica, Colombia, Scotland, France, and the United States. In essence, the representation and usage of words do matter. In contrast to Alfred's deduction, however, the Dulegaya term *urigan* is, in fact, a "literal equivalent for the English term" warriors (Alfred 80). Aiban Wagua clarifies that *urigan* are combative Dule fighters trained to defend Gunayala (Wagua, *Así lo vi* 150–151). Wagua eloquently describes:

> Los urigan eran nuestros abuelos que combatían contra los invasores, contra los europeos, contra los wagas. Los urigan eran defensores de esta tierra, nuestros combatientes. Como se trataba de muerte, de peligro, les decían urigan. Eran seleccionados entre los mejores cazadores, entre los mejores flecheros y arqueros, entre los que corrían más, entre los que conocían mejor los escondites de las selvas, entre los que no tenían miedo a morir. Los urigan eran sometidos a baños medicinales para correr mejor, para esconderse rápidamente, para no perderse en las selvas.
>
> ("The urigan were our grandfathers who fought against invaders, against Europeans, against wagas. The urigan were defenders of this land, our fighters. Since this was death, danger, we called them urigan. They were selected among the best hunters, among the best arrow makers and archers, including those who were running more, among those who knew better hiding places in the forests, including those who were not afraid to die. The urigan were undergoing medicinal baths to run better, to hide quickly, to avoid getting lost in the jungles"; my trans.; Wagua, *Así lo vi* 135–136).

In addition to Wagua's findings, Colman describes what happens to an *uri* after a battle and returns to his/her community. He clarifies: "Sean preparados esas personas y cuando ellos regresan, la propia comunidad los aísla por varios meses lejos de la comunidad en un lugar tranquilo como para humanizar de nuevo a las personas que fueron a combatir" ("These people are prepared and when they return, the community itself isolates them for several months away from the community in a quiet place in order to humanize again the people who went to fight"; my trans; Colman).

Most specifically, days after the 1925 Dule Revolution, the *urigan* stayed away from the community-at-large to perform "purification to rid them of the pollution of blood and danger from their victims' souls, detaching them from war and effecting their reentry into life" (Howe, *A People* 272). It is important to note that an *uri* never wants to enter into battle unnecessarily, but if there is a threat of invasion, the *uri* would be obligated to defend territory and culture as demonstrated throughout the Dule history, from the Spanish invasion to the 1925 Dule Revolution (Colman).

In other Dule stories, similar generational linkages are made that serve to erase time and allow the people to sit with one another. These stories allow great, great, great grandparents to speak to their children. For instance, Green describes the Dule drinking a liquor drink, fermented cane, used in Dule ceremonial practices (26). With the description that a Dule drinks, Green writes:

por eso el Tule bebe esa caña fermentada hasta la saciedad	That is why a Dule drinks that fermented cane to satiety
porque beber es recordar el camino de los mayores	because to drink is to remember the elders' ways
es embriagarnos con nuestra historia.	it is to intoxicate us with our history (my trans; 26).

In the poem, the Dule represents the people. In honoring the Dule as a nation, it is only right for one to drink the "caña fermentada" (fermented cane liquor also known as chicha used in ceremonial practices) (Green 26). It is a way to pay respect to our elders who have gone before us/them (Green 26). The power of the chicha drink is understood as something magical, thus defining a realm in which history and reality meet. The intoxication that one experiences, therefore, is not the liquor itself but all the intergenerational knowledge and history that older generations have paved for and share with new generations. The act of consuming the fermented beverage serves as a catalyst and an extension of Dule ontology. It inhabits and evokes indigeneity in ephemeral spaces shifting Dule ontological history from thought to memory and from language to speech. Regardless, these shifting words and historical memory invocations, like the tinaja, fortify and unite Dule people in multilayered existences.

Iddisig: Looking a Little Further

To close, I would like to emphasize the empowering nature of poetry and politics. As the Dule artist and storyteller José Colman highlights during our personal interview: "la poesía y la política no pueden aislarse" ("poetry and politics cannot be separated"; my trans.;

Colman). Certainly, poetry and politics cannot be inaccessible either (Colman). In most Western communities, poetry and politics are fragmented and separated (Colman). In comparison to Dule traditional political-spiritual leadership, Western society's political and religious leaders function in separate areas that force communities to operate and develop as individualist rather than progressing as a collective entity (Colman). Solidarity and collective participation are the essence of Dule governance, everyday life, and history. Similarly, we find a binding connection of poetry and politics—via the tone and rhythm of words—as well as cultural ceremonies and customary practices that cannot be divided from each other. If these components are separated, then there is the possibility that Dule indigeneity in one form or another would be dismantled, rendered incomplete, or eventually erased. The connectivity of poetics and politics in Dule orality and writing is unbroken and inseparable political-cultural practices in space and time. They are layered expressions of spoken word that transcend and inspire contemporary Dule written poetry. The assemblage of words—spoken and written—ties and unties Dule solidarity in formats that pay homage to Dule oral tradition. Contemporary Dule poets, like Manipiniktikiya Abadio Green and Aiban Wagua, are similar to our Dule leaders the *saglas*. That is, both contemporary poets and *saglas* as poet-rulers live in multidimensional worlds of Dule lands and urban spaces. Their poetry and politics are the expressive renderings of Dule orality on paper. Their work of lexical art is often overlooked and invisible. Yet their gatherings of verses blend architecturally with their urban environment and their calling upon Dule ontology and histories. Contemporary Dule poets are the urban *saglas* of our Dule gathering house, *onmaggednega*, who bridge multidimensional worlds on paper, much as our *saglas* bridge Dule lifeworlds and knowledges in spoken word. Thus, we stand to learn much by linking the works of Dule poets in Panama and Abiayala, while fostering a hemispheric approach to Native Studies and Indigenous Abiayala Literature. Itogua.

Annex

Below is a list of Dule poets whose poems are published in Panama, but little acknowledgment is shown both in and outside of Panama. Dule poets published in the first and only poetry anthology, *Antología de poetas kunas* (Editorial Urrigan, Panama, 2015) include Arysteides Turpana Igwaigliginya, Aiban J. Velarde Chiari, Taira Edilma Stanley I., Plinio Chiari, Inawinapi Cebaldo De León, Manigueuigdinapi Stanley, Sue Patricia Haglund, Austin Hernán, Kinyapiler F. Johnson G., Inawilipe Diwigdi, Abdil Brenes, Dimitry Díaz Smith, and Maninaindi Roldán. Dule poets who published poetry books: Aiban Wagua, with several poetry books published: *Kaaubi* (Kuna Yala: Privately Printed, Panama, 1997) and *De la tinaja kuna* (Ustupu, Kuna Yala: Privately Printed, Panama,1987). Aiban Velarde Chiari published several poems that appear in *Antología de novísimos poetas panameños*, INAC, Panama, 1998 and several poetry books: *Las aventuras del vigilante* (2015), *Napa Tierra* (2017) and *Peregrinas del sol* (Editorial Mariano Arosamena, Mi Cultura, Panama, 2021). Maninaindi Roldán published in 26 Lágrimas de Luz, Antología de taller (PROFE, 2018) and poetry book, *Demonios en mi desierto* (editorial El duende gramático). Other poems written by Dule poets Irik Limnio, Leadimiro González, and Awibe Harmodio Vivar Icaza published their works in Panama's national newspapers such as *La Prensa* and other virtual venues.

Note

1. The Dule (spelling variation also seen as Tule) refers to the original inhabitants of Gunayala, Panama. In Dule language, it means the original people. Other terms used by the Dule and non-Dules are "Guna" and the spelling variation of "Kuna" or "Cuna." For my own work, I use the term "Dule."

Works Cited

Alfred, Taiaiake. *Wasáse: Indigenous Pathways of Action and Freedom*. Broadview Press, 2005.

Byrd, Jodi A. "(Post)Colonial Plainsongs: Towards Native Literary Worldings." *Unlearning the Language of Conquest: Scholars Expose Anti-Indianism in America*. Edited by Don T. Jacobs, U of Texas P, 2006, pp. 81–93.

Colman, José. Personal Interview by Sue Patricia Haglund, March 2, 2009.

Green, Manipiniktikiya Abadio. "Tinaja." *El Siglo* (Panama), October 12, 2003, p. 26.

Haglund, Sue P. "Dule Molas: The Counterpoint-Counterplot Practice of the Traversable Cloth in (Non)Digital Realms." *Indigenous Interfaces: Spaces, Technology, and Social Networks in Mexico and Central America*. Edited by Jennifer Gómez Menjívar and Gloria Elizabeth Chacón, U of Arizon P, 2019, pp. 56–78.

Howe, James. *Chiefs, Scribes, and Ethnographers: Kuna Culture from Inside and Out*. U of Texas P, 2009.

———. *The Kuna Gathering: Contemporary Village Politics in Panama*. 2nd ed. Fenestra Books, 2002.

———. *A People Who Would Not Kneel*. Smithsonian Institution Press, 1998.

Iguanape Purbagana. Personal interview by Sue Patricia Haglund, March 6, 2009.

Leis, Raul. Preface. *De la tinaja kuna (Poemas)* [*From the Kuna Clay Jar (Poems)*]. Ustupu, Kuna Yala: Privately printed, 1987, pp. 1–2.

Martínez Owen, Roberto. Personal interview by Sue Patricia Haglund, March 7, 2009.

Tice, Karin E. *Kuna Crafts, Gender and the Global Economy*. U of Texas P, 1995.

Wagua, Aiban. *Así lo vi y así me lo contaron: Datos de la Revolución Kuna Versión del Sailadummad Inakeliginya y de kunas que vivieron la revolución de 1925* [*This is how I saw it and this is how they told me: Facts about the Kuna Revolution Sailadummad Inakeliginya's Version and the Kuna who lived through the 1925 revolution*], 2nd ed., Nan Garburba Oduloged Igar, 2007.

———. *De la tinaja kuna (Poemas)* [*From the Kuna Clay Jar (Poems)*]. Ustupu, Kuna Yala: Privately Printed, 1987.

———. *Kaaubi: Selección de algunos poemas 1972–1992* [*Kaaubi: Selected Poems 1972–1992*]. Kuna Yala: Privately Printed, 1997.

CHAPTER 13

Utah, más allá de Aztlán, Sión y otros reclamos colonialistas de colonos

Carolina Bloem and James Courage Singer
Salt Lake Community College

Salt Lake City, la capital del estado de Utah, se conoce como "the Crossroads of the West" en honor a la primera línea férrea transcontinental completada en 1869. Como caso de estudio interdisciplinario entre Estudios Indígenas y Estudios Hispánicos, y partiendo de su contexto histórico y geográfico, este ensayo presenta un análisis de colonialismos superpuestos de diferentes comunidades que habitan Salt Lake City. El contexto de Utah presenta una oportunidad de diálogo única no sólo en términos de disciplinas sino de idiomas. Los discursos históricos y sociales del estado han creado narrativas disasociadas que dificultan una conversación consciente de las partes involucradas. Este ensayo no pretende ser sino la continuación de muchas conversaciones, buscando oportunidades de incluir voces indígenas de los pueblos ute, goshute, paiute o shoshone. Tampoco pretende ser una crítica a ideas previamente presentadas donde Utah se proyecta, por ejemplo, como *Aztlán* o *Sión*, sino un espacio de consideración y análisis sobre los diversos discursos utilizados por algunos habitantes y su manera de relacionarse con el territorio. Para llevar esto a cabo se presentarán aspectos históricos relevantes de la formación del territorio del estado, así como una breve descripción de las interseccionalidades y limitaciones de los autores de la investigación. Se reconoce la gran bibliografía sobre estos temas, pero se busca aprovechar el espacio para dar cabida a voces recientes y disponibles para el uso en aulas y espacios con acceso internet. La conversación tejedora de puentes se desarrolla con el análisis de obras pictóricas relevantes como *American Progress* de John Gast (1872), *Navajo Long Walk* parte 1 de Shonto Begay (2005) y *Journey of Despair* de Carlos Ortiz (2012). La segunda mitad del ensayo reflexiona sobre el colonialismo de colonos (*settler colonialism*) en los esfuerzos de reclamación de identidades indígenas por parte de chican*s y mestiz*s en el territorio en cuestión.

La relevancia de este capítulo surge dentro de conversaciones en las aulas académicas donde los autores de este capítulo desarrollan sus actividades docentes, guiados por los principios tan en boga de justicia social y los eventos académicos y sociales realizados en el estado de Utah en el año 2021. Dada la importancia de este año, su relación con la caída de Tenochtitlán y una serie de eventos patrocinados y organizados por el gobierno mexicano, Utah, y Salt Lake City especialmente, ha sido sede de encuentros académicos y comunitarios que han traído al presente conversaciones históricas ligadas a la identidad mexicana y chicana.[1] Estos eventos han centrado sus esfuerzos por incluir nuevas perspectivas, sin embargo, se ha visto una brecha clara entre las perspectivas indígenas de naciones pertenecientes a este territorio y lo que surge de algunas identidades chican*s y mestiz*s. Este ensayo presenta un caso de estudio y análisis específico sobre el "indigenismo de lo antiguo" (Marez 267) y su relación con Utah y algunas perspectivas indígenas.

M. Bianet Castellanos aborda la problemática en torno a la terminología, traducción y alcance del "colonialismo de colonos" (777). Castellanos contextualiza de qué manera el término, en su original en inglés, ha servido como herramienta hermenéutica en campos académicos, así como en los Estudios Indígenas. Tal y como explica Castellanos, en el 2017 se veían dificultades en los diálogos académicos de índole postcolonial en cuanto académicos monolingües del español o el portugués enfrentaban mayores dificultades al momento de obtener traducciones de las teorizaciones pertinentes publicadas en inglés. De igual manera, hay una barrera lingüística para académic*s de Canadá y Estados Unidos para conocer las producciones intelectuales indígenas desde el sur global. Publicaciones como este libro y otras conversaciones multilingües, así como espacios virtuales y congresos multidisciplinarios propician cada vez más puentes de comunicación trans-hemisférica. Por su parte, las migraciones históricas y contemporáneas desde Latinoamérica a Estados Unidos presentan nuevas oportunidades de encuentros y diálogos que muchas veces escapan a los estudios académicos al darse en espacios intersticiales y fluidos que no pertenecen a categorías de fácil clasificación lingüística o social. Es por ello que este artículo utiliza la terminología "colonialismo de colonos", con su alcance y limitaciones, según lo describe Castellanos, respondiendo a la necesidad de explorar dinámicas de aseveración identitaria de grupos no pertenecientes a los grupos indígenas ancestrales de este territorio geográfico específico de Utah, viniendo de grupos sociales angloparlantes y colonizadores, por un lado, y de grupos de ascendencia mexicana por el otro.[2]

La doctrina del descubrimiento en Utah

Para muchos, Utah fue territorio mexicano como lo evidencia la presentación organizada por Utah Humanities *Thrive 125: When Utah Was Mexico*, organizada en enero del 2021 con el auspicio de la Universidad de Utah y el Consulado de México. En esta presentación hablaron académicos, historiadores militares y poetas. El enfoque era dar detalles sobre el período en el que los pioneros mormones, liderados por Brigham Young, se establecieron en el valle de Lago Salado en 1847 luego de huir de los conflictos en Nauvoo, Illinois (00:53:19).[3] En la presentación queda claro que Brigham Young reconocía estar invadiendo territorio legalmente mexicano (00:56:44) y cómo, luego del tratado de Guadalupe Hidalgo (00:54:29), se estableció en el territorio borrando sistemáticamente la presencia y legado español, según los topónimos utilizados (00:49:13). Sin embargo, el primer punto del sociólogo Armando Solórzano en su presentación enfatiza "Cuando Utah era territorio indígena" (00:43:31). En contraposición, el presente capítulo, haciendo eco de la perspectiva de los pueblos originarios de Utah, arguye que Utah nunca ha dejado de ser territorio indígena. El uso de la referencia al pasado evoca una presencia ancestral en el imaginario popular, pero invisibiliza y silencia a las poblaciones e individuos indígenas contemporáneos.

En el estudio histórico de Utah la expedición de los frailes españoles Francisco Atanasio Domínguez y Silvestre Vélez de Escalante se presenta como un breve episodio en 1776. El diario de la expedición cuenta con menciones a pueblos indígenas como "yuta barbones, yuta cobardes, indios navajo, indios moquinos (hopi) y cosnina (havasupai)" (Domínguez 145). Todavía no hay textos académicos comparativos entre las versiones modernas publicadas del diario de expedición en inglés y español. Basta decir que la versión en inglés incluye el mapa de Bernardo Miera y Pacheco de 1777, la traducción del diario y la lista de topónimos en inglés y español, nuevamente borrando topónimos en lenguas vernáculas. La versión en español moderno fue publicada en 2016 con una introducción larga de contexto específico del territorio y la diversidad social existente en las zonas de la exploración, el mapa de Miera y la misma lista de topónimos ya citada. La invisibilización histórica de la continua presencia de las comunidades indígenas en el territorio se ve también en las polémicas locales centradas en el uso de mascotas como símbolos de equipos deportivos e instituciones docentes. La Universidad de Utah ha seguido un largo camino para construir una relación con la nación Ute, seguir usando símbolos e imágenes que pertenecen a esa nación y no faltarle el respeto.

El Museo de Bellas Artes de Utah organizó un evento en septiembre del 2020 titulado *Manifest Destiny: The Effect of Our Sea to Shining Sea Expansion on Our Neighbor to the South*. El eufemismo para México centró la conversación en Utah para analizar la doctrina del destino manifiesto, y cómo se enseña en las instituciones de Utah y Salt Lake City en contraste con la perspectiva mexicana. La autora y abogada Susan Vogel presentó un análisis del mencionado cuadro de John Gast y sus adaptaciones dentro de edificios gubernamentales de Utah como el capitolio estatal. Se destacó el lugar marginal al que fueron relegadas las representaciones indígenas. Fanny Guadalupe Blauer, quien representó Artes de México en Utah, ofreció un análisis e información adicional según su estudió sobre el momento histórico de la cesión. James Courage Singer, ciudadano navajo natural de Salt Lake City, y coautor de este capítulo, fue invitado para dar una perspectiva indígena.

Singer es sociólogo y profesor de Estudios Étnicos en el tecnológico Salt Lake Community College. Singer ha vivido en Argentina, Estados Unidos y la Nación Navajo. Su presencia y dominio del español porteño irrumpe y desestabiliza espacios que el imaginario popular reduce a las expectativas que dictan la apariencia fenotípica. Por su parte, Carolina Bloem, mestiza e inmigrante en Estados Unidos, y coautora de este capítulo también, es profesora de Estudios Latinoamericanos y enfoca el contenido de sus clases en resaltar la pluralidad de experiencias desde la identificación cultural de las personas. Nuestras experiencias personales y académicas nos han llevado a desarrollar una conciencia crítica de las cuestiones de identidad y sus repercusiones en las geografías raciales.

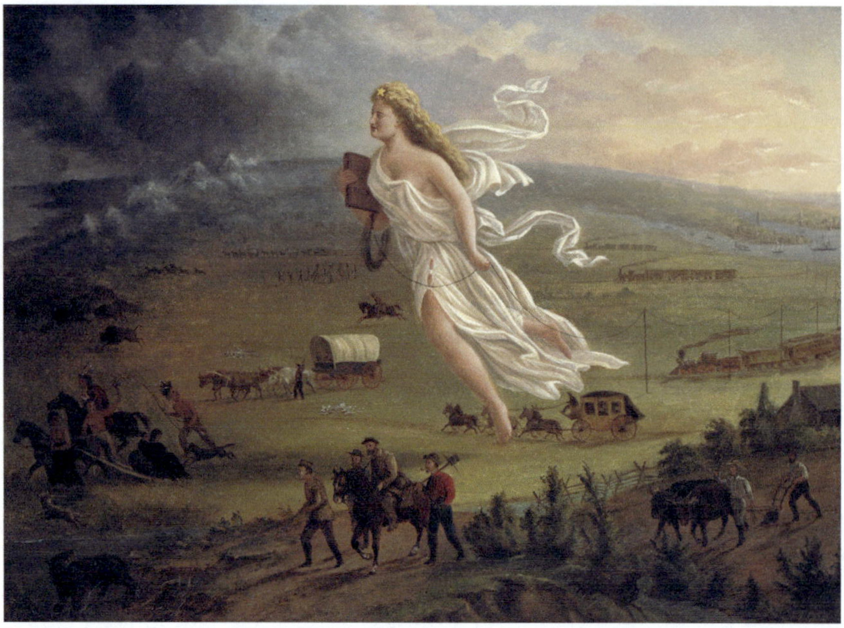

Figura 1. John Gast, *American Progress*, 1872. Oil on canvas. Museum purchase. Autry Museum; 92.126.1

Mucho se ha escrito sobre la pintura de John Gast. Sin embargo, el evento previamente citado sobre este cuadro en el ambiente específico de Utah presenta un cronotopo (Bajtín 84) de análisis único. El cuadro enfatiza el propósito divino y la inspiración que los pioneros mormones establecieron como colonialismo de colonos en este territorio, los cuales desplazaron discursiva y físicamente a las naciones indígenas, en este caso, de Utah. Como explica Patrick Wolfe, el colonialismo de colonos no se refiere a un evento aislado, sino a una invasión estructural que busca la disolución de sociedades nativas ya que destruye para reemplazar (388). La inspiración divina como doctrina central de la Iglesia de Jesucristo de los Santos de los Últimos Días indica que los pioneros llegaron a esta zona para establecer su nueva Sión. Según la historia y la doctrina de la Iglesia, luego de la restauración del Evangelio nuevamente en la Tierra en esta dispensación, sería necesario edificar la Nueva Jerusalén (*La Perla de Gran Precio*, Art. 10). Como en otras ocasiones, las escrituras indican que a veces es necesario el sacrificio de pocos para la salvación de los muchos. Así, la desposesión de comunidades indígenas, por la fuerza de ser necesario, se justifica para que Sión sea edificada. Los nuevos colonos solo acatan designios divinos inexorables. En 1851 las *Leyes y ordenanzas del estado de Deseret (Utah)* indican que cuando los pioneros dirigidos por Brigham Young llegan, estas tierras estaban bajo control de la República de México y no estaban habitadas, salvo por un "orden menor de indígenas" (i). En la actualidad existe un debate legal y político en Utah sobre la enseñanza de ciertas corrientes de pensamiento crítico y el rol de la raza, las cuales amenazan con exponer tales estructuras opresoras y sus repercusiones sobre la sociedad dominante. Sin embargo, hay que tener en cuenta que el colonialismo de colonos va más allá de una sucesión de momentos históricos en el pasado. Son estructuras que invisibilizan a las sociedades indígenas modernas.

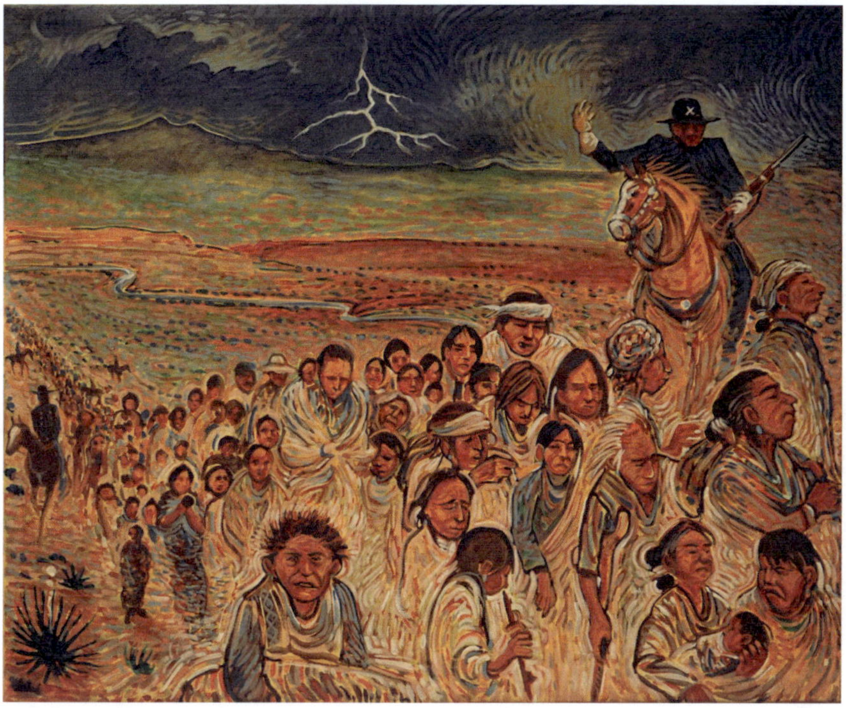

Figura 2. *The Long Walk Part I.* Artwork by Shonto Begay, Diné, 2011, Courtesy of New Mexico Historic Sites.

Dentro de los momentos más dolorosos para los pueblos indígenas están los desplazamientos forzosos y genocidios a los que han sido sujetos. Uno de esos momentos es el cuadro *The Long Walk Part I* (Figura 2) que representa los años de 1864 a 1866 cuando los navajos fueron forzados a cincuenta y tres marchas hasta *Hwéeldi* (navajización del término hispano *Fuerte*) o Bosque Redondo, Nuevo México. Las imágenes incluidas aquí buscan dar una representación visual de la magnitud del sufrimiento y violencia de ese episodio en particular. El cuadro plasma la magnitud del desplazamiento forzado en la caravana humana que se transporta a pie mientras que los oficiales del gobierno van a caballo. La manera en la que los oficiales cuidan la procesión deshumaniza a los rehenes y recuerda más a un técnica de pastoreo. Una técnica fría y despiadada que muestra cómo los navajo van a la merced de los elementos, en ocasiones sin protección contra el frío, mientras que los oficiales cuentan con sombreros y guantes. Vemos cómo esta procesión no respetaba edades, pues bebés, madres y ancianos son llevados a la fuerza apesadumbrados. En Tsaile, Arizona se encuentra el Diné College, centro de estudios superiores de la Nación Navajo. Su edificio principal fue construido siguiendo el modelo de la vivienda tradicional, el *hooghan*. En algunos de sus pisos se encuentran murales alusivos a estos desplazamientos donde no solo se ven las caravanas humanas, sino personas aterrorizadas, desmembradas, escapando y escondiéndose de los cañones de las fuerzas estatales. Claramente las opciones eran desplazamiento o exterminio.

Este triste y cruel episodio es uno de los muchos que quedan por fuera de la experiencia familiar y cultural de chican*s, mestiz*s y latin*s dentro de sus historias familiares, aunque

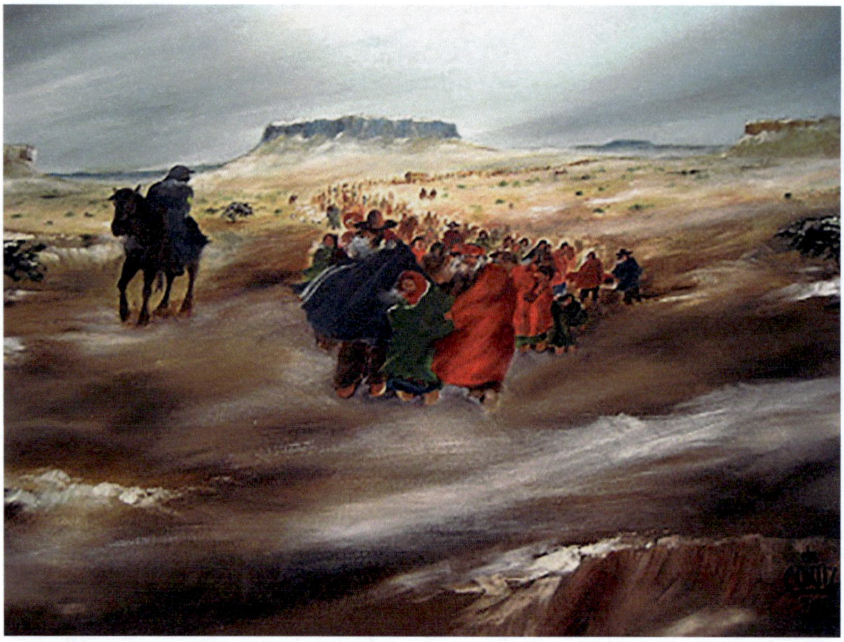

Figura 3. *Journey of Despair.* Artwork by Carlos Ortiz, Diné, 2005, Courtesy of New Mexico Historic Sites.

no niega que estas poblaciones tengan sus propias historias de abuso y epistemicidios. Los lazos culturales y familiares de estas atrocidades continúan en el patrimonio oral y los traumas generacionales de las comunidades indígenas que descienden de estos grupos. Por eso, si consideramos las voces y perspectivas de chican*s, mestiz*s y latín*s como voces indígenas que intentan reclamar su acervo ancestral, surge una tensión, como indica Lourdes Alberto: "cuando la chicana habla como mujer indígena, mujeres indígenas propiamente dichas son silenciadas" (44). Es decir, aunque las voces de chican*s expresan historias de sufrimiento por efectos de la colonización, no son equiparables al continuo histórico de presencia y opresión en el territorio y las consecuentes relaciones dentro de las comunidades indígenas.

El reclamo chicanista de la identidad indígena es colonialismo

Este capítulo confronta la aseveración de que Utah fue o era México. Utah ha sido y continúa siendo territorio indígena. Lo que llegaría a ser el reino de España, el Virreinato de La Nueva España, y eventualmente el Imperio Mexicano, y subsecuentes nombres, en el territorio que hoy es Utah, no fue conquistado militar ni culturalmente por ninguna de estas naciones. Por el contrario, el territorio ha tenido presencia ininterrumpida de utes, paiutes, shoshone, goshutes y navajos. La simplicidad de esta declaración resuena en lo contundente de su mensaje.

Para James Courage Singer fue duro y difícil vivir en territorio que una vez fue parte de las naciones tehuelche, mapuche y guaraní. Saber de las campañas de exterminio en esas tierras como las que vivieron sus coterráneos navajos.[4] Esto complicó la manera en la que se relacionaba con los argentinos en cuanto veía los estigmas que tenía la sociedad hegemónica argentina hacia los indígenas como noción de un pasado histórico distante, desconectado de su presente. El desplazamiento de las naciones indígenas por nuevas sociedades está marcado por lo que la historiadora ojibwe Jean O'Brien llama "los últimos (indígenas) y los primeros (colonos)", o sea, los últimos en vivir y los primeros en re-fundar (consultado en Dunbar-Ortiz 9). Estar en Argentina era recordar el horror expresado en el cuadro *Journey of Despair* (2012) (Figura 3) de Carlos Ortiz y saber que aún permanecemos así.

En las confluencias de las dificultades de pueblos indígenas, si se quiere de Abiayala, hay que marcar las diferencias. Por ejemplo, en los Estados Unidos, las 574 naciones indígenas soberanas reconocidas a nivel federal se diferencian en el carácter político de sus ciudadanos frente a aquellas no reconocidas por el gobierno. Este modelo de reconocimiento y legitimización es un arma de doble filo ya que crea divisiones entre grupos indígenas y sus miembros. Si bien el español y el inglés nos permiten crear puentes cuando ambos poseemos una de esas lenguas, al momento de sopesar el delicado vaivén de la unión, identificación y luchas es necesario tener extremo cuidado al asumir una identidad indígena panamericana que puede resultar en un nuevo colonialismo de colonos. En el contexto del chicanismo, se entiende que en muy raras ocasiones asumir estas identidades no viene de un acto deliberado de desplazamiento, sino en un intento de aseverar lazos de conexión, en este caso, a la tierra de Utah. Sin embargo, esto no se hace desde la inmediatez de la presencia continua, sino del "indigenismo de lo antiguo" (Alberto 39).

En "Indigenous but not Indian? Chicana/os and the Politics of Indigeneity", María E. Cotera y María J. Saldaña-Portillo presentan un excelente análisis histórico y político de los sujetos indígenas y mestizos en el contexto mexicano desde tiempos del Virreinato de La Nueva España, y las repercusiones del Tratado de Guadalupe Hidalgo sobre estos sujetos en el marco estadounidense frente a la concepción legal indígena. Este estudio elabora la diferencia entre los modelos de gobierno y sociedad mexicanos y el modelo resultante de la conquista angloparlante donde, a nivel federal, "los mexicanos no podían ser indígenas, y los indígenas no podían ser mexicanos" (562). Esta separación dio origen a lo que ellas llaman el "duelo mestizo". La negación y anihilamiento de todo nexo con lo indígena para conseguir un acercamiento a la blanquitud que les permitiera acceso a los derechos anteriormente naturales como ciudadanos de una nación libre. Las autoras advierten que un análisis apresurado podría interpretar la identificación como indígenas por parte de chican*s y mestiz*s como una fantasía de colonos. Sin embargo, ese análisis está enfocado mayormente en el caso de Arizona, Nuevo México y Texas. Es pertinente ampliar la interpretación de la reclamación de la identidad indígena de chican*s y mestiz*s incorporando otras perspectivas desde otras nacionalidades latinoamericanas y otros contextos mexicanos. Cotera y Saldaña-Portillo aclaran que los intentos de recuperación de identidad indígena de chican*s y mestiz*s no deben verse como una complicidad con el estado colonialista (563). Las prácticas opresoras y divisionistas que estos ciudadanos, mestiz*s, chican*s y afromestz*s sufrieron a manos del gobierno estadounidense son irrefutables, pero una contraparte que ha surgido en años recientes es reconocer el rol histórico y de beneficio personal que estas poblaciones recibieron al alejarse, o ser alejados, de las comunidades indígenas y sus prácticas (Keeler).

Nuestra perspectiva sólo pretenden avanzar la conversación que dentro y fuera de la academia ha tenido lugar en Utah recientemente. En el verano del 2020, Lourdes Alberto ofreció una charla titulada "Nations, Nationalisms, and Indígenas: The Indian in the Chicano/a Revolutionary Imaginary". Esta charla formó parte de una serie de presentaciones cortas en el programa intensivo de náhuatl durante el verano auspiciado por la Universidad de Utah y el Instituto de Docencia e Investigación Etnológica de Zacatecas (IDIEZ). La doctora Alberto arguyó que uno de los daños de la retórica de reclamación de identidad indígena de chincan*s o mestiz*s es la invisibilización que ocasiona para otros individuos de irrefutable procedencia y pertenencia indígena.

Es necesario desglosar y empezar el espinoso camino del análisis de la reclamación de identidad indígena por parte de chican*s y mestiz*s. No es un camino necesariamente placentero ya que conlleva que aquell*s que nos identificamos como chican*s o mestiz*s tengamos que confrontar partes de nuestra identidad relacionadas al colonialismo de colonos y hasta prácticas similares, aunque inintencionadas. Lourdes Alberto en su ensayo "Topographies of Indigenism" indica "While Chicanas might have a distant connection to indigenous people, they are not themselves indigenous but *mestizas*" (41). Gran número de personas de ascendencia mexicana en Utah presentan una interesante tendencia en hacer referencias constantes a Aztlán y hasta equiparar el estado al mítico lugar de origen con "una mirada nostálgica al pasado" (40).

Este puede ser un punto álgido dentro de las identidades chican*s y mestiz*s. Parte de esas identidades, en el contexto del suroeste estadounidense, equiparan el territorio actual de Utah con el mítico Aztlán. Parte de lo problemático de esta propuesta está en que l*s chican*s y mestiz*s adscritos a esa perspectiva intentan validar su pertenencia al territorio por sus raíces indígenas. Sandra González en su ensayo "Colonial Borders, Native Fences: Building Bridges between Indigenous Communities through the Decolonization of the American Landscape" explica, "the U.S. Mexico border is the polarizing force that shapes two different and oppositional national identities, preventing native people who have common history from seeing themselves as part of pan-indigenous diasporas" (312). Sin embargo, la tendencia actual de simplificar, o aun romantizar, los nexos entre personas de ascendencia mexicana con un supuesto único linaje azteca o nahua bajo la premisa de que los utes y los nahuas hablan idiomas pertenecientes a la familia lingüística de los yutoaztecas, solo resulta en un nuevo ejercicio de colonialismo de colonos. Es decir, chican*s y mestiz*s que reclaman una identidad indígena y por tanto un vínculo al territorio actual de Utah como un regreso a la tierra de origen, refuerzan el colonialismo de colonos al invisibilizar y reemplazar a los utes y otras naciones indígenas originarias de la zona para imponer una presencia de supuesto legado azteca.

Utah como Aztlán también es reclamo neocolonialista

En el verano de 2022 se organizó un evento cultural y académico auspiciado por la Universidad de Utah, el Consulado de México en Utah y Artes de México en Utah titulado "When Utah Was Mexico". El evento virtual reunió varias perspectivas que analizaban distintos ángulos de interpretación sobre la formación del espacio hoy denominado Utah. El sociólogo Armando Solórzano trató varios temas de gran interés para este capítulo, el cual busca crear puentes interdisciplinarios enfocados en preservar las perspectivas e integridades indígenas que desafían ciertas nociones de identidad para los chican*s y latin*s, en especial dentro del campo de Estudios Latinoamericanos o Hispánicos. En su presentación, Solórzano habla de lo que identifica como "la cuestión de Aztlán" (01:08:34). Describe a Aztlán como el lugar sagrado del origen de los aztecas y cómo se dio el movimiento chicano en Utah al final de las décadas de los 60 y 70 (01:09:03). Solórzano arguye que chican*s y mexican*s en el territorio actual de Utah son ejemplos de "historias vivientes". Para Solórzano, Utah representa el territorio donde pioneros mormones y descendientes de mexican*s, por extensión de aztecas, proyectan su conexión al territorio según sus historias mitológicas respectivas que validan su presencia (01:10:05). Para Solórzano, la narrativa chican* y mexican* precede a la pionera, y por tanto, establece lazos con el territorio con anterioridad. Sin embargo, esta perspectiva continúa siendo otra manera de invisibilización de la presencia y continua vida de pueblos originarios como los utes y las otras naciones indígenas del territorio. Solórzano también indicó que un grupo de los utes caminó hacia el sur fundando eventualmente la ciudad de Tenochtitlan (1:10:24). Expertos historiadores y lingüistas no apoyan esta teoría.

El Centro de Estudios Latinoamericanos de la Universidad de Utah y el Consulado de México organizaron una ponencia durante el verano de 2021 titulada "Linguistic Connections of the Americas—Nahuatl and Ute". En la ponencia participaron el lingüista del idioma ute Dr. Dirck Elzinga de Brigham Young University y el Dr. Abelardo de la Cruz, profesor de antropología y náhuatl (variante de la huasteca veracruzana). El tema de la presentación fue la romantización de los lazos entre las culturas e idiomas de la familia lingüística uto-azteca. De la Cruz comparó una selección de vocabulario en ocho idiomas de la familia uto-azteca: ute, tübatulabal, luiseño, hopi, tohono o'odham, tarahumara, cora y náhuatl. Por su parte, Elzinga aclaró que no hay, a ciencia cierta, una propuesta del lugar específico del origen del proto-utoazteca a la par que mencionó a Aztlán, los hopi y que nada de esto es prueba del origen de ningún pueblo en cuestión (00:33:34). Uno de los asistentes preguntó sobre la conexión entre la familia lingüística y el mito de Aztlán ligado a la interpretación local de estar en Utah (01:02:13). La respuesta de Elzinga se centró en la narrativa de la migración aclarando que no tiene fundamento en su campo. En contraste, de la Cruz mencionó que como persona nahua ha escuchado sobre el mítico Aztlán pero sin exactitud (01:04:23). De igual manera, en la presentación para el Instituto Nacional de Antropología e Historia en el 2021 titulada "Conferencia del arqueólogo Eduardo Matos Moctezuma. Aniversario del Hallazgo de la Coyolxauhqui" se menciona que hay investigadores que postulan que Aztlán no existió como sitio físico, sino como ente simbólico (00:08:27).

Este ensayo no pretende entrar en el debate sobre el lugar certero de Aztlán ni la veracidad de la migración como hecho histórico. Más bien pretende entablar diálogo con la perspectiva chican* o mestiz* de validar su presencia en este territorio al exponer vínculos de herencia indígena utilizando la narrativa de Aztlán en Utah. Esta dinámica invisibiliza y silencia la presencia continua de pueblos originarios en la zona. Dentro de este discurso, como explicó Solórzano, se reconoce la identidad indígena primigenia del territorio. Pero rápidamente se vuelca en un debate de colonialismo de colonos entre descendientes de pioneros y mestiz*s o chican*s. Una falla en esta dinámica es la celebración del "indigenismo de lo antiguo" (Marez 268) que funciona –como indica Alberto– como una espada de doble filo y arma neocolonial (50). El indigenismo de lo antiguo presenta una aserción de la identidad anacrónica, problemática por sus efectos de negación en el cronotopo exacto de su ejecución sobre las poblaciones nativas de ese entorno específico.

En los últimos meses, el punto más álgido de la equiparación de Utah a Aztlán y las identidades mestiz*s y chican*s fue la presentación "The Salt Lake Region in the Aztec-Mexica Migration Story Codices and Historic Maps: Facts or Conjecture?", donde el profesor Roberto Rodríguez utilizó una serie de mapas del siglo XVIII para justificar su propuesta de que Utah era Aztlán. Extremadamente peligrosa la aseveración dado que el mapa principal que utilizó, el mapa de Miera y Pacheco de 1777, tiene errores topográficos ya corroborados. En la tradición eurocéntrica y logocéntrica, libros, tratados, relaciones y crónicas donde abundan registros de los utes, shoshone, paiute y goshute son escasas. El *Diario de la expedición Domínguez-Escalante por el oeste americano (Nuevo México, Colorado, Utah y Arizona)"* (1776) sería una de las fuentes más probables de información. Sin embargo, esa expedición no llegó hasta lo que es la Ciudad de Lago Salado en la actualidad, sino que una de las comunidades indígenas más septentrionales que habrían visto serían "los yutas timaponogos".

Así, como mestiza y docente viviendo en este territorio es muy importante guiar las conversaciones en las aulas, y cuestionar el porqué buscamos orígenes en el pasado indígena remoto, muchas veces inasequible para nosotr*s mestiz*s. Se nos ha dicho que, si ese pasado es irrecuperable, quizás debamos tener nuestro duelo por la ausencia, pero ¿cómo conciliar la motivación del saber y el pertenecer? ¿Qué actos descolonizadores de resistencia podemos ofrecer? Muchas veces estos despertares identitarios amplían las conversaciones en torno a las identidades concebidas como entidades fijas y monolíticas que merecen ser ampliadas y reconfiguradas.[5]

En una conversación con el poeta wayuu Miguel Ángel López Hernández (Vito Apüshana), él indicaba que no se trata de volver a un punto cero pre-colonizado. Hay que tener en cuenta aspectos principales en torno a la descolonización y las identidades indígenas. La descolonización requiere lentes críticos constantes que miren dentro de sí para evaluar los momentos de aporía donde las técnicas de descolonización fallan y terminan recreando un neocolonialismo. Las identidades indígenas deben ser aceptadas en sus formas de constante cambio y adaptación. De ahí la importancia de buscar y escuchar las voces indígenas de las comunidades contemporáneas. He ahí el peligro de algunas formas de identificación indígena por parte de chican*s y mestiz*s: "la paradoja de la conciencia mestiza que depende de las ruinas de indigeneidad sin cambio para operar como una posición de sujeto dinámico" (Alberto 44).

Conclusión

Este capítulo presenta casos de estudios concretos que tienden puentes interdisciplinarios y buscan continuar conversaciones difíciles en torno a las identidades y su descolonización.

Como arguye Silvia Rivera Cusicanqui proponemos estar conscientes de lo indígena en el mestizaje sin tener vergüenza de ser mestiz*s (00:51:56). Es el reconocimiento de ese legado indígena, pero sin la necesidad de re-colonizar nuevos espacios para aseverar la identidad propia. Se trata de un llamado a tener en cuenta la posibilidad de reemplazar una estructura opresora que, al mismo tiempo, margina a pueblos vibrantes y vivos. El hecho de que estos pueblos no pertenezcan a nuestro entorno no significa que nuestra presencia física y nuestro deseo de pertenecer deban silenciarlos. No debemos sentir un duelo fatídico e inminente al querer recuperar nuestras raíces y antepasados indígenas. Podríamos explorar la opción de transitar esos caminos siguiendo la guía de los pueblos indígenas vivos. Podemos conocernos y recuperarnos de manera consciente sin inconscientemente silenciar. La especificidad de la colonización de Utah en sus diferentes etapas lo hace un estado muy particular en el suroeste estadounidense. Los grupos demográficos que lo han habitado históricamente presentan una oportunidad única de plantear nuevos diálogos de reconocimiento mutuo que busquen identificar y solventar las tensiones latentes que se han presentado a medida que la sociedad local se diversifica y cuestiona su relación con la tierra en la que habitan. Como herramienta hermenéutica, este capítulo ha buscado abrir diálogos desde la perspectiva individual -y a su vez colectiva- en torno a las tensiones en el espacio geográfico emanadas de la(s) experiencia(s) tangible(s) y simbólica(s) dentro de la relación individuo/tierra.

Notas

1. A lo largo del ensayo se hará mención a estos eventos organizados por el Utah Museum of Fine Arts, University of Utah, Center for Latin American Studies, Artes de México en Utah y el Consulado de México en Utah.
2. Bianet Castellanos expone la redundancia de las traducciones en español del término “settler colonialism” dado que ambas traducciones implican tanto asentamiento como colonialismo.
3. El nombre oficial de la iglesia es “la Iglesia de Jesucristo de los Santos de los Últimos Días”, mas el término “mormón” se usa aún en los estudios mormones y referencias al mismo.
4. Algunas consultas complementarias recomendadas que se enfocan en el reconocimiento de la violencia como herramienta en el colonialismo de colonos y sus críticas modernas incluyen “*In Mexico, Pope Slams Country's Treatment of Indians*” y “*Mexico: U.N. Calls for Better Treatment of Mexico's Indigenous Peoples*”. Ver también los artículos de Ramón Grosfoguel, “Transmodernity, Border Thinking, and Global Coloniality: Decolonizing Political Economy and Postcolonial Studies” y el de Aníbal Quijano, “Coloniality and Modernity/Rationality”.
5. En “Studying in Relation: Critical Latinx Indigeneities and Education”, Dolores Calderon y Luis Urrieta Jr. presentan más ejemplos y diálogos que yuxtaponen experiencias de latinidad e indigeneidad que amplían y diversifican las conversaciones de personas pertenecientes a ambos grupos y que comparten sus experiencias en el proceso de concientización de su(s) identidad(es) y conflictos relacionados a esos procesos.

Obras citadas

Alberto, Lourdes. “Nations, Nationalisms, and Indígenas: The Indian in the Chicano/a Revolutionary Imaginary.” Summer Nahuatl Brown Bag Series, 14 de julio de 2020, University of Utah, Zoom.

———. "Topographies of Indigenism. Mexico, Decolonial Indigenism, and the Chicana Transnational Subject in Ana Castillo's *Mixquiahuala Letters*". *Comparative Indigeneities of the Americas, Toward a Hemispheric Approach*. Edited by M. Bianet Castellanos, Lourdes Gutiérrez Nájera and Arturo J. Aldama, U of Arizona P, 2012, pp. 38–52.

Bajtín, Mijaíl. *The Dialogic Imagination, Four Essays*. Edited by Michael Holquist, U of Texas P, 2008.

Begay, Shonto. *The Long Walk, part 1*. 2005, Fort Sumner Historic Site/Bosque Redondo Memorial, NM.

Calderon, Doleres, and Luis Urrieta Jr. "Studying in Relation: Critical Latinx Indigeneities and Education". *Equity & Excellence in Education*. Routledge, 2019. pp.1–21.

"Conferencia del arqueólogo Eduardo Matos Moctezuma: Aniversario del Hallazgo de la Coyolxauhqui". *YouTube*, INAH TV, February 22, 2021. https://www.youtube.com/watch?v=OIr_GhWTy0s&ab_channel=INAHTV

Cotera, María Eugenia, and María Josefina Saldaña-Portillo. "Indigenous but Not Indian? Chicana/os and the Politics of Indigeneity". *The World of Indigenous North America*. Routledge, 2014.

Cultural Survival. *Mexico: UN Calls for Better Treatment of Mexico's Indigenous Peoples*. 2018, https://www.culturalsurvival.org/news/mexico-un-calls-better-treatment-mexicos-indigenous-peoples. Accessed January 8, 2021.

Domínguez, Fray Francisco Atanasio, and Fray Silvestre Vélez de Escalante. *Diario de la expedición Domínguez-Escalante por el oeste americano (Nuevo México, Colorado, Utah y Arizona)*. Edited by Javier Torre Agudo. Miraguano, 2016.

Dunbar-Ortiz, R. *An Indigenous Peoples' History of the United States*. Beacon Press, 2014.

Gast, John. *American Progress*. 1872, Library of Congress.

González, Sandra. "Colonial Borders, Native Fences: Building Bridges between Indigenous Communities through the Decolonization of the American Landscape". *Comparative Indigeneities of the Americas: Toward a Hemispheric Approach*. Edited by M. Bianet, Lourdes Gutiérrez Nájera Castellanos y Arturo J. Aldama, U of Arizona P, 2012, pp. 307–320.

Grosfoguel, Ramón. "Transmodernity, Border Thinking, and Global Coloniality: Decolonizing Political Economy and Postcolonial Studies". *Revista Crítica de Ciências Sociais, Eurozine*, 2008, pp. 1–24. https://www.eurozine.com/transmodernity-borderthinking-and-global-coloniality/ Accessed December 15, 2020.

"In Mexico, Pope Slams Country's Treatment of Indians". *CBS News*. February 16, 2016. https://www.cbsnews.com/news/chiapas-mexico-pope-francis-treatment-of-indians/ Accessed January 18, 2021.

Keeler, Jacqueline. Personal interview. August 30, 2022.

"Linguistic Connections of the Americas—Nahuatl and Ute". *YouTube*. International Area Studies, University of Utah, June 29, 2021. https://www.youtube.com/watch?v=MJYjCrVuPpw&ab_channel=InternationalandAreaStudies-UofU

López Hernández, Miguel Ángel. Personal interview, May 14, 2019.

M. Bianet, Castellasnos, Lourdes Gutiérrez Nájera y Arturo J. Aldama, eds. *Comparative Indigeneities of the Americas, Toward a Hemispheric Approach*, U of Arizona P, 2012.

"Manifest Destiny: The Effect of Our Sea to Shining Sea Expansion on Our Neighbor to the South". *Vimeo*, Utah Museum of Fine Arts, October 2020, https://vimeo.com/470024774

Marez, Curtis. "Signifying Spain, Becoming Comanche, Making Mexicans: Indian Captivity and the History of Chicana/o Popular Performance". *American Quarterly*, vol. 53, no. 2, 2001, pp. 267–306.

Ortiz, Carlos. *Journey of Despair*, 2012, Fort Sumner Historic Site/Bosque Redondo Memorial, NM.

La perla de gran precio. La Iglesia de Jesucristo de los Santos de los Últimos Días, 2013.

Quijano, Aníbal. "Coloniality and Modernity/Rationality". *Cultural Studies*, vol. 21, no. 2, 2007, pp. 168–178.

Rivera Cusicanqui, Silvia. "Conversa del mundo: Silvia Rivera Cusicanqui y Boaventura de Sousa Santos". *YouTube*, ALICE CES, March 12, 2014.

"Thrive 125: When Utah Was Mexico". *YouTube*, Utah Humanities, January 30, 2021, https://www.youtube.com/watch?v=Dzi-SXeme-c&ab_channel=UtahHumanities

Vélez de Escalante, Silvestre. *The Domínguez-Escalante Journal: Their Expedition through Colorado, Utah, Arizona, and New Mexico in 1776*. Translated by Angelico Chávez, edited by por Ted J. Warner, U of Utah P, 1995.

Wolfe, Patrick. "Settler Colonialism and the Elimination of the Native". *Journal of Genocide Research*, vol. 8, no. 4, 2006, pp. 387–409.

CHAPTER 14

Restorative Indigenous Jurisprudence in Anishinaabe and Tsotsil Maya Fiction

Sean Sell
University of California, Davis

The Anishinaabe scholar Lawrence Gross states: "The Western legal system is oriented toward confrontation and punishment. The Anishinaabe approach is spiritual growth and establishment of social harmony" (233). The Anishinaabe author Louise Erdrich's Justice Trilogy, consisting of the novels *The Plague of Doves* (2008), *The Round House* (2012), and *LaRose* (2016), all deal with situations in which the United States justice system fails Native Americans, who then may seek alternatives based to some extent on their Indigenous traditions. They do not always find spiritual growth and harmony, but that is the goal. Far to the south in Chiapas, Mexico, the Tsotsil Maya writer Nicolás Huet Bautista presents narratives where Indigenous people must deal with transgressions within their community, and his stories show both the benefits and the limitations of Indigenous systems in the face of the ongoing, if not always overt, colonialist power structure. Huet suggests, as does Erdrich, that nature finds a way to restore balance, and that human justice should work within nature's balance—the desire for revenge is counterproductive. Yet the problem may arise over what to do with someone who threatens the community, like a *wiindigoo* in Anishinaabe epistemology. Although answers are not easy, even in these cases the authors suggest that seeking revenge is more destructive than helpful. These works explore justice consistent with Indigenous perspectives that focus on promoting growth and harmony rather than punishment. I examine the first two works in Erdrich's Justice Trilogy in comparison with the first two stories in Huet's collection *La última muerte* to show how these authors emphasize the need for community-based healing even when desire for revenge may seem overwhelming.[1]

The term *wiindigoo* is a complex one. Anishinaabemowin language is verb based, so generally it does not have terms like "criminal" that would redefine a person based on their acts. Gross explains that "In the Western context, and most especially in the area of the law, people who are convicted of a crime undergo a change in ontological status. Thus, an individual is a rapist or a murderer, not, as might be expressed in Anishinaabemowin, 'one who raped someone before,' or 'one who murdered someone before'" (233). This leads to a focus on healing rather than punishment: "The idea is for both parties to undergo spiritual growth and so move beyond the issue at hand and reintegrate both parties into society" (233). But even the Anishinaabe recognize that some people cannot be reintegrated. In *Returning to the Teachings: Exploring Aboriginal Justice*, Rupert Ross says that "community welfare had to come first, and if a particular individual resisted (or was beyond) community efforts aimed at healing, then banishment to the wilderness was a viable, if regretted option" (14). *The Round House* addresses an even more severe option, and this is where the term *wiindigoo* comes into play, seemingly an exception to the rule against words that change someone's ontological status. In *The Wetiko Legal Principles*,[2] Hadley Louis Friedland says the concept "is impossible to definitively or permanently define," but for a "working definition," she offers the following: "The major theme that the *wetiko* concept appears to connote across time, space and changing contexts is: *people who are already, or are at risk of becoming harmful or destructive to themselves and/or others in socially taboo ways*" (32–33, emphasis in original).[3] We will see such characters in the works of Erdrich and Huet, and we will see what their communities do to address them.

The Lynch-Mob Mentality

The opening scene of *The Plague of Doves* features five members of a settler family shot to death, with only an infant girl inexplicably left alive, too young to remember any of it.[4] When the authorities see the scene, many of them think of it as a sin crying out for vengeance. This wrathful urge leads to the lynching of three of the four Anishinaabe men who found the family and saved the baby girl from dying of starvation. That they were at the scene, and Indian, seems all the evidence necessary for the lynch mob. The fourth one, Seraph Milk, is spared due to family connections, and it is through his telling it to his grandchildren that we learn the story. His account includes disagreement among the white people—a sheriff tries to stop the lynching and has his horse shot in the process (74); a teenage boy's disapproval leads him to a fistfight with his father (76). When a colonel on the sheriff's side points out that one of the Indians is just a boy, a man named Wildstrand responds, "Don't you have no conscience... Didn't you or didn't you step in that house?" (73). So conscience, for Wildstrand, goes directly from crime to punishment, without any due process or questioning if the punishment is appropriate. The cry for vengeance creates more murderers. The family's real killer, though eventually identified for readers, is never found and "brought to justice." And we never know the motive.

Nicolás Huet Bautista's short story "Ti slajebal lajele/La última muerte" (The last death) also deals with the murder of a family and no apparent legal repercussions. It is set in the Tsotsil-Maya community of Huixtán in some not-too-distant past time when Indigenous councils had little direct outside interference but significant indirect colonialist influence. Five men conspire in the murder, and in this case their motive is clear, if misguided. Manuel

Bolom is a respected healer in the community, but Pedro Ok'il persuades four other men that his powers are dangerous, that he uses them to harm people.[5] In this case two children from the family of five survive the attack, and one of them, the story's narrator, was old enough to remember. All the characters are Indigenous, but as the Tsotsil scholar Miguel Ruiz Gómez notes, the killers have taken on a colonizer's mentality:

> Organizan la masacre con armas y machetes, herramientas que evocan la imagen del colonizador cuando entra en América con violencia, desatando la muerte sin piedad con la intención de obtener el poder absoluto, incluso con la muerte de los hijos es el símbolo del desarraigo y la memoria que elimina al "oponente" para imponer su poderío sobre los más débiles. (102)

These Indigenous men seem more kindred to the white *Plague of Doves* lynch mob than to the Indigenous victims of that lynching. They blame Bolom for many deaths. Ok'il says, "Cuántos niños se han muerto? ¿Cuántos de nuestras familias han desaparecido? Es culpa de algún compañero, por un señor, sabemos quién es, el viejo Manuel Bolom" (39). Ok'il offers no evidence to prove his accusations. So, as with Wildstrand in Erdrich's novel, the existence of cruel fortune seems to justify the violent response. Also as in that case, there is dissension, as one man protests, "A mí nadie me ha hecho daño, tampoco soy Dios para castigar a un compañero sin saber qué hace, qué piensa, realmente no sé qué decirles" (39). While the *Doves* lynch mob needed to violently remove the sheriff, in this case the threat of violence is enough to overcome the objection: Ok'il responds, "Mira señor Antonio, tú estás con nosotros, no se vale traicionarnos; tú tienes que acompañarnos, si no primero te eliminamos" (39).

A key aspect in both works is that those seeking vengeance are able to convince themselves, if not all others, that they are in the right. This comes up more explicitly in *The Round House*, as the narrator Joe, a thirteen-year-old boy, learns from the reservation priest Father Travis that Catholic doctrine acknowledges "Sins Crying Out to Heaven for Vengeance" (250), and Joe later says, "I was dedicated to a purpose which I'd named in my mind not vengeance but justice" (260). Because his cause is justice, Joe feels he can violate other moral standards: "I was building up lie upon lie and it all came naturally to me as honesty once had" (260). I discuss Joe and *The Round House* in more detail later.

The mobs in *Plague of Doves* and "La última muerte" similarly feel so driven by their quest for vengeance they equate with justice that they engage in other violent acts, or threaten to, in order to achieve their goals. They may believe they are right, but they prevail due to their might. In contrast, no one seeks revenge against them. No member of the lynching victims' families seeks legal or extralegal punishment for what under the law is clearly murder. Of course the racist system being what it was at the time, they would perhaps have felt they had no choice, but consider what comes of this lack of accountability. The Anishinaabe community endures. Descendants of victims and descendants of perpetrators live among each other and may even marry. One perpetrator's granddaughter becomes a nun and takes a job teaching at a school attended by some of the victims' descendants. She is a sympathetic and nurturing figure. Erdrich suggests that nature works to reset the balance, and a system of justice based on traditional beliefs works with nature to help. Indeed, it is part of that nature.

Rupert Ross explains how Indigenous people in Canada have been working to promote such traditional systems of justice: "Justice processes involve all people within the webs of relationships that surround every offender and every victim" (270). Perhaps when official justice proves inadequate, the webs of relationships can work to bring healing and a sort of resolution through time. In *Doves*, eventually we learn that the killer lived out his life as a farmer without causing any more harm, although he was mentally unhinged: "It got so his opinion was avoided, for fear he would fly into a sick, obliterating rage" (309). After he is trampled by a bull, his family takes him, despite his resistance for two weeks, to the local doctor, none other than the little girl who survived his attack. Neither she nor anyone else knows he committed the slaughter, but she says, "When I first came to treat him, he'd reacted to the sight of me with a horror unprecedented in my medical experience" (309). He grows to accept her, however, and she learns from the family that "he'd shuck off his forbidding and strange persona just for me" (309). Perhaps the bull provided some sort of cosmic retribution, or perhaps his reluctance to see the doctor was a form of self-punishment—she also mentions that he refused morphine. When he does die some years later at an advanced age, it is from a natural cause, a blood clot, but he collapses during a violin performance by Corwin Peace, a descendant of one of the lynching victims. The book suggests that the forces of nature, including human nature, do better than angry human impulses if the purpose is restoring balance.

As for Huet's "La última muerte," as a short story it leaves many details open for speculation. We do not know what happens to the boy Miguel after his family is killed, only that he grows up and continues living in the community, possibly taking over his father's role as healer—he now wears his father's suit for the fiesta. We see no indication that finding and punishing the killers interested him. He has devoted his time, he says, to "el *ch'ulel* y la sabiduría de mis padres" (47). The word *ch'ulel* is somewhat equivalent to "soul" or "spirit," so the idea of spiritual growth, as Gross mentions, seems to matter more to Miguel than pursuing punishment. We do not know what happens over the ensuing days and years to those five men who attacked, except for one closing detail. At a town fiesta, a now adult Miguel sees "un pobre viejo sentado, pareciera doblarse en dos, sí, Pedro Ok'il" (47). The man asks his name. He says:

> –Me llamo Miguel Bolom, hijo del finado Manuel Bolom.
>
> El anciano respiró con ansiedad; con pasos sigilosos dio media vuelta, caminó con dificultad rumbo a donde se oculta el sol.... Durante veinte años he robado el aire en este espacio, he ensuciado la madre tierra, el esplendor de la palabra me ha fortalecido, aprendí del rugir del viento y del canto de las aves que el respeto a los pequeños dioses de la tierra es más poderoso que la venganza. (49)

Those are the story's closing words. The violent man seemingly gets away with a crime that cries out for vengeance, but as Ruiz Gómez asserts, "Miguel Bolom detiene la violencia pero también el poder que influye en él de Pedro Ok'il, ... liberarse de la cadena que lo ata históricamente, de la colonia y lo neocolonial" (104). Part of the colonial chain is the idea, derived from a perhaps corrupted version of Christianity, that existence is a struggle between good and evil. Maya cosmovision places greater emphasis on respect for all beings. By focusing on his own *ch'ulel* rather than on avenging a terrible crime, Miguel can find respect with "los pequeños dioses de la tierra"—the little gods of the earth. Gloria Chacón interprets this phrase to mean "humankind," and she sees in the ending a shift toward "a human rights discourse for indigenous people and spirituality as recognition of an individual's agency, rather than as a struggle between good and evil" (60). This idea fits with Huet's Tsotsil text, where the Spanish *Dios* or *dioses* usually appears as *Kajval* ("my Lord") or *jch'ultotike* ("our holy fathers"). However, in the last sentence, he uses *jchi'iltaktik* (78), which would translate more as "my companions." These companions can include human and non-human members of his community, like the wind and the birds he has just mentioned. To them, and not on revenge, is where he must focus his respect. Both Erdrich and Huet seem to argue that vengeance would not lead to healing, would not help strengthen a community, and would not help a person grow in their *ch'ulel.*

We might look at *ch'ulel* as inversely related to *wiindigoo*—if one becomes disconnected and self-serving, a Tsotsil might say their *ch'ulel* has become lost or corrupted, as we will see with Huet's second story. This may be akin to becoming a *wiindigoo.* In both cases, the situation need not be permanent.

Even *Wiindigoos* May Be Healed

In *The Round House,* set in 1988, Erdrich presents an Indigenous protagonist/narrator who does pursue vengeance. Thirteen-year-old Joe Coutts learns his mother has been raped and nearly murdered while trying to protect a young woman who is now missing. Once they identify the assailant, the problem becomes what to do with him, as the US Supreme Court ruled in *Oliphant v. Suquamish* (1978) that "Indian tribes do not have inherent jurisdiction to try and to punish non-Indians." Because it is not clear exactly where the crime took place, it is also unclear what law applies, and in this confusion the defendant is released. "I wish I could hang him," Joe's father, a tribal judge, says. "Believe me. I imagine myself the hanging judge in an old western; I'd happily deliver the sentence. But beyond playing cowboy in my thoughts, there is traditional Anishinaabe justice. We would have sat down to decide his fate" (196). Like the men in the mobs, Judge Coutts feels the urge to punish. This urge takes over when he and Joe encounter the man in a grocery store, and we again see the negative impact of revenge. Judge Coutts attacks the man, and in the struggle suffers a heart attack (244). The man seems undisturbed, even smiling during the attack. Later some of Joe's family and friends visit the man to try to warn him away. "They messed him up good, man. He won't come around you," says Joe's best friend Cappy (247). But on the contrary, the attack seems to encourage him, as he immediately visits and taunts Joe's uncle. This is not a person who will fade into the background. He is an ongoing threat, and thus possibly what the Anishinaabe consider a *wiindigoo.*

It is Joe's grandfather Seraph Milk who provides Erdrich's explanation for what a *wiindigoo* is. He narrates the account of the lynching in *The Plague of Doves*, and he appears in *The Round House* as "Mooshum," Anishinaabemowin for grandfather. Again he is a storyteller, telling Joe the story of Akii, a woman thought to be a *wiindigoo*. This time, however, Erdrich has Mooshum narrate the story from his sleep while Joe is sharing the room with him during his mother's recovery. Thus, it comes from another reality, yet Mooshum fixes it in time and place, as "the year they forced us into our boundary. The reservation year" (179).[6] Food is scarce, farms take time to cultivate, and the government reneges on its promise of supplies. "Some people in these hungry times became possessed," Mooshum says. "A wiindigoo could cast its spirit inside of a person. That person would become an animal and see fellow humans as prey meat" (180). Akii's husband Mirage decides this is happening to her, and with *wiindigoos*, the death penalty is possible, "but not before you had agreement in the matter. You couldn't do it alone. There was a certain way the killing of a wiindigoo must be done," which included that "the only person who could kill a wiindigoo was someone in the blood family" (180). Mirage gives a knife to their son Nanapush, but the boy refuses to use it against his mother. After many other developments, which include help from fish and a buffalo, Akii succeeds in proving she is not a *wiindigoo*.

Joe's information about *wiindigoo* law may come from his sleep-talking grandfather, but Erdrich's comes from more academic sources: in her acknowledgments she credits Anishinaabe scholar John Borrows and Hadley Louise Friedland, whose *The Wetiko Legal Principles* I quoted earlier. Regarding the execution of *wiindigoos*, or *wetikos*, Friedland says: "The most consistent principle in *wetiko* legal processes is that decisions regarding the *wetiko* must be made openly by the collective in order to be seen as legitimate" (75). Friedland does not concur exactly with Mooshum that a family member is the "only person" who can carry out the killing, but she does say that "the closest family members," along with leaders and medicine people, must be among the "authoritative final decision-makers" (75). Friedland also notes that those accused of being a *wiindigoo* have certain rights, such as the right to be heard and the right to receive help, for it is possible a *wiindigoo* could be healed (100–101). Indeed, Friedland states, "The vast majority of recorded *wetiko* cases demonstrate the most conventional response to a *wetiko* has always been healing" (86). The only mention Mooshum makes of a possible cure is when he says "The cure for a wiindigoo was often simple: large quantities of hot soup" (214). But Mooshum does note that people could be falsely accused, as Akii was, and that is why following the proper procedures is so important. Friedland agrees, saying, "When an individual killed someone because they claimed he or she was a *wetiko*, secretly and without group input, this drastic course of action was considered suspect or illegitimate" (76).

And this is just what Joe sets out to do. He gets a gun to try to kill the man. Joe is not related to him and does not seek approval from authorities for his plan. The nearest he comes is to ask Father Travis about sins, as mentioned previously, and to offer to help the priest shoot gophers, as Joe needs to work on his aim. Father Travis discerns Joe's obvious motive, but rather than address it directly he tries to dissuade Joe by explaining that good can come out of evil, depending on how one handles it (254). Joe has no interest in this teaching. So Joe hears both Catholic and Anishinaabe warnings against seeking rash revenge, and he ignores both.

Without revealing the story's conclusion, I will say it strongly suggests Joe would have been better off worrying about spiritual growth rather than revenge, like Miguel does in "La última muerte." As Mooshum says, "Wiindigoo justice must be pursued with great care" (187).

The Rupturing Effects of Colonial Justice

In *The Plague of Doves*, the perpetrator is never directly punished but the victim seems to find peace; in *The Round House*, the perpetrator is but the victims don't. Together the two books call into question the value of a justice defined as revenge. The remaining stories in Huet's collection reach similar conclusions—although some people may act like *wiindigoos*, committing crimes that seem to cry out for justice, vengeance does not serve to better the individual or the community. We have seen how Miguel Bolom prospered by focusing on spiritual growth while his adversary withered. The other two stories examine this idea further. I will just address the second one, "Tsajal chuvej," a phrase Huet does not translate to Spanish but that means roughly "red delirium" and refers to a type of poison. A young man named Manuel is accepted as the newest town *mayol*, part of the traditional Indigenous council. An older man Andrés, "el del nagual poderoso, quien goza de mala reputación en el pueblo" (65), offers Manuel a drink of pox[7] to celebrate. The pox is actually *tsajal chuvej*. Manuel drinks some, but "en descuido" he lets much of it spill to the ground (65). It is unclear how intentional this carelessness is—Manuel suspects the older man's motives, but not enough to refuse the drink altogether. Some hours later Manuel starts hallucinating, and his *ch'ulel* sickens, "embriagándose de poder maligno" (67). He succumbs to paranoid delusions, thinking his wife is the man who poisoned him:

> Las ollas, el metate, comenzaron a tomar vida: pequeños seres bañados de sangre, con los intestinos de fuera, los arrastraban de un lado a otro, sentía el olor a muerte, el mundo se convirtió en terror e infierno; me maldecían. Mi compañera poco a poco transformándose en el viejo Andrés Pérez con una escopeta en su mano. (71)

Manuel runs into the forest and collapses. A healer finds and is able to restore him, partly because Manuel did not drink all the poison, and partly because he had earlier demonstrated proper humility before the town's guardians, both human and spiritual.

While we might not say Manuel becomes a *wiindigoo*, as his short-lived condition does not lead him to any acts of malice, he may have been headed in that direction. Ultimately his strong *ch'ulel* and the efforts of the healer help him recover. Arturo Arias notes, "*Ch'ulel* connects everyone and everything together" (259), so it is not surprising that this man who honors connections with his community can then benefit from the intervention of a community healer.

The theme of pride bookends the narrative. Manuel as narrator and Huet as author spend much more time contemplating pride than considering revenge. "El orgullo tsotsil es poderoso," declares the opening sentence (53), without saying whether this is good or bad.

Then come details of Manuel's preparations to seek his council position. While Manuel is always respectful and deferential in this process, that opening suggests pride is part of his motivation—and the quality of his pride both puts him in danger and helps save him later. Andrés appeals to this pride to persuade Manuel to drink: "Ahora eres señor mayol, el señor carguero, peleando prestigio y honor con los grandes señores, ya veremos si cumples. ¡Toma esta copa de trago!" (65). As the poison begins to take him over, Manuel acknowledges his problematic pride: "En mi vida siempre me ha acompañado la valentía y el orgullo. El florido cargo pareciera en vano, mi deseo morirá conmigo" (67). After the healer has saved him, giving credit to Manuel's humble prayers, he asks if Manuel would like to seek revenge, and Manuel answers simply "No, señor" (77). The healer approves. The story closes with his saying to Manuel, "Si te sirve, te regalo mi bastón, puede fortalecer tu respeto y tu orgullo por servir" (77). So pride can be good if it is balanced with respect, as in being proud to serve. Capturing and punishing the poison bearer, whose pride without respect led him to envy Manuel's achievement, does not merit the narrative's attention. This absence reflects Gross's views on Indigenous justice: "There may not even be any attempt to reconcile the two parties and somehow coerce the one person to forgive the other" (233). Neither punishment nor forgiveness are necessary for Manuel to grow.

One last point of contrast with colonial justice involves the one non-Indigenous character who appears in Huet's story collection. Earlier in "Tsajal chuvej," news comes that a man has been killed, and Manuel goes with other council members to assist the municipal secretary Heladio Ortega, a Ladino, to deal with the body. Here we see the colonial power structure at work. Although Ortega, an agent of the law, is not exactly an enemy, as he works in cooperation with the Tsotsils, still Manuel calls him "el descuartizador de indios, los destaza sin compasión para averiguar las causas de la muerte" (59). In this case the dead man has already been sliced with, Ortega determines, thirty-two stab wounds. The cause of death seems clear enough, but Ortega still performs more slicing: "Hizo la señal de la cruz rozando ligeramente el cuerpo, comenzó a cortar sin compasión, en poco tiempo, con las manos llenas de sangre sacó los últimos intestinos; la casa fue invadida por olor a sangre, me pareció un verdadero mal sueño" (63). This foreshadows Manuel's hallucinations, when he imagines creatures' intestines coming out and smells again the odor of death, so in that sense the killing and examination of this man fit into the overall narrative; still, we could have had Manuel's *tsajal chuvej* experience without them. It may seem gratuitous. But recall Mikel Ruiz Gómez's commentary regarding Pedro Ok'il in "La última muerte," that the guns and machetes he uses "evocan la imagen del colonizador cuando entra en América con violencia, desatando la muerte sin piedad con la intención de obtener el poder absoluto" (102). In the quest for absolute power, it may not be enough to kill; one must also physically destroy the conquered.

Or maybe the destruction is more important than the killing. Ortega doesn't kill anyone, but once someone has died, he takes control of the body and tears it apart, as colonizers tear apart the unified communities of the Indigenous. Indigenous people who kill and steal out of pride and envy also tear apart their own communities, unless those communities can respond with healing and the restoration of balance and connection. Caring for the dead is a vital cultural act in any community. Ortega still allows the Tsotsils to do it—Manuel says, "después introdujo los intestinos al interior del cuerpo del difunto, medio costuró la herida, sólo por afán de impresionarnos cumplía sus leyes de *jkaxlanetik*" (65)[8]—but he first imposes governmental intrusion and dissection to show that the colonizers have power over Indigenous bodies even after death. And this may be more evidence that the Indigenous who engage in violence are following the colonizers' lead, while those who seek healing paths for justice are honoring their own traditions. In Arias' analysis of Huet's stories, he interprets the tearing, "blood-dripping" violence in each as showing how "a colonial violence that fractured empathy is the ghost in the machine of contemporary Tsotsil communities" (267). Yet Arias also notes that the main characters in each case can see beyond violence and revenge: "they all come to understand the link between the relationship of the self not only to itself but also to the ethics that should define the collective if any semblance of communal beingness is to be maintained" (270). The violence we encounter in Huet's stories, prior to their uplifting conclusions, suggests this form of Indigenous justice may be more aspirational than representative, but the roots are there.

Conclusion

The Anishinaabe and Maya literature and scholarship reviewed here suggest that no matter how powerful and universal the urge for revenge may be, the equally universal longings for healthy connections and spiritual peace are more effective ways of dealing with even the most horrific transgressions. Louise Erdrich chronicles generations of hurting and healing among Anishinaabe people and the whites who live among them, making clear the damage that comes from nurturing grudges and the healing possibilities of reaching out to others. The killer in *The Plague of Doves* finds some peace when he connects with the daughter of his victims, and she is able to bring the story to a peaceful resolution when she learns how the man dies, brought to peace by a character named Peace. Joe in *The Round House* instead pursues revenge, acting mostly alone, and suffers life-changing loss as a result.

The importance of human connection is made flesh in Nicolás Huet Bautista's story collection. A healer's body is destroyed, but his son seeks no revenge, focusing instead on his connections with the earth and the community, while the killer seems to weaken in body and spirit. A man whose pride kept him outside the community tries to kill someone who is a part of it, but his intended victim's ability to focus pride toward respectful service helps save him. While the colonial government agent sees bodies as things to be torn apart for examination, those Indigenous people with healthy *ch'ulel* can prevail through the power of community.

The Anishinaabe and the Tsotsil-Maya are only two of the many Indigenous cultures of America, and this chapter examines literature by only one writer from each. Ideally the view of jurisprudence they present, along with analysis by both Indigenous and non-Indigenous scholars, can help bring community-based justice into wider discourse. Both the US and Mexican judicial systems face problems of corruption, discrimination and recidivism. With help from Indigenous peoples, those in the judicial system might look beyond notions of retribution and incarceration as the key to justice and move toward more practices of restorative healing.

Notes

1. My approach to both the Anishinaabe and the Tsotsil cultures is as a student, not as an expert. I welcome those with more knowledge, or different knowledge, to comment on my ideas.

2. I follow Erdrich's spelling "wiindigoo" except when quoting Friedland, who uses "wetiko" but acknowledges that other spellings exist (20n2).

3. Robin Wall Kimmerer's *Braiding Sweetgrass: Indigenous Wisdom, Scientific Knowledge and the Teachings of Plants* (2013) is another good source for information and analysis regarding *wiindigoos*.

4. Erdrich sets these events in 1911, although they are based on an 1897 lynching.

5. As the 2020 killing of Tata Domingo Choc in Guatemala shows, fear of witchcraft as an excuse for murder happens not just in fiction ("Domingo Choc").

6. Though this reservation is fictional, Erdrich is enrolled in the Turtle Mountain Band of Chippewa, whose North Dakota Reservation dates to 1882.

7. Pox is a distilled liquor made from corn, wheat, or sugarcane.

8. *Jkaxlanetik*: Tsotsil for non-Indigenous Mexicans.

Works cited

Arias, Arturo. *Recovering Lost Footprints*. Vol. 2: *Contemporary Maya Narratives*. SUNY UP, 2018.

Chacón, Gloria Elizabeth. *Indigenous Cosmolectics: Kab'awil and the Making of Maya and Zapotec Literatures*. U of North Carolina P, 2019.

"Domingo Choc: La brutal muerte del sanador maya al que acusaron de brujería y quemaron vivo en Guatemala." *BBC News Mundo*, June 10, 2020. https://www.bbc.com/mundo/noticias-america-latina-52988801.

Erdrich, Louise. *LaRose*. Harper Perennial, 2016.

———. *The Plague of Doves*. Harper Perennial, 2009.

———. *The Round House*. Harper Perennial, 2013.

Friedland, Hadley Louise. *The Wetiko Legal Principles: Cree and Anishinabek Responses to Violence and Victimization*. U of Toronto P, 2018.

Gross, Lawrence W. *Anishinaabe Ways of Knowing and Being*. Ashgate Publishing, 2014.

Huet Bautista, Nicolás. *Ti slajebal lajele / La última muerte*. Escritores en Lenguas Indígenas, 2007.

Kimmerer, Robin Wall. *Braiding Sweetgrass: Indigenous Wisdom, Scientific Knowledge and the Teachings of Plants*. Milkweed Editions, 2013.

Ross, Rupert. *Returning to the Teachings: Exploring Aboriginal Justice*. Penguin Canada, 1996.

Ruiz Gómez, Miguel. *El* Lekil kuxlejal *(Buen vivir) y la heterogeneidad literaria: Dos categorías para leer el cuento maya tsotsil "La última muerte" de Nicolás Huet Bautista*. Master's thesis. Austral Universidad de Chile, 2014.

CHAPTER 15

Searching for Relatives: Assimilation and Global Indigenous Resistance to Boarding Schools in Xhon (Zapotec) and Jigalong (Martu) Fiction

Paulina Pineda
Princeton University

Engaging and analyzing Indigenous texts beyond local and national borders offers a rich comparative framework to understand the effects of coloniality and the various forms of resistance rising from within Indigenous communities. Employing a trans-Indigenous global approach, the current chapter brings together two novels written in seemingly disparate contexts. In so doing, I discuss experiences of Indigenous physical and epistemological displacement associated with boarding schools in relation to two Indigenous communities: Zapotec from the Sierra Norte of Oaxaca, Mexico, and the Martu people from the desert regions of West Australia.[1] Javier Castellanos Martínez, a Zapotec writer, and Doris Pilkington Garimara, a Martu author, emerge under distinct circumstances as novelists connected to non-official languages and the experience of colonialism and state marginalization, in Mexico and Australia respectively. The motivation for placing the novels *Cantares de los vientos primerizos/ Wila che be ze lhao* (1994) and *Caprice: A Stockman's Daughter* (1991) in dialogue with each other is the similarities in themes as their reading provide insight into how Indigenous communities in different geographies, navigated and resisted assimilation practices of the government at boarding schools that sought to obliterate Indigenous and Aboriginal communities. Some of the pressing questions guiding this inquiry include, How do the main characters in these novels negotiate their familial and community ties as they face the effects of forced separation and national assimilation? How do the novels provide a counternarrative to Eurocentric hegemonic discourses as we think through global Indigenous resistance to colonial subjugation through the unlearning and relearning processes of the protagonists?

Doris Pilkington Garimara published her first novel, *Caprice: A Stockman's Daughter*, in 1991, after winning the David Unaipon Award in 1990.[2] The novel follows three generations of Martu women from Western Australia. The story centers Kate, the younger of the three women and her search for answers about her grandmother Lucy and her mother Peggy. Kate, racially marked by the Australian government as "half-cast" for having an Aboriginal and a white-settler parent, first receives an education at a boarding school and then a missionary school. Many years later, she starts inquiring about her family and their community. She begins to investigate and visits the places where her grandmother and mother lived, eventually returning to the settlement where the remainder of her relatives reside. Though a work of fiction, the narrative seems to contain biographical elements about the author and her family's history (Ravinder 2021). Pilkington Garimara was born in Balfour Downs Station in West Australia. Similar to the main character in the novel Kate, the government took Pilkington and her sister to the Moore River Native Settlement at a young age. After working as a nurse for several years, she became a writer, and a movie and television producer.

Javier Castellanos Martínez's work *Cantares de los vientos primerizos/Wila che be ze lhao* became the first novel to be written in both Spanish and Xhon, a language most commonly known as Zapotec from the highlands of northern Oaxaca. Castellanos was born in the town of Yojovi in Oaxaca in 1951, and he started his studies in a community school and later moved to the city to continue his education. The literary work follows the life of Jaime, whose parents sent him to obtain an education in the city away from his community. After his parents die, Jaime stays in the school system until he graduates as a teacher. He eventually obtains a government job in the city after working as a farmer with his wife's family, ending his marriage and finding temporary employment as a teacher in various Indigenous communities. He lives in the city for years until he returns to his hometown sent on assignment by the government to gather cultural information about his people, where he meets Trhon Lia and falls in love.[3] The novel contains three distinct narrative voices: Jaime narrating his life, Trhon Lia speaking while intoxicated as she shares her "revelations," and a third person who records their stories, an enigmatic figure who appears only at the very end of the novel.[4]

Indigenous Writers on the World Stage

Cantares de los vientos primerizos/ Wila che be ze lhao (1994) and *Caprice: A Stockman's Daughter* (1991) emerged in the literary scene during the 1990s, a significant era for the visibilization of Indigeneity and self-representation on a global scale, one that coincides with the raise of the Zapatista movement.[5] Following the end of the twentieth century, the label "Indigenous" has become a capacious term, a "name [that] does not presume cultural similarity or essence but rather refers to comparable experiences of invasion, dispossession, resistance, and survival" (Clifford 15). The two authors discussed in this analysis have used the space created through the efforts of social movements and pressure by Indigenous groups, to bring attention to issues like the consequences of colonial and state oppression and the struggle toward culture and language re-acquisition. Castellanos, for example, has gained a global presence through his participation in international literary forums and conferences, while his work is disseminated and translated by numerous academics and cultural promoters in various countries.[6] In one such conference, he criticized current language revitalization state policies in Mexico, highlighting the devastating destruction the government had caused just a few decades before through its monolingual and Spanish imposition programs.[7] As a response to these challenges, Castellanos has pointed to the importance of artistic production by Indigenous people; in an interview, he spoke of the decolonial potential of his own work, hoping that his books, poetry, lectures, and so on will aid in the preservation of the history of his community and the Zapotec languages (Castellanos 2016). He also communicated his solidarity with other groups attempting to do the same and his desire to continue seeing efforts around the world that help maintain Indigenous cultures alive. In the same vein, Doris Pilkington's work has brought wider attention to the issue of boarding schools in Australia through her literary and film production, especially the movie adaptation of her second novel *Follow the Rabbit-Proof Fence*. She became a fierce advocate for creating visibility to what later became known as Australia's Stolen Generation, children forcibly removed from their families like the author. It was during the decade of the 1990s that conversations connected to the reconciliation process began in the Australian Parliament, with increased pressure for the government to issue an official apology, and the eruption of debates against unjust laws dealing with native claims to land.[8] In a Sorry Day speech Pilkington gave in 2003, she articulated the common oppression shared by Indigenous groups at the hands of their governments, making reference to her meeting with Ainu elders in Japan ("Journey to Healing Sorry Day").[9] The stature, commitment and reach of these authors allow for a global approach to decolonizing as an ongoing effort that involves a large number of Indigenous groups working toward the same goal: denouncing ongoing colonial and state subjugation while attending to local particularities and contexts.[10]

The intention of this chapter's engagement with the imposition of nationalist, and often Eurocentric, education is not to perpetuate a Western versus Indigenous knowledge binary; rather the comparison seeks to highlight the multiplicity of Indigenous presents that exist globally, in a fight that seeks to defend plurality and pluriversality against the ongoing universality imposed by nationalist discourses and coloniality.[11] In fact, Chadwick Allen proposes the framework of trans-Indigenous methodologies to highlight the richness of Indigenous textual production and self-representation while maintaining a "literary scholarship that is Indigenous-centered on a global scale" (378). Although the differences between the cultural background of the two novelists and historical context seem striking, it is precisely that juxtaposition that allows for an exploration of how these communities and individuals opposed assimilation. The government's manipulation of education as a system of oppression and the main character's complex journey back to their communities to (re)learn about their culture become the underlying themes that bind the stories together.

Foundational decolonial theorists like Linda Tuhiwai Smith have explained the significance of Indigenous peoples' writing and being part of their own narratives; Smith's foundational work touches on the importance of Indigenous people creating literature that portrays their experiences, including fictional work (149–150). The texts engaged in this chapter, written at the end of the twentieth century by Indigenous artists, stand in sharp contrast to literary production created in the nineteenth and twentieth centuries by non-Indigenous writers denouncing abuses committed against Indigenous people. These problematic narratives became popular in both Mexico and Australia, especially in relation to the genres of indigenismo and aboriginalism.[12] Authors in these traditions often belong to the national elite and frequently represent Indigenous people through a romantic lens, as noble savages, or as agentless victims of colonial and state violence. In addition, in Mexico, the creation of bilingual texts—Spanish and the author's Indigenous language—marked an important distance between Indigenous literature and indigenismo production (de la Cruz 1993). Mesoamerican writers, including Zapotec authors, also articulated their ties to literary forms, including works of fiction, not through a western lineage but pre-Colombian practices like diidxaguca' and diidxaxhuiihui.[13] These shifts have not only brought up questions about a new space of enunciation for Indigenous people and the representation of their struggles, one where Indigenous communities are no longer being spoken for, but setting the stage to imagine a new kind of audience: Indigenous readers.[14] As Burdette rightfully points out in her reading of Castellanos work, "[The novel] simultaneously issues a warning against the cooptation of indigenous knowledge by dominant society and a call to Native readers to recuperate their own lost histories of resistance. By anticipating and redirecting the terms of its reception, *Wila che be ze lhao* imparts a critique of political indifference and a call to action directed to Native and non-Native readers alike" (47).[15] These books that create richer portraits of indigenous characters are read by a global audience that includes people across Indigenous communities, containing those in the diaspora like myself. As this chapter shows, the works of Castellanos and Pilkington contribute to the decolonizing process by writing about their own communities and their experiences through the novels *Cantares* and *Caprice* which serve as invitations for current and future generations.

Breaking Family Ties

In the 1900s the Mexican and Commonwealth Australian governments used boarding schools as a tool to assimilate Indigenous and Aboriginal people into the larger nation. The history of boarding schools in Mexico can be traced to the end of the Revolution. At the beginning of the twentieth century, the SEP (Ministry of Public Education) opened the Casa del Estudiante Indígena in Mexico City in 1926, and a few years later the Casa closed and the SEP opened *internados indígenas*. By the 1970s, these had been replaced by *escuelas albergues,* which continue today (Dawson 82–83). The government aimed to educate Indigenous children in boarding schools so they could become teachers that would go back into their communities; institutions sought "pure Indian" children who had the potential to influence their societies, help with assimilation efforts, and bring modernity to their towns (Giraudo 522). Boarding schools became an important strategy to pacify and incorporate Indigenous communities into the nation (Dawson 83). Interestingly, the state project of encouraging children to go back as teachers failed, as graduates stayed in cities and became part of the wage-labor economy instead, unintendedly aiding the capitalist system and providing a labor force to urban spaces (Ramírez Castañeda 141). Through these educational systems the government intended to integrate Indigenous communities into mestizo culture and eliminate the use of Indigenous languages while replacing it with Spanish, relegating Indigeneity to the past and celebrating European heritage connected to colonial contact.

In Australia, the history of boarding schools can be traced back to the *Aborigines Act 1905* when the position of Chief Protection of Aborigines was created, giving the government authority to remove Aboriginal children from their families, a law that remained until 1964 (Buti). As a consequence, many boarding schools were established during the early 1920s; after they began to close, the government sent children to missions to continue their education, by the end of the 1980s those too closed (Buti). Boarding schools sought to completely separate the "half-caste child" from their Aboriginal culture and family, as expressed by the state during an assembly: "This conference believes that the destiny of the natives of aboriginal origin, but not of the full-blood, lies in their ultimate absorption by the people of the Commonwealth, and it therefore recommends that all efforts be directed to that end" (Commonwealth of Australia, *Aboriginal Welfare-Initial Conference of Commonwealth* 3). Graduates became sources of labor force for the white dominant population, as they had been trained as domestic servants and as laborers for farms and ranches at the boarding schools (Jacobs 209). This episode in Australia's history has labeled these children the "stolen generation," as thousands of children never saw their families again. A number of groups, including Aboriginal and Torres Strait Islander Reference Group (ANTAR), the Australian Human Rights Commission, and several Link-Ups and Aboriginal and Islander Child Care Agencies, have documented the separations and seek to reunite families. It must also be understood that the policies mentioned here only briefly recount the long and violent history of Western education and imposition in Indigenous communities; before state-mandated education, it was religious institutions that separated Indigenous communities from their ways of knowing in both geographies.

The novels *Cantares* and *Caprice* create vivid fictionalized descriptions of one of the most violent aspects of boarding schools, the separation between children and their relatives. *Cantares de los vientos primerizos* describes how Jaime's first school housed orphan children and young criminals; later, when he escaped, the reason reveals insightful information: "Un año estuve en esa casa, ya no pude soportar más el mal trato que nos daban las señoras que mandaban ahí y, gracias a que en ese tiempo aún vivían mis padres, me atreví a escapar de ese lugar para regresar a lo mío" (Castellanos 20). The character's words allow the reader to imagine the situation Jaime faced, as he finds himself far from what he calls "lo mío," signaling his family and community, and how much harder this separation becomes as he undergoes abuse at the hands of those who are meant to act as caregivers. This scenario also points to his parents' desperation; they were led to leave their child at a place filled with criminals so he could obtain an education, "Salí gracias a la pobreza que padecemos, salí porque mis finos padres ya no querían que yo viera los sufrimientos por los que ha pasado nuestro pueblo" (19). It is the promise of escaping poverty and the current situation in their hometown, through the possibility of upward mobility and integration into the national economy, that motivates Jaime's parents to send him off to boarding school. Jaime eventually accepts his parents' choice by staying in school when they take him back and by enrolling in another institution to continue his education even after their death. In this new context, Jaime continues experiencing poor living conditions where not even the most basic needs are met: "Aquí aprendí el español, aquí aprendí a sobrevivir cuando no hay que comer, cuando hay frío y cuando hay dolor" (Castellanos 21). Spanish, too, like the school itself, becomes a site of violence and pain; while attempting to separate from the precarious conditions of his hometown, he suffers from being cold and hungry at the institution. This physical separation and his education ultimately disintegrate Jaime's bond with the community while providing the promise of opportunities in a different place. After Jaime graduates as a teacher, he concludes, "Y es que para nosotros, estudiar es sufrir y hacer uno lo que no se debe con tal de avanzar" (21). The shift here from the first-person singular to the plural, the use of the "nosotros," highlights the paradigmatic position of the character being represented here: an individual who narrates an experience that directly connects to a larger and collective struggle: Jaime's experience represents other Indigenous children who attend those schools and the suffering of the community who stays behind in the hopes of providing their children with a better future. These representations of Jaime's family allow us to also reflect on state dynamics that relegate Indigenous traditional sustenance practices to integrate Indigenous communities to wage labor economy through boarding schools. In Mexico, boarding schools were not compulsory in the same way that this occurred in Australia, the United States, and Canada, still, the changing economy and modernization of Mexico have often forced Indigenous parents to send their children to *internados*. The anthropologist Bianet Castellanos states that the new economic situation made "families more susceptible to state interventions in family life and to assimilationist projects disguised as educational programs" (78). Although Bianet Castellanos's work speaks about Mayan families, other Indigenous groups, including Zapotec communities, underwent a similar process.

In *Caprice: A Stockman's Daughter*, Pilkington points to the excessive level of violence used to remove half-Aboriginal children from their homes. The narrative uses the establishment of the Moore River Native Settlement boarding school in 1918 as an example:

> The inmates present at the beginning were brought down from stations in the north under the ministerial warrants and confined against their will in this strange place amongst strangers. For these children this was no doubt the most traumatic experience in their young lives, and even more so for their bewildered mothers, grandmothers and other relatives left behind to grieve. The wailing and the moaning went on for a long time- until time and tears wiped out all memories of their lost children. . . . Many mothers never saw their children again. (Pilkington 49)

The author strategically uses the image of the school as "prison" and children treated as "inmates" to denounce the crimes and injustices against Aboriginal families committed by the state at these institutions. It is through official means, "the ministerial warrants," that these children are "confined against their will," words that too present the reader with a group of children actively resisting and opposing this separation. Much like Castellanos's work, Pilkington marks a difference between the child's community and their new environment, being a "strange place" while forced to live "amongst strangers." The fragment not only evokes the pain of the children, but of the community, the "bewildered mothers, grandmothers and other relatives left behind to grieve," where women's voices, in the form of cries, are present as this long painful scene unfolds. One of the most striking images comes at the end, as Pilkington writes that "many mothers never saw their children again," as community and children taken, alike, eventually bury the memory of their loved ones after much pain and grief. As historical accounts confirm, the laws concerning education for Aboriginal children did not exist to protect the welfare of the minors, rather they were created to reinforce the power of the elites through the continued exploitation of Aboriginal labor, all while separating families and attempting to weaken Aboriginal populations. Margaret D. Jacobs points out that half-Aboriginal populations were especially threatening to the white population, as they could potentially alter the social order that had existed since the settlement of Europeans in Australia (205). The racial language employed to speak about these children reveals an important difference between the Mexican and Australian contexts, in Mexico many of the children taken from their communities were "indios puros" meant to come back to the community to educate the population and become assimilated in mestizo culture, while in Australia, Aboriginal groups were meant to slowly disappear and only half-Aboriginal children, also called half-caste under the law, were taken to assimilate with the rest of the population.

Imposition of Western Culture in Education

Both *Cantares* and *Caprice* demonstrate and denounce government oppression through the imposition of hegemonic Western culture and the marginalization of Indigenous epistemology through education. In *Caprice,* the educational institutions explicitly attempted to eliminate Aboriginal legacy and substitute it with Western culture. This process is dramatized in the novel as the narrator speaks of the material seen in class, "there were stories to be heard, stories not about Dreamtime heroes, but about the European heroes such as William Tell, Robin Hood, the Scarlet Pimpernel and others" (Pilkington 54). This sentence illustrates how the educational system forced children like Kate to replace their own culture by displacing local references and storytelling and emphasizing European History and Literature. In the novel, this leads the protagonist, Kate, to reject her heritage and herself: "Foreign and colonial words such as 'uncivilized,' 'primitive,' and 'savages' were bandied about in the compound and the school playground. This was a subtle indoctrination based on fear and superstition that gave birth to one of the damaging concepts in this so-called new Aboriginal society discrimination against our own people" (Pilkington 51). In this character's experience, indoctrination is happening in every space of the institution, including the school's backyard where children adopt the language of the state—not only English, as they are forbidden from speaking their languages—but adopting words that demean Aboriginality to treat each other. Making denigrating terms "foreign and colonial" highlights the process of internalization of hegemonic discourses learned in schools that portray Aboriginal communities as inferior in comparison to the "superior" and "preferable" European culture, and that imprinted the kind of damage that would take years, and even generations, to unlearn.

Cantares describes the imposition of a European-centered education, through mestizo national discourses, found in Mexican boarding schools, by bringing attention to a void left by the absence of Indigenous knowledge in the main character Jaime. While becoming a citizen of the nation, Jaime relegates Indigenous values to the past, on this Chacón states that "the novel illustrates that Jaime's desire to adapt to the Western capitalist norms blinds him to Zapotec conventions about counting, intimacy, and family traditions" (138). This is exemplified when Jaime speaks about his decision to leave his pregnant girlfriend as a young man: "Aquí empecé a mostrar mi nulidad, aquí se vio mi horfandad [orfandad] de consejo, de respeto y de amor, en mi cabeza entonces (...) solo había idea de pasear, conocer, ganar dinero; que iba yo ha estar pensando en agradecimientos" (22). By speaking about his "horfandad [orfandad] de consejo" the narrator references the fact that he never received lessons from his family or his community, since he arrived at the boarding school at such a young age. Orphanhood becomes a rich metaphor for the condition of not belonging, alienization, and loss of tradition; in Jaime's case, this appears in the form of cultural and moral deficiency, where his formal education did not provide him with the relevant cues necessary to engage in Zapotec social conventions, nor an understanding of his responsibility towards others. Rather, Jaime thinks in an individualistic way, with little concern for those around him, a way of thinking typically associated with a strand of European and capitalist ideology. Jaime's orphanage and alienation from his community further materialize as he comes back to the community and attempts to reconnect to his relatives to complete his work assignment, he is no longer interested in what happens at home, nor able to speak Zapotec (40). Jaime's limitations become even more pronounced as he interacts with his partner, Trhon Lia, a woman who never left the community, nor learn to read and write. As Bustos Fernández points out in her own analysis of the novel, "El rol de Thron en el relato es, asi, el de desestabilizadora del código idiológico que ha marcado la vida de Jaime niño/adulto" (95). In an episode in the novel, during a dispute, Trhon Lia references Jaime's ignorance of Zapotec history; Jaime assumes the Zapotec were freed during the Mexican Revolution, Trhon Lia rejects that conclusion and makes fun of his education: "Tú no sabes, maestrito, desde dónde nació lo nuestro, pero ahora te lo voy a decir, pero, así también te anticipo, no esperes escuchar cosas que hacen reír a los niños o cosas que asustan a los que quieren asustarte, hoy vas a escuchar lo que pasó realmente entre la gente de donde yo soy, de donde viene mi descendencia" (71). Trhon Lia's words begin to foreground all that must be unlearned to reestablish a relationship with the community and its history; they reveal how Jaime was trained to adopt a nationalist vision with little connection to Indigenous experience.

Searching for Relatives: Resistance to the State's Education

The comparison of the novels brings forth the resistance Aboriginal and Indigenous communities demonstrate to governmental efforts of assimilation imposed through the educational system. Both characters embark on complex and distinct journeys to reconnect with relatives while (re)learning about their community and finding a connection to Zapotec and Martu culture. In *Cantares,* Jaime does not choose to go back to his town; instead, the government sends him on an assignment to write about his community in Zapotec (Castellanos 24). As Jaime sees his town and interacts with the people, he reflects: "Escuchar todo eso [las conversaciones sobre los animales y los problemas del pueblo] me hizo pensar que ya no me iba a hallar en este pueblo aunque quisiera, y además ya no venía a quedarme" (40). Jaime yearns to go back to the city and his life there, again illustrating his feelings of alienation and orphanhood in relation to Zapotec culture and ways of life. However, after living in the town and meeting Trhon Lia, his attitude completely changes as he decides to leave behind his city plans and stay with her; indeed, Chacón in her analysis of the novel connects Jaime's decolonial process to his sexual desire and relationship to this female character (140–141). Trhon Lia becomes a connection to Zapotec culture through her drunken revelations, where mezcal becomes the conduit for the protagonist, and the audience, to learn a history omitted and ignored in Jaime's formal education. Various scholars have importantly pointed out how including Trhon Lia's drunken trances within the narration, creates a counter-narrative to stereotypical images of alcohol consumption in Indigenous communities (Chacón, Burdette, Vázquez-Gonzalez). In the novel, it is the knowledge found through this female character that serves as proof that Zapotec people continue to preserve their roots, providing them with an epistemic grounding for the present. This gains even more significance when Trhon Lia reveals her role as a "yi'bedao," an individual bestowed at birth with the responsibility to protect the Zapotec world, part of a centuries-long tradition of those who pass on knowledge from one generation to the next through orality (76). The novel is clear about the temporalities it treats through the example she provides in relation to the Spanish arrival and the forced migration of her ancestors:

> Cuando ellos [los ancestros zapotecos] llegaron a estas tierras, trataron de conservar esa sabiduría que se le había herenciado y de allí es que venimos y vengo yo. Y el andar en ese camino muchos se han desanimado o se han caído en ese caminar, porque son muchos los obstáculos y también son muchos los que han sido fuertes y han logrado mantener vivo esa luz que trajeron nuestros abuelos. (75)

Thron's words, not just in the example above but in the rest of the revelation, carry the responsibility of maintaining Zapotec intellect, what she calls "esa luz que trajeron nuestros abuelos." The reference to the "abuelos," of course, is not one reduced to blood lineage in connection to grandfathers, but to the ancestors, those who are wise. In fact, in a different revelation, Trhon Lia extends this relationship to the more-than-human: "aquellos sa que lo mismo eran águilas, tigers, relámpagos o grandes árboles" (133). The revelations represent a shared commitment that connects Trhon Lia to various generations of Yi'bedao who have resisted coloniality by maintaining their ways of knowing alive and, at other times, by physically fighting off the invaders, including Trhon Lia's older sister Lia Kaxhon (102). The lesson is not merely a historical one and serves as a reference to how Indigenous communities will continue preserving the light of the elders to guide the path of the present. The teachings Jaime acquires during his time with Trhon allow him to engage with his community's culture, the Zapotec language, and the oral tradition that aids in preserving the rich and complicated history of resistance represented in the novel.

The (re)learning in Pilkington's book takes a slightly different form, though like in *Cantares*, the protagonist's connection to history and aboriginal legacy emerges in moments of interaction with women. In *Caprice* the recuperation of aboriginal knowledge comes as Kate retraces her maternal line, in an attempt to restore her ties to her kin. A quote by Annette Hamilton from *Women's Role in Aboriginal society* strategically placed at the beginning of Pilkington's novel points to the importance of those familial relationships: "In the life of an Aboriginal women, no one is more important than her mother when she is young, her daughters when she is old." This serves as a reference to understand how the narrative is structured, as the novel is divided into three sections that follows the lives of the three generations of women, as Kate is introduced to her family history. The process of retracing her ancestry allows Kate to regain her connection to Aboriginal culture and her own identity toward the end of the narrative, despite heavy efforts by the government to make her reject it; this is illustrated when she states: "I realize now that I have a past, a history that I am extremely proud of. I even have a genuine skin name. I am a Milangga, the same skin name section as my grandmother Lucy Muldune. This is my birthright and no one can take this away from me" (Pilkington 71). These sentences exemplify how her connection to her grandmother allows Kate to embrace her Indigeneity as she fights years of oppression and indoctrination that lead her to reject that part of herself. The connection, though, goes beyond familial ties since a skin name contains information about a person's kinship, both indicating their bloodline and their relationship and responsibilities to other members of the community.[16]

Although this matrilineal connection proves essential in Kate's relearning process, her story also points to earlier forms of resistance to the state's assimilation. The narration describes how throughout her years in school, Kate and the other girls managed to maintain a part of their Aboriginal culture through the oral tradition shared by older women in the settlement:

> The myths and legends would always be in their [the women's] hearts and stored away in the back of their minds, awaiting that special moment when they would be recalled and passed on to others. (...) The forbidden topics were whispered in hushed tones in the privacy of the dormitory in the evening or discussed on the grassy banks near the river under the shade of the huge river gum. (Pilkington 55)

Like *Cantares*, Pilkington's text points to the importance of oral tradition as a means to maintain knowledge. Remembering the context of the classroom and the schoolyard, it becomes fitting that it is whispers and late-night conversations amongst girls that become the modes of transmission for Aboriginal knowledge; small but powerful spaces of resistance and cultural preservation as the institution prohibited children from participating in rituals and speaking their languages. The comparison of the two narratives points to how the reeducation of these characters illustrates the resistance that Indigenous and Aboriginal groups have shown since the time of "first contact" with European settlers. Although there are differences in how the characters experience the reintroduction and connection to their culture, there are striking similarities including the significant role of oral traditions and how women are portrayed as the link to Indigenous and Aboriginal culture. The narratives provide an alternative to the absolute assimilation that the state intends; an engagement with others ways of knowing through the efforts of racialized females characters in the novel[17]. Though Indigenous and Aboriginal groups continue to face epistemic violence, their history and cultural practices endure, displaying resistance and a will to survive. The novels reveal this process of reeducation and resistance through Kate and Jaime as they reencounter their relatives and communities' knowledge, and reestablish a connection that was taken from them as children.

How to Preserve the Light of the Ancestors?

These narrations highlight the divisions and the struggles that continue to exist in Indigenous communities in relation to colonialism and the various efforts to resist and relearn through decolonizing efforts. In *Cantares*, in her first revelation Trhon articulates the lasting effects of Spanish invasion on the Zapotec population. She describes how "se perdió el respeto" became an expression after the European arrived and how the different pueblos became divided when they could not agree on how to deal with the new circumstances—helping or rejecting the newcomers—a separation that continues to exist (Castellanos 131). Her narrative illustrates the complex dimensions of a decolonizing process due to the deep divisions that remain in the Zapotec community after five hundred years of oppression. Her revelation shows no consensus on how to move forward nor the action that should be taken in relation to the groups that oppressed Indigenous communities. Even in the portrayal of her character, Trhon Lia is a yi'bedao who has renounced her duty by attempting to live her life as a wife and mother before meeting Jaime, only being brought back to this calling when she drinks mezcal and speaks her revelations. In Pilkington's work the difficulty of a decolonizing effort emerges when the character Kate speaks about the great number of people who continue to ignore and reject their aboriginality: "I was like hundreds of European oriented Aborigines, those without a tradition or a past, those who had undergone (successfully I might add) conditioning to lose our memories of our families and heritage.... Here I was unjustly condemning a culture that had survived and practiced for over 40,000 years" (Pilkington 70). These sentences highlight the reality faced by hundreds of people who have not made, and might never make, the journey back to their relatives, to regain the memory of what the government took from them as children. Both novels point to all the work being done inside and outside of communities to engage in decolonizing efforts that include both material and nonmaterial goals.

There are, of course, limitations to the claim that fiction and literary engagement can contribute to decolonizing processes when we seriously engage critiques that include Tuck and Yang's "Decolonization Is Not a Metaphor." Still, their intervention becomes relevant as we reflect on how boarding schools in Australia and Mexico remain open, and though they no longer serve as a tool for coercion in the way this text has explored, they continue to be a space of physical and epistemic violence for Aboriginal and Indigenous populations. In Mexico, this ranges from bilingual institutions that lack the proper support for such education (Pineda Santiago) to violent repression of teaching institutions that prioritize Indigenous learning, including the well-known case of the disappearance of the normalistas at Ayotzinapa. In Australia, boarding schools are often seen as the only option for Aboriginal and Torres State Islander children to obtain a "proper education" isolating them from their culture and families (Higgins; Commonwealth of Australia, "Study Away Review"). It must also be pointed out that though the current analysis takes place in the two colonial languages imposed by the educational structures discussed here, English and Spanish, the use of these languages has allowed the novels to reach a global audience that includes Indigenous communities, this too happening inside classrooms where they are taught.[18] Reading Indigenous authors who have subverted such imposed languages, and repurposed tools associated with colonial education to tell their own stories and those of their communities becomes an important invitation for many. As both a white-passing Latina and a daughter of the Zapotec diaspora on my father's side, I know from experience how access to such texts can propel meaningful unlearning/relearning journeys.[19] I first read *Cantares de los vientos primerizos/Wila che be ze lhao* and *Caprice: A Stockman's Daughter* at the beginning of my own unlearning and relearning journey, back when I knew little about my family's connection to zapotekeidad as an undergraduate student in the United States. Though my paternal grandparents belong to a different Zapotec community than that of Javier Castellanos, my engagement with these novels opened a space in my family for talking about our story of dispossession which reflects that of so many others who migrated from their towns, and later, moved me to travel to the region my grandparents were forced to leave in an attempt to seek "better opportunities." Though my grandfather did not attend a boarding school, he did stop speaking Diidxazá—Zapotec from the Isthmus of Tehuantepec—after migrating from his hometown of Ixhuatán and being called an indio in school, creating a silence that lasted two generations.

What the novels *Cantares de los vientos primerizos/Wila che be ze lhao* and *Caprice: A Stockman's Daughter* highlight is not only the painful need of reckoning with colonial and state violences at educational institutions in order to denounce and assign responsibility to the state, but also the necessity of understanding resistance and learning differently. As Leanne Simpson has pointed out, theorization of resistance that has kept cultures, languages, and systems of governance alive must go beyond large-scale political mobilizations to include what happens at the family unit level (19) and, as this chapter has shown, in small, and even clandestine, spaces. In placing the novels next to each other, or in proximity to use Māori scholar Alice Te Punga Somerville's term, I hear the voices of such resistance speaking to each other and creating larger echoes: from Trhon Lia's revelations after drinking mezcal to the whispers of women at Kate's boarding school to the global audience who reads the words of these female characters. Fictionalized voices that make culture, language and political organizations remain alive so that present and future generations can search for their own decolonizing paths.

Notes

1. "Jigalog" refers to a particular aboriginal community in Australia, while the term "Martu/Mardu" is a category that encompasses a number of aboriginal groups that share a language and certain cultural traits spread along the West Australian desert (Tonkinson and Tonkinson). "Zapotec" has been used as an umbrella term for various Indigenous groups who share a number of cultural traits, a common past, and a linguistic root, while "xhon" refers to a the specific group of people and their language who mainly reside in the northern highlands of Oaxaca and across the diaspora in cities like Mexico City and Los Angeles. Smith Stark points out that Zapotec is not a homogeneous unity and has been classified into four main groups due to substantial economic, cultural, and geographical differences: the northern highlands of Oaxaca, Sierra Madre Oriental, Zapotecs from the Valley of Oaxaca, and the Isthmus of Tehuantepec (Smith Stark).

2. This award is given to emergent Indigenous authors in Australia and named after David Unaipon (1872–1967), an aboriginal preacher, inventor and author.

3. Throughout the novel, the spelling of the character's name changes: Trhon Lia, Tron Lia, and Trhonlia.

4. Other literary critics have focus on the identity of this narrator as part of their analysis: for example, for Bisbey, Jaime's situation and what he sees as this ethnographer figure allow Castellanos to create a parody of the *testimonio* genre (47), while Burdette argues that this narrator can be read as a "metafictional device through which Castellanos Martínez reflects on his own position as an indigenous author in present-day Mexico" (52).

5. The Zapatista uprising took place on January 1, 1994 in Chiapas, Mexico, gaining international attention. The Ejército Zapatista de Liberación Nacional sought visibility for Maya groups from the Lacandona jungle and other marginalized communities, coinciding with the beginning of the North American Free Trade Agreement. In addition, numerous literary projects also appear on the scene including the foundation of the Association of Writers in Indigenous Languages (ELIAC) in 1993.

6. For examples, see work by Day and Vázquez-Gonzalez.

7. In the conference he stated: "Imagínense ustedes a un hombre que le quitan los pies, le cortaron los dos pies, eso es como el mal, ¿no?, después de 50 o 60 años se dan cuenta que hicieron algo malo, y le dicen: "¿Sabes qué? Vamos a hacer una ley para que a nadie más ya le corten los pies y al que le cortamos el pie ahora si que vaya a donde quiera, ¿no? Aquí hay leyes, ya, y vamos a hacer un instituto para que para esos que les cortamos los pies puedan ir a donde quieren" ¿A donde va a ir si no tienen pies? Eso es lo que han hecho con nosotros, hoy que casi ya desmembraron a nuestras lenguas indígenas es terriblemente difícil volver a hacer algo." See Castellanos Martínez (2010)

8. In 1991 Council for Aboriginal Reconciliation was established. The Native Title Act passed in 1993 and five years later it was amended. *Bringing Them Home*, an extensive report on the Stolen generation, was released in 1997.

9. Australia commemorates National Sorry Day on May 26; it is meant as a time for reflection, mourning, and commitment to justice for the thousands of Aborigines and Torres Strait Islanders families affected by the forcible removal of children during Australia's assimilation era.

10. "Decolonizing," understood as a verb, is an ongoing process. For detailed discussion on the subject, see Gulsah Capan, Sebastian Garbe, and Michaela Zöhrer.

11. Central to this is the notion of pluriverse, "Un mundo donde quepan muchos mundos," based on the Zapatista movement. This notion, as engaged by Arturo Escobar, allows for a criticism of universality, monolingualism, and the damage continuously caused by the narrative of progress and development. Furthermore, it provides an opening for speaking about the multiplicity of Indigenous languages, and the worlding practices embedded in them, beyond the liberal categories of "diversity" or "multiculturalism," which have been co-opted by institutions, including states, seeking to neutralize and capitalize upon the disruptive force of Indigenous cultures and knowledges without altering the material and symbolic logics of the modern and colonial universe.

12. The problematic nature of these representations has been widely discussed by academics, including in the book *The Inner Life of Mestizo Nationalism* and the article "Indigenism, Populism and Marxism" by Diaz Polanco. In Australia the issue of aboriginalism, which can be seen as parallel to indigenismo, has gained attention; the term, coined in *Dark Side of the Dream,* describes the assumption that white people must speak for aboriginal communities and record their stories, based on the belief that aborigines are a "dying race" (Hodge and Mishra, 27). In Australia there has also been a long history of non-aboriginal writing about Indigenous communities in fiction and representing them in various books. There has also been an increased awareness on how non-aboriginals have appropriated a large number of aboriginal elements and mythology that have further the exploitation of aboriginal communities, as argued by *Tiptoeing through the Spinifex: White Representations of Aboriginal Characters* by Margaret Marrilees.

13. In his seminal work *Guie' xti diidxazá/Flor de la palabra*, Víctor de la Cruz, Zapotec writer and intellectual, discusses various Indigenous literary genres utilized to describe storytelling and literary genres. "Diidxaguca' (?)-diidxaxhiihui'" is used to describe works of fiction, like short stories and novels; these terms describe storytelling practices used for entertaining, such as the creation of stories known to be made up or to be elaborate lies told to amuse an audience (35). Some of these categories have been recuperated by engaging with colonial texts, including *Vocabvlario en lengva çapoteca* originally published in 1578. For more, see Víctor de la Cruz *Flor de la palabra/Guie' xti diidxazá* (2003) and Gloria Chacón's *Indigenous Cosmolectics* (2018).

14. This of course is connected to important debates in relation to subaltern studies and Spivak's canonical work, "Can the Subaltern Speak?"

15. Contrary to this reading, in relation to bilingual editions that include Indigenous languages in Mexico, critics have pointed to the irony or contradiction contained in bilingual texts that will not be read by their respective Indigenous communities. For a detailed account, see Bisbey.

16. Skin names express complex social systems that bound people to their family, community and other groups. McConvell and Ponsonnet explain that the "The 'skin' name [of the child] is different from the skin of either parent but the parents' skin identities determine that of the child. Each of the eight categories has a particular kinship relationship with a person (an Ego). This means that when a person with a particular identity meets someone, even a stranger, they can immediately call each other by an appropriate kinship term, based on kinship links—known or supposed" (273). For an in-depth discussion and situated examples of this term see *Skin, Kin and Clan: The Dynamics of Social Categories in Indigenous Australia*, edited by Patrick McConvell, Piers Kelly and Sebastien Lacrampe.

17. Numerous thinkers who engage decolonial theory have pointed to the valuable contribution of racialized females in the spheres of praxis and politically grounded theory related to anticolonial movements and in the face of state violence. For examples see Rivera Cusicanqui (2010) and Curiel (2007).

18. Various academics have spoken about the importance of teaching Indigenous texts in global context at the university level, including comparatists Alice Te Punga Somerville and Chadwick Allen (2007).

19. This statement was inspired by Julietta Singh and Laura Rodríguez Castro's engagement with their positionality (Singh 65–94; Rodríguez Castro 59–76).

Works Cited

Allen, Chadwick. "Decolonizing Comparison: Toward a Literary Studies." *The Oxford Handbook of Indigenous American Literature*. Edited by James H. Cox and Daniel Heath Justice, Oxford UP, 2014.

Bisbey, Brandon P. "Cantares de los vientos primerizos: La ironía de una novela zapoteca en español." *Revista de Literatura Mexicana Contemporánea*, no. 40, 2009, pp. 39–48.

Burdette, Hannah. *Revealing Rebellion in Abiayala: The Insurgent Poetics of Contemporary Indigenous Literature*. U of Arizona P, 2019.

Bustos Fernández, María José. "Memoria histórica de los pueblos zapotecos en una novela de Javier Castellanos Martínez." *Revista de Literatura Mexicana Contemporánea*, no. 12, 2000, pp. 93–101.

Buti, Antonio. "The Removal of Aboriginal Children: Canada and Australia Compared." *University of Western Sydney Law Review*, vol. 26, June 2002, http://www.austlii.edu.au/au/journals/UWSLawRw/2002/2.html.

Castellanos, Bianet M. "Creating Wage Workers: Indigenous Boarding Schools in Rural Yucatán, Mexico." *Indian Subjects*, edited by Brenda J. Child et al., SAR Press, 2014, pp. 73–90.

Castellanos Martínez, Javier. *Wila che be ze lhao/Cantares de los vientos primerizos*. Editorial Diana, 1994.

———."La lengua zapoteca hoy." *Foro Lingüistico*, CEDELIO, 2010. https://www.youtube.com/watch?v=N8R-K_5TDBE

———. Personal communication with the author during the First Indigenous Literature conference in Los Angeles, July 30, 2016.

Chacón, Gloría E. *Indigenous Cosmolectics: Kab'awil and the making of Maya and Zapotec Literatures*. U North Carolina P, 2019.

Clifford, James. "Among Histories." *Returns: Becoming Indigenous in the Twenty-First Century*. Harvard UP, 2013.

Commonwealth of Australia. *Aboriginal Welfare-Initial Conference of Commonwealth and State Aboriginal Authorities held at Canberra, 21st to 23rd April, 1937*. Commonwealth Government Printer, c. 1937, http://nla.gov.au/nla.obj-52771316/view?partId=nla.obj-88456768.

———. "Study Away Review: Review of Support for Aboriginal and Torres Strait Islander Secondary Students Studying Away From Home." 2017, https://www.niaa.gov.au/sites/default/files/publications/study-away-review_0.pdf.

Dawson, Alexander S. "Histories and Memories of the Indian Boarding Schools in Mexico, Canada, and the United States." *Latin American Perspectives*, September 2009.

Day, Ida. "The Preservation of Indigenous Knowledge in Contemporary Mexico in *El cultivo del maize en Yojovi* by Javier Castellanos." *IK: Other Ways of Knowing*, vol. 1, no. 1 2015, pp. 9–14.

de la Cruz, Víctor. *Guie'sti' diidxazá/La flor de la palabra*. Centro de Investigaciones y Estudios Superiores en Antropología Social, UNAM, 2013.

———. "Literatura indígena: El caso de los zapotecos del Istmo." *Situación actual y perspectivas de la literatura en lenguas indígenas*. Edited by Carlos Montemayor, CONACULTA, 1993, pp. 139–154.

Escobar, Arturo. *Sentipensar con la tierra: Nuevas lecturas sobre desarrollo, territorio y diferencia*. UNAULA, 2014.

Giraudo, Laura. "De la ciudad 'mestiza' al campo 'indígena': Internados indígenas en el México posrevolucionario en Bolivia. From Mestizo City to Indian Countryside: Indian Boarding Schools in Postrevolutionary Mexico and Bolivia." *Anuario de Estudios Americanos,* February 2010.

Gulsah Capan, Zeynep, Sebastian Garbe, and Michaela Zöhrer. "How Do We Teach the World? A Conversation about Decolonization, Processes of Unlearning and "Aha Moments' in Institutions of Higher Education." *Acta Academica*, vol. 52, 2020, pp. 76–88.

Higgins, Isabella. "Indigenous Boarding Schools Help Close the Gap, but as NAIDOC Week Kicks off a Study Shows There Are Highs and Lows." *ABC News*, November 7, 2020.

Hodge, Bob, and Vijay Mishra. *Dark Side of the Dream: Australian Literature and the Postcolonial Mind*. Allen & Unwin, 1991.

Jacobs, Margaret D. "Indian Boarding Schools in Comparative Perspective: The Removal of Indigenous Children in the United States and Australia, 1880–1940." *Faculty Publications, Department of History*, December 21, 2006.

McConvell, Patrick, and Maïa Ponsonnet. "Generic Terms for Subsections ('Skins') in Australia: Sources and Semantic Networks." *Skin, Kin and Clan: The Dynamics of Social Categories in Indigenous Australia*. Edited by Patrick McConvell et al. ANU Press, 2018, pp. 271–316.

Ochy, Curiel. "Crítica poscolonial desde las prácticas del feminismo antirracista", Nómadas 26 (2007).

Pilkington Garimara. Doris. *Caprice: A Stockman's Daughter.* U Queensland P, 2002.

———. "Journey to Healing Sorry Day 2003." *Solidarity Philippines Australia Network, KASAMA*, vol. 17, no. 2 (2003), http://cpcabrisbane.org/Kasama/2003/V17n2/Sorry.htm.

Pineda Santiago, Irma. "La literatura de los Binnizá. Zapotecas del Istmo." UNAM, 2008.

Ramírez, Castañeda, Elisa. *La educación indígena en México*. UNAM, 2006.

Ravinder, Nandita, and Angkayarkan Vinayakaselvi. "A Critique of Western Educational Policy for Aboriginals in Australia as Represented in Doris Pilkington's *Follow the Rabbit-Proof Fence* and *Caprice: The Stockman's Daughter.*" *Turkish Journal of Computer and Mathematics Education*, vol. 12, no. 11 (2021), pp. 2083–2089.

Rivera Cusicanqui, Silvia. *Ch'ixinakax utxiwa. Una reflexión sobre prácticas y discursos descolonizadores.* Tinta Limón, 2010

Rodríguez Castro, Laura. *Decolonial Feminisms, Power and Place Sentipensando with Rural Women in Colombia.* Palgrave Macmillan, 2021.

Singh, Julietta. *Unthinking Mastery: Dehumanism and Decolonial Entanglements.* Duke UP, 2018.

Simpson, Leanne. *Dancing on Our Turtle's Back: Stories of Nishnaabeg Re-creation, Resurgence and a New Emergence.* Arbeiter Ring Publishing, 2014.

Smith, Linda T. *Decolonizing Methodologies: Research and Indigenous Peoples.* Zed Books, 2012.

Smith Stark, Thomas. "Algunas isoglosas zapotecas." *Clasificación de las lenguas indígenas de México. Memorias del III Coloquio Internacional de Lingüística.* UNAM, Instituto de Investigaciones Antropológicas, Instituto Nacional de Lenguas Indígenas, 2007, pp. 69–134.

Somerville, Alice Te Punga, and Chadwick Allen. "An Introductory Conversation." *Journal of New Zealand Literature (JNZL)*, no. 24, 2007, pp. 12–19.

Tarica, Estelle. *The Inner Life of Mestizo Nationalism.* U Minnesota P, 2008.

Tonkinson, Robert, and Myrna Tonkinson. "Mardu." *Encyclopedia of Sex and Gender.* Springer, 2004.

Tuck, Eve, and Wayne Yang. "Decolonization Is Not a Metaphor." *Decolonization: Indigeneity, Education & Society*, 2012.

Vázquez-Gonzalez, Leonor. *Una visión del mundo indígena en la literatura zapoteca contemporánea.* PhD diss., Texas Tech University, 2003.

Webby, Elizabeth. *The Cambridge Companion to Australian Literature.* Cambridge UP, 2000.

CHAPTER 16

Voces y tensiones entre mundos: Aproximación a algunos temas de la novela *Alonso Mariano* del escritor p'urhepecha Ismael García Marcelino[1]

Sue Meneses Eternod
ENES-UNAM Morelia

En 2004 sale a la luz la primera novela escrita en versión bilingüe p'urhepecha-español titulada *Alonso Mariano* del escritor Ismael García Marcelino.[2] Sin embargo, a pesar de la excepcionalidad de este hecho tanto para la literatura en lenguas originarias de México como para la literatura p'urhepecha,[3] la obra ha pasado prácticamente inadvertida por la crítica y la academia, lo que no es extraño para gran parte de esta literatura. *Alonso Mariano* aborda como eje narrativo principal la incursión de varios personajes al espacio urbano, fuera de su comunidad, lo que permite al autor plantear una serie de conflictos y tensiones en la vida de los personajes que surgen de la confrontación entre dos visiones de mundo: una sostenida por el sistema de poder moderno-colonial que se potencia en el espacio urbano, y otra forma de existencia, p'urhepecha, que tiene que navegar entre este sistema en el contexto actual, en el que los pueblos no pueden sustraerse de la modernidad, pero tampoco están dispuestos, con toda justicia, a renunciar a sus formas de existencia.

El objetivo de este capítulo es analizar estas tensiones epistemológicas que surgen en la novela a partir de este movimiento de los personajes fuera de su territorio, así como el translenguaje tanto en su versión en p'urhepecha como en español; para esto recurro a una lectura que se basa en ciertos rasgos del contexto cultural y social los cuales permiten contrastar y comprender epistemologías propias. De manera particular se abordan las nociones de educación, colectividad, ritualidad y fiesta, y autonomía temporal, para ser contrastadas con la visión moderno-colonial. Para analizar estas tensiones me baso en la noción de "visiones de cabeza" propuesta por Miguel Rocha Vivas para el caso colombiano, la cual se refiere a diferentes formas de autorrepresentación llevadas a cabo por autores indígenas que buscan subvertir las miradas hegemónicas sobre sus pueblos. La reflexión sobre estos temas me permite proponer que, aunque la obra se encuentra situada en un contexto local –y aunque ha sido escrita ya hace algunos años–, coincide en muchos planteamientos con la agenda de otros escritores indígenas en América Latina, pues contribuye de diferentes maneras a: 1) develar los efectos del sistema de poder moderno-colonial; 2) poner en disputa los estereotipos y representaciones que la sociedad dominante tiene sobre lo indígena; 3) poner en marcha procesos de autorrepresentación desde una mirada crítica; y, 4) apuntar hacia la demanda de soberanía, sobre todo política, en el caso de la novela que analizamos. Si bien la novela coincide en lo general con estos objetivos, los aspectos particulares que esta aporta en cuanto epistemologías p'urhepecha es importante en sí misma y en el campo de la literatura escrita en lenguas indígenas en México, pues se trata de una literatura que no cuenta con tanta visibilidad y reconocimiento como la literatura maya, zapoteca o náhuatl.[4]

Antes de incursionar en el análisis, presento algunos datos biográficos del autor, los cuales contribuyen a situarlo dentro del movimiento literario en lenguas indígenas de México. Esta información me permitirá también establecer algunos puentes entre la vida del autor y la novela.

Ismael García Marcelino nació en Ihuatzio, Michoacán, en 1964. Vivió varios años en la capital del estado, Morelia, pero actualmente ha regresado a Ihuatzio a cumplir con una serie de compromisos en su comunidad. Además de escritor, García Marcelino ejecuta varios géneros de la tradición oral p'urhepecha, en particular los discursos ceremoniales y el canto lírico (*pirekua*), expresiones por las que es reconocido a nivel local. Sobre los discursos ceremoniales –tan vitales en su comunidad a pesar de la pérdida de la lengua p'urhepecha en muchos otros ámbitos–, García Marcelino ha escrito un hermoso libro en versión bilingüe (aún inédito) donde da cuenta pormenorizada de su composición y su sentido. Hacia el final de este ensayo hablo sobre la presencia de estos discursos en la novela *Alonso Mariano*.

Ismael García Marcelino ha escrito poesía, cuento, novela y ensayo, tanto en p'urhepecha como en español, y ha sido colaborador en diferentes medios impresos y en radio, en donde se ha caracterizado por ser un fuerte crítico lo mismo de las políticas de estado y de las prácticas e ideologías que la sociedad dominante tiene sobre los pueblos indígenas, que hacia las problemáticas que se dan al interior de las comunidades. En estos medios, además, suele abordar temas de relevancia local y nacional sobre todo en el ámbito de las políticas culturales y la literatura. Muchas de sus ideas actuales sobre estos temas se encuentran ya presentes en *Alonso Mariano*.

En el contexto mexicano, a García Marcelino se le puede ubicar como parte del movimiento de revaloración de las artes verbales en lenguas indígenas que impulsó el escritor Carlos Montemayor en muchas regiones de México en los años ochenta y noventa. En Michoacán, este impulso lo hizo Montemayor en colaboración con el intelectual p'urhepecha Irineo Rojas Hernández, de la Universidad Michoacana de San Nicolás de Hidalgo, la universidad pública estatal. Como resultado de esta colaboración se llevaron a cabo algunos talleres literarios; sin embargo, solo algunos de los participantes continuaron con un trabajo creativo y muchos de ellos se desarrollaron más bien en la academia o en los medios de comunicación. García Marcelino, por su parte, continuó con su formación en distintos talleres literarios. Además, su participación en este movimiento le permitió convivir con escritores de distintas regiones de México y América en diversos encuentros, con lo que le ganó cierto reconocimiento a nivel nacional.

García Marcelino fue acreedor en dos ocasiones a la beca nacional del FONCA para Escritores en Lenguas Indígenas. Producto de la primera beca (1997), escribió el manuscrito sobre discursos ceremoniales ya mencionado y, gracias a la segunda (2003), escribió la novela bilingüe *Valentina Espíritu* (2013). En 2004, García Marcelino publicó *Alonso Mariano* en la colección Letras Indígenas Contemporáneas de la Dirección General de Culturas Populares e Indígenas del CONACULTA (Mendoza 238). Esta trayectoria ejemplifica el tipo de relaciones que se han ido tejiendo entre ciertas políticas de estado y los escritores en lenguas originarias en México, las cuales, por razones de espacio, no problematizo aquí. Aunque no es fácil tener acceso a algunas de sus publicaciones, unos cuantos poemas y ensayos pueden ser consultados en línea. Al final de este capítulo se refieren algunas páginas donde se puede encontrar algo de su trabajo.

Además de su labor como creador, García Marcelino imparte cursos de lengua p'urhepecha y talleres de creación literaria y escritura tanto en español como en p'urhepecha, lo mismo en su comunidad que en instituciones estatales y federales, lo que habla de la capacidad para transitar entre lenguas, aspecto que también se resalta en este ensayo cuando se aborda la cuestión del translingüismo en la novela.

Visiones de cabeza

Como ya he referido, *Alonso Mariano* aborda como eje principal una serie de conflictos y tensiones en la vida de los personajes de un pueblo p'urhepecha que surgen a partir de su salida de la comunidad –Ch'urhinkuarhu– al espacio urbano. Es este movimiento el que permite al autor contrastar epistemologías y prácticas entre visiones de mundo. La novela se ubica principalmente entre 1979 y 1983, aunque se prolonga hasta veinte años después, los suficientes para presenciar una transformación tanto del pueblo como de los personajes. La historia, sin embargo, no es lineal. Dividida en dos partes, la primera parte de la novela inicia con el entierro de nana Cele, tía de Alonso Mariano y se nos narra la vida de este joven fuera de la comunidad, en San Pedro del Río, en una casa de estudiante. La segunda parte comienza donde empieza la primera, en el entierro de la tía de Alonso Mariano, y esta es la única vez que oímos a Alonso en su propia voz (aunque a lo largo de la novela se le cita directa e indirectamente). En general esta parte narra los acontecimientos que se desatan a partir de la muerte de la tía del personaje principal y muestran el regreso a su pueblo y su proceso de transformación: de estudiante que se resiste a los tiempos y modos de la comunidad a autoridad comunitaria. Además de la de Alonso Mariano, a lo largo de la novela se nos van contando fragmentos de la vida de diversos personajes dentro y fuera de Ch'urhinkuarhu. Para esto, el autor recurre a un narrador que va cambiando de capítulo en capítulo y que relata lo que observa, lo que siente y/o lo que sabe de otros. Es en este juego polifónico que vamos reconociendo las relaciones entre los personajes que aparecen en la novela y uno de los aspectos más desafiantes e interesantes tanto para el autor, en su búsqueda por darle a los personajes una voz propia a través de la cual ver el mundo, como para el lector, que tiene que ir resolviendo el asunto de quién es el narrador en cada capítulo. Esta estrategia narrativa tiene el efecto, además, de hacernos empatizar con los personajes al presentarnos su punto vista: sus deseos, sus tristezas, sus inquietudes, su intimidad, incluso su sexualidad, pero también de ofrecernos una mirada crítica sobre diversas situaciones o personajes vistos desde la subjetividad de otros personajes.

Para analizar los conflictos y tensiones en la novela, recurro a la noción de "visiones de cabeza" propuesta por Miguel Rocha Vivas, la cual resulta útil para acercarse a distintos actos discursivos interculturales que presentan a la sociedad dominante desde un punto de vista históricamente silenciado, cuestionándola e interpelándola. Visiones de cabeza que ponen en disputa los estereotipos o las representaciones sobre lo indígena, a la vez que reivindican el derecho a la autorrepresentación y a una visión del mundo y una existencia propia:

> Las visiones de cabeza son expresiones de dinámicas de subversión de imágenes y textos, así como de enunciaciones desde múltiples orillas lingüísticas y culturales. En efecto, se resimbolizan en primera medida a partir de un cambio posicional: lo de arriba queda abajo, de cabeza. (Rocha 15)

El objetivo de este capítulo es, pues, mostrar la manera en que en esta novela se abordan diferentes cambios de posición que surgen del contraste con prácticas y epistemologías otras. Aunque el final de la novela apuesta por una autonomía política a través de formas de gobierno tradicionales, la obra está lejos de ser una idealización de la vida comunitaria, más bien lo que busca es mostrar los cuestionamientos, las contradicciones y los desgarramientos que surgen del contacto asimétrico entre sistemas de mundo, así como las diferentes resoluciones que plantean los personajes frente a este conflicto intercultural. En este sentido, la novela no solo se dirige a los lectores no p'urhepecha (público potencial mayoritario al menos de la versión en español), sino de manera importante ofrece una reflexión dirigida a la propia sociedad p'urhepecha, para que asuma críticamente su relación frente al sistema moderno-colonial.

Esta crítica se lleva a cabo, principalmente, a través de algunos de los personajes de la novela que salen del pueblo para encontrarse con ciudades hostiles a las que, sin embargo, se esfuerzan por pertenecer. Las historias de Clemente, Silvano, Paula y su hermana Carmela son, en este sentido, duros testimonios de la forma de vida en los márgenes de las ciudades en las que, sin embargo, también hay pequeños espacios para el amor, el placer, la compasión y la ternura. Pero ¿qué es lo que hace que estos personajes quieran migrar y permanecer en estas ciudades? En parte las condiciones de vida, en parte también el deseo de conocer otra forma de existencia que se ofrece como "mejor", pero también por una especie de orgullo por no mostrar que se ha fracasado fuera del pueblo. Así lo dice uno de los narradores:

> A lo mejor es por eso que algunos no quieren volver tan así de fácil; porque no quieren que se sepa que se encontraron las cosas más difíciles de lo que habían pensado. Viven bastante mal en la ciudad, pero aunque no tengan qué comer, aunque no tengan qué vestir, dónde vivir, no les da la gana volver y no vuelven. (*Alonso Mariano* 259)

Por otro lado, mucha de la gente que suele salir, "vuelve sin regresar" (*Alonso Mariano* 334), aculturizada. Así lo ironiza en una de tantas ocasiones tata Jesú, el padre de Alonso

Mariano: "Hay otra señora que fue a visitar a su hijo a México, se tardó por allá como una semana y cuando regresó ya no quería lavar en la orilla porque el agua estaba 'muy sucia'. ¡Y apenas hacía una semana que se bañaba ahí!" (*Alonso Mariano* 241). De esta manera, a través de estos personajes el autor lleva a cabo una autocrítica a los procesos de aculturación, de decapitación simbólica –en los términos de Rocha Vivas– aunque sin dejar de reconocer los desgarramientos y las tristezas de estos desencuentros interculturales que surgen al enfrentarse al espacio urbano.

A diferencia de estos personajes que salen del pueblo por razones más bien personales, Alonso Mariano se mueve al espacio urbano para estudiar, pues considera que de esta manera puede mejorar las condiciones sociales de su comunidad; para lograrlo, Alonso Mariano tiene que irrumpir tanto física como simbólicamente, al interior de la "ciudad letrada";[5] sin embargo, la única manera de hacer frente a ese espacio tradicionalmente negado a los indígenas y campesinos es organizándose con otros jóvenes como él para formar una casa del estudiante,[6] ubicada en una casona abandonada justo en el centro de la ciudad. De esta forma, en una visión de cabeza, se erige en el centro mismo del espacio urbano un espacio de resistencia y de vida comunitaria tan incómodo a las élites urbanas.

Como hemos dicho, a Alonso Mariano –como a otros personajes– lo vamos conociendo a través de la mirada de otros personajes. El segundo capítulo de la novela toma en gran parte el punto de vista del mejor amigo de Alonso Mariano y aborda el discurrir de los estudiantes cuando se encuentran alrededor de la escasa comida en la casa del estudiante. El capítulo resulta de particular interés porque en él se plantea el sustento histórico e ideológico que justifica la actuación del personaje principal. Así, en su charla, Alonso Mariano y sus compañeros hablan sobre su condición "de indígenas y campesinos", una condición con la que tienen que luchar no porque renieguen de ella, sino porque es una condición que ha sido históricamente definida desde un pensamiento e ideología moderno-coloniales que los ha colocado sistemáticamente en una posición de subordinación la cual niega sus derechos fundamentales. Un poco más adelante y siguiendo este argumento, el narrador aborda la cuestión de la diferencia colonial que ha colocado ciertos conocimientos o lenguas por encima de otros de la siguiente manera:

> Nada malo es que estos estudiantes fueran indígenas, sino que para cualquier mortal de San Pedro del Río un indio es lo que había sido siempre: aquel hombre o aquella mujer que mal habla el español y que, por no saber de leyes, todo mundo cree que no sabe de justicia, o que por no saber español, todo mundo cree que no sabe ni tiene nada importante que comunicar. (*Alonso Mariano* 202)

Así, aquí y en diferentes capítulos de la novela se van poniendo al descubierto estas miradas convencionales, estereotipadas que definen desde la idea del poder moderno-colonial qué saberes, qué prácticas, qué discursos y qué lenguas tienen derecho a existir. Frente a estas miradas hegemónicas es necesario defender el derecho a la existencia desde una manera propia de ver y entender el mundo, de gestionar la vida. Este reclamo por una existencia propia es expresado por Alonso Mariano a sus compañeros en esta visión de cabeza: "[Un indígena es] un 'raro hombre y una rara mujer' que no quiere ser como todos los mexicanos, porque, sobre todo, no quiere dejar de ser como es" (*Alonso Mariano* 203). Así, contraria a la ideología dominante que ha considerado, explícita o implícitamente, deseable que la población indígena se asimile a la sociedad mestiza bajo los supuestos de unidad nacional, progreso y modernidad coloniales, el autor afirma contundente que los pueblos indígenas no quieren dejar de ser lo que son (sin que esto signifique aislarse del mundo actual, como comentaremos más adelante).

Y es que esta manera propia de existencia está sustentada en un principio ético y de justicia fundamental presente en el pensamiento p'urhepecha que es la "honorabilidad" o "dignidad", que en este contexto no significa otra cosa que el hecho de que todo lo que existe tiene derecho a existir (*sesi ampeni* "es cosa buena"). Así lo explica el intelectual p'urhepecha Moisés Franco:

> El p 'urhépecha mantiene como un valor ético la "honorabilidad" [...] Así, los hombres, los animales, las plantas, los elementos de la naturaleza, los astros y todo lo que existe son honorables [no solo las personas]. Por ello deben ser reconocidos, respetados, venerados e invocados. La honorabilidad en el hombre implica una autoapreciación y autodefensa, debe ser reconocido y respetado por "el otro" hombre. Ser como se es y como se quiere ser, es honorable, por ello debe ser reconocido por "el otro" hombre porque es tan honorable como ese "otro". (*Alonso Mariano* 224)

Aunado a esto, está la cuestión de cómo articular la vida comunitaria en el contexto actual, es decir, cómo conciliar la vida moderna, con dignidad y justicia, y desde esta forma de existencia propia. Domi, la pareja de Alonso, y Antulio, su mejor amigo, expresan este conflicto y contradicción de la siguiente manera:

> –En parte tienes razón, pero he estado reflexionando que no es sólo saliendo sino quedándose en casa como puede ganar firmeza nuestro pueblo.
> –Pero si nos quedamos, no vamos a conseguir nada de afuera.
> –Pero si nos vamos, no vamos a conservar nada de adentro.
> –Pero, ¿no estamos marginados precisamente por lo que nos falta de afuera?
> –En parte, pero porque no hemos entendido lo que nos vale lo de dentro, lo propio; y es ahí donde está fincada nuestra lucha. (*Alonso Mariano* 293)

Ahora bien, si hay un espacio en donde estas tensiones y contradicciones entre lo de adentro y lo de afuera se exacerban es justamente en la escuela. Así, a la vez que esta ha sido la institución por excelencia por medio de la cual se han impuesto las políticas lingüísticas y culturales de castellanización y aculturación desde la época de la Colonia y de manera más intensa en el México moderno, también ha sido considerada por la población indígena como una de las pocas vías para poder mejorar sus condiciones de vida.[7] En este contexto y a pesar de las duras críticas a lo largo de la novela en torno a las prácticas escolares que fomentan el individualismo y que reproducen desigualdades de todo tipo, Alonso Mariano y sus compañeros de la casa del estudiante ven en la universidad una posibilidad para poder transformar la situación de sus comunidades; sin embargo, como hemos dicho, no se asimilan del todo a esos espacios, sino que se apropian de ellos organizándose bajo ciertos principios que les son característicos, entre otros, la colectividad, la conciencia de la lucha, el compromiso con los pueblos de origen y un pensamiento crítico al sistema capitalista.

En otro sentido, si bien Alonso Mariano piensa que muchos de los problemas que enfrenta su pueblo se deben a una estructura que histórica y sistemáticamente ha marginalizado y subalternizado a los pueblos indígenas, también cree que muchos de ellos se deben a ciertas prácticas internas a las comunidades que no las deja progresar, como aquellas relativas a las fiestas, ritos y ceremonias, o a la falta de educación.

Contrario a esta visión, tata Jesú, el padre de Alonso Mariano lamenta el proceso de aculturación que sufre su hijo y que lo aleja de los valores y la forma de vida comunitarios, expresando su opinión sobre la escuela de la siguiente manera: "Porque en Santiago vale más un niño que ayuda a su papá en el campo, que otro que quiere saber de letras. Es bueno eso de las letras, pero luego no quieren trabajar en sus casas. Yo tengo un hijo que mejor se fue para San Pedro del Río, dizque para hacerse ingeniero. ¡Ja, ya quisiera!" (*Alonso Mariano* 240).

Este conflicto entre visiones de mundo expresado por tata Jesú tiene que ver con formas diferentes de entender la educación. En p'urhepecha, la educación está fuertemente ligada al concepto de la *kaxumpekua*. De acuerdo con Jacinto Zavala, este término "generalmente se traduce como cortesía, buenas maneras, buena educación, etc., y designa por implicación, al que sabe comportarse en la sociedad p'urhépecha de acuerdo con las enseñanzas de los mayores" (104). La expresión mínima de la *kaxumpekua* es el saludo, que reconoce al otro como ser social honorable (existente); pero el espacio en donde se magnifica la *kaxumpekua* (es decir, las formas corteses y respetuosas de hablar y de comportarse) es en las fiestas y ceremonias y todos sus rituales, de ahí que tata Jesú no entienda cómo puede ser que la escuela "no enseñe a respetar el lugar donde se nace" (*Alonso Mariano* 295), pues una parte importante de este respeto, de la *kaxumpekua,* se logra por medio del cumplimiento de compromisos religiosos y civiles dentro de la comunidad, algo que Alonso Mariano rechaza en principio porque no alcanza a comprender su importancia para el sustento de la vida comunitaria.

Junto con la *kaxumpekua* está la conciencia, que es un valor superior al conocimiento (escolar). Sin ella, el conocimiento solo podrá servir para reproducir el sistema de poder colonial capitalista. Dice Alonso: "Mientras no pongas a trabajar tus capacidades de lucha y pensamiento, no eres conciencia, no eres persona, eres objeto y te puedes hacer mercadería" (*Alonso Mariano* 208). Así, sin conciencia individual y social, dice Alonso Mariano, no se alcanza a ser persona y es que, en p'urhepecha, la palabra para "hacerse persona" es *k'uiripeni,* que es la misma palabra que se utiliza para traducir la palabra "crecer" del español e implica una serie de rasgos, entre ellos la conciencia individual y social, así como el reconocimiento de los demás y a los demás como personas existentes; así los niños, por ejemplo, no solo crecen en términos físicos, sino se hacen personas en términos sociales. Sin conciencia, el conocimiento que pueda ofrecer la escuela pierde sentido. Así, el autor nos ofrece nuevamente una visión de cabeza, al subvertir los valores moderno-coloniales sobre la educación, y mostrar su sentido desde la visión p'urhepecha.

Finalmente, respecto a la cuestión de la educación, Alonso, en su proceso de reapropiación cultural, cae en cuenta de que su "lucha tiene varios rostros" y de que, si bien "uno de ellos es el derecho a la formación" (*Alonso Mariano* 333), otra forma de lucha se da caminando según los principios y valores de la comunidad. Así lo expresa Alonso Mariano en una de las cartas que envía a sus compañeros de la casa del estudiante: "Hay que ser alguien en su pueblo, con su pueblo y fuera de él, en ese orden [...]. El pueblo sabe lo que hace. Uno no siempre está listo para comprender esto porque confunde conocimiento con la conciencia, pero el tiempo que se desperdicia en la escuela, viviendo en el pueblo, de regreso, pronto se recupera" (*Alonso Mariano* 334–335). De esta manera, en su proceso de retorno, Alonso Mariano va descubriendo los valores y formas de organización que dan sentido a la vida comunitaria (entre ellas las fiestas y ceremonias), que al inicio cuestiona duramente y desde las que también se puede organizar la existencia. En este sentido, Alonso Mariano pasa por un proceso de rearticulación, de reapropiación cultural y de relocalización.

"Ser alguien en su pueblo y con su pueblo" es una idea que nos conduce nuevamente a la noción de colectividad. Como hemos mencionado, Alonso Mariano, junto con otros jóvenes, principalmente indígenas y campesinos, organizan una casa del estudiante para poder hacer frente, en comunidad, a la ciudad. "En una casa del estudiante ese sentido [de colectividad] está presente en casi todos nuestros actos porque es algo con lo que nacimos, dado el origen de casi todos los compañeros" (*Alonso Mariano* 334).

El servicio gratuito, el trabajo colectivo, el consenso en la toma de decisiones, la tierra comunal, la reciprocidad y la ayuda mutua, los ritos y ceremonias que exaltan las diferentes formas de relación de lo que existe, incluidas las de los hombres con las divinidades, son algunas de las cosas que distinguen a los pueblos indígenas de otros grupos de personas y que, de manera particular, les dan *identidad*, según lo reflexionó el activista ayuujk Floriberto Díaz al desarrollar el concepto de comunalidad. Todas estas características tienen que ver con una forma de existencia que apuesta por el bien común y no por el individual, como tiende a ser en las sociedades occidentales.

A lo largo de la novela, estas dos visiones están representadas, una, en el personaje de Héctor Mena Garcidueñas, un muchacho mestizo de la ciudad y, la otra, en el de Alonso Mariano y los estudiantes de origen indígena y campesino. Así, al inicio de la novela, en la casa del estudiante, Antulio, el amigo de Alonso, increpa así a Héctor:

> No es por eso que está usted en una Casa del Estudiante amigo [...]. La filosofía que fundamenta nuestra lucha es la colectividad y se me hace grave, aparte de contradictorio que usted promueva que cada quien se rasque con sus propias uñas. Si nuestra lucha fuera de individuos, no tendría la mínima razón de existir como Casa del Estudiante. Sería suficiente que cada de nosotros se ocupara de ser buen estudiante. Sólo eso. (*Alonso Mariano* 207)

Y, de manera circular, al final de la novela, en el último capítulo titulado "Nosotros" se aborda el encuentro, veinte años después, entre el Jefe de Tenencia de Ch'urhinkuarhu (es decir, la autoridad comunitaria), Alonso Mariano, y el ahora candidato a un cargo político promovido por uno de los partidos de estado, Héctor Mena Garcidueñas. Domi, la compañera de Alonso en la casa del estudiante y en su regreso a la comunidad, describe el (des)encuentro entre estas dos visiones, entre lo colectivo y lo individual, que también es una diferencia política, de la siguiente manera: "Había que notar la claridad con que Alonso hablaba de nosotros en la misma situación donde el candidato hablaba de sí mismo, yo. Eso me convenció para siempre de que por más que aquellos dos hombres hablaran, no iban a entenderse jamás" (*Alonso Mariano* 341). De esta manera, en Alonso ocurre una recuperación del sentido de lo colectivo, que tiene una lógica propia y un sentido político, y que opera por encima de la voluntad individual.

Ahora bien, si hay un espacio y un tiempo en el que se exaltan valores como el de la colectividad es en el de la fiesta o, como prefiere llamarla el propio Ismael García por los malentendidos que provoca (comunicación personal), la celebración. Entre los p'urhepecha, las fiestas y ceremonias son un conglomerado de rituales en donde se activan distintos códigos de participación, relación y compromiso que permiten la reproducción y permanencia del grupo. Además, las fiestas a los santos y las diversas ceremonias son espacios en los que se acentúa y se pone en escena una serie de valores sociales que sustentan la identidad p'urhepecha, tales como la reciprocidad, el acompañamiento y el respeto a los otros, incluidas las divinidades. Frente a su importancia, otras obligaciones quedan en segundo plano. Dice Garrido Izaguirre a propósito de la importancia de la fiesta y sus rituales en la comunidad p'urhepecha de Ocumicho:

> El tiempo en Ocumicho está marcado por el ritual: las fiestas en honor de los santos y vírgenes, los robos de las novias, las bodas, bautizos, egresos de la escuela y demás, se insertan en una red de compromisos familiares y de compadrazgo que ocupan el tiempo de los hombres y mujeres de la comunidad. Ayudar es un "derecho", palabra que sustituye a la de obligación y ante la que el trabajo queda relegado.[8] (130)

De acuerdo con Villar Morgan, entre los p'urhepecha, tres nociones dan sentido a la fiesta y organizan las acciones e interacciones de los que participan en ella: el *eyakwarhini* (el compromiso), la *pámpintani* (el acompañamiento) y la *porhémpikwa* (la visita).[9] Entre ellas, el acompañamiento es "el compromiso de participar en las prácticas rituales de los ceremoniales o fiestas" (Villar 53), es decir, es estar presente para los otros con los que se tiene una relación de parentesco familiar o ceremonial. A mayor acompañamiento, mayor prestigio, "más ayuda, más gasto y mayor evidencia del soporte social en el que está anclado aquel que 'hace la fiesta'" (Garrido 292). La sola idea de hacer una fiesta sin recibir ayuda y sin hacerse acompañar de los padrinos o compadres o la familia es prácticamente impensable y una gran ofensa para las personas; más que una concesión o una cortesía de parte de los acompañantes, el hacerse acompañar es una obligación. Este acompañamiento es, pues, una de las múltiples formas en las que se expresa el sentido de colectividad y es justamente esta dimensión ritual y festiva de lo colectivo la que se le escapa a Alonso Mariano quien en un principio no comprende la profundidad de la fiesta para la vida social, atribuyendo más bien a estas tradiciones la culpa de su "atraso".

Como la mayor parte de la sociedad mestiza que tiene algún tipo de contacto con las comunidades p'urhepecha, Alonso Mariano no entiende cómo la gente puede invertir tanto tiempo y dinero en estos eventos, relegando otras obligaciones e invirtiendo recursos que en realidad no sobran, en lugar, por ejemplo, de ir a la escuela. Así, con profunda ironía, el protagonista y su amigo platican:

> Lo que pasa es que luego, los padrinos tienen muchas funciones. Los llaman en una fiesta y ahí les toca, creo, cumplir con una lista de compromisos. A mí, la verdad, todo eso no me gusta. Luego eso los amarra porque no se pueden abandonar los deberes de los ahijados. Imagínate que si trabajo con alguna empresa y luego tengo que ir a una fiesta con un ahijado como padrino o con un padrino como ahijado, no les voy a decir a mis jefes que voy a faltar a trabajar porque "tengo que asistir a una fiesta".
>
> –No, pues no; si yo fuera tu patrón o tu jefe, te diría: Ándele que le vaya bien, que se divierta. (*Alonso Mariano* 269).

En contrapartida, como hemos dicho, tata Jesú, el padre de Alonso Mariano, expresa una profunda decepción por su hijo, quien no entiende que su hijo desprecie aquello que es tan valioso para la vida comunitaria. Sin embargo, hacia el final de la novela, cuando Alonso Mariano es forzado a regresar a su comunidad, en su proceso de reapropiación empieza "a mirar cosas que [...] no había volteado a ver" (*Alonso Mariano* 334), como aquellas relativas a la importancia de las fiestas y sus compromisos en diversos ámbitos de la existencia p'urhepecha. De esta manera, en los términos simbólicos que emplea Miguel Rocha Vivas, Alonso Mariano va recuperando la cabeza, es decir, va recuperando la capacidad "de pensar por cuenta propia y colectiva los procesos de autorrepresentación y rearticulación comunitaria" (25), los cuales, en este caso, dependen de una organización social que encuentra una de sus manifestaciones más claras en las fiestas, ceremonias y rituales.

Otro aspecto relacionado con la fiesta tiene que ver con el tiempo. Ya hemos dicho que en las comunidades p'urhepecha el tiempo está marcado por el ritual. Esta cuestión del tiempo y el ritmo propio de las comunidades contrasta con el de las ciudades o sus instituciones, creando otra visión de cabeza. Así, por ejemplo, a lo largo de la novela se alude a la importancia de "sentir profundo y pensar despacio". Por su parte, Antulio –el poeta, amigo de Alonso– habla así de un lugar como Santiago:

> Cuando uno conoce un pueblo como Santiago y la vida lo pone en una casa como ésta, puede uno darse cuenta que hay pueblos viejos que por costumbre caminan de puntitas. Sobreviven por sobre y a pesar de los otros pueblos que se han dejado crecer [...]. Un pueblo así, tan engrandecido, no puede caminar despacio, corre cada día. Santiago Ch'urhinkuarhu camina despacio. Vienen ratos y se queda callado; callado y tranquilo, como si estuviera pensativo. Se está tan quieto como cuando no se tiene a dónde ir. Y no tiene a dónde ir. (*Alonso Mariano* 277)

Y es que, a diferencia de una concepción lineal del tiempo, en la comunidad este tiene mucho más de repetición, de ciclicidad que de un supuesto progreso hacia ninguna parte. Ahora bien, no es raro que el tema del tiempo y el ritmo estén muy presentes en el pensamiento del autor de la novela, quien también es músico y *pireri* (cantante). Él, por ejemplo, atribuye las transformaciones actuales de la *pirekua* tradicional a un cambio en la concepción del ritmo y del tiempo comunitarios y le he oído comentar en diversas ocasiones que estos cambios temporales han traído consigo transformaciones en la realización de los rituales comunitarios que tienden a apresurarse o a eliminarse algunas de sus partes para dar lugar a otro tipo de prácticas no tradicionales o para ajustarse a los ritmos externos, por ejemplo, los impuestos por el turismo. La cuestión sobre el tiempo y el ritmo es un tema importante que aparece también en algunas obras de los escritores indígenas analizados por Rocha Vivas como Hugo Jamioy y Efrén Tarapués, quienes, además de cuestionar y criticar "los tiempos y ritmos propios de las sociedades hegemónicas", demandan una especie de "soberanía temporal". Dice Rocha Vivas: "en tal orden de ideas, la consideración sobre un tiempo propio también es la afirmación de un ritmo particular y sobre todo de una historia propia" (260). La cuestión de la soberanía temporal es un reclamo profundo y fundamental porque es una de las principales dimensiones, junto con el territorio-espacio, en el transcurrir de la existencia. Como hemos dicho, el tiempo se detiene en la fiesta y está marcado por el ritual, la construcción de relaciones de parentesco social y ceremonial requieren de un tiempo especial; la manufactura de textiles y otros productos, los ciclos agrícolas, todo tiene un tiempo que no se ajusta al tiempo del sistema mundo capitalista en el que lo que prevalece es la productividad.

Relacionada con la cuestión del tiempo y como parte de la textura de la novela sobre la que se teje la historia de los personajes, está presente una particular elaboración del paisaje visual y sobre todo sonoro de la comunidad. La música, las canciones, las radionovelas, el silencio, el ruido, las campanas de la iglesia, el perifoneo a través del que se anuncian todo tipo de cosas constituyen una parte importante del texto. En este sentido, algo que cabría resaltar es el hecho de que, a la par que presenciamos el retorno y transformación de Alonso, hay una paulatina modificación, en sentido inverso, del paisaje visual y sonoro de Santiago Ch'urhinkuarhu. Tata Jesú describe así el pueblo: "el paisaje de Santiago está hecho de cercas de piedra que saludan con hojas de maíz escurriendo de agua" (*Alonso Mariano* 240). En contraste, Alonso, años después, dice: "algunas -ya solamente algunas- cercas de piedra se extienden a lo largo de las calles empedradas y chuecas, todas chuecas" (*Alonso Mariano* 267). Junto con las casas de adobe y teja, aparecen las casas "que parecen cajas de tabique y concreto. Frías, inacabadas, cuadradas" (*Alonso Mariano* 267). El lago está amenazado por la basura. Las reuniones en las esquinas convocadas alrededor de una buena plática, unas *pirekuas* o unas canciones rancheras van siendo sustituidas por músicos de banda que tocan canciones de moda y que no tocan ni componen buena música y que "se conforman con tocar fuerte y reconocer que tocan fuerte". El silencio es sustituido por "los aparatos de música que se oyen por todas partes, a todo volumen" (*Alonso Mariano* 342). Así, frente a la decidida rearticulación del pensamiento comunitario que asume Alonso Mariano, avanza un paulatino, y pareciera, inevitable y desalentador deterioro del medio ambiente, uno más de los aspectos a los que tienen que hacer frente los pueblos originarios en los tiempos actuales en su lucha por asegurar su existencia.

Sobre la naturaleza bilenguajeante de la novela

Finalmente, un último aspecto que quisiera abordar en este texto es la cuestión del bilingüismo o, para decir mejor, *bilenguajeo* en la novela. *Alonso Mariano,* al igual que la mayoría de la literatura escrita en lenguas originarias en México, fue publicada en versión bilingüe.[10] Respecto a ambas versiones, más que señalar sus diferencias, lo que me interesa subrayar aquí es el bilingüismo de la versión en p'urhepecha, en contraste con el aparente monolingüismo de la parte que está en español. Así, la sección supuestamente monolingüe en p'urhepecha contiene una serie de cambios de código entre el p'urhepecha y el español en diferentes grados: desde palabras y frases hasta párrafos completos, lo que no sucede en la versión en español. Los cambios de código en la parte p'urhepecha ocurren fundamentalmente en contextos en los que los personajes hablan español porque no hablan p'urhepecha, porque los interlocutores no hablan p'urhepecha, porque esos cambios de código forman parte del habla cotidiana, o bien, porque se incluyen fragmentos de géneros discursivos en español que forman parte del paisaje sonoro cotidiano p'urhepecha (canciones, radionovelas, anuncios); por lo demás, tanto el narrador como los otros narradores-personajes hablan en p'urhepecha. Propongo que, si bien este fenómeno puede interpretarse como un rasgo de verosimilitud, también puede leerse como una propuesta estética sobre la naturaleza híbrida, bilenguajeante, es decir, producida a través y entre lenguas, donde cada una infecta a la otra, y que fundamentalmente tiene la intención de desafiar el esencialismo lingüístico que se impone tanto a la literatura escrita en español, como a la literatura indígena en México, la cual obliga a tener una versión bilingüe del mismo texto, como si se tratara de dos lenguas separadas. El bilenguajeo, como dice Mignolo, no es una cuestión gramatical, "sino una preocupación política en la medida en que el propio foco del bilenguaje es reparar la asimetría de las lenguas y denunciar la colonialidad del poder y del conocimiento" (231, traducción mía).

La cuestión de los géneros, por otro lado, también es una expresión de este tránsito entre tradiciones lingüísticas y lenguas; así, mientras el autor adopta el género novelístico de tradición occidental, el cual por su naturaleza heteroglósica permite dramatizar "una complejidad social, cultural, política y lingüística imposible de articular a través de otros géneros" (Chacón 45), de igual manera aparecen integrados en la novela algunos discursos ceremoniales que caracterizan los actos rituales de la comunidad p'urhepecha de Ihuatzio y que, en el caso de la versión en español, tienen el efecto de descolocar al lector monolingüe al presentarle un texto que, aunque está traducido al español –la lengua que domina– no termina de comprender, pues no cuenta con las claves culturales para hacerlo. Aquí reproduzco solo un pequeño fragmento de un discurso que aparece al final de la novela en el que el carguero de la fiesta de San Francisco va a visitar a sus padrinos de bautizo (los padres de uno de los personajes femeninos) para saludarlos y preguntarles cómo han amanecido, después de que lo acompañaron en los rituales que el cargo obliga y que continúan ese día en el que se está llevando la entrega del cargo.[11]

> Y puede quizá que el señor Moro Capitán fue llamado un poco para que fuera a prenderle una vela un rato de un año señor... Y quizá cumplió ya un año y así llegó el día que hubo

> que llevarle las gracias a tata San Francisco, un poco, un rato hacerle un juego, señor, a tata San Francisco darle alegría señor. Así también quizá como les es sabido, compadre, puede que tata Moro Capitán no pudo saberse por solo, señor; e ir solo un poco a las autoridades a despedirse, a avisar... (*Alonso Mariano* 301)

Lo primero que habría que decir de estos discursos es que estos son enunciados originalmente en p'urhepecha, nunca en español; que se activan en ceremonias y rituales tanto civiles como religiosos y forman parte de la tradición oral de Ihuatzio. Además, estos discursos los elaboran especialistas que no solo tienen conocimiento de la palabra ritual, sino del procedimiento del ritual mismo. Estos personajes son reconocidos en la comunidad, además, no solo por conocer las formas corteses de hablar y de actuar, sino porque "saben hablar bonito" y lo que dicen "es bonito" "por lo que dice, habla de vivir bien, de cosas buenas, éticamente bellas" (Garrido 458). Así, el sentido estético de estos discursos –que también es ético– descansa tanto en su forma como en su contenido, el cual se activa en un contexto de producción particular, algo difícil de aprehender en conjunto por quien no pertenece a la cultura.[12] Este tipo de discursos se usa para hacer invitaciones, saludos (como en el caso del que aquí presentamos), peticiones, agradecimientos, entre otros. En estos contextos, los especialistas de la palabra hablan en nombre de las personas y familias involucradas y se refieren a su interlocutor como *señor* o *compadre*.[13]

En cuanto al contenido, "Moro Capitán" se refiere al carguero de la fiesta de San Francisco (*Sambranku*) que ese año guía la danza de moros; durante un año, una de las obligaciones del carguero es mantener las velas encendidas para alumbrar al santo; el juego se refiere a la fiesta o celebración que realiza el carguero en agradecimiento al santo por los bienes recibidos y para que éste esté contento; finalmente, "no pudo saberse por solo" se refiere a que, como obliga la costumbre, el carguero debe hacerse acompañar por su familia extensa y, sobre todo, por sus padrinos: nunca nadie hace algo solo, ni por sí mismo, y hacerlo resulta en una gran ofensa para las personas con las que hay un vínculo ceremonial, aspectos que ya fueron comentados líneas arriba cuando se habló acerca del sentido de lo colectivo. Por lo que toca a la traducción, esta trata de mantener algunos rasgos pragmático-discursivos presentes en el género p'urhepecha, por ejemplo, el uso de atenuadores como *poco*, *un rato* y también las expresiones *quizá* o *puede que*, que no se utilizan, como en español, para marcar duda o posibilidad (pues lo que se dice realmente sucede), sino para atenuar lo dicho y expresar así humildad.

Un cuestionamiento que podría hacerse aquí es el de que, como indicio de la imposibilidad de traducir el sentido estético de estos discursos, el autor podría haberlos presentado en p'urhepecha. Considero, sin embargo, que la propuesta de traducción funciona al permitirle al lector hispanohablante no-p'urhepecha un acercamiento que lo descoloca por su extrañeza –aun estando en su propia lengua, la lengua hegemónica–, algo que difícilmente sucedería si el texto solo apareciera en su versión p'urhepecha sin posibilidad para que el lector monolingüe pueda transitar más que en términos puramente semióticos por él.

Ahora bien, para efectos de la ficción, es interesante observar que tanto al final del primero como del último capítulo de la novela hay dos eventos en los que aparecen fragmentos de estos discursos: un entierro y una boda. En este sentido, estos discursos contribuyen, por un lado, a la construcción del paisaje sonoro de la novela, al incluir la sonoridad ritual que aportan este tipo de eventos y, por otro, a la reconstrucción del contexto comunitario particular p'urhepecha en el cual se desenvuelve la historia de los personajes.

Finalmente, otro rasgo de la naturaleza bilenguajeante en la novela es la presencia de un español ap'urhepechizado. Ejemplo de estas expresiones son: "Vénganse a llegar a la casa un rato" por "Vengan a la casa un rato"; "¿Dónde lo mandaste a tu señora?" por "¿A dónde mandaste a tu señora?", "Ya me voy a venir de vuelta" por "Ya me voy a regresar", "Y ahí entonces te lo voy a avisar" por "Y ahí entonces le voy a dar tu recado". Es importante notar que esta variante del español no es muy usada por Alonso Mariano ni por sus compañeros quienes, fuera de su comunidad, hablan un español que podría definirse como urbano y universitario, retando así el uso de las variantes estigmatizadas del español en contacto que se suelen atribuir a los hablantes de pueblos originarios. De esta manera, tanto Alonso Mariano como al autor pueden ser caracterizados por su plurilingüismo, en términos de las distintas lenguas y variedades lingüísticas por las que transitan.

En fin, la traducción de los discursos ceremoniales, junto con la aparición de algunos rasgos característicos del español ap'urhepechizado en la versión en español, lo mismo que los cambios de código de la versión en p'urhepecha y el juego entre géneros, así como las otras propiedades lingüísticas enunciadas, demandan un modo de lectura bilenguajeante e intercultural que pone en disputa la creación y crítica literaria hegemónica monolingüe canónica en español que ha caracterizado la literatura y los Estudios Literarios en México.[14]

A manera de conclusión

A lo largo de este trabajo hemos expuesto algunos de los conflictos y tensiones entre visiones de mundo que se ponen de manifiesto en la novela *Alonso Mariano*. Para abordar estos puntos de conflicto y tensión resultó útil la noción de "visiones de cabeza" con la que Miguel Rocha Vivas nombra el tipo de expresiones que dan la vuelta a las representaciones que la sociedad mayoritaria tiene sobre lo indígena, y que critican el pensamiento hegemónico y la forma de vida capitalista. Así, la perspectiva p'urhepecha sobre la educación, el sentido de colectividad que está presente en las fiestas y ceremonias, así como en diversas formas de organización social, la concepción cíclica del tiempo y la demanda de una soberanía temporal son algunos ejemplos de "visiones de cabeza" que contrastan conceptos, nociones y formas de entender la vida con el sistema mundo moderno-colonial. Algunos de estos temas tienen su correlato en otras novelas de escritores indígenas: la cuestión de la educación y el retorno, por ejemplo, está planteada en novelas como *Cantares de los vientos primerizos* (1994) de Javier Castellanos; y, en la novela *Teya, un corazón de mujer* (2005) de Marisol Ceh Moo hay una apuesta por la autonomía política, como argumenta Gloria Chacón. La cuestión de la soberanía temporal, por su parte, es un tema abordado por Rocha Vivas al analizar a algunos poetas colombianos, así como la cuestión del retorno.

En suma, considero que una de las aportaciones de este trabajo es la propuesta de que los temas que se analizan aquí pueden ser vistos como caminos de interpretación para ingresar en las narrativas de otros autores indígenas que, al ser contrastados con las narrativas de autores no-indígenas, pueden permitir develar epistemologías propias. Queda profundizar en cada uno de estos temas, en su abordaje por distintos autores, así como analizar más obras que permitan tender puentes entre diversos creadores, géneros y temas del Abya Yala.

Por otro lado, en este capítulo también se resaltaron las cualidades lingüísticas de un texto que solo puede ser elaborado por quien vive en ese constante tránsito y frontera entre lenguas (lo que Mignolo llama bilenguajeo), lo cual reta de diversas maneras tanto la producción monolingüe en español, como la bilingüe lengua indígena-español (como si se trataran de dos lenguas separadas), características de la literatura producida en México.

Por último, si una de las funciones de la literatura es la de acercarnos a otras realidades que nos interpelan y nos cuestionan, que nos hacen ver el mundo desde otro punto de vista, sin duda *Alonso Mariano* cumple a cabalidad este objetivo, en un contexto, además, en el que se ha vuelto urgente e inaplazable escuchar estas voces históricamente silenciadas en la construcción de nuevas formas de relación frente a la realidad plurinacional de los países de América Latina.

Notas

1. Agradezco a los editores de este volumen sus innumerables lecturas y sugerencias para que este trabajo pudiera ser publicado. Cualquier error, sin embargo, es responsabilidad absolutamente mía.

2. El p'urhepecha es una lengua hablada por cerca de 141,000 personas en el estado de Michoacán, México, aunque también hay hablantes en otros estados y en Estados Unidos debido a la migración.

3. Un excelente compendio sobre la novela en lenguas originarias en México puede encontrarse en Arturo Arias. Como se puede ver ahí, en realidad son pocas hasta ahora las novelas escritas en estas lenguas desde una visión propia, a diferencia de la novela indigenista que, por su propia naturaleza, no puede acercarse al otro más que desde una visión y una lengua ajena.

4. El auge de estas literaturas quizá pueda deberse a una o varias de las siguientes razones: la formación de generaciones de escritores en talleres dirigidos por los propios creadores en lenguas indígenas, la publicación continua de sus trabajos en revistas literarias propias, la creación de premios a nivel local, una visión clara del papel de la cultura y la lengua en sus movimientos sociales, mayores posibilidades de educación y de inserción en espacios de poder, así como redes que han tejido con diversas instituciones y personas en el ámbito nacional e internacional, todo lo cual le ha faltado en mayor o menor medida a la literatura p'urhepecha. Así, en el caso de esta literatura, lo que se puede observar son unos cuantos autores que han recibido algún reconocimiento nacional, con formaciones y trayectorias de vida muy diversas y algunos espacios eventuales en los que llegan a coincidir. Entre estos escritores podríamos mencionar, entre los más reconocidos a nivel regional y nacional a Ismael García Marcelino, Joel Torres Sánchez, Elizabeth Pérez Tzintzun y, más recientemente, a Rubí Huerta. Si consideramos que México cuenta con 68 pueblos indígenas, en realidad, la resonancia que ha tenido la literatura maya, zapoteca o náhuatl a nivel nacional e internacional es más la excepción que la regla.

5. Así llama Ángel Rama (1985) a un espacio real e imaginario instaurado a partir de la época colonial en América Latina y desde donde se concentra, se ejerce y se reproduce el poder, del centro a la periferia, a través del predominio de la escritura. En los márgenes de esta ciudad ha estado la población rural e indígena, analfabeta a los ojos de la élite, quienes, al escribir en diferentes momentos en lenguas o variantes históricamente marginalizadas, han transgredido los límites y fronteras impuestas por este poder.

6. En Morelia, la capital del estado de Michoacán, las treinta y cinco casas del estudiante que reciben recursos de la universidad pública estatal han permitido a estudiantes de distintas regiones del país, muchos de ellos indígenas y campesinos de escasos recursos, tener la posibilidad de acceder a estudios superiores. Como otros espacios de esta naturaleza, las casas de estudiante son constantemente estigmatizadas y combatidas por las élites políticas o económicas del estado quienes no ven con buenos ojos la presencia de estos grupos en el espacio urbano; sin embargo, para otros sectores, las casas de estudiante representan importantes bastiones de lucha y resistencia de las clases menos favorecidas.

7. De igual manera lo son la migración y, más recientemente, con terribles consecuencias, la incorporación al crimen organizado.

8. No es posible en un espacio tan breve hablar del sentido y la importancia de las fiestas y ceremonias en las comunidades p'urhepecha, sin embargo, el lector puede remitirse al libro de Lorena Ojeda *Fiestas y ceremonias tradicionales p'urhepecha* para una introducción al tema.

9. El compromiso es "la fuerza moral que da sentido a las normatividades que deben cumplirse para mantener y reproducir las redes y relaciones sociales estructurantes de la vida familiar, comunitaria e intercomunitaria" (Villar Morgan 52), tales como la realización de fiestas, las ayudas, el servicio. Mientras que la visita se entiende, según Villar Morgan, como "el compromiso entre comunidades, en el nivel oficial (visita entre autoridades y/o representantes de la comunidad) y familiar (visitas entre parientes o conocidos) de acudir principalmente en las fiestas patronales" (55), aunque también se refiere en el nivel intracomunitario a las visitas que se llevan a cabo para realizar invitaciones o agradecimientos.

10. La cuestión sobre la escritura monolingüe, ya sea en español o lengua indígena, la traducción y la autotraducción hecha por autores indígenas es un tema que ha generado bastante discusión y reflexión entre los propios escritores y los estudiosos de estas literaturas y que, por razones de espacio, no abordaré aquí.

11. Un acercamiento al género de los discursos ceremoniales p'urhepecha, aunque de otra comunidad, puede consultarse en De Jesús Rosas y Meneses.

12. Como ha dicho Sherzer, es justamente en el discurso y el arte verbal "donde se activan en todo su potencial los recursos de la gramática y los significados y símbolos culturales, y donde se torna prominente la esencia de las relaciones entre lengua y cultura" (31), de ahí también su dificultad de traducción.

13. En la versión en p'urhepecha, el vocativo es también el préstamo *senior* y no *acha* que sería la correspondiente palabra p'urhepecha. En este sentido, es interesante notar, como parte de la naturaleza bilenguajeante de las formas de expresión en la lengua indígena, la presencia de dobletes, es decir, de una forma en español para el arte verbal y su correspondiente forma en p'urhepecha en el habla cotidiana. Por ejemplo, en los discursos ceremoniales de Ihuatzio se utiliza el préstamo *recibirini* "recibir" y nunca *xóokani* que es la palabra correspondiente en el p'urhepecha cotidiano. Aunque este fenómeno bien puede estar asociado al prestigio que se le atribuye al español, es innegable, aun así, su diferenciabilidad con fines estéticos.

14. A diferencia de otras literaturas indigenistas, en México no existe algún autor como José María Arguedas en Perú que refleje las variantes del español en contacto, de ahí también la relevancia de obras como esta en el panorama de la novela mexicana.

Obras citadas

Arias, Arturo. "La novela en las lenguas originarias de México". *Enciclopedia de la literatura en México*, 2019. http://www.elem.mx/estgrp/datos/1370

Castellanos Martínez, Javier. *Wila che be ze lhao: Cantares de los vientos primerizos*. Diana, 1994.

Ceh Moo, Marisol. *X-Teya, u puksi'ik'al ko'olel/Teya, un corazón de mujer*. Conaculta, Letras Indígenas Contemporáneas, 2008.

Chacón, Gloria. "El nacimiento de la novela indígena y el rechazo a la integración eurocéntrica". *Revista de Crítica Literaria Latinoamericana*, vol. 91, 2020, pp. 39–58.

De Jesús Rosas, Gloria, and Sue Meneses Eternod. "Discursos de matrimonio en la comunidad purépecha de Cuanajo: Una primera aproximación a su contexto, forma, contenido y función". *Revista de Literaturas Populares*, vol. 19, no. 1, 2019, pp. 75–108.

Díaz, Floriberto. *Escrito: Comunalidad, energía viva del pensamiento mixe Ayuujktsënää yën – ayuujkwënmää ny- ayuujk mëk äjtën*. Edited by Sofía Robles Hernández and Rafael Cardoso Jiménez, Universidad Nacional Autónoma de México, Dirección General de Publicaciones y Fomento Editorial, 2014.

Franco, Moisés. "Sïruki: La tradición entre los p'urhépecha". *Relaciones: Estudios de Historia y Sociedad*, vol. 15, no. 59, 1994, pp. 209–238.

Garrido Izaguirre, Eva María. *"Donde el diablo mete la cola": Antropología del arte y estética indígena*. Universidad Nacional Autónoma de México, Laboratorio Nacional de Materiales Orales, 2020.

Jacinto Zavala, Agustín. *Mitología y modernización*. El Colegio de Michoacán, Gobierno del Estado de Michoacán, 1988.

Mendoza, José, dir. *Diccionario de autores michoacanos I. Literatura*. Secretaría de Cultura, Gobierno del Estado de Michoacán, Centro de Documentación e Investigación de las Artes/Red Utopía Jitanjáfora, 2011.

Mignolo, Walter. *Local Histories/Global Designs: Coloniality, Subaltern Knowledges,and Border Thinking*. Princeton UP, 2000.

Ojeda Dávila, Lorena. *Fiestas y ceremonias tradicionales p'urhepecha*. Gobierno del Estado de Michoacán, Secretaría de Cultura, 2006.

Rama, Ángel. *La ciudad letrada*. Fundación Ángel Rama, 1985.

Rocha Vivas, Miguel. *Mingas de la palabra: Textualidades oralitegráficas y visiones de cabeza en las oralituras y literaturas indígenas contemporáneas*. 2d ed. Editorial Pontificia Universidad Javeriana/Ediciones Uniandes, Universidad de los Andes, 2018.

Sherzer, Joel (2000). "Una aproximación a la lengua y a la cultura centrada en el discurso". *Forma y Función*, vol. 13, 2000, pp. 31–54. https://revistas.unal.edu.co/index.php/formayfuncion/article/view/17181/18033

Villar Morgan, Karla Katihusca. "La kw'inchikwa como tema de conversación: Un estudio de la relación entre discurso, ideología y cultura en una comunidad purépecha". Master's thesis, Universidad Nacional Autónoma de México, 2008.

Obras del autor o dónde consultarla

García Marcelino, Ismael. "Uarhikuani ch'anakutsperi/Escape a la muerte". *Relatos Purépechas. P'urhépecha Uandantskuecha*. Consejo Nacional para la Cultura y las Artes/Dirección General de Culturales Populares, 1995, pp. 51–59. (Colección Lenguas de México 12). Una versión en inglés de este cuento puede encontrarse en la siguiente página: https://www.wordswithoutborders.org/article/escape-from-death

García Marcelino, Ismael. *El habla y la poesía de los discursos ceremoniales que los uantariicha pronuncian en los ceremoniales en Ihuatzio*, 1997. Manuscrito.

García Marcelino, Ismael. *Alonso Mariano*. Consejo Nacional para la Cultura y las Artes. Dirección General de Culturas Populares e Indígenas, 2004. (Colección Letras Indígenas Contemporáneas)

García Marcelino, Ismael. *Valentina Espíritu*. Dirección General de Culturas Populares-Programa para el Desarrollo Integral de las Culturas de los Pueblos y Comunidades Indígenas (PRODICI), 2013.

García Marcelino, Ismael. Columna "Letralia". *Yunuencita* https://yunuencita.com/category/letralia/

Página Purépecha. "Tatá Ismael García Marcelino (Poeta P'urhépecha) originario de Ihuatzio, Michoacán, México". https://www.purepecha.mx/threads/3196-Tat%C3%A1-Ismael-Garc%C3%ADa-Marcelino-(Poeta-P-urh%C3%A9pecha)-originario-de-Ihuatzio-Michoac%C3%A1n-M%C3%A9xico. Accedido el 23 de abril de 2021.

Segundo, Abdías (pseud.). Columna "Introversiones". *Yunuencita* https://yunuencita.com/category/introversiones/

CHAPTER 17

Literaturas indígenas en Brasil: Migrar a las letras[1]

Miguel Rocha Vivas
Universidad Javeriana, Bogotá

As sagradas plantas dos pés,
o pequeno assento arredondado
do Vazio Inicial
enraizou seu desdobrar (florescer)
Tradición oral guaraní

Povos indígenas devem caminhar com seus próprios pés.
Eliane Potiguara

Brasil: Cambio, viraje y vuelta

En 1922 Brasil experimentó un cambio, un viraje y una vuelta de pies. La Semana de Arte Moderna de São Paulo dejaría al descubierto un grupo de cinco artistas, quienes transformarían con sus obras la visión que el país tenía de sí mismo. El grupo de los cinco estaba conformado por las pintoras Tarsila do Amaral y Anita Malfatti, los poetas Oswald de Andrade y Menotti del Picchia, y el poeta-narrador Mário de Andrade, en cuya novela *Macunaíma* (1928) retoma elementos de la mitología indígena amazónica para reflejar el carácter, o *nenhum caráter*, del brasilero. Se gestaba así un cambio de actitud en la concepción del Brasil, un viraje en la atención a la expresión nacional, y cierta mirada de vuelta a los orígenes nativos pre-brasileños.

El Brasil que comenzó a dibujarse con el tratado de Tordesillas en 1494 respondía en realidad a la separación arbitraria de Sudamérica entre los reinos de España y Portugal. Tordesillas puede considerarse una de las primeras reparticiones efectivas del llamado mundo occidental, y un anticipo temprano de las "Conferencias" de Berlín realizadas en 1884 y 1885, cuando las potencias europeas decidieron repartirse África como si fuera un pastel.

Desde el arribo oficial de Pedro Álvares Cabral en abril de 1500, y con las subsiguientes expediciones colonizadoras del siglo XVI, Brasil comenzó a gestarse como un imperio de asentamientos en las costas, un país de espaldas a los sistemas fluviales y selváticos más enormes del planeta tierra. Brasil miraba a Portugal y daba la espalda a la Amazonia. La cabeza era Portugal, el cuerpo era Brasil, y la Amazonia era esa parte interna del cuerpo que no se puede ver. En esa Amazonia inicialmente infranqueable, en ese universo de agua y árboles que cubren el cielo, se replegaron por siglos cientos de lenguas y culturas indígenas que fueron explotadas, diezmadas, a veces absorbidas, y con frecuencia rechazadas.

Brasil, a diferencia de los demás países sudamericanos, pasó de ser colonia a reino. Ante la avanzada expansionista de Napoleón Bonaparte a principios del siglo XIX, el reino de Portugal se trasladó a Brasil en 1808. De tal suerte, el destino de Brasil dejó de ser momentáneamente eurocéntrico para convertirse en Europa misma que se trasladaba por completo a América. Así que era Portugal la que se volvía americano-céntrica, Brasil-céntrica. Con todo, el traslado de las estructuras de poder de Portugal a Brasil implicó un proyecto de europeización más marcado. Tras la independencia de 1822, con el nombramiento de Pedro I como primer emperador de Brasil, curiosamente un 12 de octubre, se realizaba una separación fáctica de la corona de Portugal, al tiempo que se renovaba el orden colonial y subrepticiamente se le perpetuaba mediante el emperador heredero. Durante el siglo XIX no siempre fue necesario diferenciarse radicalmente de Portugal, sino continuar a Portugal de una manera diferente, es decir, una colonialidad brasilera propiamente dicha, en donde "el negro" seguía siendo esclavizado y "el indio" inferior, salvaje y desconocido. En suma, negro e indio son producciones coloniales.

Desde México hasta Argentina las élites criollas continuaron en general orbitando psicológica y culturalmente en torno a sus orígenes europeos, al tiempo que negando al indígena contemporáneo y al esclavizado traído del África. La bipolaridad entre civilización y barbarie se tornó en equivalente de lo europeo culto versus lo salvaje americano. La llamada barbarie, gentilidad, infidelidad y salvajismo encarnaron en esa parte no blanca y no europeizada que los proyectos de nación pretendieron erradicar con las armas, absorber con la educación monolingüe, y extirpar con la religión misional monoteísta.

Los países iberoamericanos continuaron siendo eurocéntricos a pesar de su separación de la administración colonial española. Esta actitud se matizó de manera significativa en Brasil, en donde el centro se trasladó a la periferia colonial, y en donde lo portugués-europeo se perpetuó aun después de la independencia a través de la corte imperial de Pedro I. El hecho de que la corona imperial portuguesa se hubiera mudado temporalmente a tierras de Brasil, estableciendo su capital en Río de Janeiro, implicó una actitud diferente en su eurocentrismo, transformándolo en una especie de euroamericanismo. La continuidad del proyecto colonizador portugués, que adquirió una nueva forma con el imperio de Brasil, mantuvo las diferencias e indiferencias con las naciones indígenas. En los tiempos de la colonia quedaron sumidas las posibilidades marginales de relaciones caracterizadas por cierta mutualidad asimétrica, como las que parecían gestarse parcialmente en las misiones jesuíticas guaraníes del siglo XVIII.

En un Brasil que pasó de imperio a república en 1889, recién abolida la esclavización, los viajeros europeos de finales del siglo XIX y comienzos del XX fueron en parte los encargados de dar noticia sobre aquellos indios diezmados, acorralados, replegados en las selvas, o simplemente aún no contactados.

Yurupary: Un hito legendario para Colombia y Brasil

En 1890 el conde Ermanno Stradelli, geógrafo y fotógrafo italiano, publicó en Roma: *Leggenda dell' Jurupary*. El *Yurupary* es un texto mítico-literario basado en la tradición oral ritual de comunidades de filiación lingüística arawak, tukano y tupí-guaraní, entre otras tantas etnias ubicadas a ambos lados de la actual frontera colombo-brasilera, en particular en la cuenca del río Vaupés en Colombia, o río Uaupés en Brasil. La versión reelaborada literariamente por Stradelli al parecer fue recogida y escrita originalmente en ñengatú (una lengua general del noroeste amazónico a finales del siglo XIX) por Maximiano José Roberto, mestizo brasilero descendiente de indígenas manaos por parte de su padre y de los indígenas tariana del lado de su madre. Para Héctor Orjuela, un crítico literario colombiano de la Universidad de California Irvine, el *Yurupary* es ante todo una epopeya y puede considerarse el *Popol Vuh* suramericano (1983). Cecilia Caicedo de Cajigas, otra crítica literaria colombiana, llegó a referirse al Yurupary como el origen de la literatura colombiana (1990), lo cual es cuestionable; en tanto la obra es una producción literaria europea basada en tradiciones orales indígenas que trascienden las actuales fronteras. En Brasil el *Yurupary* también despertó interés y polémicas entre los intelectuales. Con todo, a diferencia de Colombia, la obra parece haber ganado un interés más temprano en tanto material antropológico. Para Luis da Cámara Cascudo, Maximiano José Roberto fue ante todo un "colector apasionado de centenares de leyendas maravillosas y seguras como documentación etnológica" (Câmara Cascudo 1967). De hecho, todo indica que Maximiano José Roberto recogió y escribió diversos fragmentos del Yurupary en ñengatú, y que se los "fue entregando" a Stradelli, quien los habría traducido, reorganizado, retocado y publicado por completo en el Boletín de la Sociedad Geográfica Italiana con el nombre de *Leggenda dell' Jurupary*. Buena parte de las secuencias míticas están asociadas con lugares ubicados actualmente en Colombia.

El *Yurupary* es uno de los hitos inaugurales del periodo etnoliterario en el área de frontera entre Brasil y Colombia. Es uno de los textos más célebres basados en un compendio literariamente intervenido de tradiciones mítico-literarias. A la vez posee como trasfondo una actitud y técnica que se prolonga hasta nuestros días: la escritura en perspectiva etnográfica. Este tipo de escritura anticipa lo que será el futuro trabajo de los escritores indígenas, caracterizado en parte por una visión propia sobre sus comunidades. Estamos hablando sobre el *Yurupary*, manuscrito de Max J. Roberto y E. Stradelli, pues por yurupary también se conocen múltiples ciclos mítico-rituales profundamente complejos, que hoy en día se transmiten y actualizan en numerosas comunidades indígenas del Vaupés, en lo que respecta al lado colombiano. Los yurupary poseen un marcado carácter masculino iniciático y suelen conservar su vitalidad oral-ceremonial. En cambio, los textos que conocemos como *Yurupary* suelen ser resultado de múltiples versiones transcritas (M. J. Roberto y Stradelli, Reichel-Dolmatoff, A. Guzmán y A. J. James), usualmente de procedencia tukano y arawak, en lo que respecta al lado colombiano.

Von Koch-Grünberg *zu* Andrade

Theodor Koch-Grünberg fue un etnólogo y explorador alemán que participó en expediciones a ríos como el Xingú, Negro, Yapura, Ventuari y Orinoco a principios del siglo XX. Sus exploraciones en los territorios amazónicos entre Brasil, Venezuela, y parte de Colombia le permitieron entrar en contacto con poblaciones indígenas poco contactadas como los pemón y baniwa, entre otras tantas tribus que fotografió y sobre las que informó a los lectores europeos. Sus primeros dos informes etnológicos se publicaron en 1910 y 1911 en Alemania: *Zwei Jahre unter den Indianern. Reisen in Nord West Brasilien, 1903–1905* (*Dos años entre los indios, viajes por el noroeste brasileño, 1903–1905*). Con todo, su libro más reconocido fue publicado en Alemania en 1917: *Vom Roroima zum Orinoco. Ergebnisse einer Reise in Nordbrasilien und Venezuela in den Jahren 1911–1913*. Estas dos expediciones de 1903–05 y 1911–13, y sus respectivas obras etnológicas, marcarían un hito exploratorio en el *territorio ignoto* del Brasil excéntrico. Estas exploraciones también dejaron al descubierto tradiciones narrativas desconocidas y sorprendentes. El poeta y novelista Mário de Andrade se nutrió en particular del volumen II de *Vom Roroima zum Orinoco*, en cuyas páginas Koch-Grünberg presentaba *Mitos y leyendas de los indios Taulipang y Arekuná*. Las narrativas tradicionales recogidas por el etnógrafo alemán servirían de base simbólica para la creación de un personaje de origen indígena, Macunaíma, quien migra de la selva a la ciudad en compañía de sus hermanos. En la versión cinematográfica adaptada en 1969 por Joaquím Pedro de Andrade, Macunaíma es interpretado por un actor afrobrasilero, quien en el camino a la ciudad se transforma mágicamente en un hombre blanco, y al llegar a São Paulo, se deslumbra inicialmente con la civilización.

Migrar a la ciudad, migrar a la letra

En el libro *Crônicas de São Paulo, um olhar indígena* (2004), Daniel Munduruku refresca la memoria de los paulistas, los brasileros y los latinoamericanos en general, al compartir sus recorridos por lugares con nombres indígenas en una de las ciudades más populosas y multiculturales del hemisferio. Ya en un libro anterior, *Histórias de índio* (1996), Munduruku nos contaba aún sorprendido sobre su encuentro con un ciudadano que se le aproxima preguntándole primero si él era japonés, y luego si era chileno. Si bien es cierto que *São Paulo* concentra una de las colonias japonesas más grandes fuera del Japón, y que hay chilenos viviendo en Brasil, el hecho de ser abordado como un extraño en su propio país, dejó pasmado a uno de los más publicados y reconocidos escritores indígenas brasileros. El auto-exotismo del fenotipo indígena en Brasil le dejaba claro que la ignorancia continuaba siendo la misma. De hecho, en una entrevista afirma: "Os indígenas sempre foram ocultados pelo sistema político, sobretudo militar. Nossa condição era uma vengonha e era bom que permanecêssemos longe do cénario político. Oficialmente éramos inúteis" (Ferreira y Zilberman 221).

En *Crônicas de São Paulo* la ciudad se convierte en espejo de la aldea originaria, en escenario de las remembranzas del escritor migrante. El Munduruku paseante imagina cómo fueron antes esos lugares urbanos, y qué significan los nombres indígenas que llevan, aunque nadie cuestione al respecto. Reflexionar sobre los nombres originarios de una de las grandes urbes sudamericanas, implica otorgarles voz e imagen a sus predecesores pre-brasileros. De hecho, Munduruku siente que está caminando sobre sus antepasados. Así es como ciertos sectores de la ciudad se convierten en espejos de la memoria en donde el estilo de asentamiento indígena, recurrentemente circular, contrasta con el estilo cuadrado, más bien cuadriculado, que se impuso con los portugueses, y en particular con la modernidad vestida de moles, edificios, túneles, etc. La ciudad de piedra, estresada, sin memoria, rápida, agitada, deja entrever las sombras de aquellos otrora sus pobladores:

> Homens e mulheres desmanchavam suas barracas, anunciando que mais um dia de trabalho estaba chegando ao final. Seus movimentos bruscos projetavam suas sombras em direção aos prédios, criando uma sinfonía de luz e sombra que lembrava fantasmas soltos no ar.
>
> São os fantasmas dos nossos antepassados", pensei e voltei meu olhar para os carros que entravam e saíam do túnel como canoas modernas a transportar gente de um lado para o outro. (Munduruku 2004: 21)

En 2008, Munduruku publicaría, junto con Mauricio Negro, una versión en portugués del mensaje del jefe Seattle, un nativo americano que escribió una célebre carta al presidente de Estados Unidos en 1855: *A palavra do grande chefe*. Las visiones de Munduruku y del gran jefe coinciden en su crítica a las ciudades "del llamado hombre blanco", en concepto de Seattle, al tiempo que rescatan la visión de lo que estaba antes así como de quienes habitaban primero. Con todo, lo que hace diferente la visión del cronista de la aldea munduruku, es la forma cómo se reapropia de São Paulo, al convertirla en su aldea, una gran aldea de desconocidos, en cuyas vías las canoas han sido reemplazadas por carros, en donde el metro es un gran tatu (armadillo) metálico, y en cuyos entramados él, al igual que la serpiente del bosque, va en procura de su alimento. Apropiarse de la ciudad es apropiarse de sus nombres indígenas, interpretarlos, imaginarlos, interpelarlos, interponerlos entre los mundos de antes y los de ahora.

Migrar a la ciudad es migrar a la letra. La ciudad, cual un gran libro, como el incesante palimpsesto de las identidades, es traducida, re-imaginada, vuelta a leer por el cronista y paseante indígena contemporáneo, quien la reclama suya desde un nosotros inclusivo. La gran ciudad deviene en casa indígena, en maloca, en casa comunal en donde hay espacio para todos. Sin embargo, la ciudad es apta para quienes consigan resistir su crecimiento, para los que sean capaces de vivir creativamente en su memoria, para los que sepan mantenerse en contacto con la naturaleza –de paso sin arrasar los grillos–, y sobre todo para quienes puedan reinventarse al abrir sus oídos a las historias sapienciales.

Las palabras mayores de Munduruku, y de otros escritores y escritoras indígenas, vienen desde los ríos y las selvas, así como desde un pre-Brasil más antiguo, más silencioso, un país de países que quedó aislado por el ruido ensordecedor de la invasión y la modernidad apresurada. En la mirada indígena de Munduruku la gran ciudad se vuelve aldea global. El cronista se ocupa en quitar el velo del presente para ver lo que estaba antes, para imaginar cómo fueron los que allí vivieron, cómo era la naturaleza antes que fuera cercada y cubierta su desnudez con el pesado ropaje de la modernidad.

En las márgenes urbanas del río Tietê el cronista deja fluir la imaginación. Nos cuenta que su propia aldea queda cerca a un río, y también cuenta que la vida indígena amazónica discurre en torno al agua, en relación con los ciclos de inundación-abundancia y sequía-escasez. El paseo por las márgenes del río Tietê le permite imaginar los tiempos antiguos:

> Imagino a movimentação das crianças brincando e correndo atrás umas das outras, fazendo a alegria do avô que a tudo assistia, impassível mas feliz. Quantas aldeias havia em suas margens? Quantas pessoas ele alimentava? Quantas histórias já ouviu? Quantos casais de jovens namoravam às suas margens? Quantas confissões já guardara para si? Quantos corpos tombaram ao seu redor? (Munduruku 2004, 48)

El río, aunque contaminado, es un abuelo. Un abuelo como el lago de Ibirapuera, parque que fascina al escritor "não tanto pela beleza da natureza que o circunda, mas pelo fato de ser um lugar circular, como uma autêntica aldeia indígena" (Munduruku 2004, 23).

Tatuapé es otro nombre indígena que despierta la imaginación de Munduruku. En su concepto Tatuapé significa el camino del tatu, una especie de armadillo. El metro de São Paulo resulta ser un tatu metálico. El metro sabe para dónde va, transportando personas de un lugar a otro. El tatu, en cambio, "desconhece o próprio destino mas sabe aonde quer chegar" (Munduruku 2004, 15). Es la imagen del propio hombre de la selva, acostumbrado según el cronista al silencio del bosque, al canto de los pájaros y al flujo del río. El tatu de la selva puede ser cazado y comido. Mientras que el tatu metálico sirve de transporte para que las personas de la ciudad puedan ir en procura del alimento. En suma, el cronista traza mundos y escalas diferentes con las mismas necesidades básicas por suplir.

Uno de los momentos más conmovedores del libro ocurre en Jabaquara, un nombre guaraní que Munduruku interpreta como el lugar de los esclavizados fugados. Allí imagina cómo se habrían sentido los esclavos traídos de África al Brasil. Se pone en el lugar de sus hermanos explotados e imposibilitados para volver a su propia casa:

> De um lado havia seus senhores que não davam tregua e os massacravam e exauriam de tanto trabalhar. De outro lado havia os indígenas, que os olhavam con estranheza e encanto, mas não compreendiam uma só palabra do que diziam. E à sua frente? O mar, esse gigante que lhes lembrava a impossibilidade de voltar para casa. O que lhes restava? (Munduruku 2004, 28)

Munduruku confiesa haber encontrado su alma en la ciudad. Allí se revela su vocación de profesor, o confesor de sus sueños, y cambia el arco por la palabra: "Foi assim que me tornei um transeunte da cidade e transformei o barco em trem, o arco em palabra, a mata em tabual, a escuridão em luz elétrica, a aldeia em cidade" (Munduruku 2004, 43).

Las andanzas, pesquisas e interpretaciones del cronista culminan en la reindigenización de la ciudad. En la conversión de la ciudad en aldea: "Não troquei mina aldeia pela cidade. Eu transformei a cidade em minha aldeia" (Munduruku 2004, 43).

Fogones de la literatura

Daniel Munduruku se educó con los cuentos e historias tradicionales de su aldea. Para él las narrativas originarias son sentimientos, consejos, voces que le guían. Munduruku es un autor formado en la dinámica de una literatura tradicional y sapiencial, es decir, un arte verbal de intercambio oral intergeneracional que explora y detenta el conocimiento de la naturaleza, la comunidad humana, y el interior pleno de resonancias simbólicas y oníricas en cada persona.

En el microuniverso oraliterario de Munduruku, no sólo los mayores cuentan sus historias a modo de autoridades jerárquicas tradicionales. Las niñas y los niños cuentan sobre sus peripecias, sueños y temores a sus madres, padres, abuelos y mayores. Este intercambio, antes que transmisión generacional, es la esencia misma de la educación propia, y en tal sentido cuenta con espacios privilegiados como el fogón en el centro de la casa. Educación propia y literatura tradicional son ejercicios de participación en la comunidad familiar:

> Depois do banho no río corríamos para casa, onde éramos recebidos com o saboroso alimento preparado por nossas mães. Assim, o dia passava mais uma vez e nos deixava com saudade do dia seguinte. Nós —meus irmãos e eu— nos sentávamos, então, ao redor do fogo aceso no centro da casa para alimentar nosso corpo. Ali, contávamos para todos os adultos presentes tudo o que havíamos feito durante o dia, Embora não parecesse, todos nos ouviam com atenção e respeito. Aquele era um exercício de participação na vida de nossa comunidade familiar. (Munduruku, *Catando Piolhos* 7–8)

La obra literaria de Munduruku se conecta significativamente con el proyecto de oralitura del poeta mapuche Elicura Chihuailaf (1999), así como con la idea de analfabetismo de lo indígena (Rocha 2012) expresada por Hugo Jamioy, oralitor camëntsá del Valle de Sibundoy en Colombia. Chihuailaf, quien creció en el Wallmapu en Chile, remonta su proyecto escritural al fogón, espacio en donde escuchó y compartió desde niño las historias de su gente. Jamioy, quien también se formó en el fogón con las historias de sus mayores, reconoce la importancia de educar, o alfabetizar en sentido figurado, a quienes no conocen o ignoran el mundo indígena. En la obra de Daniel Munduruku es evidente el proyecto de educar y sensibilizar a los niños, jóvenes y adultos de las ciudades, los llamados no indígenas, al tiempo que la certeza de estar compartiendo una literatura comunitaria propia de raíz oral.

Ya en la década de los setentas, a partir de materiales pedagógicos como los creados a partir de la Teología de la Liberación, se fortaleció el entrenamiento crítico en lectura y escritura para nuevas generaciones en diferentes aldeas indígenas de Brasil. En concepto de Munduruku esto

> foi ajudando os povos indígenas a tomarem consciência de sua própria condição social e a se perceber no cenário político nacional. (Mas) a dificuldade de aparecerem escritores se deu pelo fato de a escrita não ser um instrumento manipulado por nossos povos. Isso demorou mais de 30 anos até serem formadas novas gerações com experiencia de cidade e de escola.

> Escrever é um oficio e como tal precisa haver prática, treino. Muitos líderes indígenas eram grandes oradores —e muitos registros da suas falas existem— mas escreviam muito pouco. (Ferreira y Zilberman 2010, 221)

Rescatar y compartir de la memoria de mayores y líderes indígenas fallecidos, iletrados y/o relegados, son unos los motivos más profundos en obras como las de Munduruku y Jekupé. En las sorprendentes páginas de *Xerekó Arandu, a morte de Kretã*, Olívio Jekupé narra el mensaje de resistencia y el asesinato, en una emboscada, del líder kaingáng Ãngelo Kretã. Obras como ésta no sólo recuperan la memoria; ante todo la actualizan y la ponen en diálogo con la sociedad dominante: "Como sempre dizia Kretã: o índio tem que entender as coisas dos brancos" (Jekupé 2002, 36).

Diez características sugeridas de las literaturas indígenas en Brasil

Eliane Potiguara es una de las escritoras y activistas indígenas más reconocidas hoy por hoy en Brasil. Para ella la irrupción contemporánea de escritoras y escritores indígenas es muy positiva "porque mostramos ao mundo que não somos só contadores de história oral, mas pessoas capacitadas que têm a sabedoria de escrever belas histórias".[2] En efecto, dos de las características sobresalientes de estas multi-surgientes literaturas es que sus autores quieren 1) demostrar las capacidades intelectuales y artísticas de los indígenas en Brasil; y 2) des-estereotiparlos como pueblos ágrafos exclusivamente orales. Para la autora de *Metade cara, metade máscara* (2004), la literatura indígena es expresión del "pensamento brasileiro", frase con la que encabeza su frecuentado blog de internet.

Olívio Jekupé y Aldeia Krukutu son escritores guaraníes. Para ellos los escritores indígenas en Brasil "temos uma missão muito importante, conscientizar a sociedade não indígena através de nossa escrita, e fortalecer nossas crianças indígenas a preservar a cultura lendo nossos trabalhos que escrevemos e através dela nosso povo ser mais valorizado e respeitado" (Rocha 2012: 60–1). En tal sentido puede sugerirse una tercera característica de estas literaturas: 3) concientizar al interior de los pueblos indígenas (intraculturalidad), y educar hacia afuera: a los brasileros, a los no indígenas en general, comenzando por los niños y jóvenes de las ciudades (interculturalidad).

El proyecto oraliterario de Daniel Munduruku parte del hecho de que los pueblos indígenas tienen sus propias literaturas, de raigambre oral, cuya sabiduría quiere compartir con los lectores brasileros mediante antologías, libros para niños y jóvenes, novelas cortas, crónicas, etc. En una de sus entrevistas declara: "nunca fui um exímio leitor. Descobri a leitura –e não a literatura– quando já era adolescente".[3] A partir de esta reflexión en que el autor de *Crônicas de Sâo Paulo* diferencia literatura y lectura, puede sugerirse otra característica: 4) los escritores y escritoras indígenas de Brasil suelen reconocer la actual literatura indígena, que ellos y ellas producen, como subsidiaria, y/o complementaria, de una literatura mayor, oral y comunitaria.

En septiembre de 2005, la agencia EFE, reconocido servicio de noticias internacionales, difundió la siguiente noticia: "Brasil incentivará con literatura el uso de las lenguas indígenas: La literatura brasileña, que durante siglos ha sido publicada casi exclusivamente en portugués, se abrirá a ediciones en lenguas indígenas para impedir la muerte de cerca de 160 hablas autóctonas del país" (Rocha 2012: 263). Con esta política estatal se afianzaba otra característica, esta vez por parte del Estado brasilero: 5) la necesidad política institucional de promover oficialmente la literatura indígena como una forma de reconocer las lenguas y culturas nativas, ignoradas y negadas por tanto tiempo.

Aun así, muchas de las obras contemporáneas indígenas se escriben preferencialmente en portugués, en parte como una forma de captar la atención de la sociedad dominante. En Brasil, y en toda América del sur, algunos de los obstáculos que impiden que los autores indígenas publiquen con mayor frecuencia en sus lenguas originarias, tienen que ver con la evidente desaparición de muchas de éstas, y también con la falta de consenso sobre una escritura alfabética unificada. Los glosarios de palabras y conceptos indígenas, traducidos al portugués, son uno de los recursos usados con más frecuencia por los autores indígenas. En el libro *Kurumi Guaré no coração da Amazonia*, el escritor Yaguarê Yamã incluye una lista de símbolos maraguá, su pueblo de origen, además de un glosario en ñengatú. Yaguarê Yamã suele ilustrar sus propios libros. Las ilustraciones, y el lenguaje visual en general, también son un componente muy característico en libros de Munduruku y Jekupé.

Ahora bien, la interculturalidad característica de estas literaturas está estrechamente ligada a otra de sus características: 6) la literatura indígena en Brasil es una estrategia de resistencia política y cultural que convoca, aproxima y busca expresar la voz de los pueblos indígenas. Es en este sentido que Daniel Muduruku declara:

> tenho trabalho na perspectiva de que a literatura é um caminho de aproximação entre os diferentes povos indígenas. Mesmo sabendo que há uma grande diversidade de saberes e culturas, sinto que a literatura pode funcionar como elemento aglutinador, além de ser um instrumento para "soltar a voz" que tem ficado entalada na garganta de nossa gente ancestral. Nosso desafio é ajudar nossa gente a aprender a usar a escrita como porta-voz. Na medida em que isso for acontecendo, o que era apenas um murmúrio irá tornar-se um grito consciente e consistente.(Ibidem)[4]

La necesidad de una estrecha relación de la literatura indígena con la resistencia política, y el movimiento indígena en Brasil, lleva a Eliane Potiguara a afirmar que

> núcleos de pensadores e escritores devem ser também incentivados e capacitados dentro das Organizações indígenas, assim como muitas vezes, falou-se em discutir a questão de gênero, de raça e etnia nas Assembléias. Os problemas identificados devem ser imediatamente direcionados para estudos objetivando estratégias, mecanismos que busquem a solução das dificuldades, dos conflitos e das diferenças.[5]

Ahora bien, al ejercicio de resistencia política se suma la dinámica de necesaria renovación y fortalecimiento al interior de los mismos pueblos, por ejemplo en lo que atañe a la recuperación de sus propias memorias históricas. Eliane Potiguara, quien concentra parte de sus esfuerzos en las luchas por la recuperación de la memoria, afirma que "a literatura indígena cumpre o papel de resgate histórico onde a oralidade foi perdida, de preservação cultural, de fortalecimento das cosmovisões étnicas"(Ibidem).[6] Así pues, otra característica sugerida es la que concibe 7) la literatura indígena como una herramienta dinámica de la memoria, en cuanto su práctica permite reconsiderar las oralidades y preservar las culturas originarias mediante la atención a sus cosmovisiones.

En entrevista con Olívio Jekupé, la educadora Darlene Taukane de la etnia bakairi, realizó importantes apreciaciones a propósito de las relaciones entre escritura y oralidad. Su testimonio sugiere que 8) la literatura indígena actual forma parte de un proceso de negociación, compensación y mediación entre la escritura alfabética contemporánea y la elaborada oralidad de raíces ancestrales:

> Eu acho que o sistema, o uso da escrita nos seios das comunidades indígenas não debe suprimir o lugar e o espaço da história oral. O sistema oral no meio dos povos indígenas é tão antigo quanto os nossos mitos de origem. (...) O uso e a manipulaçao da escrita têm que ser sempre a nosso favor, precisamos aprender a fazer isso. Nós temos que ter a clareza dos lugares tanto da escrita como do uso da história oral no meio da comunidades da qual fazemos parte. (Jekupé 2009, 39)

En este punto cabe preguntarse ¿qué entienden los escritores y escritoras indígenas por literatura? Daniel Munduruku, uno de los líderes del movimiento de la literatura indígena en Brasil, responde desde su propia experiencia:

> Entendemos literatura indígena como o conjunto de manifestações culturais que são reproduzidas por nossa gente em seus rituais, desenhos, cantos, danças, rezas, etc. Fugimos um pouco da ideia de literatura como escrita. Queremos mostrar que este nosso jeito de comunicar é literário. Se pensarmos que no mundo literário é preciso que haja iniciados nele para compreendê-lo, podemos imaginar que nossa forma de fazer literatura é um código que a sociedade não indígena precisa aprender para poder nos compreender. Nosso esforço em compreender a sociedade brasileira passa pelo domínio das novas tecnologias (a escrita entre elas). É justo que a sociedade letrada pense no movimento de nossos corpos como literatura.[7]

Así es como surge una nueva característica, entre otras tantas que podríamos reconocer y sugerir a partir del discurso de las escritoras y escritores indígenas en el Brasil actual. Si bien es cierto que la literatura indígena suele adecuarse técnicamente a la literatura alfabética de ascendencia europea, 9) las raíces orales, gráficas, testimoniales y multilingües de estas literaturas indígenas contemporáneas, exigen una ampliación de la práctica misma de literatura. Esta ampliación implica que el lector debe aprender nuevos códigos, reeducarse en la escucha de historias como los niños, y estar dispuesto al encuentro con artes verbales que no están necesariamente separadas de artes plásticas y corporales.

Parte de la literatura indígena del Brasil se destaca por su lenguaje sencillo, profundo, interpelante y sapiencial, y aunque su producción textual privilegia el libro como formato, tiende a transmitirse con total dinamismo en el plano virtual del internet, con frecuencia mediante blogs personales de los autores. En efecto, las escritoras y escritores reconocidos poseen sus propios blogs, en los que publican textos relacionados con sus pueblos originarios, las luchas indígenas en Brasil, su bibliografía, los enlaces virtuales de otros autores indígenas, una agenda de actividades, portadas de sus libros, y a veces fragmentos de sus propias obras. En tal sentido puede sugerirse que 10) la literatura indígena en Brasil posee una particular tendencia a la difusión virtual y a la resonancia intercultural mediada por las redes sociales y el internet.

Ahora bien, al tiempo que los escritores suelen difundir las direcciones de sus blogs y correos electrónicos para el público general, también se dan cita en algunos encuentros públicos en favor tanto del movimiento indígena como de la difusión de sus propias obras. De acuerdo con Olivío Jekupé, el primer encuentro de escritores indígenas en Brasil se realizó en septiembre de 2004 en Río de Janeiro, "organizado pelo IMBRAPI (Instituto Brasileiro de Propriedade Intelectual) e FNLIJ (Fundaçao Nacional do Livro Infanto e Juvenil)" (Jekupé 2009: 19).

Para redondear

Se calcula que a la llegada de los portugueses, entre tres y ocho millones de nativos, hablantes de unas novecientas lenguas y variedades dialectales, poblaban esa inmensidad inabarcable que se nos viene a la mente con el nombre Brasil. Los años en curso del siglo XXI son testigos de la eclosión de estas literaturas escritas en portugués, y a veces en lenguas indígenas como el guaraní. Estamos ante literaturas y literaturas orales publicadas en formatos de libros, recurrentemente ilustradas, dirigidas especial mas no exclusivamente a un público infantil-juvenil, y difundidas con frecuencia en internet por sus propios autores.

A los nombres citados aquí, y hasta aproximadamente el año 2015, podían sumarse otros tan importantes como Creomar Tahuare (umutina), Lia Minapoty (maraguá), Elias Yaguakãg (maraguá), Ziel Guaynê (maraguá), Ailton Krenak (krenak), Carlos Tiago Haki'y (sateré), Ely Macuxi (makuxi), Cristino Wapixana y Rony Wasiry Guará (maraguá). En los últimos años el canal de YouTube *Literatura Indígena Contemporânea*, con la gestión intercultural de Julie Dorrico, se ha convertido en uno de los espacios de mayor difusión de los escritores indígenas en Brasil.

Notas

1. Este ensayo se basa en un primer intento de abordar las literaturas indígenas en Brasil publicado en *Revista Canadiense de Estudios Hispánicos.*
2. URL: http://www.elianepotiguara.org.br/home.html#.UTLISjdphjM.
3. Entrevista exclusiva ao Instituto Ecofuturo en http://danielmunduruku.blogspot.com/.
4. Ibidem. **<favor de integrar al texto>**
5. http://www.elianepotiguara.org.br/home.html#.UTLISjdphjM
6. Ibidem. **<favor de integrar en el texto>**
7. Entrevista exclusiva ao Instituto Ecofuturo en http://danielmunduruku.blogspot.com/.

Obras citadas

Andrade, Mário de. *Macunaíma, o hérói sem nenhum caráter.* 1928. Río de Janeiro: Agir, 2008.
Cajigas, Cecilia. Caicedo de. *Orígen de la literatura colombiana: El Yurupary.* Bogotá: Norma, 1990.
Câmara Cascudo, Luís da. "Em memoria de Stradelli". 2d ed. Manaus: Livraria Clássica, 1967.
Chihuailaf, Elicura. *Recado confidencial a los chilenos.* Santiago: Editorial LOM, 1999.
Ferreira-Pinto, Cristina y Regina Zilberman. "Entrevista a Daniel Munduruku". *Revista Iberoamericana* 76, no. 230 (2010): 219–223.
Jamioy Juagibioy, Hugo. *Bínÿbe oboyejuayëng/Danzantes del viento.* Manizales: Universidad de Caldas, Ediciones Indígenas, Juabna de América, 2005.
Jekupé, Olívio. *Literatura escritos pelos povos indígenas.* Sao Paulo: Scortecci, 2009.
———. *Xerekó Arandu, a morte de Kretã.* São Paulo: Peirópolis, 2002.
Koch-Grünberg, Theodor. *Vom Roroima zum Orinoco: Ergebnisse einer Reise in Nordbrasilien und Venezuela in den Jahren 1911–1913.* Berlin: Dietrich Reimer; Stuttgart: Strecker und Schröder, 1928.
Munduruku, Daniel. *Catando piolhos, contando histórias.* São Paulo: Brinque-Book, 2006.
———. *Crônicas de São Paulo: Um olhar indígena.* São Paulo: Callis, 2004.
———. *Histórias de índio.* São Paulo: Companhia das Letrinhas, 1996.
Munduruku, Daniel, and Mauricio Negro. *A palavra do grande chefe.* São Paulo: Caramelo, 2008.
Orjuela, Héctor. *Yurupary, el Popol-Vuh suramericano.* Bogotá: Editorial Kelly, 1983.
Potiguara, Eliane. *Metade cara, metade máscara.* Brasil: Global, 2004.
Rocha Vivas, Miguel. *Palabras mayores, palabras vivas, tradiciones míticos-literarias y escritores indígenas en Colombia.* Bogotá: Taurus, 2012.
Yamã, Yaguarê. *Kurumi Guaré no coração da Amazonia.* São Paulo: FTD, 2007.

AFTERWORD

Seven Thoughts on Indigenous Studies, Hispanic Studies, and Bodies in Relation

Joseph M. Pierce

1. Sometimes

Sometimes we have to speak the colonizer's language, and in this languaging, still somehow remember ourselves.
Sometimes we have to hide our knowledge,
Sometimes we hide ourselves.
And sometimes our bodies say more than words ever could.
Sometimes this means that our bodies vibrate, in pain, in joy, in the fullness of our memories, which is to say, in relation, and this is what guides us.

2. Beginning

I am an Indigenous person from Turtle Island, a citizen of the Cherokee Nation, who was trained in Latin American Studies. The question of how to navigate the disciplinary structures that limit and legitimize knowledge production, what the editors describe as the Eurocentrism of Hispanic Studies, reminds me that Indigenous knowledge is not simply about the production of artifacts, objects, or culture; rather, it is itself a praxis—an engagement with—a particular Indigenous worldview. This worldview, this knowledge, is incommensurable with Western epistemologies and ontologies. We must start there.

3. Enjambment

This incommensurability
    is not something
    that is going to change

is not something
that will be *bridged*
with the publication of a single volume.
Of course.
But that is not the point.

The point is that to bridge means speaking from where we are, from the positions that we occupy within, adjacent to, and outside the academy, and constantly interrogating how the forces of colonialism, capitalism, heteronormativity, and patriarchy inflect the types of knowledge that are legible within the disciplinary structures of Hispanic Studies or Indigenous Studies. But that's not all.

To bridge means interrogating how these structures also inflect the ways we go about imagining our varied and ongoing relations with land, humans, more-than-humans, with time, with ancestors, with spirituality. These ways, these doings, are themselves a form of resistance to the settler colonial conditions that predetermine what knowledge counts as disciplinary and what disciplines shape knowledge production. Bridging is an action. A verb. It is embodied. It is resistance.

4. Beginning, Again

I should have clarified: I am writing an afterword to this book, but I am imagining it as something else, something more like a *reflection on* that is also a future dream. How can I write an after-word that is also a future-word? How can I describe this book in a way that does it justice, while also, simply, telling you how it makes me feel?

Some of the chapters in this book begin with doubts: How do we relate? How can we start? What barriers must we face? What does the body have to do with it?

Some chapters begin with doubts because sometimes doubts are all we have. These doubts are the most ethical way of saying: help me. This help me is also a relate to me, an invitation to writing with and reading with that so often is absent from Hispanic Studies. To be honest, this is absent from most disciplines.

We are taught to always already have known things that are impossible to know.

And we are taught never to ask for help, never to doubt.

But we doubt. We wonder.

Other chapters begin with certainty. I am certain of some things, even though I doubt others. I am certain that colonialism is bad. It is ongoing, an ever expanding appetite. An insatiability.

We know some things for sure: relations, land, time.

We know and yet...

We have to explain.

And then some chapters refuse to explain. I love this. We cannot always explain things because settler colonialism wants to explain away guilt, violence, theft. We refuse to explain why that is deadly. We live its deadliness, and we will not assuage.

We doubt, we know, we refuse.
This is Indigenous Studies.

5. Gratitude

The real thing I want to say in this afterword/future word is thank you. I want to thank the editors, Gloria Chacón, Lauren Beck, and Juan Sánchez Martínez, for organizing, editing, and caring for a book that we desperately need. And I want to thank each of the contributors, too. Wado:

Miguel Rojas-Sotelo, for taking us on a walk, in relation, in cyclical animation, through the cultural production of *Soberanía Visual*, an act of witnessing that is at the same time an engagement with the intergenerational and transcultural efforts of Indigenous art, politics, and community.

Mikeas Sánchez y Violeta Percia, por mostrarnos cómo el diálogo puede ser no solo una metodología vibrante y emotiva, sino también arraigada en las epistemologías indígenas; por enfocar nuestros corazones en los desbordes, los desdoblamientos, que florecen en la poesía contemporánea indígena.

Marco Antonio Huerta, por haberme enseñado que la proximidad tanto conceptual como corporal involucra tomar riesgos, y que estos riesgos valen la pena asumirlos si queremos vivir en buenas relaciones.

Antonio Catrileo y Manuel Carrión-Lira, por articular una metodología situada que no se limita a la mera comparación epistémica, dejando así intactas las presunciones coloniales, sino abriéndonos a un desdoblamiento intelectual, recíproco y transparente, capaz de transitar entre mundos.

Pedro Favaron, por insistir en la legitimidad de nuestros sentimientos poéticos, filosóficos, por apelar a una filosofía cardíaca –¡qué imagen!– la cual desencadena una serie de responsabilidades éticas para con nuestras comunidades.

Nathan Henne, for demonstrating how concepts like the K'iche' *utz k'aslemal* and the Andean *sumak kawsay* are world building devices, wording techniques that allow us to see how living a good life is to live in relation, as relation.

Ulises Juan Zevallos-Aguilar, por las reflexiones en torno a la enseñanza de la poesía y el canto quechua, por invertir el tiempo y el conocimiento en fortalecer nuestras posibilidades de mejor articular las diferencias epistémicas que surgen cuando estudiamos (en) idiomas indígenas.

Víctor Quiroz Ciriaco, Estelle Tarica y Ana Lucía Tello, por proponer una lectura del Manuscrito de Huarochirí que dé cuenta de sus características múltiples, solapadas, las cuales emergen desde una mirada *ch'ixi* que es a su vez una forma de reciprocidad, una relación con el texto mismo.

Oswaldo A. Lara Orozco, por presentarnos de modo sistemático no simplemente lo que se ha estudiado en términos de video y cine indígena en América del Norte, sino más bien mapear de modo decolonial las prácticas colectivas, individuales, académicas, políticas y estéticas, que emergen desde las mismas comunidades indígenas en esta zona.

Rita M. Palacios, Juan Ariel Castillo Cocom, and Paul M. Worley, for acknowledging the need not simply to "indigenize" Hispanic studies, but to reconceptualize the frames, terms, and methods of engagement with the land and peoples of the Americas on the terms set by Indigenous peoples as a precondition for changing both the field and canon.

Fredy A. Roncalla, por demostrarnos la base concreta, telúrica, de las poéticas andinas; por habernos recordado que la huaca es también, y siempre fue, poesía.

Sue Patricia Haglund, for asking us to consider the relational continuities—the ongoing aesthetic, political and cultural interventions—that poetry makes in the Dule language (but also across languages) for the Guna people; for asking us to imagine the spoken and written word as layered assemblages, instead of separate spheres.

Carolina Bloem y James Courage Singer, por explorar los anacronismos fundamentales de las ideologías de pertenencia mestiza y chicana al territorio indígena que los colonos hoy llaman Utah.

Sean Sell, for reminding us that vengeance is not justice; balance is not based on punishment, but spiritual and communal growth.

Paulina Pineda, for teaching me that whispered stories and shared experiences of resistance can be found even in places meant to eliminate Indigenous forms of knowing, of being.

Sue Meneses Eternod, por insistir en las múltiples visiones, formas de ver y ser vistos autóctonas, soberanas, las cuales honran nuestras culturas, nuestras lenguas, nuestras traslenguas, nuestros retornos.

Miguel Rocha Vivas, por no dejarnos olvidar que los procesos coloniales también se han estudiado desde perspectivas indígenas, como las de Daniel Munduruku, Eliane Potiguara, Olívio Jekupé y Aldeia Krukutu, entre otros, y que en sus palabras se plasman una resistencia política que vislumbra la vigencia de nuestro quehacer intelectual, cultural y artístico.

6. When We Cry Together

One thing I learned from reading this book is that when we cry together, we recognize the materiality of our bodies in relation. When we cry together. When we love. When we fight. When we listen. It takes me so many words to say this: that our togetherness, our being-in-relation, our becomings, our multi- and transdisciplinary engagements, our onto- and epistemological imbrications, our spiritual and ethical and cosmic belongings, matter. They are the mattering of us. They are the we-ing of us. I learned how to think in relational vibrations, in songs that linger, ribboning space-time into the simplest fact of our existence: the we of us.

I guess I learned to think with the heart. I guess, I always knew this. I guess it is good to be reminded. I guess this is the most important thing I can do. Which is to say, I guess I learned how to listen, again, to the stars in their becomings.

7. Resonant Implication

I have been trying to think about what it means to write about a book in a way that does not simply summarize what is there but that indicates how it has affected me. And how I hope it affects you, too. Perhaps this is a confession, an opening. I think this is a more Indigenous way of doing things. To say that the end is not an ending, but a becoming, an ongoingness that reflects the properties and investments of a collection of thought, which is itself also, ongoing. The final word is thus, not final, but resonant. And in that resonance, I hope you feel yourself implicated, taking these words as part of a resonant implication, a gesture that continues.